PUBLIC HEALTH POLICIES AND SOCIAL INEQUALITY

Public Health Policies and Social Inequality

Charles F. Andrain
Professor of Political Science
San Diego State University

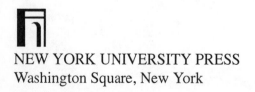

NEW YORK UNIVERSITY PRESS
Washington Square, New York

362.1
A55p

© Charles F. Andrain 1998

cp

First published in the U.S.A. in 1998 by
NEW YORK UNIVERSITY PRESS
Washington Square
New York, N.Y. 10003

This book is printed on paper suitable for recycling and
made from fully managed and sustained forest sources.

Library of Congress Cataloging-in-Publication Data
Andrain, Charles F.
Public health policies and social inequality / Charles F. Andrain.
p.   cm.
Includes bibliographical references and index.
ISBN 0–8147–0676–2
1. Medical policy—Social aspects.   2. Discrimination in medical
care. 3. Health services accessibility.   I. Title.
RA393.A53 1998
362.1—dc21   97–48835
                                                              CIP

Printed in Great Britain

Contents

List of Tables

Preface

In contemporary industrialized nations, social inequality influences public health policies and their outcomes on people's health. No matter how egalitarian the country, the most active policy participants — managers, administrators, professionals — have the most education, income, and organizational ties. Their public health programs shape the degree of social equality. Since World War II health care has become more available to all citizens, thereby lowering infant mortality rates and raising life expectancy. Lower-income persons benefited from these policies. Yet groups with the highest socioeconomic status still secure the best-quality health care. Despite the growth of comprehensive plans, they gain greater access to urban specialists. Everywhere rural residents, the urban poor, individuals with little formal education, and ethnic minorities receive the fewest benefits relative to their health needs. Increased access to health care facilities has hardly produced equal health among diverse socioeconomic groups. During the 1990s cost-containment measures placed higher priority on efficiency than on equal access, equal treatments for similar health needs, and programs to achieve more equal health among the population. Government officials reduced services, raised taxes, and enacted higher copayments, premiums, deductibles, and user fees. Low-income groups suffered the most from these policies.

Several features characterize this analysis of public policies, social inequality, and health. First, the book takes a cross-national approach. Part I compares eight industrialized nations according to three general models. The United States embodies an entrepreneurial market model. German policy processes reflect the organic corporatist model. Swedish leaders have implemented health programs derived from a social democratic model. All three societies, as well as the five other countries, reveal aspects of diverse models. Although less influential today, the corporatist tradition has shaped Sweden's contemporary health policies. Canada combines entrepreneurialism with a few social democratic practices. German corporatism features private activities associated with the market model. The weaker French corporatism operates along with a strong liberal commitment to physicians' clinical autonomy. Japan blends corporatism with private-sector entrepreneurialism. In England and even Sweden, market concepts have gained greater importance. The Dutch health care system, with its extensive pluralism, relies on all three models.

This comparative approach uses general variables that pertain to diverse cases across historical time and geographic space. Probing interactions within nations as well as between countries, it applies these ordinal variables to specific situations. The main tasks revolve around formulating equivalent cross-national concepts and devising operational indicators that measure the same variable in similar ways across diverse situations. If effectively used, such a comparative approach helps realize several analytical goals: accurate description, valid explanation, insightful evaluation, and the discovery of feasible, desirable health policies applicable to many industrialized societies.

Second, rather than just describing health policies according to different models, this volume explains policy contents and their outcomes. Explanatory theories comprise general propositions that specify the conditions (cultural, structural, personal) producing some outcome. We explore two general effects: the administrative, fiscal, and benefits policies as well as the health status of nations, social groups, and individuals.

Comparing health policies in eight industrialized nations, Part II uses three types of theories to explain these programs. The political culture approach analyzed in Chapter 5 probes the meaning of causal attributions and policy preferences about health and health care services. Formulated by Aaron Wildavsky and Mary Douglas, cultural theories clarify the framework of political discourse — for example, the meaning of health, the causes of illness, the ability of public policies to improve health, and possible solutions to the problem. This approach can help explain why the United States has less comprehensive, egalitarian health care policies than do most other industrialized nations.

Structural theories explore the political power of organizations to secure policy changes. As noted in Chapter 6, the pluralist framework of Paul Sabatier emphasizes the formation of policy coalitions as a key to understanding programmatic changes. By analyzing the groups participating in these coalitions, we can partly account for the more egalitarian health policy changes that occurred in the Netherlands than in the less pluralist German system. Institutionalism assumes the dominance of state agencies over social groups. It clarifies why the British government, compared with the French and Japanese, implemented more rapid, far-reaching policy changes from the early 1980s through the 1990s. Marxist theories provide insights into class alignments and historical policy changes. For example, why after 1950 did Sweden administer more generous, egalitarian health benefits than did Canada and particularly the United States?

Chapter 7 investigates the relevance of rational choice theory to explain the degree of efficiency in health care markets. Why do empirical outcomes diverge from theoretical assumptions? What marketing strategies lead to unintended consequences? How can we best measure the efficiency of health care programs, particularly the link between costs and benefits (quality of services)? What impact does market competition wield on medical professionalism, patient satisfaction, economic efficiency, and access to health services? Rational choice theorists offer answers that focus on concepts like expected utility, self-interest, strategic behavior, and instrumental rationality.

In Chapter 8 a theory of social opportunities elucidates the relationships between public policies and health. This explanation assumes that cultural values, sociopolitical structures, and individual behaviors shape the origins, processes, and effects of public policies. By providing meaning to political activity and motivating people to participate in the policy process, cultural values affect their opportunities to attain policy priorities. From the structural perspective, the power of the government, political parties, social groups, and transnational organizations not only constrains policy effectiveness but also facilitates opportunities for individuals to achieve their goals. Along with these cultural-structural macrodimensions, such microvariables as personal attitudes, motivations, and perceptions shape an individual's influence over the health policy process. The interaction of these three dimensions also explains the degree of health realized by nations, groups, and individuals. Cultural values about health-promoting behavior become institutionalized in structures and internalized by individuals. Certain structural dimensions — high income equality, low unemployment, safe working conditions, well-built housing — expand opportunities for health improvements. The health experienced by particular individuals depends not only on these cultural and structural conditions but on certain behavioral variables: genetic predispositions, individual orientations (information, attitudes, motives, perceptions), personal lifestyles, contacts with social support networks, and the individual use of health services. These personal conditions may increase or limit opportunities for health.

Third, this volume examines health policies from an interdisciplinary perspective. Rather than use a biomedical model or neoclassical economic framework, it applies a holistic approach to explain health programs and their outcomes on people's health. The holistic overview synthesizes the findings of political scientists, sociologists, economists, psychologists, and health science researchers. Aggregate data from statistical yearbooks and survey data from national samples indicate the complex interactions among cultural values, structural conditions, and personal information, attitudes, motivations, perceptions, and actions. From the holistic perspective, sociopolitical conditions, not only personal behaviors, produce better health. Assuming that illness stems partly from social causes, holists support public policies that expand the structural and cultural opportunities for healthy living. Public policies that provide preventive services and egalitarian access to comprehensive, universal programs can promote health improvements more effectively than policies relying on curative medicine. Using this holistic framework, Chapter 9 evaluates public health policies according to several criteria: public satisfaction with national health programs, their effectiveness in improving health, and equality of access, treatment, and outcome.

Like making public health policies, producing a book is a collective endeavor that involves several individuals. At San Diego State University, I received a sabbatical grant that enabled me to gather information in the 1994–1995 academic year. During the last decade three Political Science Department chairmen have provided intellectual support. They include William A. Schultze, Louis H. Terrell, and E. Walter Miles. SDSU graduate students Dean Marrone and John Perretta helped prepare the manuscript for publication. I also appreciate the encouragement of T. M. Farmiloe, publishing director of Macmillan, and Niko Pfund, director of the New York University Press. This volume represents the fourth one that Anne L. Leu has processed for me since 1987. As always, she performed her work with efficiency, patience, and grace.

1 Introduction: Politics and Health

Henrik Ibsen sketched a close linkage between politics and health. Published in 1882, his play *An Enemy of the People* highlighted the dependence of doctors on government policies. Purists and pragmatists battled over the safety of the local water supply in a town along the Norwegian coast. Dr Thomas Stockman uncovered poisonous bacteria polluting the water works ('Baths') and endangering the community with typhoid fever. Dr Stockman urged his older brother Peter, who served as town mayor, chief of police, and chairman of the Board of the Baths, to rebuild the water pipes and sewage system. Yet this policy would entail higher taxes, greater unemployment, and lower profits for businessmen, mainly because the town operated as a resort area. Mayor Peter Stockman rejected his brother's demands to close the Baths. A public meeting occurred to discuss this issue. As a purist, Dr Stockman championed the cause of public health. Challenging government authorities with justifications based on moral right, civic virtue, and ultimate ends, he viewed the dispute over the water supply as a conflict between good and evil. For him, bacteria polluted the water. Lies, opportunism, and eagerness to compromise polluted the spiritual values of the community. As he told the public meeting: 'I have made . . . the discovery that all our *spiritual* sources are polluted and that our whole civic community is built over a cesspool of lies. . . . It's no longer just the water-supply and the sewers now. No, the whole community needs cleaning up, disinfecting.'[1] With his powerful will, Dr Stockman championed the cause of individual conscience, truth, and righteousness. Attacking bureaucrats, party politicians, and lobbyists, he pointed out the long-term policy consequences of building new waterworks: physical, moral, and spiritual public health.

Opposed to this purist stance, the town pragmatists, such as the mayor, newspaper editor, and head of the taxpayers' association,

1

upheld material interests. The Baths' operation brought economic prosperity: rising property values, lower unemployment, and reduced taxes. Closing the Baths and relaying the water pipes would lead to devastating short-term consequences, including higher public costs and declining prosperity. Hence, town leaders had to calculate the risks of taking precipitous actions. To what extent would the short-term costs outweigh the benefits? Rather than challenge public opinion, town policymakers advocated a pragmatic strategy. Follow the majority will. Enact moderate programs that heed the importance of dominant cultural values and existing structural conditions. Against these pragmatic appeals, the purist Dr Stockman lost the cause to town officials and most residents at the meeting, who indicted him as an 'enemy of the people'. The directors of the Baths fired him as medical officer. The taxpayers' association convinced town residents to refrain from visiting his office. Yet the pragmatists' success hardly resolved the problem of the polluted water supply. Community health deteriorated.

Like Dr Stockman, political theorists have drawn an analogy between the human body and the 'body politic'. Classical Greek philosophers (Plato, Aristotle), medieval theologians such as St Thomas Aquinas, and classical conservative thinkers — Edmund Burke, G. W. Hegel, Adolph Wagner, François Chateaubriand — likened a healthy political system to a harmoniously-functioning human organism. Just as the mind rules the body, so the head of state should govern the people. Genetic codes partly determine human behavior. Similarly, constitutions represent legal codes that regulate the behavior of individuals who participate in public policymaking. Harmony among the bodily organs produces human health (order, equilibrium). Political order depends on harmony among groups and individuals who often hold divergent values, attitudes, and interests. Medical personnel try to maintain an individual's health by extracting certain impurities — germs, viruses, bacteria, carcinogens, pathogens — from the body. Disease arises when organs malperform or show disequilibrium. For instance, the pancreas secretes no insulin. Cancer results when cells grow too rapidly. By analogy, political disease emerges under conditions of inequitable role allocation. Leaders influenced by their selfish appetites govern everybody else. The 'best and brightest' — those with superior knowledge — wield limited influence over the policy process. Political disorder (disequilibrium) thrives. According to organic statists, just as a doctor must direct the patients' behavior, so enlightened government must rule over the body politic. Only when these hierarchical elites extract abnormal conditions, polluted ideas, and evil people will a healthy system emerge. Public policymaking involves a purification or cleansing of infected elements.[2]

Although rejecting the organic state, most contemporary policy analysts in democratic societies still perceive a resemblance that links the practice of medicine to the exploration of public health programs. Both health personnel and policy analysts engage in anatomy, physiology, and morphology. They dissect the parts (variables) of the body (health system), probe their functioning, and classify different structures. As diagnosticians, they try to explain the causes of disease and health. Medical treatments revolve around the prevention of disease, curative practices, and the alleviation of physical, emotional, and mental distress. Policy treatments refer to programmatic solutions that will effectively resolve health programs and lead to improved general health. Prognoses attempt to predict the impact of current treatments (policies) on desired future outcomes, such as greater equality of health among individuals and groups.

SOCIAL CHANGES AND HEALTH POLICY

During the late twentieth century, the social changes linked to modernization shape public health policies throughout the industrial world. Protests arise against the inequalities resulting from the modernization process in the cultural, structural, and behavioral dimensions of life. Culturally, modernization involves a movement from consummatory values (ultimate ends, revelation) to greater instrumental rationality, with its emphasis on efficiency, planning, and concern for long-term material consequences of public decisions. Professional expertise takes precedence over medical amateurism. The universalism of health care standards becomes more important than local, particularistic criteria. Greater impersonalization associated with large-scale structures supplants the intimate, personal ties linked to small-town ties linking doctor to patient. Mass communications media transmit these universalist values that transcend face-to-face personal interactions. Reason, globalism, and competitive market capitalism become dominant media values. As a reaction to instrumental rationality, protesters seek a life that offers more personal warmth, communal spontaneity, simplicity, amateurism, and local solidarity. Alternative medicines such as homeopathy, acupuncture, herbalism, biofeedback, hydrotherapy, and holistic spiritual healing reflect this protest against neomodernism.

The structural conditions of the world capitalist economy entail growing functional differentiation, stratified roles, and medical specialization. As evidenced by the multinational corporation and the medical-industrial complex, economic institutions become more centralized. Income inequalities widen as the corporate economy makes the transition from manufacturing to service provision based on information processing. The communications media, educational institutions, and urbanized life feature greater diversity, complexity, specialization, secularization, and centralization. Political structures reveal contradictory tendencies. A centralized bureaucratic state competes for scarce resources with decentralized government agencies in regions and cities. Political parties trying to reconcile diverse interests clash with single-issue social movements that propound widely-divergent messages. As more and more groups participate in the health policy process, social pluralism expands. Yet business and professional organizations continue to wield dominant influence. Even though the nation-state still regulates domestic health care, multinational corporations and such transnational intergovernmental institutions as the European Union and the North American Free Trade Agreement exert rising policy influence. Health care becomes more internationalized. Most pharmaceutical industries operate as multinational corporations. The European Commission issues directives about drug manufacturing, marketing, safety, and prices. The European Court of Justice adjudicates disputes over cross-national trade of pharmaceuticals within the European Union. Health ministers from EU nations hold ad hoc meetings where they discuss occupational safety, universal standards for medical equipment, appropriate prices for the same drug in different countries, and the mobility of medical personnel from one nation to another. The European Parliament has established a Health Intergroup composed of different political party members who consider transcontinental hospital standards, pharmaceutical industries' operations, tobacco consumption, contraception, and care for the elderly. A nonprofit association — the European Public

Health Alliance — supplies specialized information to the Health Intergroup.

Behaviorally, modernized societies face a tension between the dominant role played by professional-administrative leaders and increased activism by formerly underrepresented groups — women, ethnic minorities, the disabled — in social movements. Managers, administrators, professionals, and their allies in academic research institutes stress elitism. Their sphere of control revolves around the government civil service, corporate bureaucracies, legislatures, and coalitional political parties. By contrast, populist activists in social movements uphold more egalitarian values that stress direct personal involvement, local concerns, and spontaneity. Health clinics, local health councils, and rape crisis centers become centers for expanding participatory rights to those groups formerly excluded from the health policy process.[3]

From the late 1980s through the 1990s, health policy changes reflected these contradictory tendencies in neomodernization. Administrative policies revealed centralization, decentralization, and a blurred distinction between 'public' and 'private' health sectors. Governments both centralized their regulatory control, particularly over finances, and decentralized implementation of health care programs to regions (states, provinces, counties) and municipalities. As private medical corporations grew more concentrated and internationalized, informal, local healing movements gained popularity. Not only under market-oriented health programs but also in corporatist and social democratic systems on the European continent, private health providers became closely involved with public officials. Government subsidies financed private health care agencies. The operating practices of forprofit firms, nonprofit organizations, and government health institutions showed many similarities. Fiscal programs experienced a conflict between the drive to expand access to health care services and pressures to contain costs. Efficiency took priority over equal access, equal treatments for similar health needs, and programs to achieve equal health status among diverse groups. Cost containment programs promoted privatization, competition among suppliers, and greater freedom of consumer choice. Contracts between health providers and purchasers of health care tried to restrain expenses. Although the rate of expenditure growth declined during the 1980s, compared with the

1970s, costs for health care continued to increase in the 1990s. As a result, government leaders reduced benefits, raised taxes, and enacted higher copayments, premiums, deductibles, and user fees. Reimbursements fell for hospitals, health personnel (physicians), pharmaceuticals, and administration. Even if expanded access to health care coverage occurred in most industrial nations except the United States, economic recession and the rising popularity of market models curtailed public benefits. Competitive market mechanisms and means-tests allocated fewer services than during prosperous times. Low-income groups suffered the most from reduced benefits. Social stratification thus continued to influence public health programs and their outcomes on individual health.[4]

POLICYMAKERS, CITIZENS, AND POLICY ANALYSTS

Citizens, policy analysts, and particularly government officials help shape the health care system. Policymakers, who play the leading role, stress action-oriented goals, feasible strategies, and the immediate consequences of government decisions. For them, gaining power, maintaining control over political institutions, and realizing certain policy objectives take priority. They identify health problems, specify the community's health needs, and review alternative programs for handling problems. Discovering a cure for cancer assumes greater concern than financing basic cell research. Tactics for making decisions focus on the interpretation of information from personal experiences, political party cues, interest group communications, media messages, public opinion surveys, and academic reports. After formulating a policy, government officials evaluate its implementation to ascertain the degree to which the actual outcomes correspond with policy intentions. Today political leaders have the potential power to wield extensive impacts — sickness or health for millions of people. Their success in achieving intended consequences depends on their ability to use resources that overcome opposition, coordinate dispersed actors in a coalition, and mobilize apathetic individuals behind a cause, such as a more effective health care system.

Like the policymaker, citizens seek remedies to practical problems — for example, improved health at the lowest personal cost. They participate in churches, unions, businesses, political parties, and voluntary associations dedicated to health improvements. These organizations may work for changes outside the policy arena, or they may pressure government officials for more generous, comprehensive, accessible, and inexpensive health programs. Unless individuals actively participate in an organization that can effectively influence the policy process, they will likely wield only a limited impact over the specific programs that finally emerge. Citizens' policy influence also derives from their socioeconomic status, information, ideological commitments, and congruence between their policy preferences and the preferences of key personnel: cabinet ministers, government civil servants, political party activists, and interest group leaders. Because these political elites are usually wealthier, more highly educated, better informed, and more ideologically aware than the general citizenry, they articulate more detailed policy views, issue preciser instructions, and wield greater influence over the health policy process.

Although many policy analysts try to shape government decisionmaking, basic theoretical research assumes a high intellectual priority. They aim at accurate descriptions and explanations of policy operations. How and why did a set of interacting variables — business fragmentation and leftwing party cohesion — produce a specific outcome, such as the enactment of a health care law that expands the access of comprehensive services to the whole population? Policy analysts describe and explain the impact of government decisions on economic efficiency, public satisfaction, equality of treatment, and effectiveness in improving the national population's health. Evaluation of different policy options also becomes a major preoccupation. By estimating the impacts of each alternative, analysts try to blend core values — criteria of worth — with issues about feasibility. Linking theory to practical policy issues, they suggest alternative policy solutions, indicate the success of policy options adopted in the past, and often justify government decisions.

However great their expertise, few health researchers can transform all their policy preferences into government decisions. Policy analysts have the greatest influence over framing the political agenda. They identify key issues like health inequalities or inefficiencies, highlight their importance, articulate assumptions about government's role in the health care arena, and formulate causal attributions behind the problem, for example, the individual and environmental sources of illness. Analysts wield less impact over specific public policies made by elected officials. Civil servants, however, remain more responsive to health researchers' studies and recommendations. Both university-educated groups value specialized knowledge. In social democratic systems like Sweden and in organic corporatist states — Germany, France, Japan, — policy analysts achieve more influence than in the entrepreneurial United States, where civil servants play a less dominant role over health care decisionmaking.[5]

CONCLUSION

Focusing on the links between social inequality and public health, this book probes four key issues. First, what groups wield the greatest influence over the policy process? How elitist, pluralist, and populist are policy formulation and administration? Three models — the entrepreneurial, organic corporatist, and social democratic — highlight the power relationships among government agencies, political parties, and interest groups. Second, which groups gain the greatest benefits and suffer the fewest economic losses from fiscal policies? How regressive are programs for financing the health care system? Third, how comprehensive and generous are the health services covered under public health plans? How egalitarian is the provision of high-quality health benefits, particularly to poorer individuals?   Fourth,   what variables explain the relationship between social stratification and health? Why are some groups healthier than others? In most contemporary industrial societies, higher socioeconomic status brings healthier populations, as measured by infant mortality, life expectancy, and incidence of diseases. Women live longer than do men; female babies face lower infant mortality rates. The health status of ethnic groups depends on their socioeconomic status, especially living and working conditions. Social stratification affects health and the effectiveness of public policies in mitigating the impact of social inequalities. To what extent can public health policies improve people's health and change the social stratification system? Policy success stems from the impact of public programs on the cultural, structural, and personal conditions that produce improved health. The institutionalization and internalization of health-promoting values lead to greater resilience in performing daily activities. Policies aimed at changing structural conditions focus on reducing income inequalities, expanding education, increasing provision of social services (prenatal care, health care for the elderly), and more effectively regulating health risks — for example, polluted air and water, hazardous wastes, unhealthy food, dilapidated housing, unsafe working environments. From the behavioral perspective, personal orientations (cognitions, values, attitudes), individual lifestyles, contacts with social support networks, and use of health services influence the effect of cultural values and structural conditions on individual health.

The causal relationships that link public policies to national, group, and individual health remain difficult to ascertain. Analysts need to know the actual impact of both policy and nonpolicy variables on improved health. Which variables can policymakers most effectively control? They can more easily change managerial processes, alter financial incentives, expand health-related information, increase environmental regulations, reduce physician/patient ratios, and decentralize administration than they can transform personal lifestyles, individuals' genetic predispositions, or dominant cultural values. Particularly in democratic political systems, where countervailing pressures constrain official actions, government leaders cannot directly control all the environmental conditions or individual behaviors that cause health. Hence, policy analysts face difficulties ascertaining the probability that a specific program will actually secure more equal health among nations, social groups, and individuals.[6]

Part I

Models of Health Care Systems

From the end of World War II through the late 1970s, the supply of public health services expanded. Structural administration became more concentrated. Central governments gained greater authority over local and regional agencies. Public institutions assumed responsibilities that private organizations — families, churches, mutual aid groups, unions — used to exercise before the war. Furthermore, governments enacted higher expenditures and taxes for health care as a proportion of the national income. The scope of services also increased. Benefits became more generous. More people — young and old, rich and poor, urbanites and rural residents — gained coverage under the generous programs for hospital, ambulatory, and dental care.

At the beginning of the 1980s, the government supply of health benefits reversed course. Regional governments — Canadian provinces, German Länder, Swedish counties, American states — secured greater policy influence vis-à-vis the central government; they both came to share similar responsibilities. Plans for privatization and deregulation gave private health care agencies more autonomy from direct government control. Government expenditures for health care as a share of the national income rose less rapidly than during the era from 1960 through 1980. Austerity programs lessened the range of health benefits available to individuals. Benefits reflected a less generous and inclusive policy commitment.

Despite these convergent patterns of health policies throughout the industrialized world, significant differences still marked Japan, West European nations, and North America. The United States pursued the least comprehensive, inclusive, generous, and egalitarian programs. Although other nations like England and the Netherlands implemented 'managed competition' policies, citizens still enjoyed fairly equal access to public health services. Swedish policymakers undertook limited privatization. The Canadian federal government decentralized health care responsibilities to the provinces; even the reduced health benefits remained more accessible to a wider range of people than in the United States. German leaders have blended decentralized administration with comprehensive, generous health services that are unequally distributed. Despite France's reputation as a cohesive, centralized state, French officials regionalized authority over health care issues; private hospitals and private physicians still exercise considerable autonomy from tight central government control. In Part I we will explore these similarities and differences among industrial societies by using three models — the entrepreneurial, organic corporatist, and social democratic — to compare public health programs in eight countries.

In *The Three Worlds of Welfare Capitalism,* Gøsta Esping-Andersen formulated three models of social service administration: the liberal entrepreneurial, conservative corporatist, and social democratic. Although he applied these models to employment policies and cash benefits — pensions, disability insurance, unemployment compensation, poor relief, — they also have relevance for understanding health care policies. Each model reveals distinctive ideological and structural characteristics.[1]

Ideologically, the entrepreneurial model stresses 'liberal' promarket values. Government functions to preserve and expand the health care market. Opposed to a bureaucratic state, entrepreneurialism upholds voluntarism, free choice, equal opportunity, and equality before the law. Of all three models, the entrepreneurial one gives the highest priority to competitive individualism. Policy actors view the national interest as the sum of particular interests. Agreement on legal procedures supplies the moral solidarity that restrains the competition among economic interest groups. According to entrepreneurs, freedom must assume priority over equality, especially equality of income. In a competitive market, both patients and health providers should have wide choice over resources and their use, free from bureaucratic state interference. The liberal entrepreneurial model supports equal opportunity if it enables individuals to maximize their choices on the health market.

From a structural perspective, the entrepreneurial model reflects fragmented, dispersed power arrangements. Neither a powerful bureaucratic state nor strong political parties coordinates the policy process. Decentralized government agencies assume major responsibilities for making and carrying out health programs. Private organizations, particularly business corporations, prevail over public institutions. The former handle many activities that exert a societal impact. Under the pluralist arrangements, several groups compete for policy influence. Through exchange interactions, they make decisions based on estimated costs and benefits. Even though business firms wield dominant influence over the health policy process, other groups —

medical associations, unions, ethnic/linguistic organizations, senior citizens' associations — also exercise some leverage over health policymakers. Under this fragmented power structure, the market, rather than the central state, supplies integration. Access to the market determines the comprehensiveness and generosity of health benefits. Those with the most money purchase generous services from private health insurance corporations, which view the wealthiest as the healthiest and hence the lowest actuarial risks. Low-income people must rely on public health programs for their health care services. Based on means-tests, these programs usually supply niggardly benefits. Entrepreneurial health policies thereby stratify people into different tiers depending on their income and political power. According to the entrepreneurial market model, the central government performs only limited activities. It lacks the power to achieve tight regulation over the extensive private health care sector. As a result, public health policies secure incremental, marginal changes. Major changes in health programs arise from the private sector and local-regional governments, not from the central nation-state.

By contrast, the organic corporatist model highlights classical 'conservative' principles. Government should maintain social order, harmony, and sacred values linked to the family and religious institutions. Interactions between leaders and followers exemplify hierarchical relationships. Paternalistic elites have the duty to care for their subordinates' health needs. Group obligations take precedence over the rights of individuals, who must defer to state officials, ecclesiastical hierarchs, family heads, and corporation executives.

Structurally, the organic corporatist model features a more monistic pattern of elitist power than does the entrepreneurial paradigm. A powerful government bureaucracy often coordinates the policy process. Despite this unified control, extensive decentralization also occurs. Regional governments and churches make and implement health care decisions partly financed by the national government. Hence, a blurred distinction links central with regional authority. Similarly, the interactions between private and public agencies also reveal fuzzy boundaries. Private groups implement government health programs. Under this pluralist power structure, extensive social differentiation marks group interactions. Religious, ethnic-linguistic, and occupational associations share decisionmaking authority. By including diverse interest groups in the policy process, government officials try to accommodate divergent preferences so that a policy consensus emerges. Yet this process is more elitist than populist. Interest group leaders, not rank-and-file members, participate in policy forums. The emphasis on accommodation conflicts with group inequalities. Lower-status individuals play a passive role. Health policies secure different benefits for diverse groups. Wealthy individuals and those working in high-status positions such as the civil service gain more generous services than do less advantaged people. Given these elitist, decentralized arrangements, policy changes occur incrementally. Even though the central/regional governments regulate nonprofit insurance agencies and subsidize their activities, public officials lack the power to institute immediate, transformative health policies. Instead, extensive time elapses before all policy participants — government leaders, party activists, insurance executives, medical personnel, labor union heads, clergy — reach accommodations.

Unlike organic corporatism, the social democratic model can institute more rapid, comprehensive policy changes because of clearer accountability and stronger commitment to egalitarian values. Democratic socialists hold that government should enhance socioeconomic equality and the dignity of workers, whatever their occupational status. Public policies ought to increase the freedom and equality of women, low-income people, the marginalized, and those of low status. Individuals should not only gain equal opportunities to health care but also enjoy egalitarian health treatments and health conditions. Whereas liberal entrepreneurs highlight competitive individualism, social democrats view individuals as more altruistic and cooperative. Viewing society as a fellowship, they assume that people will realize improved health only in a socialist system governed by democratic procedures. Instead of an aggregate of individual interests, the public good emerges from a cooperative process of reconciling divergent preferences according to solidary principles.

Power arrangements under the social democratic model establish clear sources of political accountability. A strong socialist, social democratic, or labor party, along with a cohesive cabinet of ministers and state bureaucracy, coordinates the policy process. Although governing centralized unitary states, social democratic officials delegate authority over health issues to regional and local institutions, which maintain some autonomy and financial resources from tight central control. Among the three models, the social democratic one shows the greatest dominance of the public over the private sector. Neither private commercial insurance corporations nor nonprofit insurance associations assume an activist role in providing health services. Instead, government health agencies negotiate with medical associations over health issues, including fees, charges, and types of health benefits offered to individuals. In this pluralist system, class ties take precedence over communal affiliations. Labor unions and cooperative societies play an especially active role. Business corporations and medical associations wield less influence than under the organic corporatist or liberal entrepreneurial models. The government performs an extensive scope of activities. It owns a large share of hospitals, employs a high proportion of health personnel, plans health programs, and regulates the provision of health care services. Government expenditures for health constitute a large percentage of total expenses. High progressive income taxes finance these programs. Because of extensive cohesion in the decision process, incumbent government officials remain accountable for policy contents and their outcomes. Hence, they can institute fairly comprehensive changes in a brief time. Nation-states governed by democratic socialists have implemented the most comprehensive, generous, inclusive, egalitarian health programs: hospital and physician services, preventive care measures, child care, family allowances, parental leaves, disability insurance, and sickness benefits.

Chapters 2, 3, and 4 use these three models to analyze the administration of public health policies in eight countries. Rather than empirical descriptions of concrete societies, models represent abstract representations — cognitive maps or pictorial representations — that simplify the dominant modes of public policymaking. In actuality, all societies feature a mixture of different models. Often within a single country, leaders upholding divergent models compete for policy supremacy. Particularly during the last decade, those supporting the liberal entrepreneurial model have gained greater policy influence over organic corporatists and particularly social democrats. We explore these conflicts among advocates of competing models by examining the structural power of several key organizations: governments (national, regional, local), political parties, and social groups, including business firms, labor unions, and medical associations.

Three related issues assume particular significance. First, who governs the health care systems? Which organizations wield the dominant policy influence? Second, what structural conflicts face policymakers? Third, how does the conflict between integration and differentiation explain the type of policy changes realized by government leaders?

The power of government agencies over health programs shapes the type and rate of changes emerging from the interactions among all these structures. A powerful nation-state — one with high coordination, centralization, autonomy from social groups, and scope of activities — can implement rapid, transformative changes if its political leaders show the will to undertake innovative health programs. Less powerful political systems with fragmented authority, dispersed decisionmaking, and limited scope may formulate flexible programs adapted to local conditions. Yet under the dispersed power structure, conservative elites retain the opportunity to block policy innovations that threaten their interests. Hence, policy changes stem from private organizations or local/regional governments. The policy process generates incremental, rather than transformative, changes.[2]

2 The Entrepreneurial Model

The entrepreneurial model gives the highest policy priority to market principles. The goals of efficiency, increased productivity, and cost containment take precedence over equal access to health services and equal treatment by medical personnel. To attain these goals, entrepreneurs support decentralization, competitive markets, and limited state intervention into the health care market. According to this model, sharp distinctions separate the private from the public sector, with government playing a subordinate role. The market responds to diverse needs and preferences. Purchasers, providers, and consumers enjoy extensive market freedom. Managers in private health insurance corporations make decisions based on cost-benefit analyses. Physicians and hospital personnel have clinical autonomy to treat patients, who choose their health providers from competing plans. The individual assumes personal responsibility for health care needs. Healthy persons finance their medical expenses through private insurance plans. Whereas the healthy pay low insurance premiums, higher-risk sick people must pay more expensive premiums. Means-tests determine eligibility for public health care benefits, which government officials allocate mainly to those with low incomes. These entrepreneurial values reinforce a socially stratified health care system based on extensive income differentiation.[1]

Canada and particularly the United States best illustrate the entrepreneurial model. Both nations have a decentralized federal system, extensive pluralism, high civil liberties, and a private enterprise market economy. Public policies emerge when political leaders can form coalitions and negotiate compromises based on exchange relationships. Despite these similarities, the two North American societies have pursued divergent health policies since the 1960s. Canadian health programs provide more universal, comprehensive, and generous benefits. The parliamentary system, which fuses legislative with executive powers, enables a majority governing party to coordinate the policy process and hence

19

implement comprehensive programs preferred by the top leaders. Profit-oriented health insurance corporations wield less veto power over public health policies than in the United States. Even if liberal entrepreneurial values have become more dominant during recent years, social democratic and organic corporatist principles still retain some influence on Canadian public officials. In the United States, the dispersal of government powers provides several opportunities for opposition groups to impede the enactment of comprehensive, egalitarian, inclusive public health policies. At the federal level the president, Congress, and courts share decisionmaking authority. Within each branch competing factions contend for policy dominance. These federal officials must share responsibilities for health programs with state government agencies, which also lack cohesion. Given the fragmented political systems, private businesses gain extensive policy leverage over government decisionmakers. Forprofit organizations — private health insurance corporations, hospital conglomerates, nursing homes, pharmaceutical industries — implement public health plans.[2]

THE UNITED STATES

Since the 1970s the United States has moved toward a profit-oriented health system that stresses managed care but negates several entrepreneurial values such as individual choice, professional autonomy, and competition among small-scale organizations. Private insurance corporations and federal government regulatory agencies, especially the Health Care Financing Administration, wield centralized control over physicians, hospital personnel, and patients. Greater bureaucratic standardization has emerged, as reflected in uniform standards for medical treatment and categorization of illnesses. Under managed-care plans in health maintenance organizations, health providers and their patients face more restricted choices than before. Managers in government agencies and oligopolistic insurance corporations make key health decisions. Rather than clearly separated, the private and public health sectors reveal fuzzy boundaries. Managers move from government health agencies to private health insurance corporations. In both sectors, they base their decisions on cost-effective considerations. The same tendency has emerged in nonprofit health institutions, which give cost containment a higher priority than equality of health care.[3] Even though the entrepreneurial model upholds a clear differentiation of the private from the public health sectors, both reveal reciprocal interactions, interdependence, and fusion. The government finances private agencies but wields ineffective controls over them.

Four private structures — health insurance corporations, pharmaceutical manufacturing industries, hospital conglomerates, and the American Medical Association — exert dominant policy influence. Concentrated industries have arisen from the mergers and joint ventures among health insurance corporations, health maintenance organizations (HMOs), hospital chains, and suppliers of medical equipment and drugs. Profit-oriented firms have become more important at the expense of nonprofit agencies, such as Blue Cross insurance firms and local hospitals run by religious institutions. Specialized managers have gained rising influence over medical professionals. Whereas physicians stress clinical autonomy based on medical expertise, managers uphold technical expertise based on productivity and instrumental rationality. This trend toward increased managerial influence over health decisions stems from economic and political changes. National and world capitalism has experienced a rapid growth in medical technology, greater specialization, and the globalization of markets, as reflected in higher world competition, increased foreign trade, and more overseas investment. Politically, the decline of the Democratic Party, the rise of the suburbs, and the greater power wielded by social movements stressing antistatist, inegalitarian policy preferences and support for expanded individual consumption have also promoted the commercialization of the health care sector.[4]

Since World War II federal government policies promoted the movement toward forprofit health insurance corporations and exerted only limited regulation over their operations. The 1945 McCarran-Ferguson Act prevented the national government from enforcing antitrust laws against insurance corporations. The 1974 Employee Retirement Income Security Act (ERISA) deterred state governments from regulating health insurance plans offered by employers. In 1981 the Omnibus Budget and Reconciliation Act authorized state governments to use HMOs for Medicaid recipients. During that decade public policies also encouraged Medicare patients to join HMOs. Under Reagan administration directives, the Office of Health Maintenance Organizations in the Department of Health and Human Services allocated federal grants only to forprofit HMOs.

Private health insurance corporations have lobbied Congress to block the enactment of proposals for a universal, comprehensive, egalitarian health care program. Major contributors to US congressional representatives and presidential candidates include the National Association of Life Underwriters, the American Council of Life Insurance, the Independent Insurance Agents of America, the American Family Life Insurance Company, Travelers, Prudential, and Metropolitan. They contribute to incumbent congresspeople from both political parties and mainly to Republican candidates for president. Business lobbies articulating small companies' interests — the Health Insurance Association of America, the National Federation of Independent Business, local chambers of commerce — oppose public health plans that mandate employer benefits. Widespread advertising by these organizations over the mass media help sway public opinion and legislators against egalitarian policies. The growth of forprofit health insurance corporations and managerial control by them has secured few benefits for low-income, high-risk individuals: part-time employees, immigrants, workers who frequently change jobs, the disabled, poor children in rural areas and the inner cities, cognitively-impaired aged persons, home health care givers, and unskilled service workers for small firms. Largely uninsured, these consumers wield little influence over health care policymakers.[5]

Pharmaceutical industries also play a major role shaping public health policies. Unlike other health care suppliers, which finance both incumbent Democrats and Republicans, the major pharmaceutical manufacturers contribute primarily to Republican candidates — political leaders who reject tight government regulation of commercial health industries but support market-based programs that ensure high profits for private enterprises. During the last decade, drug industries, like health insurance corporations, became more concentrated. Whereas before the 1900s vendors moved from one town to another selling patent medicines, today transnational oligopolies dominate both the production and the distribution of pharmaceuticals. Mergers have strengthened the power of such firms as Merck, Eli Lilly, SmithKline Beecham, Bristol-Myers Squibb, and Pfizer. They not only manufacture and sell drugs but they also have leverage over corporate chain pharmacies, laboratory diagnostic tests, biotechnology, and medical equipment.

Federal government agencies exert little control over drug production and prices. Even though the federal government finances drug research, the National Institutes of Health have abandoned their authority to require that pharmaceutical industries charge 'reasonable' prices for their products. While granting rebates to hospital conglomerates, pharmacy chains, and forprofit HMOs, drug companies levy higher prices on their products sold to the government. Except for aged citizens who have joined an HMO, the elderly must pay high out-of-pocket expenditures for drugs. Often the same pharmaceutical manufacturer produces both generic and higher-priced brand-name drugs; both types sell at prices above production costs. Many pharmaceutical corporations operate in Puerto Rico, where they pay low federal taxes or gain a tax exemption. The Food and Drug Administration conducts minimal testing of new drugs, which need FDA approval. Instead, it delegates authority over drug testing to major universities such as Duke and the University of North Carolina. University physicians and research scientists receive funds from the pharmaceutical manufacturers to finance these tests. Hence, federal subsidization occurs with only limited regulation over production or prices.[6]

Like the pharmaceutical industries, hospitals have recently experienced the same trend toward more mergers, chains, conglomerates, and forprofit investor-owned institutions. Before World War II city governments and churches owned most hospitals. Their boards of directors comprised physicians, priests, nuns, nurses, and urban officials, not businessmen. Private regulations and local control shaped hospital operations. Volunteer assistance and philanthropic financial support kept costs fairly low. Providing a community service, these nonprofit hospitals supplied health care for low-income people and the working class. After 1970 more centralized hospital conglomerates emerged. Particularly in the rural areas and inner cities, nonprofit private and public hospitals closed or merged into forprofit hospital conglomerates. Centralized management replaced the decentralized control formerly exerted by physicians, clergy, volunteers, and local leaders.

Today federal government officials from the Health Care Financing Administration and corporate managers determine hospital decisions, along with the business executives, lawyers, and bankers who dominate hospital boards of directors. Business managerialism triumphs over medical professionalism. Physicians wield less clinical autonomy as hospital administrators pursue strategies to contain costs, raise efficiency, expand technology, and secure the highest possible profits in a competitive environment. Whereas locally-controlled hospitals used to cooperate with each other, the newer hospital conglomerates compete for profitable patients, not the poor. Greater inequalities and social differentiation have resulted from these trends toward hospital concentration. Many emergency departments that used to treat low-income sick persons have closed. Remaining urban public hospitals treat indigent and Medicaid patients for serious physical injuries. Especially in the Southern, Southwestern, and Western states, investor-owned, private forprofit hospitals treat wealthier individuals, who undergo profitable treatments like heart surgery.

Even if federal government agencies wield tighter regulatory authority over hospitals than over pharmaceutical industries, this control remains limited. Joined by private health insurance corporations, the federal government during the 1980s promoted forprofit hospital chains. Nonprofit hospitals no longer secured such large benefits from their tax-exempt status. Rather than a government agency, a private organization controlled by hospitals — the Joint Commission on Accreditation of Healthcare Organizations — accredits hospitals according to lax standards. Unaccredited institutions secure no Medicare revenues. Not only the Health Care Financing Administration (HCFA) officials but employers and private insurance managers monitor the financial performance of hospitals and physicians.[7]

Although the American Medical Association and state medical associations dominated the health policy process from 1920 through the 1970s, their power waned during the 1980s. Before World War II most physicians functioned as solo practitioners, as independent proprietors who earned a fee for their services. Until the 1970s their authority rested on professional medical expertise. Through control over licensing and medical school enrollment, state medical associations regulated the supply of doctors. Exerting extensive clinical autonomy, physicians shaped the demand for health care services. High cohesion, financial resources, a large membership, and close ties with business enterprises enabled the AMA to undertake effective lobbying activities before Congress. In the 1980s the AMA's power declined. Whereas in 1975 nearly three-fourths of doctors belonged to the AMA, by 1995 its membership had fallen to only 40 percent. The AMA still contributed more money to congressional campaigns than did any other interest group. Yet lower cohesion weakened its influence over health care issues. Other medical associations — for example, the American College of Surgeons, the American College of Physicians, and Physicians for a National Health Program — articulated policy positions that diverged from official AMA stands. Growing fragmentation among general practitioners, specialists, academic researchers, administrators, and alternative medical personnel — chiropractors, osteopaths — further impeded doctors' attitudinal and organizational cohesion, thereby lessening AMA policy effectiveness. The increased importance of managed care, forprofit HMOs, private health insurance corporations, and hospital chains split the close ties that allied the AMA with private businesses. Over four-fifths of physicians now participate in managed care plans that offer services through networks of health personnel who receive a fee for each enrolled patient. Entrepreneurial concerns for efficiency, productivity, and cost containment take precedence over respect for professional medical knowledge. This trend toward cost containment, managerial dominance, and greater bureaucratic control by private health insurance corporations and the federal Health Care Financing Administration limits doctors' independence. Hence, the AMA no longer wields such dominant influence over government policymakers.[8]

Compared with private organizations, national government institutions exert limited control over health care decisions and fail to integrate the fragmented policy process. Except for veterans' health care administered by the federal Department of Veterans Affairs, the other health plans remain highly decentralized. Under contracts administered by the HCFA, over 80 private health insurance corporations administer the Medicare program for the elderly. State governments implement most other public health care programs, especially Medicaid, which covers low-income children, pregnant women, the disabled, and the elderly poor. Under Medicaid, the federal government issues general guidelines for eligibility, authorizes minimum benefits, and finances from 50 percent to 80 percent of state expenditures. State government leaders make decisions about optional benefits, payments for services, and specific groups deemed eligible for Medicaid benefits. Yet most states show only limited compliance with federal standards. Insufficient financial resources, reluctance to raise taxes, and pressures from the business sector limit coverage and benefits. Poor people, especially children, face the greatest difficulties gaining access to health care services. The elderly fare better. High administrative costs for Medicaid exacerbate these socioeconomic inequalities. Only in wealthy states led by a Democratic governor and Democratic legislators do elected officials implement generous Medicaid programs.[9]

Of the two major parties, the Democrats have supported more activist government policies to improve public health. Democrats scored their greatest successes during the 1960s and early 1970s, when they controlled both houses of Congress. The Medicare-Medicaid legislation passed in 1965. Most regulatory laws promoting workplace safety and a healthy 'clean' environment were enacted at the start of the 1970s. Influential interest groups such as the civil rights movement, labor unions, ecological associations, and senior citizens' groups, especially the American Association of Retired Persons, actively supported congressional Democrats in their drive to enact these health policies. By the 1980s, however, Democratic party cohesion waned. Unions and civil rights organizations no longer wielded such political influence. The Republican party, allied with powerful private businesses and evangelical Christian churches, became stronger. Its congressional leaders during the 1990s advocated privatization, vouchers for private health insurance plans, medical savings accounts, block grants to state governments for Medicaid, and limits on expenditures for public health care programs, including reduced government funds for Medicare, Medicaid, the National Institutes of Health, and the Agency for Health Care Policy and Research. Opposed to abortion and antismoking laws, congressional Republicans backed pharmaceutical industries' efforts to gain speedier approval of new drugs by the Food and Drug Administration. They also supported bills to deregulate health, safety, and the environmental institutions, such as the Food and Drug Administration, the Environmental Protection Agency, and the Occupational Safety and Health Administration. Most Democratic congresspeople opposed these Republican measures to weaken regulatory agencies, reduce public health expenditures, and limit the enforcement of laws against pollution. Yet faced with pressures for cost containment and dependent on private businesses for financial contributions, congressional Democrats have accepted less severe cuts in government expenditures than those backed by Republicans. Few Democratic proposals for health care reforms have leaned toward a single-payer system administered by the national government. Instead, most Democratic bills favor more comprehensive programs administered by either private insurance corporations or state governments, with federal agencies supplying guidelines and overseeing policy implementation.[10]

In sum, many different types of structural conflicts pervade the complex, differentiated US health policy process. Conflicts occur both within an institution as well as between such structures as governments, political parties, and social groups. At the national level, government agencies compete with each other for policy influence, even within the same branch. For example, the Office of Management and Budget tries to reduce expenditures by federal regulatory agencies. Numerous congressional committees propose divergent health bills. Led by Chief Justice William Rehnquist, the Supreme Court limits the right of federal courts to challenge the actions of hospitals endangering their patients. Conflicts between the presidency, Congress, and the Court also give organizations against transformative policies the opportunity to veto these changes. The federal system exacerbates intrastructural and interstructural conflicts. Governors from different states struggle to secure scarce resources for their health programs. Wealthy states compete with poorer states. Ideological conflicts pit the Northeast against the more 'conservative' South. State officials often reject compliance with federal government mandates. Both major political parties experience internal policy fragmentation between those preferring more extensive public programs and others supporting private provision of health care services. During the last decade ideological polarization between Democratic and Republican activists has hindered the ability of legislators to secure compromises. When a different party controls the presidency than the Congress, accommodation becomes more difficult. Group conflicts animate political life. Intragroup factionalism, conflicts between groups, and hostile relations among groups, political parties, and government agencies fragment decisionmaking authority. For example, unions of health personnel — the Service Employees International Union, the National Union of Hospital and Health Care Workers, the American Nurses Association — bargain to secure higher wages, more generous fringe benefits, and better working conditions. Physicians' associations seek greater professional autonomy from the private health insurance corporation managers who have increased their power over medical treatments. Opposed to liberal Democratic congresspersons, private business executives ally with Republicans behind increased privatization and deregulation of public health programs, with a focus on measures that will curtail employer costs. Yet within the business sector, cleavages fragment employer solidarity. Corporations articulate divergent policy preferences from smaller firms. Unlike large-scale enterprises, small businesses employ sicker workers and incur higher administrative costs enforcing government health regulations. Hence, they express stronger opposition to employer mandates and employer-insured health plans that raise firms' overall health costs. Small business executives instead support Republican plans to expand medical savings accounts with low premiums and high deductibles. Despite this business fragmentation, private enterprises, commercial health insurance corporations, and medical associations retain greater cohesion than most other organizations. No comprehensive public health programs will emerge without their passive support or at least indifference.

Because the US health care system functions with high differentiation, complexity, group inequalities, and numerous veto points, few comprehensive, generous, and egalitarian policies have occurred at either the federal or state government level. Opponents of comprehensive change retain greater cohesion than do its supporters. Policy stalemate usually prevails. Government officials can implement policy changes only when their attitudinal and organizational solidarity exceeds the opposition's cohesion. Even under this condition, new programs bring incremental modifications, such as government regulation of private health plans that provide enhanced benefits for pregnant mothers, the elderly, and individuals with preexisting medical conditions. The most significant changes originate in the private sector, not in government institutions. During the early 1990s the fear of interventionist government actions by a Democratic administration, rather than the passage of innovative legislation, stimulated private businesses and health insurance corporations to undertake changes in their health plans.[11] The movement toward managed competition reflected the continuing US commitment to entrepreneurial values.

CANADA

Whereas the United States more fully embodies the entrepreneurial model, Canadian health policies have blended liberal entrepreneurialism with features from organic corporatism and democratic socialism. Canadians operate an even more decentralized and pluralist system than do Americans. Yet under parliamentary government, the governing party in the cabinet coordinates the policy process at both the federal and provincial levels. To a greater extent than in the United States, regional governments assume primary responsibility for health care issues. Provincial health ministries, rather than private health insurance corporations, manage medical care and wield an extensive scope of public authority. The decentralized, pluralist Canadian system stresses liberal values: free trade, a market economy, civil liberties, the rule of law, autonomous churches, and individual rights. Compared with American officials, however, Canadian leaders place greater emphasis on health care as a public good available to all residents, not just as a private benefit purchased on the market. Nonprofit institutions, particularly hospitals and nursing homes, assume greater importance than in the United States. Instead of administering health care services, private insurance corporations offer plans that supplement benefits secured from the provincial government. Upholding both individual freedom and social equality, Canadians have extensive choice to select their own physician, who functions as a private entrepreneur. The public health program also features egalitarian access and treatment. All citizens participate in the same provincial health plan. They secure access to basic benefits: hospital services, medical care, and long-term nursing.[12] In short, Canadian public policymakers administer a more comprehensive, egalitarian, generous, publicly-financed program than operates in the United States.

Although before World War II the Canadian policy process functioned under a strong national government but weaker provincial authorities, today the ten Canadian provinces wield greater influence vis-à-vis the federal government than do the 50 American states. The provincial prime minister, the cabinet, and senior civil servants take major responsibility for most social services, including health care, education, housing, and family programs. Federal government powers revolve mainly around the specification of national policy guidelines, tax collection, disbursement of unrestricted funds to the provinces, and foreign relations. However important the decentralizing trends, the national Supreme Court under the 1982 Constitution Act secured greater authority to regulate the conflicts between the federal and provincial government as well as to promote individual rights against government restrictions, such as the right to an abortion. Yet the 1982 Canadian Charter of Rights and Freedoms gave provincial governments the authority to enforce laws that violate Charter provisions.

Both within the Canadian nation and each province, extensive decentralization occurs. The federal Department of Health and Welfare issues general standards and more specific regulations about provincial health plans, especially their need to provide comprehensive, universal, portable benefits administered by a nonprofit public agency. Provincial health ministers, finance ministers, other cabinet members, and the premier wield dominant influence over health issues. Usually a single party controls the one-chamber provincial legislature. With tight party discipline in legislative voting, it helps coordinate the policy process.

Even if the provincial health ministry exerts the greatest power, health authority boards at the regional and district levels influence some local decisions. They assess the health needs of citizens, set policy priorities, recommend budget reductions, and oversee the operation of hospitals, nursing homes, community support services, and home care. Yet these boards wield limited authority, especially over revenue enhancement and physicians' budgets. The provincial government's health ministry usually appoints their members, controls their budgets, and specifies their operational procedures. Although board members view themselves as representatives of the local citizenry, their elitist background (high incomes, university education) and lack of information about citizens' preferences for health policies mean that low-income people gain little empowerment over local decisionmaking.

Agencies in cities and towns also cannot effectively shape general health care provision. District health councils, community health centers, and community clinics stress preventive services, practice holistic medicine, assist low-income individuals, and promote citizen participation. Typical activities include health education, home health care, and help to drug addicts, youth, and the disabled. Most prevalent in areas governed by the socialist New Democratic Party or by the Parti Québécois, community health centers secure strongest participation from women physicians, doctors under 30, immigrant physicians, and nurse practitioners. Nevertheless, most poor people seek health care from emergency departments in urban hospitals, rather than in the few available community health centers. Provincial medical associations, general practitioners, health administrators, and ministers of finance and treasury oppose their operation. For example, in the Quebec province, conflicts have arisen between different types of control. Administrators within the Treasury Department and the Ministry of Health and Social Affairs prefer managerial control, with a focus on efficiency, effectiveness, and respect for hierarchical authority. Physicians want to maintain their professional control based on clinical autonomy. Participants in the *centres locaux de services communautaires* and in the *conseils régionaux de la santé et des services sociaux* seek expanded, more egalitarian populist control. Elected party legislators from either the Parti Québécois or the Liberal Party who head the provincial Ministry of Health and Social Affairs in Quebec City stress the need for party political control, especially the need to make public health policies that will help them win reelection. In these role interactions between managers and employees, professionals and patients, and elected politicians and citizens, managers, physicians, and elected political leaders gain the dominant position.[13] Despite a few populist pressures, entrepreneurial practices based on managerial-professional control shape Canadian health policies.

Under pluralist Canadian arrangements, several groups — medical associations, business corporations and labor unions — share policy influence. Among these, the Canadian Medical Association and provincial medical associations play the key role. Particularly before 1965, they remained independent from direct provincial regulation. Even though the provincial health ministries licensed physicians, doctors shaped health policies and often held the top positions in these ministries. After 1965, however, the influence of provincial medical associations waned, while the power of the provincial health ministries increased. Managers, accountants, economists, and planners, rather than physicians, made the key regulations within the health ministry. They negotiated fees with the provincial medical associations, financed medical schools, hospitals, and nursing colleges, limited admissions to medical colleges, and placed limits on physicians' fees and hospital expenditures reimbursed by provincial governments. Provincial colleges of physicians and surgeons lost their previously strong authority to shape decisions taken by both the provincial government and by other medical personnel, such as chiropractors, nurses, and laboratory technicians. Extensive fragmentation weakened the medical profession. Divergent interests pitted the Canadian Medical Association against provincial medical associations, general practitioners against hospital specialists, medical doctors against chiropractors, and those in private practice (over 90 percent) against those in public health, administration, and medical colleges. In Quebec general practitioners, specialists, medical interns, medical students, and English-speaking physicians organized their own separate associations. This lack of cohesion impeded physicians' efforts to shape provincial health policies, especially about doctors' fees, billing practices, and prospects for instituting voluntary plans, rather than a mandatory public program in each province.

Whereas private health insurance corporations exert weaker influence than in the United States, unions assume greater policy significance. Most nursing homes and hospitals function as nonprofit institutions financed by the provincial government; only a few operate under a profit orientation. Offered mainly by employers, private health insurance plans provide only those benefits, like a private hospital room, dental care, and medicines, unavailable through the public provincial program. Although unions of health personnel scarcely exert the same impact over public policymakers as do medical associations, in the provinces hospital employees, nurses, and nurse practitioners can attain some of their goals, particularly in public sector agencies. Union ties with the New Democratic Party governing the provinces of Saskatchewan and British Columbia increased their influence over regional policies.[14]

Faced with extensive group differentiation, political parties assume the major responsibility for integrating the policy process. The parliamentary government and high party discipline in legislative voting behavior strengthen cohesion at each government level — federal and provincial, — but not between levels. National parties cannot control regional parties. Yet within each province a single party usually holds a majority of seats of the one-house chamber. Rather than form interparty coalitions, as in the United States, Canadian members of the same party vote the same way. Hence, the party controlling the provincial assembly and the cabinet can see its policy preferences translated into binding public policies. At the federal level minority governments have been more common, particularly from 1957 through 1984. During this period, the federal House of Commons enacted four health measures that guaranteed all Canadian residents access to physicians' services and hospital benefits as well as regulated their provision under a publicly-administered plan. When the governing Liberal party held a minority of seats in the House, it supported NDP proposals for higher expenditures on health care and for more comprehensive health programs. This strategic alliance arose only when the NDP was rising in popularity. When its popular appeal declined, then Liberal cabinet members refused to implement NDP proposals. Such a situation occurred during the 1993 federal election, when the NDP secured only 7 percent of the total popular vote and merely nine seats in the House of Commons. Winning 60 percent of the seats, the majority Liberal party enacted health care policies that decreased federal funds to the provinces and placed greater reliance on private revenues, which led to lower provincial benefits.

The health policies adopted in 1995 marked a trend toward a more entrepreneurial model. The federal government reduced its payments to the provinces, which received block grants for health, postsecondary education, and income maintenance services. Provincial government ministers had to decide the specific ways to allocate the decreased funds among these three general programs. Whereas in 1975 the federal government financed about two-fifths of total public health expenditures, by the mid 1990s that share had fallen to one-third. Public opposition to higher taxes led provincial officials to reduce spending. Individuals bore a greater proportion of health expenses; copayments, deductibles, and user fees increased. Some provincial health programs no longer covered such services as dental care for children, eye examinations, physical therapy, and certain prescription drugs. Instead, employers and private insurance companies began to provide these health services. As a result of the policy changes, greater inequalities emerged. Low-income individuals suffered the most from decreased public health expenditures and reduced benefits.

Both national and international structural conditions explain these recent policy changes. Like most industrialized nations, Canada suffered from a low growth rate during the 1990–1993 period. Unemployment escalated to over 11 percent of the labor force. The fiscal deficit at all government levels rose from 3 percent of the gross domestic product in 1989 to over 7 percent four years later — double the US figures. Federal government officials faced pressures to curtail expenditures. The intense regional, ethnic, and linguistic conflicts exacerbated the political pressures about the allocation of government revenues. Governments and social groups competed for scarce resources. Conflicts occurred between the federal and provincial governments as well as among the different provinces. Regionalism pitted the West against the East, Ontario against Quebec, and poorer provinces in the Maritimes against wealthier western provinces like Alberta. Ethnic-linguistic tensions also animated political life, as the English-speaking Canadians, French speakers, native peoples (First Nations), and immigrants from Eastern Europe, Asia, and the Caribbean sought to attain their interests and values through public policies. Yet the high fiscal deficits impeded the realization of group demands. The waning power of the socialist New Democratic Party and the rise of two regional parties — the West-based Reform Party and the Bloc Québécois — also weakened the policy commitment to comprehensive health services. Quebec citizens more strongly identified with their province than with the Canadian nation or federal government. Pledged to enhancing western provincial autonomy, the Reform Party allied with regional medical associations in their efforts to curtail government regulation over physicians and to expand private provision of health care services. The growing Canadian integration within the United States market also increased support for entrepreneurial values based on private enterprise. The North American Free Trade Agreement pressured Canadian leaders to contain government costs, especially for social services like health care. Along with NAFTA, greater competition in the world capitalist economy limited union influence over enterprise and government decisions but increased business leverage. Most Canadians read books published in the United States and especially watch US television programs. These media highlight liberal entrepreneurial values, such as private enterprise, free markets, free trade, individual competition, and personal choice. All these values discourage the implementation of comprehensive, generous, inclusive, and egalitarian public health policies.[15]

In sum, as the entrepreneurial model has grown stronger in Canada, the commitment to principles associated with social democracy and organic corporatism has weakened. With its greatest strength in Saskatchewan, the New Democratic Party (NDP) implemented health policies that expanded social services: dental care for children, medical equipment for the disabled, prescription drugs for the elderly, joint health and safety committees for workers, higher pensions and disability benefits to injured workers. Although workers gained the right to obtain information about toxic chemicals and to participate in decisions about reducing workplace hazards, the NDP government still limited employee control over the enterprise. In accordance with market liberalism, managers and professionals made the key decisions about the pace of work, investment, and use of technology. Safe working conditions in the mines assumed lower priority than high profits for joint mining ventures between the provincial government and private corporations. The NDP relied on these high profits and the market economy to finance its comprehensive social service programs. Hierarchical managerial authority, not egalitarian workers' participation, reflected the dominance of the entrepreneurial model, even in provinces governed by the New Democratic Party.

Organic corporatism no longer exerts such an important impact on public health policies. Linked to Tory principles, organic corporatism stressed a paternalistic social service state, communal obligations, deference to professional authority, and consultations between elite groups and government officials. Even if dominant before World War II among Progressive Conservative Party leaders, these values have declined with the growth of liberal entrepreneurialism. Although negotiations still take place between provincial medical association heads and government health ministers, medical associations now wield less authority over these ministries. Managerial dominance by provincial government accountants and planners has increased at the expense of deference to physicians' authority. Efforts to restrain costs mean that communal obligations recede. In Ontario the Conservative Party won the 1995 provincial election on a platform that promised lower income taxes, a balanced budget, reduced expenditures for social assistance, and the enactment of laws that would curtail union influence. The Tory government led by Prime Minister Michael Harris closed nonprofit hospitals but promoted the expansion of private commercial ones. Private health insurance corporations, such as Liberty Health, a branch of Boston's Liberty Mutual, expanded their influence over health service provision. They financed dental care, pharmaceutical purchases, home assistance, eye care, and hospital management, especially information technology processing. Pressured by the Ontario Manufacturers Association, the provincial government in 1997 abolished the Occupational Disease Panel, which focused on the medical needs of miners and automobile workers who had incurred lung cancer and other diseases at their workplace. These policy developments reflected the growing importance of the entrepreneurial model.[16]

Conclusion

Although US and Canadian government leaders have pursued somewhat divergent health policies since World War II, their programs became more similar during the 1990s. Both nations decentralize political power to regions and cities. Several agencies share responsibility for formulating health programs. Overlapping jurisdictions fragment the policy process, which reflects the preferences of many participants with divergent values and interests. Central party elites wield little influence over regional officials. However great the dispersion of power in the two North American societies, Canada features greater provincial autonomy. Provincial governments, especially their health ministries, wield the dominant influence. In the United States, however, the fifty state governments have less authority over the federal government, even if they do share extensive decisionmaking responsibilities. Private health insurance corporations integrate the administration of health care services. The growth of mergers, joint ventures, and conglomerates has reinforced this trend. They play a key role formulating and implementing not only private but public health programs.

Canadians live under a more decentralized system than the Americans and participate in a more pluralist policy process. Private businesses and medical associations exercise the greatest leverage over the US health policy process. These groups also shape Canadian public programs but share power with unions and local citizens' groups. Community health centers, councils, boards, and polyclinics expand the opportunities for various groups to wield some influence, however limited, over the provision of local health services.

Despite its decentralized pluralist arrangements, Canada operates a coordinated political system. Under the parliamentary structure that fuses legislative with executive powers, a majority party can enact its program without the need to make alliances with opposition parties. Interest groups such as private business corporations and medical associations gain fewer opportunities to veto public health proposals. Yet policy cohesiveness hardly eliminates political negotiations, compromises, and coalition formation. Facing pressures from a private enterprise economy, Canadian leaders, whatever their political party affiliation or ideological preferences, must uphold the rights of private businesspeople and medical professionals to conduct their activities free from tight government control. All Canadian parties — Liberals, Progressive Conservatives, New Democrats, Reformists, and activists within the Bloc Québécois and Parti Québécois — have supported a market economy and the need to curtail expenditures for social services, including health care. Similar tendencies have occurred in the United States, which has less cohesive political institutions. Even though the two major American party activists articulate a polarized rhetoric and the Republicans favor a more privatized, deregulated health care system, both congressional parties want to maintain policies that delegate crucial responsibilities to state governments and private health insurance corporations — a stand that reflects the dominance of entrepreneurial principles. Canadians value devolution but more to public agencies — the provincial government — and to such nonprofit private institutions as hospitals and nursing homes, which in the United States operate under greater profit-oriented management.

Fiscal policies illustrate the stronger politicized features of Canadian health programs. Whereas in Canada public expenditures for health care as a share of total health spending exceed 70 percent, in the United States that proportion amounts to around 45 percent. Canadian governments rely on income and sales taxes to finance their health programs. American policymakers choose less egalitarian measures, primarily social security taxes for public programs, especially Medicare, and health insurance premiums for private plans. Both employers and employees receive tax credits for purchasing private health insurance, since they can deduct the value of these premiums from their incomes and hence pay lower income taxes. This tax subsidy reinforces economic inequalities.

As a result of these administrative and fiscal dimensions, the Canadian governments implement more comprehensive, universal, generous, and egalitarian policies. Canada has a simpler system administered primarily by the provincial governments. All residents participate in the same provincial program that provides physician and hospital services. Other benefits vary by province. Compared with US state government leaders, Canadian provincial leaders supply greater prenatal care for mothers and more public assistance for the elderly. Faced with the extensive influence of private health insurance plans, Americans receive less egalitarian or comprehensive public benefits. Full-time, highly-paid employees in large private corporations and government agencies receive the greatest benefits from private health insurance. Part-time, temporary low-paid workers in small firms suffer the most; their employers have the least financial resources to supply private health insurance. For these marginals, health care becomes a scarce fringe benefit unavailable on either the private or public markets. The complex public health system operates different programs for divergent groups: Medicare for the elderly, Medicaid for some low-income individuals, the veterans' hospitals for the armed forces, and the Bureau of Indian Affairs for Native Americans. Under these programs, the working poor and children fare the worst. The drive to reduce expenditures for the 'undeserving poor' has meant stricter eligibility requirements and reduced benefits for Medicaid recipients. Over 50 percent of the population with incomes under half the US median income receives no Medicaid benefits. Canadians live under a less stratified, inegalitarian health care system. Yet, during the early 1990s Canada faced a fiscal crisis produced by low growth rates, high unemployment, and sizable fiscal deficits. At both the provincial and federal levels, government officials reduced expenditures for health care. As a result, benefits became less comprehensive and generous. Geographical and income inequalities widened as poorer provinces lacked the revenues to finance health services. Individuals and private insurance companies assumed greater responsibility for paying health care costs.[17] Even if the two North American nations have not converged toward identical health policies, their programs reflected more similar features stressed by the entrepreneurial model.

3 The Organic Corporatist Model

Whereas liberal entrepreneurs stress individual rights in a market economy, organic corporatists focus on more collectivist principles regulating the market. According to these classical 'conservative' values, communal obligations, order, hierarchy, and social differentiation take precedence over individual rationalism, equality, homogeneity, social leveling, and income redistribution. Societies form an organic whole, rather than an aggregate of individual atoms. Communal institutions like the church and family help preserve a society's historical continuity. Along with the government, they maintain order amid group diversity.

Structural conflicts revolve around the tensions between integration and differentiation. The state bureaucracy provides hierarchical policy coordination. Negotiations among elites who head various organizations — government agencies, sickness funds, insurance societies, physicians' associations, hospitals, businesses, unions — supply a more pluralist form of coordination. The same structures that differentiate the policy process also integrate it. The need to reconcile the divergent group interests and values accounts for the slow rate of policy change. The civil service plays a key role trying to harmonize differences and transcend policy stalemates.

This elitist process produces inegalitarian health policies. Depending on their geographic residence or occupational status, different groups secure divergent health insurance plans. High-status employees in wealthy urban areas gain the most health services, whereas lower-status rural residents have less access to generous benefits. Employer and employee contributions to the health insurance programs finance a large share of health expenditures; these payroll taxes are more regressive than national income taxes.

If we define corporatism as the participation of highly-organized groups in public policymaking, Germany and the Netherlands show more corporatist features than does France or Japan. Particularly in Germany, which embodies the organic corporatist model, the state authorizes group participation. Participating organizations — business, labor, physicians' associations, hospitals, pharmaceutical industries, sickness funds — function under hierarchical, elitist leadership. Dutch policymakers follow a more egalitarian type of pluralism; a greater variety of groups participate in committees, councils, national government agencies, and local organizations. Although historically the French bureaucracy pursued a centralized, statist strategy, during the 1980s the French policy process decentralized; regional governments assumed greater authority over health issues. A unitary state, Japan has also concentrated powers in the central bureaucracy that followed the Prussian model at the close of the nineteenth century. Yet as in the other three societies, the regional governments and especially the cities handle preventive care measures. Unlike the entrepreneurial model, which draws a sharp distinction between the 'private' market and the 'public' government, under organic corporatism the boundaries between structural sectors seem fuzzier. Central, regional, and local governments intermingle as their leaders participate in policy consultations. 'Private' groups formulate as well as implement 'public' health policies. When group leaders and government officials cannot harmonize their divergent policy preferences, policy stalemates emerge. The accommodation of group differences takes extensive time. As a result, the corporatist decision process achieves mainly incremental, rather than transformative, changes.[1]

GERMANY

The operation of the health care system in the Federal Republic of Germany best illustrates the organic corporatist model. Influenced by Catholic conservative values, German society and government operate in a pluralist, decentralized, but hierarchical way. Men enjoy higher prestige than women. Indigenous Germans look down upon migrant workers from Turkey. Unionized workers remain subordinate to managers, corporate executives, financiers, and professionals. Nurses defer to physicians, who dictate orders to patients. In this differentiated society based on status, elites stress the need for harmony, relying on several structural mechanisms to secure integration.

Policy integration takes place through hierarchical government regulation and more pluralist negotiations among health providers and other group participants. The federal government and especially the Länder (regional) governments regulate the activities of health purchasers (sickness insurance funds) and providers — physicians, dentists, hospitals, pharmacists, and pharmaceutical industries. Sharing overlapping responsibilities, federal and regional government officials draw no sharp distinctions in their functions. Both formulate uniform standards for physicians' performance and hospital construction. The federal government decides on specific drugs that deserve reimbursement and sets the maximum prices for them. Länder governments finance hospitals' capital expenditures. After specifying these standards of health care performance, government officials monitor their implementation. Corporatist values become realized in various consultative committees among group ('corporate') actors. These include negotiations between health providers and insurance funds in the Federal Committee of Physicians and Health Insurance Funds. The Concerted Action in Health Care provides opportunities for more varied groups to take part in health care policymaking. Composed of over sixty members, it represents the policy preferences of several elite groups: federal government ministries, Länder governments, federal association of municipalities, sickness funds, private insurance companies, physicians' associations, federal dental chamber, German Hospital Association, pharmaceutical industry, federal association of pharmacists, trade unions, employers' association, and civil servants' association. Composed of medical researchers, economists, and social scientists, a Board of Experts appointed by the federal Ministry of Health analyzes the delivery of health services, estimates likely outcomes, and suggests ways to curtail costs. At the regional level, similar commissions include representatives from hospitals, sickness fund physicians, mandatory sickness insurance funds, and Länder governments. They negotiate physicians' fees and charges for hospitals' operating expenses. City governments handle care for the elderly, children, and the disabled. Until 1996 municipal officials imposed means-tests for the elderly receiving home health care services. Limited benefits exacerbated the deprivation faced by low-income, stigmatized aged individuals. During recent years, the drive to contain rising health care expenditures has increased the power of government regulators over negotiators in such committees as Concerted Action. Regulations have lowered physicians' incomes, limited medical school admissions, reduced hospital expenses, restrained the volume of prescribed drugs, and reduced drug prices. Under this elitist pluralist system run by professionals, managers, administrators, experts, specialists, and scientists, government regulators have expanded their policy leverage over health care issues.

German health policymaking reflects the high structural differentiation associated with elitist pluralism. Policy influence, wealth, and social status congrue. In the medical role hierarchy, specialists enjoy higher status and money than do general practitioners. A few well-paid hospital consultants wield dominant authority over more numerous junior doctors. Although in scarce supply, nurses have low status and inegalitarian relations with physicians. The health insurance system also differentiates people according to their occupational status. Separate insurance agencies function for different groups. Before 1996 low-income employees, unemployed persons, students, pensioners, farmers, craftspeople, and disabled individuals had to join a mandatory insurance fund; legal provisions of health care legislation assigned them to particular insurance agencies according to their place of work, not residence. A few blue-collar workers as well as most white-collar employees had a choice about joining a particular insurance fund. Not until 1996 did all Germans gain this freedom. High-income individuals usually select a private commercial plan that levies higher premiums than the primary mandatory funds but grants more generous benefits. German hospitals are also functionally differentiated among public, nonprofit independent, and private commercial. Owned mainly by the Länder, county, and municipal governments, public hospitals are most numerous. Catholic hospitals provide services to southern and western residents. Private commercial hospitals, often owned by physicians, constitute a growing sector, with over one-third of total beds.

Populist representation within the German corporatist health system seems limited. Groups advocating egalitarian policy preferences have achieved less success than more elitist institutions. Allied with the business sector, the dominant Christian Democratic Union has focused on cost containment measures, rather than on programs to attain greater equality of health benefits. Representing workers' and union interests, the Social Democrats have sought safer, healthier working conditions for employees. Yet under the codetermination program, unions and works councils exercise weaker influence than do the more highly-organized employer associations. Health specialists and academic scientists represent employer concerns; they gain respect for their technical expertise. Managers dominate most companies; workers have far less say about healthier strategies for organizing production. Of all the major parties, the Greens most enthusiastically articulate populist, egalitarian health messages that stress the need for a cleaner environment. Although their strength has grown during the last decade and they now participate in some Länder/city coalition governments with the Social Democrats, Green power has yet to bring transformative changes to the German health care policy process.

With its numerous veto points, the German corporate system undergoes incremental change. Even though health policies provide comprehensive benefits — physicians' care, hospital services, dental care, maternity care, physiotherapy, eyeglasses, medicines, and even stays at health care resorts (spas), — the elitist model of administration continues. Adopting a paternalistic outlook, these administrators assume that elites have the obligation to assist less fortunate members of the national family. They stress the importance of government social services, especially old-age pensions and child allowances, that strengthen the patriarchal family. Even if German corporatists want government to regulate the health sector, they reject public policies that secure more income equality through progressive taxes or egalitarian expenditures. Regressive taxes finance the health programs; most revenues derive from the equal shares contributed by employers and employees. Pledged to maintain a diverse society, corporatists support different insurance programs for distinct occupations. Hence, lower-status employees receive less generous, comprehensive benefits. Policymakers have devoted little attention to providing long-term care for the low-income elderly who live in nursing homes. The focus on curative medicine assumes precedence over preventive medicine, particularly education about the desirability of healthier diets and less cigarette smoking. This emphasis on curative hospital treatments and excessive drug prescriptions partly derives from the extensive policy influence of medical associations and associations of sickness funds. The administrative costs of operating the diverse insurance funds also impose economic burdens on the poor, who scarcely benefit from high managerial expenses.

In sum, the German health care system has achieved less integration than differentiation. The policy process remains fragmented; elitist groups with a vested interest in the status quo dominate decisionmaking. Political elites downplay conflict by stressing the need to harmonize differences. Given group stalemates, government officials at the federal and Länder levels have secured greater regulation over hospitals, physicians, pharmaceutical manufacturers, and insurance associations. The Health Care Act of 1992 did introduce incremental changes, such as the right of all employees, not just white-collar workers, to choose their insurance fund. Yet as patients' choice expanded, their copayments also rose. Neither increased mergers nor greater competition among insurance funds seemed likely to reduce prices of health care services, especially for low-income individuals.[2]

THE NETHERLANDS

The Dutch health system functions under a more egalitarian pluralism than the German one. A greater variety of groups participate in the policy process. Compared with German clergy, Dutch Catholic leaders voice more egalitarian, less hierarchical values. Although gaining slightly fewer popular votes than the Christian Democratic Appeal (CDA), the Labor Party often participates in a coalition government with the CDA. Socialist unions have allied with Protestant and Catholic labor movements. As a result of this differentiation and integration secured through extensive negotiations, public health policies in the Netherlands provide relatively generous, comprehensive, and egalitarian benefits. Policy coalitions and compromises among contending groups lead to incremental changes.

Policymaking in the Netherlands illustrates the operation of several distinct models: organic corporatism, entrepreneurialism, and social democracy. Under corporate arrangements, Dutch civil servants wield less authority than do their German colleagues. Historically, independent churches and private business firms limited the power of the central bureaucracy. A similar trend continues today as central government control declines over physicians' fees, hospital charges, and the activities of insurance companies. The national government still limits hospital expenditures, sets maximum prices for health providers, specifies benefits covered under insurance plans, and authorizes similar insurance premiums for the same health care services, regardless of a patient's health status or risk. Nevertheless, extensive negotiations among all health care participants reflects a corporatist process that limits regulatory control. For example, the Health Insurance Funds Council includes insurance association heads, government officials, employers, employees, health professionals, and representatives from hospitals and nursing homes. Its members allocate funds to public and private insurance companies, formulate a benefits' package, and recommend insurance premiums to the Ministry of Health. The Central Agency for Health Care Charges (COTG) negotiates health providers' fees and charges, which the Ministries of Health and of Economic Affairs then approve. Lengthy negotiations among all these groups aim to achieve a consensus among the conflicting interests. Yet the dispersed power arrangements impede the search for mutually-beneficial exchanges. Policy stalemates often result. Incremental changes emerge when a coalition realizes the sufficient cohesion to transcend the fragmented policy process.

Historically, liberal entrepreneurialism has also influenced Dutch policymaking. The Dutch value civil liberties and tolerance. Protestant and Catholic churches retain autonomy from tight state control. Along with Protestants, Catholics, and Socialists, the Liberals represent one of the four 'pillars' of Dutch politics. Drawing support from nonreligious voters, they uphold a market economy, free trade, government deregulation of business, and a secular outlook. Private entrepreneurs function in a market setting. Numerous Dutch exporters sell their goods on the world market. In 1993 exports amounted to around 45 percent of the gross domestic product — one of the highest percentages in the OECD. Private physicians function as independent entrepreneurs who negotiate contracts with sickness funds and private insurance companies. Individuals can choose their general practitioner, who then refers the patient to a hospital specialist. Under the Dekker reforms, policies encourage greater competition among insurance agencies for customers, who purchase their plans as individual residents, rather than as employees of a private or public institution. Especially in the cities, citizens have enhanced opportunity to choose their insurance company and hospital. Rural dwellers secure fewer benefits from declining regional monopolies. All these policy changes illustrate key features of the entrepreneurial model.

Not only liberal market principles but social democratic values shape the Dutch health care system. Even though under 30 percent of the labor force belongs to a union and the Labor Party (Partij van der Arbeid — PvdA) rarely wins more than one-third of the popular vote, union representatives participate on numerous consultative councils, agencies, and committees with businessmen and government officials. Since World War II the Labor Party has joined several coalition governments with the Christian Democratic Appeal, which articulates a more egalitarian policy stance than the dominant Christian Democratic Union/Christian Social Union in Germany. As a result of the center-left coalitions, the Dutch government has enacted higher expenditures for social services, including health care, as a share of the gross domestic product than do most other OECD nations except Norway and especially Sweden — two nations usually governed by social democratic/labor parties. Dutch policymakers authorize the provision of generous, comprehensive health care benefits. Mothers receive prenatal-postnatal assistance with nutrition, hygiene, and screening for possible diseases. Silver Cross societies manage well-baby and toddler clinics subsidized by the government. Nearly all children secure immunizations against polio, diphtheria, tetanus, measles, and rubella. Funded by city governments and the national government, school health services provide assistance to teenagers. Family planning clinics and easy access to inexpensive oral contraceptives induce a lower abortion rate and fewer teenage pregnancies for every 1000 women than in the United States, Canada, France, and England. The elderly benefit from public financing of nursing homes and extensive home health care. Most individuals gain equal access to all these services, with the possible exception of rural residents and refugees from Turkey and Morocco. Yet a Refugee Health Care Center does provide free assistance to those from North Africa, the Middle East, and Vietnam. Policies for financing these generous, comprehensive benefits are less progressive than in Sweden or Britain. Regressive payroll taxes raise most revenues; progressive income taxes finance less than 10 percent of total health care costs. The Dekker reforms, however, authorized a more progressive financial system under which insurance premiums paid to a Central Fund depend on individual income; hence, wealthier persons pay a larger share of their incomes than do poorer people.

All these generous health policies have emerged in a highly differentiated, pluralist society. Both government and social groups reveal considerable dispersed power. Central government agencies — mainly the ministries of health, social affairs, and economic affairs — coordinate policies, finance their implementation by regional-local governments and social groups, and oversee all the negotiations among concerned participants, especially issues about expenditures for health care. The 12 provincial governments and 600 elected city councils then implement policies negotiated at the central level. Besides handling preventive medicine, immunizations, and vaccinations, municipal authorities license primary care physicians.

Three different types of pluralism operate in the Netherlands: liberal, communal, and radical. Liberal pluralism becomes manifest in the strong commitment to civility, which highlights the need for tolerance, mutual respect, empathy, and political dialogue among individuals with conflicting policy preferences about health care. Civil values maintain a shared attachment to the political role of a citizen and to general political institutions that equitably treat diverse groups. The rule of law and a concern for general well-being transcends the more particular interests of ethnic, linguistic, religious, and economic groups. In the Netherlands dispersed, noncumulative cleavages reinforce civil values. All four 'pillars' — Catholics, Protestants, Socialists, Liberals — include rich and poor, workers and employers. Hence, economic differences do not accentuate communal religious conflicts, which have declined since the early 1970s. Protestant and Catholic churches own over 50 percent of all hospitals, which the government subsidizes. At the local level, radical pluralism flourishes to a greater extent than in Germany. Radical pluralists prefer a policy process based on equality, decentralization, and widespread popular participation. Several health programs provide opportunities for marginal groups to participate. For example, low-income women play a key role in the Network of Health Cities Social Renewal program. Working in partnership with the Municipal Health Office, it supplies preventive health services such as health education to urban residents. Financed by the

Ministry of Health, the Federation of Dutch Junkie Unions treats people with AIDS. It educates about 'safe sex,' supplies condoms, and oversees the exchange of clean needles and syringes. The Association of Parents of Children with Motor Handicaps pressures local health policymakers to expand benefits for the disabled. In sum, Dutch pluralism not only reflects an egalitarian type of differentiation but also promotes individual rights.[3]

In this highly differentiated policy process, how does integration occur? By helping to reconcile the policy preferences of different parties, coalition governments promote national integration. From 1979 to 1994 the largest party, the Christian Democratic Appeal, always participated in the coalition with either the Liberals or the PvdA, the second largest party. This alliance encouraged government officials to reconcile their partisan policy differences. Coalitions between the CDA and Labor facilitated egalitarian health care measures. Another structural mechanism for integration focuses on the extensive negotiations among policy participants that take place in such forums as the Health Insurance Funds Council and the Central Agency for Health Care Charges (COTG). These structures provide an opportunity for several groups with contending policy preferences to participate in a general dialogue. Government officials, health experts, labor unions, business corporations, and associations of general practitioners, medical specialists, and insurance agents take part. In these negotiations, neither the civil servants nor representatives from physicians' associations play as dominant a role as in similar German consultations. Unlike their German colleagues, Dutch physicians are less well organized. In the negotiating process, the associations of social health insurance funds, private health insurers, and public health insurers usually ally with the Ministry of Health against the efforts of hospital doctors in the Association of Medical Specialists to secure higher fees for medical treatments and office expenses. COTG decisions more often uphold the preferences of insurance associations than physician demands. Most insurance companies function as nonprofit organizations as do nearly all hospitals. Thus private profit-oriented business corporations wield limited control over public health care policymaking. Although supporting individual rights, Dutch corporatism gives greater weight to collectivist, egalitarian values, particularly the mutual obligation to provide similar basic health services for all citizens.[4]

JAPAN

Although Japanese leaders stress their unique cultural approach toward public policymaking, in several respects their health care system resembles the organic corporatist model practiced in Germany. Under the Meiji restoration that began in 1868, Japanese administrators modeled their political institutions after Bismarckian arrangements. Despite the greater German decentralization, bureaucrats dominated both systems. They industrialized society through a powerful state that regulated private corporations, which acted as subordinate partners to the civil service. Autonomous unions and socialist parties held little influence, especially in Japan. Collectivist, hierarchical values took precedence over equality and individual rights. Group loyalties proclaimed the need for individuals to pledge their duty to the nation and family. Paternalistic values accorded women few rights. Obedience to hierarchical authority meant that lower-status people deferred to elite expertise. Harmonizing group differences behind national solidarity deterred less powerful groups from mounting overt conflicts that challenged the ruling elite.

Over one hundred years after the founding of the Meiji regime, these values still shape the health policy process. Like Germany, Japan today has a health insurance program based on occupational membership. Contributions by employers and employees finance the largest share of costs. Regional and city-town-village governments implement decisions originally formulated by the national Ministry of Health and Welfare. At all governments, civil servants base their decisions on recommendations made by advisory councils, which include most participants involved with health care issues. Stressing the importance of consensus, compromise, and national solidarity, conflicts remain muted. Negotiations occur in secret, rather than in open forums. Physicians play a key role negotiating agreements. As in Germany and the Netherlands, they retain extensive autonomy, even if public-private consultations regulate their fees. With a focus on the need to reconcile contentious group interests, incremental policy changes usually result from the extensive consultations. Given the tendencies toward group stagnation, health administrators have the greatest influence to realize far-reaching changes.

Under the elitist Japanese system, the Ministry of Health and Welfare (MHW) integrates the policy process. Rather than regulating the provision of health services, it primarily exerts economic control by setting reimbursement rates for physicians' fees, hospital charges, and drug prices. Attached to the MHW, several agencies participate in making decisions about the Reimbursement Fee Schedule. Composed of around 20 members, the Central Social Insurance Medical Care Council wields the most influence. It includes representatives from the government, private corporations, unions, health providers, and the professions of law and economics. Physicians from the Japan Medical Association exert the most policy leverage on this council, which contains no representatives from the Japan Hospital Association, an organization upholding the interests of hospital administrators and specialists. Through extensive negotiations, the council makes recommendations to the MHW about benefits, maximum fee increases, and allocation of funds. Along with the Ministry of Finance, the MHW then decides the final policies ultimately approved by the Japanese legislature, the Diet. Because regional prefectural and city governments implement national policies, the central Home Ministry also participates in the public health care policy process. Monitored by the Home and especially the MHW ministries, the prefectural government insurance division registers physicians, administers the Government-Managed Health Insurance plan, and monitors claims for payments from physicians. City government insurance offices, which manage the Citizens Health Insurance (CHI) programs for the elderly, self-employed, and unemployed, determine CHI premiums largely subsidized by the national government. Not only at the national levels but also in the prefects and cities, advisory councils composed of employers, employees, health providers, and medical scientists recommend policy proposals to government insurance offices. Local medical associations play a key role on these councils.

Among all the interest groups that interact with the MHW, the Japan Medical Association (JMA) exercises the greatest influence. Representing the interests of office practitioners and physicians in clinics (medical facilities with fewer than twenty beds), the JMA maintains close ties with large corporations and with the Liberal Democratic Party, which governed Japan from 1955 through 1993 and still functions as the dominant party. Even though reimbursed fees are low, physicians earn a high income through prescribing and selling drugs to their patients. Doctors often own medical equipment used for making diagnoses. Laboratory tests and physician ownership of clinics and small hospitals further enhance doctors' earnings. As professional experts, they receive deference from their patients for occupying a high-status position. This wealth and prestige increase their access to political elites in the Liberal Democratic Party and the Ministry of Health and Welfare. Political leaders often use medical terminology to underscore the need for consensual decisionmaking. For example, the term *yuchaku* means 'healing'; in political discourse it refers to cooperative relations between government bureaucrats and 'private' elites who work as partners.

Despite the policy leverage exerted by the JMA, civil servants in the Health Ministry still retain extensive authority. Like the Liberal Democratic Party, the JMA functions as a faction-riven organization. Conflicts arise between general practitioners in smaller offices — usually older doctors who control the JMA — and younger hospital specialists. Divergent interests also pit physician owners of clinics and hospitals against doctors who work as employees. Because of this factionalism, the influence of the JMA has recently declined. Against JMA opposition, ministers in the Finance and Health agencies have reduced physicians' reimbursed fees. Just as the Finance Ministry and the Ministry of International Trade and Industry constitute 'pilot' agencies guiding Japanese economic development, so the MHW operates as the pilot for health planning.[5]

Unlike the Netherlands, Japan operates a more elitist form of pluralism. Government officials share power with corporate executives. Labor unions function as company organizations dedicated to close cooperation with business management. Large corporations (*keiretsu*), along with government bureaucrats and Liberal Democratic Party leaders, have dominated economic policymaking since the early 1950s. Over health decisions, however, private forprofit insurance companies play a less prominent role than in the Netherlands or France. Pressured by the Ministry of Finance, the Ministry of Health and Welfare has tried to decrease reimbursement rates for drugs. Yet faced with the close personal ties that link representatives from the Japan Pharmaceutical Manufacturers Association and the Federation of Japan Pharmaceutical Manufacturers with MHW officials, government policies reduced reimbursement rates for old drugs but allowed higher prices for new drugs. During the early 1980s MHW officials authorized the sale of contaminated blood coagulants manufactured by major pharmaceutical corporations. As a result, hemophiliacs who used these clotting agents developed the human immunodeficiency virus. Not until 1996 did the MHW admit its complicity and did five drug companies agree to compensate patients who had filed suits. Hence, even if government bureaucrats wield extensive regulatory authority over health issues, their economic control remains checked by powerful social groups that participate as partners in the Japanese corporate state. Government regulation hardly brings hegemonic control. Bureaucratic integration takes place in a differentiated society.

Populist influence is weaker in Japan than in the Netherlands. Patients and consumers gain only limited access to administrative officials. Although citizens have a free choice of physicians and hospitals, most Japanese must select a plan linked to their occupation. Around a quarter belong to the Society-Managed Health Insurance program offered by large-scale enterprises with over three hundred workers. A Government-Managed Health Insurance program supplies health benefits to employees of medium- and small-sized firms; these members include 30 percent of the population. The Citizens Health Insurance (CHI) program administered by the municipal government serves self-employed persons, the unemployed, and retirees — groups that comprise a third of Japanese. Remaining public programs enroll national civil servants, local government officials, schoolteachers, and sailors. Only a few private commercial health insurance companies exist; they provide benefits such as more nutritious meals and better rooms in hospitals that supplement services offered under the public programs.

However limited the policy influence of 'ordinary' Japanese, they receive generous health care benefits. Elites operate the system as a paternalistic family. National heads have a duty to help their family members. Basic services include hospitalization, physician care, dental care, nursing, and provision of prescription drugs. Mothers receive extensive prenatal and postnatal care. Public health centers, clinics, and hospitals provide thorough screenings. Public health nurses make visits to the home, where children secure vaccinations and checkups. The elderly fare less well. With its tradition of the extended family caring for the aged, Japan has established few nursing homes. The few existing ones face long waiting lists, a shortage of night nurses, and little privacy for residents. Hence, most sick aged individuals endure long hospital stays or remain with their families. Yet hospitals offer limited nursing care, physical therapy, and opportunities for rehabilitation. Public health programs subsidize only a few home health aides; family members must pay for the expenses of caring for their elderly relatives. Despite this lack of institutional facilities for the aged, most Japanese enjoy fairly equal access to health services. Public policies subsidize insurance plans for lower-income people, the elderly, the self-employed, the unemployed, and workers in small firms. Employees in large enterprises and government officials — those who earn the highest incomes — receive no government subsidies. Yet they also secure the greatest benefits (for example, free screenings, subsidized vacations at sanatoria) and pay lower premiums as a share of their income than do members enrolled in CHI and government-managed plans. Whereas bankers, insurance agents, and civil servants gain the most benefits, coal miners and textile workers secure the least services. Hence, even in a society with an egalitarian income distribution, social stratification marks the provision of health care services.[6]

FRANCE

Whereas the Japanese health care system secures a balance between differentiation and integration, in France greater conflict pits the integrative French state against social groups. The French policy process remains more fragmented and incohesive; under the complex, dispersed power arrangements, various institutions and groups contend for dominant influence. A blurred pattern guides interactions between the public and private sectors as well as among the central, regional, and local governments. Given this low coordination, the central state bureaucracy tries to integrate policymaking. Yet elitist administrative practices provoke popular demonstrations, strikes, and boycotts, even by high-status groups like physicians. In this highly stratified, inegalitarian process, the tension between state integration and group differentiation explains policy changes. Groups that dominate the social stratification system wish to maintain their policy privileges, whereas subordinate groups struggle to secure more equality.

Even if the central government seems to wield extensive formal authority over health care, during the last two decades the policy process has become more decentralized. Several private influential health care institutions — physicians' associations, hospitals, insurance companies, pharmaceutical industries — also assume responsibility for providing services. These structures limit the hegemonic power of the central government, which focuses on financial support and regulation. Key ministries include health, social affairs, and economy and finance. They appoint top officials, such as directors of public regional hospitals and the head of the *Caisse Nationale d'Assurance Maladie des Travailleurs Salariés* (CNAMTS), the major health insurance fund. CNAMTS officials make financial decisions based on consultations with physicians' associations, employers, and labor unions. By determining payroll contributions, providers' fee schedules, drug prices, and benefits, the central government ministries shape the programs enacted by these quasi-independent nongovernmental insurance funds. Doctors who prescribe fewer drugs receive larger increases in their reimbursed fees. The Ministry of Health determines not only the prices charged for reimbursed pharmaceuticals but also patients' copayments. Besides regulating physicians' fees and drug prices, the national government controls both public and private hospital activities when it targets their maximum expenditures or 'global' budgets. However extensive the central government's formal authority, regional governments gained greater policy influence during the 1980s. They regulate local sickness funds and help manage regional hospitals. The city mayor serves as president of the local hospital board, which oversees several locally-owned hospitals. Governments in the *départements*, cities, and *communes* also handle preventive medicine: health education, vaccinations for children, and care for the elderly.

Not only local-regional governments but numerous private associations check the central state bureaucracy's power over the health sector. French pluralism reflects high social differentiation and stratification. Over 80 percent of physicians conduct private practices that provide them a fee for their services. Salaried hospital specialists often have some private patients, whom they see two half-days a week. Doctors retain clinical autonomy over diagnosis, treatment, and prescription of drugs. Even if they retain the right to charge fees for their services, negotiations among state officials, medical associations, and insurance funds determine the fee schedules. Despite fragmentation among physician associations, during the 1980s doctors' yearly fees increased faster than did hospital charges. Physicians now belong to two different sectors. In sector 1, they accept the reimbursed fees negotiated for specific types of services. Sector 2 physicians, which now comprise over a third of all doctors, can charge higher than the standard fees but must pay larger social security contributions. These higher-status sector 2 doctors include mainly gynecology and dermatology specialists who practice in Paris, Lyon, and Marseilles. Their patients come from wealthy, professional, urban backgrounds; most range from 18 to 24 years old. By contrast, sector 1 physicians function as general practitioners in the rural areas. They treat lower-income, older individuals, especially unskilled workers, farmers, and the unemployed.

French hospitals also reveal considerable stratification. Around 65 percent of beds are located in public hospitals owned by regional and lower governments. Three powerful persons dominate public hospital administration: the elected mayor of the commune or president of the regional general council, a physician who serves as president of the *commission médicale d'établissement*, and the hospital director appointed by the Minister of Health. These three represent distinct interests: the general political interest, medical needs, and the drive for cost containment. Whereas local communal hospitals that offer general care have lower status, the greatest prestige lies with the public regional hospitals linked to medical schools in Paris, Lyon, and Marseilles. With the most beds, physicians, and advanced technology, they meet various medical needs, including medical research, psychiatric counseling, major surgery (cardiovascular, neurological), care for the poor, treatment of AIDS patients, pediatric care, and long-term stays for the elderly. Even though subordinate to public hospitals, forprofit ones owned by corporations have shown a fast growth rate; they now house over half of all beds in private hospitals. Individuals go to private hospitals mainly for minor surgery. Nonprofit hospitals are further divided into those linked to the public insurance fund and those that do not participate in this fund.

Various insurance funds finance hospital charges, physician fees, and other health benefits. All French must enroll in some sickness fund based on occupation. Around four-fifths participate in the *régime générale* — CNAMTS, the general insurance plan for salaried employees. The remaining 20 percent belong to other mandatory funds for farmers, miners, railway workers, sailors, armed forces, professionals, and the self-employed. Because most health services require copayments ranging from 20 percent to 35 percent of total costs, over four-fifths of citizens obtain supplemental coverage from private insurance agencies, mainly from nonprofit ones called *mutuelles*. A growing private commercial insurance sector also offers health plans. French who hold supplementary insurance see more specialist physicians and use more prescription drugs than do those without supplemental coverage, who tend to be poorer and older (over 40 years old).

Faced with the highly-stratified health care system and insurance programs, the French secure unequal access to health providers. Income, occupation, ethnic status, and geographic residence, rather than medical need, determine choice of health benefits. In principle, the health insurance funds offer generous services: medical care, hospital care, drugs, dental treatments, physiotherapy, rehabilitation, nursing, and maternity benefits. Children and their mothers receive particularly comprehensive services, such as prenatal and postnatal care, maternity leaves, family allowances, preventive measures for children under two years old, and school health services for those over six years old. Yet married mothers, indigenous French, and employed women use these medical services more than do teenage single mothers, immigrant workers, and the unemployed. Among adults occupational status further stratifies access to health care. Manual workers, farmers, the self-employed, and shopkeepers are less likely to consult a specialist, see a private physician, gain dental care, and secure preventive care services than are executives and professionals. Similarly, geographic residence affects opportunities to receive medical care. Low-income rural residents — especially farmers and manual workers in the northeast — remain dependent on general practitioners and communal public hospitals. Urban professionals and engineers who live in the south or the wealthiest Parisian suburbs have greater access to specialists, private office practitioners, and dentists. As a result, they experience better health and lower mortality rates.

Given the fragmentation, stratification, and elitist administration of the health care system, individual citizens and even organized groups enjoy limited influence over the policy process. Although individuals can choose their physician, whether a general practitioner or specialist, and have some discretion over hospital selection, they cannot select their own health insurance fund. Instead, their occupational status mainly determines this choice. Because of their fragmentation, associations cannot easily challenge bureaucratic power. Ideological splits divide the two leftwing parties: the larger Socialists and the smaller Communist Party. The major conservative parties are divided between the *Rassemblement pour la République* and the *Union pour la Démocratie Française*. Three or four unions try to organize the working class. At least two unions represent the interests of nurses, who suffer from low salaries, bad working conditions, and a nonprofessional identity. Even though businesses can exercise more policy leverage than unions, conflicts between large corporations and small firms as well as between exporters and enterprises producing for the domestic market fragment business cohesion. Physician associations also lack solidarity and financial resources. French doctors attain less organizational cohesion than found among the German and Japanese medical profession. Several different associations articulate doctors' policy preferences. Because a more cohesive administrative corps controls access to the policy process, the fragmented physicians' associations often fail to attain their preferences through consultations with government ministries. As a result of bureaucratic resistance, physicians often have relied on direct action tactics — strikes, boycotts, demonstrations — to articulate their policy demands for larger reimbursements. For similar reasons, nurses' organizations have also staged protests for improved working conditions and higher salaries. This tendency to rely on direct action partly stems from the French ambivalence toward the state administration. On the one hand, they have historically relied on the state, more than intermediate associations, to fulfill basic needs. On the other hand, their revolutionary heritage leads them to challenge arbitrary bureaucratic decisionmaking. Hence, popular protests, even by high-status physicians, seem more common in France than in other corporate states such as Germany and Japan.

Despite the comprehensive bureaucratic control, government ministers and civil servants hardly wield hegemony over the health care sector. True, since the establishment of the Fifth Republic in 1958, the policy influence of doctors has waned while state managers have increased their authority over hospital charges, physicians' fees, and drug prices. Yet France remains a pluralist society differentiated by autonomous social groups. Organizations that hold socialist and entrepreneurial values retain influence. The Socialist Party governed France from 1981 through 1993 (except for a brief interim in 1986-1988) and regained the prime ministership in 1997. It decentralized health care policymaking to the regions and expanded access to health services. Liberal entrepreneurial values shape the activities of several health policy participants. Most physicians conduct private practices that charge a fee for service; they form what the French call '*la médecine libérale*'. Although nonprofit hospitals and insurance companies dominate the health care market, forprofit corporate-owned hospitals and commercial insurance companies have recently become stronger. Along with the antiauthority stance taken by French toward the state, these intermediary associations check the power wielded by the central government. The fragmented, understaffed Ministry of Health cannot effectively regulate the differentiated health care system. Inexplicit, unclear bureaucratic rules, overlapping jurisdictions among government agencies, and the further dispersal of power among several private organizations produce incremental policy changes.

Major health problems stemming from an inegalitarian social stratification system still plague France. High hospital expenditures, sizable administrative expenses, and the overprescription of drugs exacerbate costs. Paid low salaries, nurses remain in short supply. Policymakers give insufficient attention to the need for preventive medicine and home health care. Most important, economic inequalities impede access to health care services by low-income people, particularly those in the northeast and rural areas. High copayments, extra-billing by second-sector physicians, and regressive financing policies reinforce stratification. Direct payments, private insurance premiums, and employee payroll taxes finance around two-thirds of total health expenditures. These revenue sources are less egalitarian than employer contributions, which constitute a smaller share. In the French corporatist state, elitist administration has thus enacted few policy changes that reduce the inequalities of the stratified health care system.[7]

CONCLUSION

What similarities and differences do the four corporate states show in the administration of public health policies? Germany, the Netherlands, Japan, and France all have occupation-based insurance programs to which employers and employees make joint financial contributions. Administered by autonomous, nongovernmental agencies, these health insurance funds blur the distinction between public and private. Even if formally 'private,' they undergo government regulation by civil servants who strive to restrain costs and ensure the delivery of certain health services. Although physicians, dentists, and hospital administrators retain autonomy to provide services, government regulators negotiate with health providers about reimbursed fees. Moreover, no clear distinction separates the national from regional-local governments. All these health care systems have decentralized authority to regions and municipalities during the last two decades. Regional governments oversee public hospital and health insurance fund operations. City governments handle preventive medicine, children's health needs, and care for the elderly. Elites, mainly managers and administrators in the government and health insurance funds, govern these pluralist organic systems. Individual citizens and spontaneously-formed associations wield little influence over the policy process. Despite the lack of citizen 'input,' policymakers implement generous health care benefits. In all four societies, women form a lower share (55 percent to 60 percent) of the total labor force than in Canada, Britain, the United States, and especially Sweden.[8] Public health officials pay particular attention to meeting the health needs of mothers and children; extensive public prenatal and postnatal care represents one policy example. Elderly people face greater problems. They receive care from their extended families and hospitals. Government financing for home health care and nursing homes remains limited, despite the high demand for this assistance.

The four corporate regimes differ in their degree of integration, differentiation, and stratification. With its small size and homogeneous population, Japan features the strongest integration of health care decisionmaking. Along with the Japan Medical Association, ministries of Health and Finance coordinate the policy process. In Germany and particularly France as well, civil servants play the integrating role. They, however, wield less power over Dutch policymaking; in the pluralist, differentiated Netherlands, social groups retain autonomy to shape health care decisions. The Dutch, who live in an egalitarian society with a historical tradition upholding civil liberties, experience the most egalitarian health care system among the four corporate states. Dutch political leaders wield less elitist authority; citizens enjoy fairly equal access to health care benefits. Germany, France, and Japan reflect greater stratification based on income, occupation, and geographic residence. Stressing the need to harmonize differences, all these corporate systems prefer consensual decisionmaking, with the Japanese and Germans placing the greatest attention on conflict avoidance. As a result of the need to reconcile the divergent policy preferences of numerous public and private actors, policy changes occur incrementally. Given its revolutionary heritage, France has faced the most open conflict between state bureaucrats and protesters; nurses and even physicians have staged strikes, demonstrations, and boycotts that articulate their economic grievances. Yet in France, incremental change results, however militant the dissidents' rhetoric. There, as in the other societies except perhaps Germany, physicians' policy influence has waned. Civil servants and administrators in the insurance funds exercise more authority to initiate changes than heretofore. Reflecting the organic corporatist model, extensive consultations with physicians and other health providers still help shape public health policies.

Public health policies in the four nations feature aspects linked not only to the corporatist system but also to the entrepreneurial and social democratic models. Germany best exemplifies organic corporatism, with Japan and particularly France promoting fewer consultations with other interest groups such as labor unions. France has faced more open policy conflict than Germany or Japan. All four societies are market economies, where private enterprisers and consumers retain extensive freedoms. These corporate systems represent regulated or 'social markets'. Laissez-faire values attract less support among elites than in the United States or Britain. Nonprofit agencies operate the health insurance system. Most hospitals operate on a nonprofit basis. Commercial pharmaceutical manufacturers act according to the profit motive; yet the government regulates the reimbursed prices for their drugs. Socialist parties hold the greatest strength in Germany and the Netherlands, where they have formed coalition governments with the Christian Democrats. Particularly in Germany, however, Social Democrats' parliamentary influence declined after the 1970s, even if they did govern several Länder governments. Several political parties compete for power in the Netherlands, where the Labor Party secures almost as many seats as the Christian Democratic Appeal. Hence, they could wield some influence over health care programs. Except for a brief period (March 1986–June 1988) of *cohabitation*, from 1981 through 1993 the French Socialist Party controlled the presidency and the National Assembly, thereby giving it the opportunity to decentralize policymaking and expand access to health services. Yet in none of these four societies have social democrats wielded the extensive influence over health policies that they did in Britain and particularly Sweden after World War II.

4 The Social Democratic Model

Policymakers who advocate the social democratic model of the public health process try to reconcile supposedly conflicting values. Blending individualism with communal cooperation, social democrats support personal freedom in the collective context. For them, public health policies must combine material interests with moral values. Perceiving health as a public good, not a private benefit, they try to 'decommodify' health services. Health providers should seek to serve the public in an altruistic way, instead of maximizing their revenues. However great their attachment to moral values, social democrats also pursue material interests. Income redistribution measures become a key policy for expanding equal access to health care services, securing egalitarian health treatments, and realizing similar health outcomes. Social democrats implement health policies that reconcile any tensions between freedom and equality. Assuming that all people share human dignity, they want everyone to gain equal access to health care services, equal treatment by health providers, and equal health status. Progressive methods for raising finances minimize costs to the poor. Physicians retain extensive freedom over diagnoses and treatments. Patients have some choice of their general practitioner.

Social democrats handle health policy issues under structural conditions that blend integration with differentiation. Central government guidance allows considerable local control. National government health ministries formulate general standards for health providers and purchasers. Regional and city governments then implement health programs, partly financed by central revenues. Although pluralistic, societies governed by social democrats feature limited privatization. Public hospitals and public insurance plans supply health benefits. Yet several different groups — businesses, medical associations, and especially labor unions — participate in making health decisions. Along with

63

government officials, group representatives meet regularly in committees, councils, and public agencies to form a consensus on health programs. A strong socialist/labor party as well as the government cabinet integrate this pluralist policy process. Social democrats form the strongest party elected to legislative office; they dominate the cabinet, often in coalition with smaller legislative parties. As a result of their policy priorities and cohesive structures, social democrats implement universal, generous, and egalitarian health care benefits. Regardless of wealth or social status, citizens gain access to similar services provided throughout the nation.[1]

The health systems in Britain and especially Sweden combine elements of the entrepreneurial, organic corporatist, and social democratic models. Sweden best exemplifies the social democratic paradigm. Except for nine years, the Social Democratic Party (SAP) governed Sweden from 1932 through 1997. Yet beginning in the early 1980s the social democratic influence over public policymaking began to wane along with the corporatist framework. Entrepreneurial values and structures gathered greater strength. To an ever greater extent, the entrepreneurial model triumphed in Britain during the late 1970s, when the Conservative Party scored electoral victories over the Labour Party. The governing Tories implemented policies that privatized former state enterprises, deregulated state control over business activities, and relied on market mechanisms to supply social services. Despite this movement toward the entrepreneurial model, in neither Britain nor particularly Sweden have social democratic values disappeared. Assisted by powerful unions, the Labour Party implemented the National Health Service immediately after World War II. Today the British still rely on a public health system largely financed by tax revenues. Only limited privatization in the health arena has occurred. Rather than operating under extensive price competition, the health care market functions as a 'quasi-market' with considerable central government regulation. Compared with Britain, Sweden has a smaller private health sector. Most physicians work as salaried employees for the county governments, which formulate and carry out health policies. Except in the large cities, few private hospitals exist. The state owns retail pharmacies. Private health insurance corporations enroll fewer members as a share of the population than in England. In both nations, particularly Sweden, the public health care system supplies fairly generous, comprehensive, and egalitarian benefits — a reflection of democratic socialist values.

SWEDEN

From 1950 through the end of the 1970s, the Swedish policy process attained its 'golden age'. Embodying a social democratic corporate model, Sweden blended structural integration with social differentiation. The Social Democratic Party and the cabinet coordinated policies and integrated the society. Powerful labor unions and private businesses, along with numerous voluntary associations, supplied differentiation to Swedish pluralist life. Accommodative values reconciled interest group conflicts. During this period, expenditures for social services, including health care, expanded. In 1969 the parliament established a nationalized, largely public health system. High growth rates, low unemployment, moderate inflation, and greater income equality supplied the financial resources that enabled these reforms to take place. After 1975, however, economic conditions deteriorated as growth declined and consumer prices rose. The power of the Social Democratic Party (SAP) and allied blue-collar unions began to wane. Private businesses grew more powerful vis-à-vis unions and the SAP. More hostile relations developed between economic corporations and leftist organizations. Policy preferences seemed more difficult to reconcile. Public policymakers came under pressures to curtail government costs, especially for social services. User fees increased. Swedes faced reductions in their generous public health benefits. All these developments reflected the decline of the corporate and social democratic models. Values linked to the entrepreneurial model gained greater influence over health policies.

The Social Democratic Party lost its hegemonic control after 1975. A coalition of nonsocialist parties governed Sweden from 1976 through 1982 and again during the 1991–1994 era. Under the nonsocialist coalition government that lasted from late 1991 through 1994, unemployment and income inequality rose. Even though the inflation rate fell, Sweden experienced a negative growth rate in 1992–1993. General government budget deficits skyrocketed to over 10 percent of the gross domestic product. Led by the Moderate Unity Party, the nonsocialist government in 1992 reduced pensions, sickness insurance payments, and injury benefits, requiring employers and employees to make higher contributions. The national government reduced grants to municipal councils, which thus had fewer resources for such social services as day care, elder care, and home-help assistance. Swedes had to pay higher fees for these social services, which became provided by private agencies that made contracts with city governments. Under these deteriorating economic conditions and declining social benefits, the SAP increased its electoral support at the 1994 election and returned to executive office. Yet economic conditions remained grim. Faced with continuing lower growth rates, the Social Democratic government enacted austerity programs to reduce the budget deficit. Like the nonsocialists, they came under pressures to restrain wage increases and to reduce expenditures for social services, including health care benefits.[2]

These political-economic conditions account for the liberal entrepreneurial model's impact on public health policies during the 1990s, even under Social Democratic rule. Just as more collective bargaining arrangements now occur at the plant level, so the county and municipal governments have assumed greater control over decisions affecting health care. Central government agencies like the National Board of Health and Welfare formulate minimum general standards, not detailed regulations, for the local provision of health services. Besides gathering and analyzing information about medical care, central institutions supervise and evaluate the performance of county councils, which play the dominant role in the health policy process. They plan, manage, and finance public health services. Whereas the national government finances around one-fifth of total health expenditures, the county councils raise 70 percent of revenues, mainly from proportional income taxes. County governments employ most general practitioners and other medical personnel, such as nurses, midwives, and physical therapists. County councils also own and operate most public hospitals. During the last decade a trend has emerged toward delegating greater authority to municipal governments, which now handle preventive services, school health services, day care for children, and assistance to the elderly, disabled, and mentally ill. Whereas Swedes used to receive most of their health care from hospitals and specialists — services falling under county government jurisdiction, — city councils have assumed greater responsibility for managing care by general practitioners, who work at neighborhood (district) primary health care centers. Despite these decentralizing trends, the central government still retains crucial fiscal control that limits regional autonomy. Because of high general government fiscal deficits, the parliament reduced grants to county councils and restricted their authority to raise local income taxes. Decentralization also produced contradictory effects. On the one hand, each county council gained the right to enact innovative health reforms, such as those implemented by the Stockholm policymakers. On the other hand, this devolution weakened the influence of the Federation of County Councils in its negotiations with national health ministers. Hence, this intermediary association between the central and regional governments no longer wields such important leverage over national officials.

In accordance with the liberal entrepreneurial model, Swedish policymakers have recently introduced market reforms into their pluralist health care system. Although expanding, privatization still remains limited. No more than 10 percent of physicians, mainly younger ones, conduct full-time private practices. Yet most specialists, who work in hospitals, also rely on part-time private practices for increased income beyond their county-paid salaries. County councils reimburse doctors employed in private offices or private health care centers. Private physicians in corporations perform surgical operations such as coronary bypasses. Except in large cities, most hospitals function under public (county) ownership. Urban residents have access to a few private hospitals and to more numerous, smaller private health clinics that provide speedier appointments with medical personnel.

However limited the private sector, Swedish policymakers, particularly in Stockholm, recently enacted entrepreneurial programs that expand competition and patient choice. As in Britain and the Netherlands, purchasers (county councils) became more sharply separated from health providers — physicians and hospitals. Through competitive bidding, county governments contracted with private as well as public health providers, including nursing homes, diagnostic laboratories, physicians in group practices, and hospital specialists. Government regulations tried to contain costs. Using cost/benefit ratios, policy officials stressed the need to lower health care costs by cutting expenses and raising hospital productivity. County governments reimbursed hospitals according to DRG (Diagnostic Related Group) formula based on diagnoses of specific illnesses and age of patients. The elderly over 80 years spent fewer days in hospitals. After the national government reduced grants to county councils, they limited health expenditures and raised patients' copayments. Individuals secured greater freedom to choose their general practitioner, specialist, and hospital within their county or an adjacent county. Shorter waits for hospital surgery emerged. The quasi-market reforms hardly involved a powerful role for private insurance companies, which sold premiums to a fairly small share (under 5 percent) of the population, mainly senior executives in small firms. Health care funding remained largely public. In 1993 public revenues — local income taxes, social security contributions, national grants to county governments — financed 83 percent of total health expenditures. Even if higher than before, patient copayments and user fees amounted to a low share. Hence, although higher user charges meant greater inequality, the revenue system that funded health care services remained more progressive than in most other industrialized nations.

The pluralist system of representation reinforces the egalitarian dimensions of the Swedish health system. Several diverse groups participate in shaping public health policies — a reflection of social democratic corporatism. From the nineteenth century onward, the state has assumed responsibility for scientific medicine. The Swedish Medical Association (SMA), which organized in 1903, today wields less policy influence than in other Scandinavian countries. Nevertheless, with the devolution of authority for health care to the county governments, the SMA oversees hospital operations and negotiates working conditions, hours, and salaries with local officials. Functioning under the National Board of Health and Welfare, the Medical Board of Responsibility handles complaints from patients about their treatment by doctors. Composed of nine members, the Board includes representatives from the Federation of County Councils, the LO blue-collar union, TCO (a union of salaried employees), SACO (a professional association that includes health personnel), the public, and the national parliament. It compensates patients for mistreatment, delayed diagnoses, and prescription of deleterious medicines. Rather than incurring fines, most physicians receive warnings, admonitions, or reprimands. Hence, few doctors need fear the financial consequences of malpractice litigation. Negotiations between the National Corporation of Swedish Pharmacies, pharmaceutical industries, and the National Social Insurance Board decide reimbursement fees for particular drugs covered by the public health program. Besides health personnel, union representatives, businesspeople, and government officials, other groups exert some influence over health policies. These include associations of retired people and the disabled. The Noah's Ark Red Cross Foundation helps formulate plans to cope with AIDS. The national administration and the Stockholm county government fund its activities.

Within this pluralist, differentiated health system, the Social Democratic Party, cabinet, and bureaucracy integrate the various policy actors. Even though its electoral support has recently waned, the SAP still remains the dominant if not hegemonic party that coordinates the policy process. Elections to the city and county councils occur at the same time as national parliamentary elections. Hence, a national SAP victory usually means that Social Democrats control lower governments. Given the overlapping jurisdictions among the national, county, and municipal levels, the SAP can try to reconcile any policy conflicts. The cabinet and state bureaucracy also play a key coordinating role. Headed by a legislator from the governing party, the Ministry of Health and Social Affairs seeks to formulate a unified policy based on accommodation of diverse interests. Several bureaucratic agencies subordinate to the Ministry — the National Board of Health and Welfare, the National Social Insurance Board, the Medical Products Agency — further integrate the health care system.[3]

Backed by a coordinated policy process, Swedish Social Democrats have wielded the power to translate their egalitarian policy preferences into generous, comprehensive, universal health programs, especially for children, mothers, and the elderly. Sickness and maternity benefits constitute a comparatively high share (80 to 90 percent) of a worker's wage; these twin benefits continue for over a year. Parental benefits, grants for medical expenses, rebates for medicines, and travel subsidies to hospitals also help Swedes finance their health costs. Swedish policymakers highlight curative and preventive services. Administered by municipal governments, school health education programs stress the dangers of alcoholism, smoking, drug abuse, unsafe sex, AIDS, and violence. Adults gain access to prenatal and postnatal care, dental treatments, screenings for cancer, and assistance for the disabled. Policies to help old people include government-funded services rendered by general practitioners, district nurses, home-based caregivers, and staff in nursing homes. All these health services provide fairly equal benefits to people throughout Sweden. Those in the rural north secure less access to specialists than do Swedes who reside in the wealthier, southern urban regions. Even if some ethnic discrimination occurs, all individuals, whether born in Sweden or overseas, have the same legal access to health care. Foreign-born political refugees, who constitute nearly 6 percent of the population, pay the same fees for consultations with physicians. Compared with the indigenous Swedes, these immigrants more often secure treatments in the hospitals, both in emergency and specialist departments. By contrast, native Swedes more often go to private health clinics. Ethnic differences in securing primary care and hospital out-patient care remain slight.

These egalitarian health policies reflect the Swedish commitment to social democratic values. Despite the increasing influence of the entrepreneurial model, most Swedish leaders still view health care as a public good. According to their causal attributions, the environment shapes personal behavior. Hence, public programs must change social conditions, particularly the working and residential milieu, that will lead to improved general health. Programs expand access to health services. Preventive measures try to increase occupational health and safety, reduce job monotony, and educate people about the dangers of alcohol consumption, drug abuse, and deficient diets. By contrast, British policymakers assume that bad health stems more from personal lifestyles than from social structural conditions. Compared with Swedish leaders, they give stronger support to the liberal entrepreneurial model, with its stress on individual freedom, personal choice, and competition. Founded by the Labour Party in 1948, the National Health Service since then has blended social democratic principles with entrepreneurial practices.[4]

BRITAIN

Unlike Swedish policy activists, who have reconciled conflicts among social groups, political parties, and government agencies at all levels, British officials have less successfully blended the contradictions between structural integration and differentiation. The reforms in the 1990 National Health Service and Community

Care Act upheld the virtues of market competition; yet more government regulation ensured. Managerialism, with its emphasis on cost containment and efficiency, triumphed over medical professionalism. Although promising greater autonomy to physicians and hospitals, the reform actually extended central bureaucratic control. Hence, integration overwhelmed differentiation; less pluralism, populism, and local authority independence now prevail than under the original National Health Service (NHS) framework established during the late 1940s. Compared with Sweden, Britain today has a more centralized and privatized health care system. Even after the 1990 reforms, however, public features from the original social democratic model remain influential.

The establishment of the National Health Service immediately after World War II (1946–1948) stemmed from the power of the Labour Party, unions, and supportive health ministries. Winning the 1945 election by a wide margin (over 60 percent of seats in the House of Commons), Labour Party leaders favored a new health program that would provide universal coverage, comprehensive benefits, and central governing financing through national tax revenues. Supported by central government officials in the Ministry of Health and by local medical officers, Aneurin Bevan — Labour's Minister of Health from 1945 through 1951 — steered this policy proposal through Commons. Groups allied with Labour, including the trade unions, Fabian Society, and Socialist Medical Association, rallied public support. Although the British Medical Association (BMA) favored a national program, it opposed some specific features of the Labour plan. Nevertheless, negotiations between Labour officials and BMA physicians led the government to modify its proposal. The BMA gained several concessions: doctors' involvement in health care decisionmaking, retention of their clinical autonomy, and continuation of their status as independent contractors. Private businesses, especially commercial health insurance companies, exerted weak influence over the policy process. Because of its military victory, the national government held extensive authority. As a result, it could implement its health policies even against the opposition of pharmaceutical corporations, voluntary hospitals, and commercial insurance companies.[5]

During the late 1980s and early 1990s, a powerful government and ruling political party also explain major changes in the NHS

that moved Britain away from social democratic principles toward
the entrepreneurial model. At this time the Conservative Party
held nearly 60 percent of Commons' seats. Led by a powerful prime
minister, Margaret Thatcher, the government sought to uproot
socialist influences and establish greater market competition,
privatization, and deregulation. Unlike Swedish leaders, who have
tried to accommodate conflicting interests, Prime Minister
Thatcher took a more adversarial stance toward the opposition,
which included the Labour Party, trade unions, local governments,
the British Broadcasting Corporation, and the universities.
Blending traditional conservative principles with liberal
entrepreneurial values, she stressed the need for a powerful
central state and strong leadership that would uphold the
'enterprise culture': competitive individualism, market freedom,
economic efficiency, and diminution of the 'paternalistic welfare
state' that made people dependent on government 'nannies'.
Supported by Conservative Party elites, technocrats, and
intellectuals, Thatcher appointed Kenneth Clarke Secretary of
State for Health (1988–1990) to implement health care reforms.
Economists working for the Institute of Economic Affairs, the
Adam Smith Institute, and the Centre for Policy Studies proposed
plans for changing the NHS toward a greater commitment to
market freedoms, competition, productivity, and individual choice.
American economist Alain C. Enthoven assumed that an internal
health market would produce more flexibility, innovation,
efficiency, and decentralization. Under his 'managed competition'
plans, policies should separate health care suppliers — hospitals,
doctors, diagnostic laboratories — from purchasers such as district
health authorities and general practitioner fundholders. These
purchasers would choose competing providers according to
cost/benefit ratios and their quality of performance. Influenced by
these promarket intellectuals, a group of five cabinet ministers,
headed by Prime Minister Thatcher, prepared in 1989 a White
Paper *Working for Patients* outlining health reforms that became
part of the 1990 NHS and Community Care Act.

Conservative Party elites and intellectuals, rather than civil
servants, business executives, or even physicians, played the
dominant role shaping the 1990 Act. Unlike the immediate post-
World War II situation, during the late 1980s the government
failed to negotiate with the British Medical Association, three-
fourths of whose members rejected the Tory innovations. As feared

by the BMA, the Act strengthened centralized control over local accountability. Government regulators managed the health care market. Amid the structural conflicts between integration and differentiation, integration became dominant.[6] Pluralism, populism, and localism declined, at least within England. Wales and particularly Scotland continued to maintain slightly different organizational arrangements. Thus the following analysis of health care decisionmaking will focus mainly on England.

Under the internal market or 'quasi-market' reforms, the National Health Service became more centralized. The Department of Health, especially its NHS Executive (NHSE) committee, gained greater control over the health policy process. By communicating the meaning of 'health' and the proper scope for government responsibilities, it defines the political agenda. The NHSE implements Department of Health policies about AIDS, waiting lists to hospitals, and economic efficiency. Guided by the central government's Treasury Department, it determines resources and formulates plans for their allocation. Medical audits of hospitals and physicians bring greater standardization than before 1990. Administered by managers accountable to the central government, these audits specify norms of efficient policy performance evaluated by the NHSE. The 1990 Act abolished English regional health authorities and replaced them with eight regional offices of the NHSE. Upholding the need for central strategic planning, these regional offices controlled the district health authorities, which lost their former influence. The Department of Health appoints the chair of the district health authorities, which merged with family service health authorities to become local health commissions. Regional offices accountable to the NHSE appoint the nonexecutive members of these commission boards. Economic managers — district general managers (CEOs), directors of finances, directors of planning and contracts, directors of public health — constitute the executive members. They, not medical professionals, make the crucial decisions about health programs. Local managers determine budgets, prepare medical audits, control drug prescriptions, evaluate health care performance, and formulate contracts with hospital consultants. These managers maintain responsibility to the central Secretary of State for Health, the Department of Health, and the NHS Executive.

The 1990 Act did devolve some authority to local institutions, mainly the NHS hospital trusts and the general practitioner fundholders. Although centers of local autonomy, these two organizations, particularly the trusts, wield only limited autonomy apart from government regulation. Functioning as 'quangos' — quasi-autonomous nongovernmental organizations — , the NHS hospital trusts retain some independence to allocate resources. They must compete for contracts with the GP fundholders and health authorities, which lost control over public hospitals. Yet the central government finances trust hospitals as well as appoints the chair and nonexecutive members of trust boards. Tory businessmen on these boards and NHSE officials stress instrumental rationality, especially the need to increase efficiency and lower costs. Hospital specialists (consultants) are viewed as producers dealing with consumers. The trust prepares an annual business plan evaluated by the NHSE, whose regional officers monitor expenditures, finances, and the flow of funds. Limiting the degree and types of capital hospital expenditures, they prefer greater reliance on private financial institutions for credit. As public funds to the hospital trusts decrease, more hospitals close or merge. Fewer beds remain available to patients, who face shorter hospital stays. Reduced funds lead to the dismissal of nurses. Now that trust hospitals must compete for patients, hospital specialists lose influence vis-à-vis GP fundholders, who shape the demand for health care and refer their patients to specific hospitals under contractual arrangements. Many fundholders have established clinics for outpatient surgery, which further reduces consultants' influence.

According to the 1990 NHS and Community Care Act, local authorities (councils) now assume major responsibility for community care to the elderly, children, the physically disabled, the mentally handicapped, drug addicts, alcoholics, and AIDS victims. Even though local authorities, namely their department of social services, determine eligibility for benefits and payments for services, limited financial resources hinder implementation. Central government subsidies to local authorities have decreased. National social security funds no longer provide supplemental income support payments. Treasury Department officials impose limits on taxes that local councilors can levy. Higher user charges and means-tested criteria for eligibility hurt the poor. Local authorities must spend over 80 percent of their funds on private sector agencies. More private forprofit nursing homes now house the elderly.

As a result of these community care policies, greater inequalities and lesser political accountability have emerged. Increased demand for community services, combined with lower public revenues, heightens competition for scarce resources. Conflicts over proper jurisdictions arise between hospital consultants and general practitioners as well as between health authorities and local authority social services departments. For example, whereas hospital consultants seek early discharge of elderly patients, community care managers who place them in nursing homes or at home want longer hospital stays, given the shortage of nursing facilities and funds to pay for home health visitors. Overlapping jurisdictions and ambiguous, inconsistent norms from the NHS Executive impede national planning. As bureaucratic, technical expertise replaces political dialogue within local agencies, lower political accountability occurs. Managers and businesspeople dominate health authorities and hospital trust boards. The managerial ethos stresses efficiency, productivity, cost containment, and calculation of cost-benefit ratios as primary health policy objectives. From this utilitarian perspective, managers try to raise physicians' productivity by promoting medical audits, competition among providers, and quantitative computer analyses of professionals' activities.[7]

The 1990 reforms produced widespread dissatisfaction among physicians and other health personnel who opposed the greater managerial control over health care decisions. Even though the reforms increased flexibility, made hospitals more responsive to general practitioners, and authorized greater economic authority for entrepreneurial general practitioners, the act provoked grievances. Doctors resented the increased administrative burdens that stemmed from filing claims and providing information to managers who sought statistical data about physicians' performance. To many physicians, the materialistic focus on cost-benefit analyses downplayed the concern for service and the whole context of patients' wellbeing. The elevation of instrumental rationality produced greater skepticism about physicians' professional authority, knowledge, and expertise. Hence, they received more patient complaints about their treatments. Those doctors who did not join a GP fundholders practice feared the creation of an inegalitarian two-tiered system, under which the GP fundholders would secure the greatest economic resources at the expense of the nonfundholders. Other health personnel also perceived injustices under the 1990 innovations. Compared with NHS hospital consultants, who conduct private practices and spend less time with patients, junior doctors (25 to 35 years old) have lower status and salaries. The national government has reduced their numbers. Assisting more than one consultant, they must work long periods that may exceed 70 hours each week. Sleep deprivation, irritability, low morale, and frustration result. Nurses suffer even greater deprivation. Hospital nurses' salaries have risen at a slower rate than income earned by senior managers, who dismiss trained nurses and replace them with lower-paid health care assistants. Faced with understaffing, low morale, and limited opportunities for upward mobility into management positions, nurses staged protests against managerial dominance. Determined to cut labor costs, the Conservative central government favored local settlement of nurses' salaries, rather than the maintenance of national pay standards. Several nurses' associations — the Confederation of Health Service Employees, the National Union of Public Employees, the Royal College of Midwives, and even the Royal College of Nursing — resisted this proposal. Yet the fragmentation of the nurses' movement impeded the effectiveness of public protests against powerful state and managerial opposition.[8]

Faced with the conflict between increased demand for health care and limited financial resources, English policymakers concentrated on restricting demand for public services as the primary way to contain costs. Tightened eligibility rules for public health benefits, higher user fees, early hospital discharges, and reduced services represented some typical strategies for reducing costs. Public policies also redirected demands to the private sector, such as independent hospitals, private practitioners, nursing homes, and hospital suppliers. Under the quasi-market reforms, the distinction blurred between public and private provision. Public revenues financed services received at private agencies. Private funds subsidized private beds in the NHS hospitals.

However articulate the promarket entrepreneurial rhetoric supporting private health care, the public sector retains considerable influence. Despite the privatization policies pursued by the Conservative government during the 1980s, the National Health Service still remains a largely public institution shaped by social democratic Labour values. True, Britain has a larger private sector than Sweden. Physicians function as independent contractors. Most dentists, pharmacists, pharmaceutical manufacturers, and suppliers of hospital food, equipment, laundry, and cleaning function as private agents. About one-fourth of NHS hospital consultants maintain fee-for-service practices that secure greater incomes than their government salaries. Nevertheless, in the early 1990s no more than 4 percent of total hospital beds were in private hospitals; NHS trust hospitals reserved only 1 percent of their beds for private beds paid for by patients. Only 12 percent of British citizens held private insurance, mainly purchased by nonprofit companies such as the British United Provident Association and the Private Patients Plan. These private insurance plans finance payments for private NHS beds as well as surgical operations like abortion, hip replacements, and hernia treatments that require lengthy waits in NHS hospitals. In 1993 public revenues financed 83 percent of total health expenditures — the same share as in Sweden.

Compared with most other industrialized nations, Britain implemented a relatively egalitarian system of raising revenues. Taxes to finance the NHS came mainly from national insurance contributions, personal income taxes, and indirect taxes like the value-added tax. During the early 1990s private health insurance premiums and out-of-pocket personal payments constituted only 15 percent of total revenues for health benefits. Although indirect taxes, along with private insurance and personal payments, wielded a regressive impact, the national insurance contributions and especially the personal income tax were more progressive. The NHS financed most health costs, except for dental care, eye treatments, a few prescription medicines, and medical supplies. Hence, under 10 percent of health expenditures stemmed from out-of-pocket payments. As a result, the overall financial system remained slightly progressive or at least proportional. Poor people, who faced more chronic, longer-lasting illnesses, paid lower taxes as a share of their income and received greater health expenditures than did wealthier individuals. Socioeconomic status only slightly influenced the use of primary health services, with homeowners making greater use than council tenants.[9]

Despite the egalitarian financing, the 1990 Act widened the geographic, ethnic, and economic gaps in access to health care benefits. The wealthy southeastern region secured more NHS funds than did poorer northern areas. Compared with prosperous suburban districts along the coast, inner city and rural districts received fewer expenditures for such services as vaccinations, immunizations, and screenings for cervical cancer. Low-income persons in London suffered from dilapidated hospital facilities that lacked air conditioning, heating, functioning elevators, and private toilets. Lengthy waits occurred for hip surgery and cataract operations. Caring for numerous patients, elderly general practitioners lacked the staff to treat the medical needs of the urban poor. Throughout Britain renters with no car gained less access to health programs than did residents who owned their home and automobile. Older individuals endured economic loses with the transfer of financing for residential care from the NHS to local authorities, which levied income-based tests to determine eligibility for admission to nursing homes and for home health visitors. Some of the aged had to sell their own homes as a way to raise the revenues needed for entrance into a private nursing home. Impelled to cut costs and increase efficiency, the GP fundholders and NHS hospital trusts rarely sought the elderly or sick who needed long-term expensive care. These policy changes particularly disadvantaged low-income people, among them individuals originally born in Africa, the Caribbean, and South Asia. Ethnicity, geographic residence, and socioeconomic status thereby reinforced a more elitist health care system than in Sweden.[10]

CONCLUSION

Even if Sweden more fully embodies the social democratic model than does Britain, both societies remain committed to public programs. Public revenues finance over 80 percent of health care expenditures. Most hospitals function as publicly-owned institutions, as do Swedish county health agencies and British health authorities. Physicians who earn a government salary or per-patient fee also conduct private practices. Regardless of income or occupational status, all citizens participate in the same health program. Benefits cover most hospital, physician, pharmaceutical, and therapeutic appliance costs as well as such preventive services as vaccinations, nutritional education, campaigns against smoking, and screenings for diseases. Public funds pay for over 90 percent of a beneficiary's bills, including those for hospital treatments, care by health professionals, and prescribed medicine. Powerful political parties and government agencies coordinate the health policy process. In Sweden the Social Democratic Party, cabinet, and civil service have played the dominant unifying role. During the 1980s the Conservative Party, Prime Minister Margaret Thatcher, the Department of Health, the Department of Treasury, and neoclassical economists from pro-Tory research institutes wielded decisive influence over policies that moved Britain toward a more entrepreneurial model.

The greater power of the Swedish Social Democratic Party and unions account for the major policy differences that separate Britain from Sweden. From 1970 to 1990 the SAP's share of the popular vote to the Riksdag declined from 48 percent to around 42 percent. In Britain, however, the Labour Party's electoral support fell by 13 percentage points from 46 percent to only 33 percent. Similarly, British union strength decreased during this period. Whereas in 1980 50 percent of the employed labor force belonged to a union, that figure had fallen to only 40 percent by 1990. By contrast, Swedish union membership rose to over 80 percent. Women working in local government service positions — health care, education, social work — constituted an increasing proportion of the unionized work force. Due to this Social Democratic and union strength, Swedish health officials maintained their commitment to public decentralized generous services. Although during the 1990s fiscal deficits led them to cut some benefits and privatize a few programs, these changes were less far-reaching than in England. Swedish county and city governments gained greater autonomy from central health ministers. Various groups — unions, medical associations, businesses — participated in the pluralist health process. However important the movement toward a more entrepreneurial model, Swedish democratic corporatism retained vitality as policymakers consulted several diverse groups when framing decisions. The British policy process revealed greater centralization and less pluralism. Both the Swedish and English governments restricted local authorities' right to increase taxes during the 1990s. Yet the Swedes retained more local fiscal autonomy; in 1992 local taxes, nearly all raised from proportional income taxes, constituted over one-third of total tax revenues. That year the British local tax share accounted for under 4 percent, compared with over three-fourths of revenues collected by the central government. (The Swedish central proportion was 45 percent.) Social security contributions raised about 20 percent in both nations. Hence, local British councillors lacked the fiscal resources to challenge Conservative Party central domination.

Policymaking in Britain also featured less pluralism than in Sweden. Neither the British Medical Association nor even British businesses shaped national government decisions. Unions had minimal influence. At the local level, employers gained greater control over determining the validity of workers' claims for sickness and disability benefits, which remained lower than Swedish expenditures. Small business executives loyal to the Conservative Party secured representation on boards directing the health authorities and NHS hospital trusts. Consumers, patients, union leaders, and local elected officials secured minimal representation on these agencies dominated by the National Health Service Executive. Along with limited pluralism went ineffective populist control. Community health councils exerted little influence over local health policies. Local Well Women Clinics obtained few funds from the NHS, held only a few short sessions each week, and reached few working class women.[11]

Leaders' stands toward group conflicts shaped the divergent rates of policy change in Sweden and Britain. Swedish officials stressed the need to reconcile conflicts that split leaders who represented the diverse interests of national, county, and municipal governments, medical associations, unions, businesses, patients, and competing political parties. Even if they more effectively reached accommodations during the 'golden age' from 1950 through the late 1970s, the reconciliation policy style remains vital in Sweden today. Extensive consultations among all concerned actors secure final policy agreements. As a result of these pluralist negotiations, incremental policy changes have resulted. In Britain, however, Conservative Party leaders, particularly Prime Minister Thatcher, adopted a more confrontational stance toward opponents. Conflict took precedence over consensus. Determined to eliminate socialist influence from the British body politic, neither she nor her cabinet ministers consulted a wide variety of groups when framing the 1990 NHS and Community Care Act. Governing an integrated, coordinated political system that allowed little scope for differentiation, the Conservative leaders had both the will and the power to institute more transformative policy changes than in Sweden. The internal market reforms gave GP fundholders greater autonomy to secure services from hospital specialists. Private health organizations increased their activities. For example, private hospitals performed cataract operations and hip surgery. Private enterprises supplied physical therapy and such advanced medical equipment as MRI (magnetic resonance imaging) devices. People over 60 years old received tax credits for purchasing private health insurance. All these Conservative policies reflected a movement toward a more entrepreneurial model for the British health care system.

With the return of the Labour Party to government power in 1997, however, the commitment to social democratic values assumed stronger policy priority. Compared with the Tory health programs, the New Labour government's policies placed more emphasis on egalitarianism, public provision of health services, and collective government action. Instead of blaming individuals for sickness, the Labour government highlighted the environmental causes of illness: pollution, poverty, unemployment, dilapidated housing. Rather than abandon the internal market, Labour health ministers pledged to reform it. Cooperation among local general practitioners took precedence over competition as the best way to commission hospital care for their patients. More egalitarian access to health care emerged with the end of special benefits for fundholders' patients, such as shorter waits for hospital treatment. Public health care regained policy priority, as reflected in the decisions to close fewer public hospitals and to discontinue tax credits for elderly persons who purchase private health insurance.[12] Like Swedish officials, Labour Party leaders enacted incremental reforms that reflected key features of the social democratic model but maintained the entrepreneurial focus on limiting health care costs.

Part II

Explanations of Public Health Programs

Policy analysts rely on theoretical explanations to clarify the general significance of specific health care programs in different nations. Theories constitute sets of interrelated propositions that specify the conditions producing some outcome, such as changes in health policies. Even if these generalizations never fully account for the complexities and historical contingencies that shape the policy process, they offer insights into the mechanisms by which certain conditions produce some effect. General propositions show the relationships among variables — for example, the impact of public opinion vs. elite preferences on health policy changes. More specific hypotheses indicate the particular conditions under which the general assumptions apply.

An insightful theory fulfills explanatory, conceptual, and policy criteria. Evaluating diverse theories, the analyst places a priority on their explanatory power. How empirically accurate, innovative, and parsimonious are the explanations? Which ones show the greatest plausibility? Health researchers view explanatory generalizations as probability statements that explicate the likely impact of certain variables on health policies. General explanations that hold true across several nations and different historical periods carry greater weight than those applying to only a few specific contexts. An innovative theory explains more unanticipated findings, solves more analytical puzzles, and accounts for more new empirical results than does a competing theoretical perspective. By generating new predictions and stimulating original research, innovative theories inspire policy analysts to explain the political world through more creative lenses. Explaining the gap between empirical reality and theoretical expectations becomes a key concern. For instance, why do health care costs rise in systems that introduce managed competition and greater market features? Neoclassical economists prefer rational choice theories that offer parsimonious explanations. Under ideal conditions, a few general theoretical assumptions explain large numbers of events, structural conditions, and behaviors. Parsimonious explanations link simple axioms to complex political situations across time and diverse cultures. According to rational choice theorists, one such axiom is the following: 'In choosing between alternative policy options, a political leader selects the option that has the greater value and the greater probability of a successful outcome.' Such an assumption about expected utility provides a unified, comprehensive, coherent explanation of the motivations that shape health policymakers in diverse nations.

As this axiomatic example implies, theories should rest on a logically coherent foundation. Coherent generalizations deduce specific implications from general premises. If the general assumptions are true, the conclusions logically follow. The assumptions remain consistent with each other and with their consequences. Logical analysts understand that qualities of the part (micropolitical attitudes) do not generalize to the performance of the whole macropolitical system. For instance, even if most citizens support a more comprehensive, generous, universal, and egalitarian health program, government officials will not necessarily enact such policies. The structural power of sociopolitical elites — cabinet ministers, insurance corporation executives, heads of medical associations — may block the transformation of individual policy preferences into binding government decisions.

We can also evaluate theories according to practical policy criteria. To what extent do they propose effective policies that will actually realize intended outcomes? If implemented, will the policy recommendations lead to efficient goal attainment, so that the government attains certain benefits — improved health status of the general population — at the lowest possible costs? Policy analysts also want to assess the crossnational applicability of policy options. Does a program that effectively improved people's health in one nation produce similar effects in different countries? Together with explanatory and conceptual criteria, these policy standards enable us to evaluate various theories of public health programs.[1]

Part II applies cultural, structural and rational choice theories to the health care systems of eight industrialized nations. The political culture framework in Chapter 5 explores the meaning of health to medical personnel, government officials, political party activists, social group leaders, and citizens. What conditions cause illness and improve health? What role can government policies play in curing illnesses and preventing disease? These causal attributions and policy preferences partly explain the degree of government involvement, particularly the scope of benefits provided individuals. Three structural theories — institutionalism, pluralism, Marxism — explain the scope and rapidity of health policy changes. Analyzed in Chapter 6, the power of various organizations, including government agencies, political parties, social groups, and multinational corporations, becomes a crucial explanatory variable. Whereas institutionalist, pluralist, and Marxist approaches highlight the structural causes of health policies, rational choice theories stress the motives, perceptions, and actions of individuals who shape these programs. Structures operate as constraints and opportunities influencing personal choices. Rejecting a determinist position, rational choice theorists assume that policymakers retain freedom to consider policy alternatives and to select the option calculated as the most beneficial. Efficiency becomes a major policy priority. Chapter 7 uses rational choice assumptions to assess the efficiency of health care markets — an issue focusing on policy strategies that will contain rising costs.

5 Political Culture and the Meaning of Health

George Bernard Shaw viewed medicine as a new form of salvation. Written during the early twentieth century, his essays on *Doctors' Delusions* sketched an analogy between health care and religion. Physicians and priests articulated meaning to health. They perceived health as wholeness, as freedom from sin or viruses and bacteria. Physicians functioned through the General Medical Council (GMC), which resembled the College of Cardinals. Authorized by the state, the GMC cemented the union of church and government. Challenges to medical orthodoxy represented blasphemy and heresy. Just as the Church excommunicated heretics, so the General Medical Council upheld scientific medical standards by banning unorthodox practitioners (osteopaths) and new medical techniques. Physicians wielded the power of life and death over their patients, who assumed the same passive role occupied by the laity. Doctors extracted malignant cells from patients' bodies, in a similar way that priests exorcised demons from parishioners. Faith in scientific medical expertise paralleled faith in divine wisdom. Medical cures resembled spiritual miracles. Asked by a newspaper reporter if the British had lost their faith, Shaw replied: 'Certainly not; but we have transferred it from God to the General Medical Council.'[1] Challenging this hierarchical model, Shaw deconstructed the idealistic rhetoric of the General Medical Council and the British Medical Association. Although they claimed to serve the public well being, in practice the GMC sought to expand its professional power. The BMA pursued its economic self-interests. As a Fabian socialist and vegetarian, Shaw rejected the hierarchical and competitive individualist worldviews. Championing a communal, egalitarian position, he proclaimed changed lifestyles and transformed environmental conditions as the best ways to improve people's health. Consume more raw vegetables. Avoid beef. Abandon smoking and drinking. Establish a state medical service with lay control. Rally behind movements that blame illness on political persecution, class exploitation, and poverty, not on individuals' sinful behavior.[2]

CAUSAL ATTRIBUTIONS AND POLICY PREFERENCES

By shaping causal attributions and policy preferences, cultural values affect the health care programs adopted in different nations. Political culture encompasses values, norms, and interests. Values constitute general concepts of desirable conditions. Norms refer to the more specific means for goal attainment, especially the rights and obligations attached to specific roles. These rules help mediate sociopolitical conflicts. Values and norms in turn influence people's political interests — the stakes that they have in government actions and inactions. Through political interactions, individuals formulate and reformulate their interests, mainly by evaluating the costs and benefits that they expect will emerge from public policies.

As embodied in political ideologies, cultural values serve several crucial functions in the policy process. First, they prescribe the purposes, responsibilities, and priorities of government officials. Framing the political discourse, cultural values define problems and place them on the political agenda. What are the most salient issues? Which problems should take priority? What situations need the greatest improvement? These concerns over the nature of injustice focus on key government responsibilities. Policymakers with divergent values will highlight growth vs. equality, efficiency vs. equity, freedom vs. government regulation. For some leaders, high costs will seem the greatest problem. For others, the need to institute a more egalitarian health program will take precedence over cost containment measures.

Second, besides designating social problems and policy priorities, cultural values explicate the cause of the problem. Whom should we blame for poor health? Possibilities include fate, chance, God, and the Devil — all sources beyond individual control. More voluntarist assumptions place major responsibility on individual lifestyles: high-fat diets, insufficient physical exercise, imprudent sexual behavior, and consumption of alcohol, cigarettes, and noxious drugs. Collectivists blame large-scale institutions, nations, and environmental conditions. Typical examples include business enterprises, governments, foreign states, and multinational corporations. All these agencies may take actions that pollute the environment, raise unemployment, cause greater income inequality, and fail to rectify dilapidated, overcrowded, damp housing.

Third, political ideologies propose solutions to basic problems. Influenced by their distinctive values and norms, policymakers deliberate about who bears the main responsibility for resolving such a problem as poor health among low-income citizens. Should the government take action? If so, what levels — national, regional, city — must take charge of specific tasks? Or can private structures act more effectively? If so, what is the appropriate division of labor among government agencies, the family, nonprofit voluntary associations, and forprofit business enterprises? Through deliberating various policy alternatives involving administrative organization, expenditures, finances, and scope of health benefits, government officials estimate the consequences of each alternative. Values, norms, and information help shape these estimates. They also specify the best policy solution for implementation — that is, the option that seems most desirable and feasible given the structural constraints.

Fourth, political leaders use various media to justify their policies. By linking a specific health policy to a programmatic cause, they try to mobilize supporters and demobilize opponents. Rather than use empirical evidence or logical coherence to rally support, policy activists rely on general values — freedom, equality, efficiency, justice, choice. These values arouse enthusiasm among policy advocates, thereby encouraging them to back the political parties and officials associated with a specific health policy.

Fifth, cultural values supply the criteria of worth used to evaluate policy performance and outcomes. Such standards as efficiency, equality, freedom, order, and equity assess the procedures for implementing a program, the behavior of policy actors, and their success in attaining the intended outcomes. Proponents of a program that expands health services to low-income individuals highlight the positive effects, for example, the greater use of health care facilities by persons with chronic illness. Opponents cite negative outcomes, which may include increased costs and more bureaucratic regulations. From these evaluations emerge recommendations to change particular aspects of programs and perhaps even proposals to terminate a policy.[3]

The political culture approach of Aaron Wildavsky and Mary Douglas represents an insightful framework for explaining causal attributions and policy preferences across different industrialized nations. They make several general assumptions about the origins and outcomes of cultural values.[4] According to them, even though culture and structure constitute analytically distinct variables, they show a reciprocal empirical interaction. Patterns of social interaction shape cultural values, norms, and interests. In turn, political culture influences the activities of institutions, organizations, groups, and networks — all examples of role relationships. From this reciprocal perspective, social stratification conditions the type of values dominant in society. A rigidly stratified society places constraints on egalitarian choices. Upholding the need for order, ruling elites propagate hierarchical values. Through the dominant media — state, church, family, — they construct interpretations of political reality that produce shared meanings. If these elitist norms are institutionalized in dominant structures and internalized by individuals, people will accept the hierarchical order or fatalistically resign themselves to the status quo. By contrast, in a more flexible stratification system, egalitarian and individualist values have greater opportunity to thrive. Voluntary associations enable individuals not only to maintain existing health care structures but also to transform them. To understand the processes of policy change, we hence need to probe the congruence among normative worldviews, the patterns of social interaction, and individuals' behavioral strategies, especially their relative freedom to choose alternatives.

Political culture influences causal attributions and policy preferences. Based on both information as well as values and norms, causal explanations specify the conditions leading to some outcome such as improved health. When formulating a health program, policymakers consider several issues: To what extent do the conditions causing health lie within the individual or the environment? Does illness stem primarily from unhealthy personal lifestyles or from a polluted environment? A second issue revolves around the power to control these conditions. Individualist explanations involve both genetic predispositions and lifestyles; people have greater control over the latter than the former. Policymakers can more easily expand access to health services than they can change the world capitalist economy or transform citizens' attitudes about healthy living. A third issue deals with assumptions about the power to change causal conditions. Particularly in a flexible political system geared toward innovation, egalitarian leaders optimistically assume that they can change conditions that will improve people's health. Political campaigns to reduce cigarette smoking, decrease alcohol consumption, and promote greater physical exercise represent typical examples of political education. Competitive individualists perceive they can restrain health care costs by instituting competitive market features in public health programs. Fatalists and hierarchs, however, view causal conditions as more stable. Because health results from such unchanging conditions as genetic predispositions or original sin, public policymakers scarcely have the ability to implement policies that will lead to fundamental changes in people's health.[5]

Causal attributions not only locate the source of blame for a problem but also assign responsibility for a solution. Information, norms, and anticipated outcomes shape policy preferences. By specifying normative expectations — rights and obligations in particular roles, — political culture frames the discourse about the desirability and feasibility of alternative policies. Hierarchs prefer health programs that retain elitist control over the provision of health services. Competitive individualists support market strategies involving free choice, entrepreneurship, and innovation. Egalitarians like Bernard Shaw lean toward widespread participation in health care decisionmaking and toward similar health programs for all citizens, regardless of income, education, occupational status, and ethnicity. Fatalists doubt that any public or private health policy will improve individuals' health, mainly because they perceive sociopolitical life controlled by chance, luck, random conditions, and other forces beyond any person's control.

Aaron Wildavsky and Mary Douglas classify cultural worldviews according to two dimensions: strength of personal ties with the group and strength of externally-imposed rules over individual members. Collectivists strongly identify with the group, for example, the family, region, nation, race, ethnicity, class, and religion. Group ties remain weaker among individualists. Elitists advocate externally imposed rules that regulate individual actions. Accepting the need for rule differentiation, they propose that different groups in the social stratification system abide by divergent norms. By contrast, egalitarians assume that the same rules should apply to everyone, regardless of social status. Rather than deferring to the hierarchs' interpretation of rules that mediate conflict, individuals in small group settings negotiate the specific implications of general laws, so that rules adjust to *ad hoc* situations. Based on these two dimensions, four worldviews emerge. *Hierarchism* emphasizes strong group ties, deference to rules imposed by elites, and different normative expectations based on one's social status. Organic corporatists take this position. Linked to entrepreneurialism, *competitive individualism* ranks low on group identification and on externally-imposed, differentiated rules. *Egalitarianism*, which democratic socialist and Green parties support, urges individuals to participate in communal settings where widespread participation occurs. Citizens carry on political discourses about appropriate rules and policies. Programs provide equal access to health services, equal treatments, and similar health outcomes — that is, improved health status. *Fatalism* assumes an atomized view of the political world. Cynicism about others' motives deters individuals from participating in collective action. Perceiving change as futile, these fatalists resign themselves to the rules imposed by hierarchical authorities.[6] I will compare the meaning of these four worldviews by concentrating on three variables: (1) philosophical assumptions about collectivism/individualism, moral-spiritual values/material interests, freedom/equality, (2) causal attributions about sickness, health, and government responsibilities, and (3) specific policy preferences that derive from these general cultural values about health care.

Hierarchism

Oriented toward collectivist values, hierarchists seek tight group boundaries and powerful external rules that constrain individual behavior. According to them, without a powerful group network monitored by governments, churches, and families, individual liberty will degenerate into license, anarchy, and disorder. Human nature reveals perverse tendencies; hence, elites must wield sufficient authority to punish evil people and deter others from violating normative expectations. Order, regulation, and control take priority over individual freedom that challenges established authority. Elites secure compliance by stressing moral-spiritual values, especially the need for discipline and for faith in the established order. Rather than advocating equality, hierarchists assume that political systems resemble a functionally differentiated organism. Status, wealth, and power distinctions reflect individuals' divergent talents and moral qualities. Just as the head dominates the other bodily organs, so in society elites must govern everyone else so that all live in harmony.

The hierarchists' assumptions about health reflect their philosophical positions. Sickness results when people deviate from established rules for healthy living. Reckless driving, promiscuous sex, binge drinking, and overconsumption of fatty foods represent typical examples of irresponsible behavior. Only when individuals conform to the rules and defer to the experts such as physicians will health emerge. Governments have the obligation to promote health by propagating adherence to normative expectations about virtuous behavior, punishing those who violate these rules (e.g., drug addicts), and regulating the activities of both citizens and health providers. Through these programs, harmony, order, and stability in the political system generate health among the citizenry. Specific policy preferences for health care include government regulation of private nonprofit institutions, such as hospitals and nursing homes linked to churches. These agencies receive public subsidies. Health benefits depend on an individual's position in the social stratification system, with those in upper-status occupations paying more and securing greater services. Social security contributions that vary by earned income finance the benefits offered by sickness insurance funds. Based on these elitist premises, the organic corporatist arrangements in such countries as Germany best illustrate hierarchical value patterns.[7]

Competitive Individualism

Competitive individualist values linked to the entrepreneurial model contrast with the collectivist ethos articulated by the hierarchists. Individualists assert the dominance of personal responsibility, self-reliance, and self-control. Externally-imposed rules remain weak. Behaving as self-interested actors, individuals express only limited identification with collectives like the nation, race, ethnic group, or economic class. Political action occurs when individuals perceive that forming a coalition to realize mutual gains will best satisfy their own interests. Unlike the hierarchists, who urge sacrifice to the collective cause, individualists assume that the pursuit of self-interests will ensure social well-being. Norms of reciprocity that regulate bilateral bargains, exchanges, and tradeoffs mediate conflicts among the self-interested actors. Even though most people seek material gains through rational, calculating techniques, moral-spiritual values also motivate individuals' actions. Rejecting the hierarchical reliance on government sanctions or ecclesiastical religious commandments, individualists see the need for internal moral restraints to deter people from achieving unfair advantage over others. According to Adam Smith's *Theory of Moral Sentiments*, the 'impartial spectator' or conscience restrained tendencies to steal, cheat, violate contracts, and practice fraud. Yet the impartial sector did not come from God, the Church, or the government. Instead, this socialized conscience reflected individuals' need to attain small group approval and avoid disapproval. Blame brought shame. Competitive individualists like Smith assumed that these internal moral restraints based on small group praise more effectively produced just trade exchanges than did state or church regulation of economic behavior. Rather than 'interfering' in private business activities or providing generous, egalitarian, comprehensive social services, decentralized government agencies must act primarily to remedy market imperfections. Fearing a powerful state bureaucracy, individualists want governments to concentrate on protecting private property rights, ensuring contracts, deterring fraud, promoting free world trade, educating the labor force, and guaranteeing everyone an equal opportunity to advance toward unequal positions. From the individualist standpoint, personal freedom or what Adam Smith called 'natural liberty' takes priority over equality. Laws that apply to everyone will regulate competition so that producers, traders, consumers, and political actors enjoy the freedom to pursue their own interests and to form short-term coalitions that realize mutually-beneficial exchanges. Even though individualists uphold equality before the law and equal opportunity to compete in the free market, they oppose equal economic outcomes. Government policies promoting egalitarian measures for income redistribution hinder the incentive to work hard, achieve success, and thereby gain upward social mobility.

Individualists' approach to health care relies on private agencies, market mechanisms, and personal responsibility. For them, illness stems from unhealthy personal lifestyles and from government regulations that hinder a competitive market. The most effective health programs include preventive services stressing the risks of unsafe, injurious behavior, such as smoking, alcohol consumption, nonnutritious diets, and lack of physical exercise. All these habits lead to lower productivity, greater inefficiency, and the failure to satisfy personal needs. Viewing a healthy body as a means to enhance productive capabilities, individualists back political education campaigns that highlight self-control of the body. With a skeptical attitude toward government regulations, they support private provision of health benefits. Private health personnel should have the freedom to compete on the market so that they respond to consumer preferences. Contracts between health providers and insurance companies will supply benefits based on the ability to pay. The healthy and wealthy purchase a private health plan; they pay lower insurance premiums than those who practice unhealthy lifestyles, such as smokers and obese people. The poor, sick, elderly, and disabled — consumers with high actuarial risks — join public programs. Government agencies enforce minimal standards on the operation of these private and public plans. Cost-benefit analyses used by government officials evaluate the degree to which the programs effectively achieve health goals and maximize efficiency.[8]

Egalitarianism

Unlike individualists, egalitarians adopt a more communal orientation toward political decisionmaking. Committed to widespread participation in local, decentralized groups, they stress the need for everyone to cooperate with others in the pursuit of egalitarian goals, such as improved conditions for marginals — women, youths, migrant laborers, immigrants, poor people. The active, cooperative, altruistic person becomes the ideal political actor willing to make sacrifices that raise the marginals' status. To the egalitarians, the rules imposed by the political establishment, even a pluralist regime, appear as ways to maintain the privileges of the elites, who dominate the policy process through inordinate control over money, information, and the organizational-communications media. Although citizens may experience equality before the law, they still endure unequal wealth and status. As

Anatole France reminded us, '[The poor] have to labor under the majesty of the law, which forbids rich and poor alike to sleep under bridges, to beg in the streets, and to steal bread.'[9] Egalitarians aim to create a populist political system based on equality, decentralization, and widespread participation. Opposed to both the centralized bureaucratic state and private corporate oligopolies, they strive to organize the unorganized, empower the weak, and enrich the poor. From their perspective, each person can perform several different roles. Not only professional physicians but rank-and-file citizens should participate in making health decisions. Even though a nurse may lack a million dollars to press her demands on government officials, she has other potential assets — intelligence, personal efficacy, a cooperative spirit — that can help shape public health programs. Dialogue in egalitarian associations such as local health clinics and councils enables individuals to learn the norms of persuasion, consensus, mutual obligation, and civic duty needed to attain health policy changes in an orderly way. Despite the support for political decentralization, egalitarians show an ambivalence toward state authority. Even if too hierarchical and bureaucratic, activist government may secure more equal outcomes, such as greater access to finances, education, and health care facilities. For egalitarians, government has the responsibility to pursue both moral and material goals: to raise everyone's living standards, narrow the gap between rich and poor, enhance economic opportunities, and raise the moral dignity of the worker. Both democratic socialists and Green party ecologists advocate these policy preferences.

The egalitarian stance toward health care policies stems from their assumptions about elitist rule that causes illness. Like George Bernard Shaw, egalitarians believe that sickness arises mainly from environmental conditions, not from personal sins or genetic defects. Political oppression, class exploitation, and status degradation produce ill health among subordinate marginals, who lose control not only over material production but also over their human life. Rule by managerial elites, government health bureaucrats, and medical monopolies exposes the powerless to extensive health risks, such as pollution, carbon monoxide, carcinogens, toxic chemicals, unsafe work sites, unhealthy foods, and dilapidated crowded housing. Only through a transformation of these social conditions will people's health fundamentally improve. Perceiving health as a human right of citizenship, egalitarians seek community empowerment through local health centers. National governments should formulate generous, comprehensive, inclusive health service programs implemented by communal agencies that expand citizen participation. Rather than favor the proportional taxes advocated by competitive individuals, egalitarians rely on progressive income taxes for financing health care policies.[10] They optimistically expect that these plans for providing and financing health benefits will lead to widespread improvements in public health, especially for the marginals.

Fatalism

Compared with the egalitarians, the fatalists take a more cynical, skeptical, pessimistic view about the effectiveness of government policies. Excluded from membership in the political community, they must comply with rules imposed by hierarchical elites. For the fatalists, apathy, cynicism, distrust, and political withdrawal seem rational responses to the unpredictable, arbitrary, random outcomes that befall them. As isolated atoms, they shun cooperative activities. Sociopolitical life appears as a zero-sum or negative-sum game. Material interests revolve around the struggle for economic survival. Moral values focus on the need for resignation to a random universe. Neither freedom nor equality assumes primacy. Because people's situation depends on luck, chance, accidents, and the arbitrary decisions of superordinates, freedom from all these environmental restraints appears futile. Elites enjoy unfair advantages. The subjugated victims live under the egalitarian conditions of misery.

Fatalists express little hope for public policies that will enhance their health status. Sickness stems from conditions beyond individual or collective control — luck, chance, fate, God, the Devil, genetic defects, accidents, social injustices. Distrusting others and overwhelmed by institutional obstacles, fatalists feel politically inefficacious. Government institutions remain unresponsive to citizens' demands. Individuals lack the resources to wield an effective impact on public policymakers, whether through personal contacts, voluntary group activities, or political party pressures. Too many perceived constraints and too few opportunities immobilize political action. Hence, fatalists expect no long-lasting, significant policy solutions to their health problems.[11]

POLITICAL OPINION AND HEALTH PROGRAMS

From these ideological assumptions about health and government responsibilities derive testable hypotheses that explain the origins of these propositions and their more specific policy implications. Based on the assumption that general worldviews shape specific policy preferences toward health care, one hypothesis proposes that if egalitarian values assume priority, the government will enact the most comprehensive and inclusive health programs. If competitive individualism dominates the political discourse, government leaders implement less egalitarian, comprehensive, universal, and generous services; private forprofit organizations play a crucial role. If elites with hierarchical values perceive a paternalistic obligation to care for the health needs of national family members, then generous health benefits will emerge from public policies, which will concentrate on helping children, their mothers, and the elderly. If fatalistic values prevail among a nation's people, high cynicism about government's effectiveness in improving health conditions will lead to low levels of public health benefits.

Second, assuming that culture and structure interact, I hypothesize that the power of key organizations, including business organizations, labor unions, and especially political parties, shapes the impact of ideological worldviews on specific health policies. Along with union activists, leftwing party leaders — Labor, Socialist, Social Democrat, US Democrat, New Democratic Party of Canada — most fervently hold egalitarian values. Businesses and promarket parties like the Free Democrats, Liberals, and Republicans support competitive individualism. Christian Democratic and Conservative parties blend hierarchism with individualism. Among these partisans, activist members express more coherent ideological views than do individuals who merely identify with a party or just vote for it. Political inactives, mainly less-well-educated people in low status occupations, hold the most fatalistic values.

Third, from the general proposition that elite cultural values influence the public's causal attributions, we infer that policymakers' responsiveness to public opinion depends on the degree to which citizens express clear, strongly held, and unified attitudes about the causes of health. Specifically, if coherent public attitudes blame collective sources — governments, business corporations, general environmental conditions (unemployment, income inequality, dilapidated housing, unsafe work sites) — for illness, then political leaders will translate these causal attributions into egalitarian public policies. If the public takes fatalistic positions or perceives that health stems from individual actions, political elites will less likely implement comprehensive, egalitarian, generous public programs.[12] In the following sections, we probe the plausibility of these three sets of hypotheses by examining national public opinion, political party preferences, labor and business views, and attitudes of health personnel. I assume that particularly when the public holds ambivalent or fragmented positions, elites — government officials, political party activists, business executives, union heads, representatives from health provider associations — can exert greater leverage over policy formulation.

National Public Opinion

Even if the policy preferences of voters wield some impact over public health policies, national public opinion scarcely explains the major differences among the industrialized capitalist nations. Along with most Europeans, Japanese, and Canadians, Americans strongly support programs that expand government assistance for health care, increase old-age pensions, improve public education, reduce unemployment, provide job training, and enhance employment opportunities. Higher expenditures for defense, foreign aid, means-tested public assistance, unemployment compensation, cultural arts, transportation, state-owned industries, and administrative salaries arouse less enthusiasm throughout the democratic world. Even though economic problems such as high unemployment and soaring inflation take precedence over health care as salient policy issues, most citizens support higher taxes for improved health services and reject lower spending on health care as a way to reduce fiscal deficits. Health programs financed by both governments and employers, rather than by higher copayments or insurance premiums, take priority. Whether in Japan, North America, or West Europe, most individuals seek expanded benefits, especially for elderly assistance, nursing home care, prescription drugs, and dental treatments. Over two-thirds of Europeans, Japanese, and

Americans regard health services as a right that government agencies and private organizations should supply. In short, the less egalitarian, generous, inclusive, comprehensive health programs in the United States, compared with Europe, Canada, and Japan, do not stem primarily from Americans' antipathy toward government social service programs.[13]

The major difference between US public opinion and popular attitudes in other nations revolves around the greater American support for the values of competitive individualism and the weaker endorsement of egalitarianism, hierarchism, and fatalism. Compared with the British, French, Germans, and Dutch, fewer American citizens take a fatalistic view toward the causes of individual failure. For them, success comes from hard work, not from luck or impersonal forces beyond personal control. Hierarchical values also attract less enthusiasm in the United States than in such nations as Japan, where community harmony, respect for authority, and deference to elites like physicians elicit approval, especially from older, uneducated people. More than the Japanese and Europeans, Americans adopt the ideological values of competitive individualism. Around two-thirds of the US population perceive laziness, thriftlessness, alcoholism, and personal failures to take advantage of social opportunities as the main reasons for poverty. Viewing government programs as inefficient and wasteful, Americans uphold 'free enterprise,' local community control, and self-reliance. Personal freedom to pursue one's life goals takes precedence over activist government efforts to help the needy. Compared with Americans, a higher proportion of Swedes, Dutch, French, Germans, British, and Japanese perceive that the government has a basic responsibility to provide good medical care. Yet like citizens in these other nations, most Americans want to increase government spending on health programs.

Unlike other national populations, US citizens give weaker backing for government policies intended to narrow the gap dividing rich from poor. A higher percentage of Europeans, Canadians, and Japanese stress government responsibilities to assist poor people, reduce income differences, provide a guaranteed income, supply jobs, and maintain decent living standards for everyone. Swedes, British, Dutch, and Japanese give particularly strong support to these egalitarian values. More influenced by democratic socialist and Christian democratic ideologies,

Europeans hold collectivist attitudes toward government's role. They blame their personal economic miseries not only on individual failings but mainly on social injustice, environmental deprivation, unfair public policies, misguided political leaders, unemployment, and world economic pressures. Compared with Americans, who express greater reliance on private enterprise and individualism, Canadians voice greater faith in an activist egalitarian social service state that will help remedy the problems stemming from social injustice.[14]

Despite the stronger American support for competitive individualist values and the greater opposition to egalitarianism, we cannot conclude that public opinion determines cross-national health policies. Values represent general concepts of desirable conditions. Policies, however, constitute more specific programs. The same cultural values may yield divergent policy implications. Even though Americans endorse individualist principles and reject programs for securing more equal incomes, they strongly back government health programs intended to reduce personal health costs, increase access, and expand such benefits as prenatal care, diagnoses, prescription drugs, immunizations, surgery, home health assistance, financial support for catastrophic illnesses, and long-term care for the elderly. Through their control over the media, sociopolitical elites — government officials, political party spokespeople, labor union heads, health care providers — communicate the policy implications of consensual values as well as the details of specific health programs. Unlike Europe, where Social Democrats, Christian Democrats, and unions wield stronger policy influence, in the United States business groups and promarket political parties, especially the Republicans, secure greater leverage over health care decisionmaking. They shape not only public opinion but also congressional and media perceptions of citizens' attitudes toward health policies.[15] Interviewing US policymakers during the early 1990s, Lawrence Jacobs and Robert Shapiro

> found that policy makers were in fact reluctant to follow the public's policy preferences. Their inclination was to make decisions based on their own judgments and ideology. Politicians exercised substantial discretion in formulating mechanisms for financing and delivering health care . . . . It is simply not the case that public opinion has dictated policy. Rather, information and discussion among elites have largely shaped public opinion . . . .[16]

Among these elites, political party activists play an especially important role mobilizing popular support for health programs.

Political Party Preferences

In these eight pluralist democracies, political parties influence the legislative agenda; their causal attributions and policy preferences determine the decisions made by representative government. Analysts have formulated three models of representation. According to the 'mandate' model, voters communicate detailed political preferences to their representatives, who then implement these policy positions in specific legislation. The 'trustee' approach assumes that representatives form their own judgment about the best health policies to pursue. Under the 'party loyalist' model, representatives adopt the policy stands of their party's leaders in the legislature. Empirical studies of legislative voting behavior indicate that representatives most often follow the party loyalist model. Because the public holds divergent, vague, and contradictory stands on specific issues such as the details of a health care proposal, legislative party elites retain extensive discretion to frame the political agenda, guide parliamentarians' votes, and influence mass attitudes. Particularly in parliamentary systems, the need for party discipline in legislative voting ensures that few representatives deviate from their party whips' cues. On general policy issues, legislators thus follow the party mandate. Responsiveness to constituents' demands occurs when rendering specific services for them or channeling government funds to their districts.

Since World War II the main economic issues dividing political party leaders have revolved around government promotion of social equality, public control of private enterprises, and the rights of trade unions. Leftwing activists more strongly support increased expenditures for social service programs, such as health, education, pensions, and job creation, that provide generous, inclusive, and comprehensive benefits. According to the leftists, government should regulate private enterprises so that they ensure safe, healthy working conditions and avoid industrial pollution. Trade unions must gain expanded rights to secure healthier workplaces, whether in a factory or office. By contrast, rightwing party leaders voice greater opposition to comprehensive, egalitarian income maintenance, education, and health policies. They seek more government assistance (tax credits or subsidies) for private health programs, private schools, and private pension plans. Preferring to deregulate and privatize the health sector, they want private enterprise managers to gain independence from government and union control.

The commitment to these ideological programs depends on a person's degree of party activism. Passive supporters — either voters or identifiers — rarely hold coherent policy positions toward health issues. Those actively working for a party and its candidates express more coherent, consistent ideological principles. They have attained the formal education and political experience needed to interpret political issues from a comprehensive set of abstract principles — individualism, hierarchism, egalitarianism — that systematically show the interconnections among several diverse issues. Unlike passive supporters, activists not only think more abstractly and deductively but also voice more polarized stands. Just as leftwing party leaders voice more leftist stands than does their mass base, so rightwing activists also articulate more conservative orientations toward health policies than do their followers.

Partisan cleavages toward health policies are greater than differences among nations or between social groups within a country. Even if lower-income, less-formally-educated unskilled workers express the strongest support for egalitarian health policies, controls for education, occupational status, and income strengthen the impact of party ties on attitudes. Combined with class and ideological identifications, political party affiliation emerges as the key explanatory variable. As expected from these divergent ideological values, leftwing partisans most strongly prefer generous, egalitarian, comprehensive, and inclusive policies. For example, in the United States Democrats who view themselves as 'working class liberals' favor a single-payer government health program, universal access to health care, increased government spending on health services, and higher taxes to finance health insurance for all citizens. Supporting government regulation of industry, they stress the environmental causes of illness, such as pollution. Republicans, however, back a more market-oriented system that mandates less government regulation, lower public spending, reduced taxes, and more individual responsibility for health.

Of all Canadian parties, the socialist New Democratic Party (NDP) voices the greatest support for egalitarian health policies and rejects a two-tiered proposal blending public finances for basic health services with private payments for additional services. With a more competitive individualist outlook, the Progressive Conservatives and Reformists show less enthusiasm for extending public health benefits. Liberals take an intermediate position. At the federal government level, they enacted the comprehensive, egalitarian Canada Health Act of 1984 when their administration relied on the New Democrats for legislative support. After the NDP electoral popularity declined in the 1993 elections to the House of Commons, the Liberal government reduced health care benefits by decreasing funds to the provincial governments.

In Britain, Germany, and Sweden leftwingers — Labourites, Social Democrats, Greens — back activist government health programs. Supportive of trade unions, these egalitarians believe that government has an obligation to provide health care for the sick and to raise public expenditures for financing these policies. According to the Labourites' worldview, illness stems from environmental causes such as pollution, unsafe working conditions, and dilapidated housing. Hence, public policymakers should improve general health by changing the environment. The rightist parties — British Conservative, German Free Democrat, Christian Democratic Union/Christian Social Union — blend hierarchical principles with competitive individualism. Opposed to income equality, they prefer a health care system based on individual responsibility, personal incentives that reward healthy lifestyles, and market-oriented reforms. Deference to experts — physicians, hospital administrators, insurance managers — coexists with market competition regulated by government agencies. Although the major Swedish parties have achieved stronger policy consensus than the two largest British parties, during the 1980s the partisan activists on the left (Social Democrats) and right (Moderate Unity members) became more polarized. Whereas social democratic leaders favored egalitarian public health services, the Moderate Unity partisans expressed the greatest support for private competition in the health care sector.

Compared with competitive individualists and egalitarians, who participate in political party activities and work for changes in health policies, hierarchs and especially fatalists play a less active role. Japanese holding hierarchical values defer to authority, seek

community harmony, trust incumbent government officials, and
vote for the Liberal Democratic Party, which has stressed health
care programs for children and the elderly. LDP support arises
mainly from older, less-well-educated hierarchs. By contrast,
Japanese individualists lean toward opposition parties. Younger
and better educated, they have greater political interest, higher
political efficacy, and more political knowledge. Along with
egalitarians, these individualists possess the resources and
motivations to rally dissent against incumbent government
policies. Fatalists, however, take a more cynical view toward
government efforts to improve social and personal conditions, such
as health. With limited income and low education, they feel that
government does not respond to their personal needs. They neither
identify with political parties nor become active members of
voluntary associations. Unlike the competitive individualists and
egalitarians, the fatalists wield little if any influence over health
policymakers.

Despite the ideological differences between leftwing and
rightwing party activists, the health programs implemented by
diverse governing parties within the same country show only
modest variations over time. What conditions explain the gap
between party rhetoric and government health decisions? In these
pluralist democracies, the need to compromise and the demands for
political feasibility often produce interparty accommodations. First,
nearly every political party experiences attitudinal disunity. Rarely
does one party proclaim a united, coherent stand toward pressing
issues, like government's role in the health sector. Probusiness
factions compete with more egalitarian factions favoring social
service programs. This policy factionalism necessitates
compromises among diverse groups within a party.

Second, when a party holds executive power, government
officials retain discretion to mold policies that often depart from
party activists' preferences. Policymakers usually share a greater
consensus on issues than do rival party leaders. Ideological
desirability yields to the demands of political feasibility when
elected leaders bargain with other participants in the policy
formulation process. Especially from the mid-1980s through the
1990s, sluggish economic growth among industrialized capitalist
nations increased pressures for governments to control social
service spending. Even leftist parties enacted austerity policies
designed to restrain the expansion of comprehensive social service

programs and to increase private sector provision of health benefits. Rightwing party cabinet members hesitated to make drastic reductions in health care expenditures.

Third, most continental European governments comprise a coalition of parties that need to accommodate ideological differences. For example, in 1992 whereas the Christian Democratic Union controlled the Bundestag — the lower chamber of the German federal parliament, — the Social Democrats held a majority of seats in the Bundesrat, the upper house that represented Länder interests. Even though the CDU's coalition partners the Free Democrats opposed measures to curtail health providers' fees, the CDU allied with the Social Democratic Party to enact laws that reduced pharmaceutical prices, hospital budgets, and fees for physicians' services. Despite pressures from the dominant Moderate Unity party that held the Swedish premiership, in 1992–1993 the Liberal Party Minister for Health and Social Affairs refused to make drastic cuts in social service expenditures. With support from the opposition Social Democrats, he convinced the Riksdag to implement a policy expanding benefits for the disabled.

Fourth, agencies other than parties and elected government leaderships shape governments' responsibilities for health care; these include the civil service, central bank, and business corporations. Particularly in Sweden, France, Germany, and Japan, civil servants influence the content of public health policies. Oriented toward prudence, they reject drastic changes that greatly expand or limit government activities. Seeking continuity, the civil service usually favors incremental health programs often opposed by rightwing or leftwing party ideologues. Central banks retain some autonomy from the cabinet, especially in the United States, Germany, Britain, and the Netherlands. Concerned to halt inflation, these central banks constrain both monetary and fiscal policies, especially the tendency to pursue an expansionary strategy. Faced with bankers' pressures, elected leaders implement austerity policies that limit expenditures for health care. Domestic private businesses and multinational corporations seek greater privatization of the health care system, deregulation, and reduced public health benefits. Because these corporations provide investment funds and employment, government officials, whatever their party affiliation, must refrain from enacting policies that threaten 'business confidence'.[17]

Business and Labor Views

Business and labor leaders often express more polarized views toward social service programs than do political party activists. According to sample surveys in Western Europe, Japan, Canada, and the United States, business executives remain hostile to egalitarian public health policies. This corporate antagonism appears particularly widespread in the United States. Compared with European and Japanese businesspeople, US executives show weaker enthusiasm for government oversight of industrial safety standards, for government controls of environmental pollution, and for government administered health programs. They oppose universal health coverage, higher personal taxes to finance this coverage, employer mandates to provide health insurance, and government controls over hospital construction and the supply of physicians. Rejecting taxes on health insurance premiums, they prefer increased taxes on cigarettes and liquor and higher insurance premiums for individuals who engage in excessive smoking and drinking. Medical savings accounts and lower government reimbursements to health providers represent desirable ways to curtail rising health care costs. Most US corporate executives support private programs under which employers decide whether or not to provide health insurance, with workers sharing the costs of managed-care plans. Government policies should supply only partial benefits and limit public coverage to the poor and unemployed. Identifying with rightist parties, European businesspeople perceive taxes as a burden on competition, prefer user fees as the best method to finance health services, and want to extend the private provision of health care. By contrast, labor unions identify with the ideological left, favor egalitarian taxes on income, and reject privatization proposals that limit the comprehensive range of public health benefits.

Given the divergent preferences of corporate and union leaders, nations where unions exercise the greatest policy influence vis-à-vis the business sector implement the most generous, comprehensive egalitarian, and inclusive health programs. These countries include the Netherlands and especially Sweden. Since 1932 Swedish Social Democrats have controlled a high share of cabinet seats. The rightwing parties faced greater fragmentation. Over 80 percent of the labor force belonged to unions; the industrial LO allied with the Social Democrats (SAP). Coalitions with farmers and white-collar employees strengthened the SAP's popularity and its ability to enact egalitarian health policies. Even though labor unions and leftist parties are weaker in the Netherlands than in Sweden, intense electoral competition between the Dutch Labor Party and Christian Democratic Appeal has led to fairly generous public health plans. Gaining the highest share of voters at recent elections, both parties compete for the working class vote and often form a coalition government. Socialist and Christian Democratic unions collaborate. Christian Democrats assume that the government should help the needy. Rather than separated from the state, religious institutions fuse their activities with the government. Receiving government subsidies, Catholic and Protestant churches allocate health benefits. As in Sweden, pluralism in the Netherlands promotes cooperation among government officials, unions, churches, and divergent political parties. As a result, egalitarian values temper the competitive individualism linked to the market and the hierarchical ethos associated with the Swedish state bureaucracy and the Dutch Roman Catholic Church.[18]

Attitudes of Medical Personnel

Among health personnel, social stratification influences policy preferences, with nurses holding more egalitarian worldviews than do medical students and especially physicians. Surveys conducted in the United States, Canada, Britain, the Netherlands, and Japan indicate that nurses most strongly challenge physicians' professional authority, support patients' right to share in health care decisionmaking, and favor patients' access to medical information. Committed to egalitarian health policies, Dutch nurses oppose higher insurance copayments, reject special access to health facilities for high status people, and favor expanding the scope of benefits offered by public health insurance plans. Dutch physicians show less enthusiasm for all these policy options. In the United States and Canada, male surgeons back a more individualist, promarket stand than do women doctors, psychiatrists, and those in primary care: family practice, internal medicine, and pediatrics. Along with solo private practitioners, these male specialists voice stronger support for privatized health plans, higher user fees, and increased patient copayments. Female physicians employed by community health centers or health service organizations prefer the national public program ensuring equal access to comprehensive benefits. Among North American physicians, Canadians take the more egalitarian position. Committed to a national universal policy, they seem less inclined to participate in health maintenance organizations run by private insurance corporations. For them, government planning of the health system will assure a more equal distribution of needed services.

Medical school students in the United States and England express attitudes located between practicing physicians' and nurses' perspectives. Whereas US physicians prefer a voucher plan and tax deductions for private health services but reject a government-financed national health program for all citizens, American medical students lean toward more egalitarian policies that would restrain costs by reducing insurance company profits and by limiting public reimbursements for hospital stays, diagnostic tests, and doctors' salaries. According to them, higher income taxes represent the best way to finance these benefits. Women and future primary care physicians particularly favor these policy proposals. In Britain women medical students also adopt more egalitarian attitudes than do men. Supportive of nurses' and patients' autonomy, women seek increased sharing of responsibilities among doctors, nurses, and patients.[19]

CONCLUSION

This analysis of political culture in eight nations indicates the need to qualify the three hypotheses linking public opinion to health policies. First, general value differences among countries hardly explain specific national health programs. For example, Swedes and Japanese uphold such individualist values as competition, hard work, personal responsibility, and the dominance of freedom over equality. Yet they implement more egalitarian health policies than does the individualistic United States. Unlike Americans, Europeans and Japanese see individualism and equality not as irreconcilable but as compatible values. Moreover, national public opinion scarcely takes a monolithic policy position. Poor people, nurses, trade unionists, and especially leftwing partisans adopt the most egalitarian stands toward health issues. Wealthier individuals, surgeons, business executives, and rightwing party supporters back more promarket, individualist, and hierarchical policies. The particular programs emerging from the policy process reflect the preferences of those sociopolitical groups that control government ministries.

Second, even though political party identification wields the strongest impact on health policy preferences, partisan stands in ideological manifestos differ more than the specific policies implemented by divergent parties. The need to seek accommodations with other parties in coalition governments encourages government officials to compromise their positions.

Third, although citizens take a coherent stand on health policy goals, they hold less cohesive, clear, intense attitudes toward specific health policy proposals. For nearly everyone, health care represents a salient issue. Most individuals feel strongly about the need to contain personal costs, ensure access to health providers, and guarantee continuous coverage whatever one's medical condition. Yet people remain uninformed about the esoteric administrative details of particular policy proposals to achieve consensual health objectives. Specific plans encounter greater ambivalence and disunity than do the goals of restraining personal costs or expanding health benefits. Hence, sociopolitical elites assume responsibility for determining explicit programs. Through their access to the mass media, government officials, political party activists, corporate executives, technical experts, and health professionals influence the public's perspective on specific policy measures. They not only set the political agenda but also frame proposals to cope with problems deemed serious by these elites.

The major limitation of cultural analyses revolves around their failure to explain the precise mechanisms that link general, vague values to specific organizational operations and elite preferences. The framework elaborated by Aaron Wildavsky and Mary Douglas reveals parsimony and logical coherence. We can deduce specific hypotheses from a few general assumptions. The fourfold value pattern — egalitarianism, individualism, hierarchism, fatalism — offers a parsimonious way to highlight the dominant meanings among nations, groups, and individuals. Nevertheless, this cultural approach lacks explanatory power. Such cultural values as egalitarianism and individualism convey divergent interpretations. Different individuals and groups may hold the same values but interpret them in opposite ways. Because different policy implications and plans for government action may emerge from similar values, the analyst faces difficulties ascertaining the precise impact of these general principles on specific public health programs.[20] In sum, cultural analysts downplay the important way that structures institutionalize and internalize the general values uncovered in mass sample surveys. Hence, they can neither fully explain the crossnational differences among public health programs nor accurately assess the impact of public opinion on these policies.

6 Political Power and Policy Changes

Novelists highlight the structural conditions that produce illness. Written immediately before World War I, *The Ragged Trousered Philanthropists* took an egalitarian stance toward programs for workers' health. Its Irish author Robert Tressell described the working and living conditions of several residential construction workers: house painters, decorators, carpenters, plumbers, plasterers, bricklayers. Laboring in southern England, these men faced long working hours and low wages followed by lengthy periods of unemployment. Poverty, starvation, unhealthy worksites, and dilapidated, crowded, damp residential housing caused sickness, disease, and premature death. A house painter himself, Tressell died at age 40 of tuberculosis. The novel's hero Frank Owen suffered from lung disease. Yet he had the energy to proclaim egalitarian socialist ideals to his workmates, most of whom failed to view the world through a working-class consciousness. Unlike Owen, they accepted the dominant fatalist, hierarchical, and individualist worldviews. Holding fatalistic values, several perceived their world as unchangeable. God and evil human nature, not structural conditions, brought sickness, poverty, and joblessness. This fatalism bred self-contempt and low personal efficacy. Other workers assumed a hierarchical view, accepted the status quo, and deferred to their 'betters'. Influenced by the capitalist media, the individualists blamed illness on personal vices: laziness, alcoholism, thriftlessness, and other unhealthy habits. Countering all these views, Owen argued that sickness and disease stemmed from the capitalist system: competition for low wages, unsafe working conditions, residential slums, unemployment, poverty, malnutrition, economic inequality, and private monopolistic ownership of the means of production. Making an analogy between housing conditions and health, Owen explained to his skeptical workmates:

Suppose they were always ill, and suppose that the house was badly built, the walls so constructed that they drew and retained moisture, the roof broken and leaky, the drains defective, the doors and windows ill-fitting, and the rooms badly shaped and draughty. If you were asked to name, in a word, the cause of the ill-health of the people who lived there you would say — the house. All the tinkering in the world would not make that house fit to live in; the only thing to do with it would be to pull it down and build another.[1]

As an egalitarian socialist, Owen sought to replace the 'Money System' with a cooperative commonwealth based on production for use, not profit. From his perspective, policies in this new system would secure jobs for all, short working hours, high wages, income equality, comfortable housing, and healthy working conditions. Unions and a socialist party would deconstruct reactionary worldviews and overcome the employer exploitation and working class apathy that maintained economic misery. By changing structural conditions, Owen expected to construct a new house — a system free from the 'disease called poverty'.

Thirty years later the British novelist A. J. Cronin made similar assumptions about the structural conditions causing ill health. In *The Citadel* the physician Andrew Manson linked lung disease to Welsh miners' working environment. Examining the coal miners, he discovered that older anthracite workers suffered the most from pulmonary tuberculosis, which derived from the lengthy exposure to silica dust. Indifferent to this problem, corporate executives, mineowners, and even other physicians refused to support scientific studies that would uncover the causal connections between occupational stratification and lung disease. Policymakers took few steps to enact legislation that would regulate working conditions in the coal mines. Even if not a socialist like Frank Owen, Dr. Manson still supported public programs for upgrading the workers' environment — policies such as expanded education, improved public health services, better sanitary facilities, and safer working conditions.[2]

Chapter 6 compares three structural theories — pluralism, institutionalism, Marxism — that explain the variations in health policies across the eight industrialized nations. It analyzes these questions: First, who wields the dominant influence over the health policy process? Which groups, organizations, and institutions shape the key decisions? Pluralists like Paul Sabatier, who focuses on advocacy coalitions, see an interdependence among social groups, political parties, and government agencies at all levels. Institutionalists assert the dominance of the state over society. Although Marxists perceive the state as exerting some autonomy, they assume that class relationships dominate government decisionmaking.

Second, what types of conflicts pervade the health policy arena? How do policymakers deal with these conflicts based on divergent values and interests? What level of conflict do they tolerate? What strategies do they use to accommodate conflicts over values and interests? This issue relates to the degree of unity attained by various organizations participating in the policy process. Taking a pluralist outlook, Sabatier assumes that various intergovernmental agencies and social agencies try to reconcile conflicting policy preferences that stem from core beliefs. Solidarity arises during the process of coalition formation as alliance members seek mutual benefits. For him, shared values represent the most unifying element behind the coalition. Institutionalists perceive policy conflicts emerging mainly from disputes over power and interests. Riven by factionalism, government agencies and political parties compete for scarce resources. Nation-state solidarity and party cohesion derive from organizational rules and mechanisms — communications links, interlocking directorates, interdependent networks. According to Marxists, class solidarity stems from class conflict. In the modern capitalist world economy, the proletariat and bourgeoisie struggle for supremacy. Blending class consciousness articulated through the media with political mobilization waged by unions, capitalist corporations, and competing parties, they struggle to enhance class solidarity. The relative degree of class organization and consciousness shapes their influence over the policy process.

Third, how does the extent of conflict and solidarity explain health policy changes? Sabatier assumes that most policy changes in pluralist societies emerge through coalition formation. Policy actors who can most effectively establish alliances with other government agencies, political parties, and social groups will see their policy preferences transformed into government decisions. According to institutionalists, powerful political institutions headed by civil servants, cabinet ministers, legislators, and political party activists forge policy changes. Marxists view policy change as resulting from both class conflicts and class alliances. Political mobilization of supporters and demobilization of opponents strengthen the prospects for class actors to transform the health care sector.

The following sections use the three theoretical perspectives to explain the types and degrees of health policy changes among the eight nations. Sabatier's advocacy coalition framework helps us understand the more egalitarian changes that occurred in the Netherlands than in Germany during the 1985–1995 period. Institutionalism explicates the more transformative changes secured by Conservative elites in England, compared with France or Japan, from 1980 through the early 1990s. Marxist approaches stress the divergent type of class structures that enabled Swedish government officials after World War II to implement more generous, comprehensive, egalitarian health programs than did Canadian and especially United States leaders.

PLURALISM: ADVOCACY COALITIONS AND POLICY NEGOTIATION

The advocacy coalition framework (ACF) formulated by Paul A. Sabatier and Hank C. Jenkins-Smith adopts a pluralist approach toward the policy process.[3] It assumes that several different institutions, organizations, and groups participate in making decisions. Oriented around a single issue or problem like health care, they constitute a policy subsystem. Intergovernmental coalitions unite government agencies at different geographical levels: central, regional, municipal. Health, economic, and finance ministries play a key role. Important group participants include health insurance agencies, associations of health providers, and pharmaceutical industries. They often form alliances with government institutions and political parties, which represent their interests and mediate conflicts among the groups. Comprised of several different parties, coalition governments negotiate compromises as they formulate health policies.

Basic policy conflicts revolve around divergent values and interests. Sabatier and Jenkins-Smith analyze three types of values: core beliefs, policy preferences, and implementing strategies. Core beliefs represent the most stable values, which include general priorities (freedom, equality, justice, efficiency, equity) and causal assumptions about ways that the policy process operates, especially its distribution of power. These normative values and causal assumptions shape perceptions of salient problems, specific policy objectives, and possible policy solutions. Policy preferences focus on the scope of government responsibility for dealing with a problem like ill health. Implementing strategies refer to particular methods for attaining policymakers' preferences — for example, administrative rules, specific regulations, budget allocations, appointment of personnel, and interpretations of laws. Whereas core values constitute nonempirical, abstract, expressive ends (general concepts of the desirable), interests refer to more empirical, concrete stakes in government action or inaction. Because interests focus on tangible benefits (power, wealth) and pragmatic orientations, political leaders can more easily compromise interests than values. For instance, government regulatory agencies can strike deals with physicians' associations about their reimbursement fees. Negotiating with antiabortion leaders becomes more difficult, because they view abortion as murder. Hence, government policies to finance or even allow abortions violate their intensely-held core values. Particularly when struggles over competing interests become infused with core values, coalition heads face difficulties negotiating policy disputes. When two advocacy coalitions hold divergent core values, this normative polarization hinders the bargaining process. Zeal supplants the deal. Policymakers cannot enact incremental policy changes.

According to the ACF, policy changes mainly originate from external shocks occurring in the sociopolitical environment. Economic shocks include oil price hikes, recessions, high inflation, trade deficits, and other structural conditions in the world capitalist economy. Political shocks stem from wars, reunification of nation-states, and changes in the party composition of governments at higher jurisdictions. These external shocks alter the structural power of policymaking organizations: government agencies, advocacy groups, and coalitions among them. By changing the resources accruing to various coalition partners, the shocks transform their structural opportunities and constraints. For example, trade deficits, low growth, high unemployment, and accelerating inflation limit financial resources available to the government but also increase demands on policymakers for economic assistance. Economic stagflation may produce electoral defeat for a dominant governing party and enable a new coalition to assume executive power. If the new coalition has a solid majority in the legislature and upholds different core values than the party it replaced, policy changes will result. Especially in a pluralist political system, these changes will flow from the core values of the key actors, their policy preferences, and information about feedback from previous health programs. This information comes mainly from populist groups, interest groups (health providers, insurance agencies, pharmaceutical industries), and such expert groups as health scientists, economists, and professional analysts.

Three hypotheses about policy change flow from these assumptions. First, policy changes more often originate from external shocks than from internal conditions within the policy subsystem. More severe external economic shocks produce greater policy changes. If the government of a 'hierarchically superior jurisdiction' changes from control by one party to dominance by a party with divergent policy preferences, then officials at lower levels will more likely initiate policy changes. Second, policy changes originate at the subsystem level when pragmatists (brokers) dominate the ruling coalition. The higher the number of value cleavages, the more unstable the governing coalition and the less likely that brokers will achieve the power required to enact policy changes. Third, moderate conflicts produce the greatest policy changes, particularly incremental reforms, and the most learning across coalitions. Implementing strategies change more often than do policy preferences or especially deep core values. The more polarized the core values, the more difficult for leaders to institute policy changes. The greater the role of experts, professionals, administrators, economists, and brokers in the policy process, the more likely that changes will occur, mainly because decisions stem from professional norms that stress the need for accurate empirical information. The greater the role of ideological interest groups in the policy process, the more difficult for coalition leaders to negotiate policy compromises about needed changes.[4] How well do these hypotheses explain the health policy changes that occurred in Germany and the Netherlands from 1980 through the mid-1990s?

Germany and the Netherlands represent two corporatist regimes governed by coalitions among private social groups, government institutions, and different political parties; hence, the advocacy coalition framework helps us understand the changing health policies that have arisen over the last two decades. As indicated in Chapter 3, both nations disperse power among diverse structures.

No sharp boundaries separate 'public' institutions from 'private' groups. Social groups participate in policy formulation as well as implementation. Public revenues finance private health providers, most of whom operate nonprofit agencies. Government institutions regulate their activities. As a federal system, Germany allocates responsibilities among the federal government, the Länder, and municipalities; the Länder play a particularly important part regulating the provision of health services, expenditures, and revenue collection. Although a unitary state, the Dutch central government shares authority with the provinces and cities. In the two countries, the central government ministries of health, finance, and economic affairs shape national health programs. Members from these ministries, along with associations representing health providers, insurance organizations, private firms, and unions, participate in regulatory agencies that manage the two health care systems. Within these agencies — the German Concerted Action and the Dutch National Health Council, Health Insurance Funds Council, and the Central Agency for Health Care Charges, — coalitions form among public and private participants as they negotiate compromises.

Political parties establish coalition governments. In Germany two parties usually dominate the federal policy process. From 1969 through 1982 the Social Democratic Party (SPD) and the Free Democratic Party (FDP) governed the Federal Republic. An alliance of the Christian Democratic Union/Christian Social Union (Bavaria) and the Free Democrats ruled during the 1982–1997 period. Länder governments also feature coalitions of diverse parties. For example, in early 1993 the Social Democrats controlled four regional governments, allied with the FDP in one, and joined with the Greens in two. A three-party coalition of Social Democrats, Free Democrats, and Greens governed Brandenburg and Bremen. Like the SPD, the CDU united with different parties in various Länder, for example, with the Free Democrats in four and with the SPD in one. Only in two regions did the CDU rule the executive as the sole party.[5] These coalitions promoted compromises over interests, rather than core values. Similarly in the Netherlands, two or three political parties have usually formed the national coalition government. The two major parties — the Christian Democratic Appeal (CDA) and the Labor Party (PvdA) — have instituted alliances with each other and smaller parties. Between 1973 and 1994, the CDA dominated all coalition governments. From 1973 through 1977, it ruled with the PvdA and Democrats '66, a small party of social liberals. During 1977–1981 the CDA allied with the People's Party for Freedom and Democracy (VVD), which upheld promarket liberal values. After two brief coalitions between 1981 and 1982, the CDA reestablished an alliance with the VVD. That coalition lasted until 1989, when the PvdA and the Christian Democrats once again united. Following the 1994 parliamentary election, the PvdA allied with the VVD and the Democrats '66 in a coalition government, with a Democrat '66 legislator heading the health ministry. As in Germany, all these diverse coalitions necessitated compromises over values and interests.

Even if the political parties and their group allies articulate divergent values and economic interests, these conflicts remain fairly moderate and hence compromisable. In both Germany and the Netherlands, the Christian Democratic parties occupy a centrist position between the Socialists and promarket Liberals (VVD and FDP). Along with the more egalitarian wing of the Christian Democratic parties, the Social Democrats uphold solidarity: mutual trust, reciprocity, and cooperation for the common good. They seek the realization of these communitarian values in public health programs that ensure generous, comprehensive benefits available to all citizens, whatever their social status, income, or occupation. The FDP and VVD most strongly articulate promarket values: self-reliance, efficiency, and cost containment. These values encourage the spread of private health insurance plans and higher user fees. Catholics within the CDU, CSU, and CDA prefer policies based on 'subsidiarity,' the concept that local governments and private associations such as churches should manage health programs.

The economic interests promoted by Dutch and German parties derive from their stands toward equality. Backed by workers and unions, the SPD and PvdA most strongly favor egalitarian public programs that provide generous health benefits to low-income individuals. Private business corporations and health providers, especially physician associations and pharmaceutical industries, ally with the promarket wing of the Christian Democratic parties and especially with the two Liberal parties. Unlike the Christian Democrats, the FDP and VVD attract electoral support from self-employed businesspeople and highly-paid managers who do not participate in Protestant or Catholic church activities. These

Liberals reject egalitarian income redistribution measures, strong unions, and government regulation of health care industries.

Gaining votes from Protestants and Catholics of all social classes, the Christian Democratic parties campaign for a regulated welfare society based on vertical and horizontal pluralism. Vertically, the subsidiarity principle means that regional and local governments take charge of health care management. Horizontally, several autonomous 'private' groups — churches, unions, private insurance agencies, and firms — share responsibilities for initiating as well as administering health programs. Given this pluralist, communitarian framework, most health policy conflicts have revolved around divergent interests: taxes, contributions to insurance funds, premiums, patient copayments, and reimbursements to physicians, hospitals, and pharmaceutical manufacturers. Policymakers have also clashed over other implementing strategies such as interpretation of laws and allocation of health care tasks to specific personnel.

Incremental changes have emerged from these moderate conflicts and dispersed power situations. Because several political parties, governmental agencies, and social groups participate in the coalitions that make health policies, no transformative changes seem feasible. Instead, participants must compromise their diverse interests. As Sabatier hypothesized, external economic conditions such as recession in the world capitalist economy have placed cost containment policies at the top of policymakers' agenda. Under pressures from finance ministers, central bankers, private financiers, and employers, both the German and Dutch governments during the early 1990s enacted policies that limited reimbursements to physicians, hospitals, and pharmaceutical industries. Patient copayments increased. High costs for elderly care motivated German officials to transfer financing of home health and nursing home care from cities and Länder to nationally-raised social security expenditures financed jointly by employees and employers. Whereas the Free Democrats and business corporations preferred private insurance, the SPD and unions initially favored universal benefits financed by federal taxes. The prolabor wing of the CDU/CSU governing coalition, led by Minister of Health Horst Seehofer, negotiated a compromise. Acting as a broker, he convinced the SPD to accept a social insurance plan that eliminated local means tests for elderly assistance, expanded rights of all citizens, whatever their income, to choose a sickness fund, and helped low-income persons pay for insurance by basing fund subsidies on participants' age and sex — two demographic factors related to health risks. The German parliament enacted these reforms due to pressures from below, not from 'hierarchically superior jurisdictions'. As we have seen, the Social Democrats, usually in coalition with other parties, controlled a majority of Länder governments. Because the Bundesrat, the upper house of the German legislature, represents these regional governments, the SPD held more seats in that chamber than did the CDU/CSU, which dominated the Bundestag (the lower chamber) and hence wielded executive power along with the FDP, the junior partner. Because the Bundesrat can veto laws passed by the Bundestag, the SPD legislators influence health policies formulated by the governing opposition party. Federal health policies thus emerged from a bottom-up process, rather than through top-down hierarchical arrangements. Leaders in the municipalities and Länder effectively used their resources to translate some of their policy preferences into federal government decisions.

Similarly, in the Netherlands, health policy changes arise from the diverse preferences of several groups and political parties. Private insurance companies, physicians' associations, labor unions, businesses, churches, and environmental groups voiced policy demands about ways to restrain health care costs, lower fiscal deficits, maintain egalitarian access, and ensure generous, comprehensive benefits. In 1987 the Dekker Commission proposed several reforms that successive Dutch governments tried to implement. These reforms included measures to establish a single national health insurance program that would fuse sickness funds with private insurance companies. Competition among insurance agencies would give consumers greater choice of health care plans and would provide incentives for increased efficiency. Unlike Germany, however, Dutch governing coalitions have faced weaker continuity and a more fragile power base. Since 1982 the national coalitions frequently changed party representation. In 1994 the Labor Party allied with the centrist Democrats '66 and with the rightist VVD, which represents the interests of physicians' associations, private insurers, and business corporations. Disputes arose about the progressivity of the taxes needed to finance the Dekker reforms and about the level of flat-rate premiums received by a central fund. Even though the Labor Party agreed to support expanded competition among private insurers, it refused to compromise its commitment to progressive taxes and premiums. By contrast, the VVD and its business allies rejected higher, more egalitarian taxes that would help low-income persons. The need to accommodate conflicting interests among political parties, private insurers, other businesses, unions, and doctors' associations led to slow incremental policy adjustments.

Because the pluralist policy process often produced deadlock in both Germany and the Netherlands, the central governments during the early 1990s took the initiative to negotiate incremental changes with health providers. National legislation enacted moderate restrictions on hospital charges, physicians' fees, and drug prices. All these expenditure caps revolved around interest conflicts, not value cleavages. Rather than reinforcing each other, the conflicts among political parties, religious institutions, and economic class overlapped. Christian Democratic parties in both nations attracted some working class support as well as individuals who did not actively participate in a Catholic or Protestant church. The SPD and PvdA received votes from white-collar Christians as well as from their main working class base. All major parties allied with each other in policy coalitions. Union members cooperated with businesses and with the Christian Democrats. Policy participants from diverse social groups and political parties competed over access to scarce resources, not over irreconcilable values. Policy disputes centered on interests: expenditures for health providers and consumers, private vs. public financing procedures, and the impacts of income taxes, social security contributions, and premiums. Allocation of health care responsibilities to various government agencies, nonprofit associations, and commercial enterprises also consumed policymakers' attention. Experts, civil servants, economists, and health science researchers played a significant role in the policy deliberations. Providing nonideological technical advice, they lessened partisan antagonism. As Sabatier hypothesized, these moderate interest conflicts led to policy learning across coalitions and to incremental changes.

Even though both the German and Dutch coalition governments forged incremental change through their mediation of interest conflicts, Dutch policymakers enacted more egalitarian programs. The German health care system rests on status differentials; at least before 1996, enrollment in sickness funds depended on employees' occupation. In the Netherlands, however, social health insurance funds provide health plans to individuals based mainly on region, not on occupation. Higher-income people purchase private insurance as individuals, rather than through their employer. As organic corporatist regimes, both Germany and the Netherlands seek to reinforce family values. Yet Dutch government leaders have implemented more generous expenditures for home care services and for nursing homes. Progressive income-based health premiums finance egalitarian benefits for older, poorer, sicker individuals. From 1973 through 1996 the Labor Party participated in coalitions during fourteen of these years. Compared with the CDU/CSU, which has dominated the Bundestag ruling coalition since 1982, the Dutch Christian Democratic Appeal (CDA) upholds more egalitarian policy positions supported by workers and union members.

Social group participants take more egalitarian stands in the Netherlands than in Germany. The Dutch Roman Catholic hierarchs articulate humanistic orientations dedicated to helping the poor, sick, disabled, and unemployed. Even if Dutch unions enroll under 30 percent of the labor force, they actively participate in collective bargaining, works councils, and efforts to shape government decisionmakers. The dominant union federation — the FNV (Federatie Nederlandse Vakbeweging), which represents three-fifths of all unionists, — allies Catholic with pro-Labor party members. Hence, it exerts some influence over both major political parties. Unionists hold around two-thirds of positions in the works councils, which focus on regulating health and safety conditions. Although business corporations wield extensive power in both countries, German corporations, particularly financiers, central bankers, and manufacturers, attain greater dominance over the policy process. Along with the Bundesbank officials and finance ministers, they press the federal government to place cost containment at the top of the health policy agenda. Dependent on the export trade and functioning in a smaller country, Dutch entrepreneurs probably carry greater policy weight than do financiers. Compared with their German counterparts, Dutch policymakers have achieved less success curbing fiscal deficits. Social service expenditures, including those for health care benefits, reach higher levels of national income than in Germany. The Dutch not only function as egalitarian individualists but as active group participants. National sample surveys conducted in the early 1990s of citizens in the Netherlands, West Germany,

France, Britain, the United States, and Canada indicate that the Dutch have the highest rate of associational membership especially in religious organizations, education/cultural groups, environmental associations, and social welfare groups. This civic participation expands the range of policy preferences voiced to government officials, reinforces the vitality of pluralism, promotes learning across diverse coalitions, and hence partly explains the egalitarian health care programs enacted by Dutch political institutions.[6]

INSTITUTIONALISM: THE STATE AND SOCIAL GROUPS

Whereas the advocacy coalition framework regards government agencies and social groups as interdependent, institutionalists place more emphasis on the autonomy of political organizations in the policy process. According to health analysts like Theda Skocpol, Ellen Immergut, and David Wilsford, political institutions — cabinets, bureaucracies, legislatures, courts, political parties — make the key decisions. They have the resources, potential independence, and cohesion to initiate and implement policies. From this 'polity-centered' perspective, government institutions and political parties control key resources. Economic resources include finances and expertise. Political resources involve power over the public sector and authority to make specific decisions. Cultural resources refer to information and symbols. When framing health programs, policymakers rely on information obtained from censuses, yearbooks, and other statistical reports. They depend on symbolic appeals derived from law, language, and rituals to win support for their health policies. These symbols express a sense of collective identity, vision, and interpretation of political reality that helps legitimate the authority needed to make public policies. By effectively using these three resources, political leaders try to overcome opposition, mobilize apathetic supporters, and coordinate disparate activities. Differentiated from social groups, state institutions determine the distribution of resources among key policy actors, whose political strategies partly depend on the constraints and opportunities erected by political institutions. Through its cultural resources, institutional leaders shape groups' policy goals, strategies, and interpretations of their stakes (interests) in specific government activities.[7]

The power of public policies to realize leaders' objectives stems from the actual autonomy and cohesion of political institutions vis-à-vis social groups. Maintaining independent control from domestic groups and foreign organizations, autonomous institutions have the freedom to define policy problems, formulate goals, propose alternative solutions, and enact decisions believed most desirable and feasible. For example, a powerful civil service in a health ministry has several resources needed to maintain its autonomy: expertise, information, *esprit de corps*, organizational identity, positive self-image, and commitment to bureaucratic norms. Taking a unified view of sociopolitical problems, an autonomous civil service shares similar objectives and agrees on appropriate policies. Hence, it can play a key role helping cabinet ministers formulate health programs. Institutional power also reflects the degree of cohesion among diverse government agencies and political parties that form the coalition government. Cohesion derives from both organizational and attitudinal sources. Organizational mechanisms such as small group networks, interlocking directorates, and communications linkages reinforce solidarity. Consensus on shared values, norms, and policy preferences overcomes the tendencies toward institutional fragmentation.

According to the institutionalist paradigm, policy conflicts revolve around procedural disputes, power relationships, and interest clashes. Policy participants disagree on the meaning of rules, especially the role expectations that allocate government responsibilities to specific government agencies, parastatal organizations, or private associations. Clashes among different factions, agencies, parties, groups, and organizations focus on their efforts to influence the policy process, wield dominant power, and secure access to scarce resources. By establishing ways to block new proposals or to secure the passage of a new law, institutional rules shape the opportunities for interest groups such as health providers to attain their policy preferences. Institutions deal with these conflicts through coercive and consensual means. Fear of sanctions motivates compliance toward government authorities. More important, they try to achieve voluntary agreements on procedures that outline moral obligations in specific political roles and indicate routines for appropriate behavior toward other policy actors. Formal laws and informal conventions promote cooperative interactions. They emphasize the need for trust, interest accommodation, and solidarity based on such shared cultural values as civility.

How do policy changes occur? Government agencies and political parties play the crucial role in realizing incremental, evolutionary changes. A cultural lag arises between new values that challenge ideological hegemony and traditional values that no longer convincingly explain the meaning of transformed empirical realities. This value conflict may cause changes in normative expectations about the proper responsibilities for governments in tackling health care problems, whether to expand benefits or to restrain costs. Technological developments often lead to conflicts between standpatters and innovators who devise new techniques for providing health services. Cultural innovations and technological advances then lead to institutional adaptations that facilitate policy changes. External shocks like war and worldwide economic recession sensitize government leaders and party activists about the need for policy changes. Domestic conditions — corruption, inefficiencies, leaders' unresponsive behavior, general government malperformance — often bring to power new government leadership and political parties. Particularly if government agencies and parties possess the resources, cohesion, and independence to overcome opposition, they can realize intended policy changes.[8]

Three hypotheses derive from these general assumptions about the causes of policy change. First, as the activities of government agencies become more coordinated, innovative elites gain greater opportunities to enact policy changes. Second, when government agencies, especially the cabinet and civil service, maintain autonomy from social groups, they can more easily implement policy changes desired by these institutional leaders. Third, a high interdependence between government agencies (cabinet ministries, bureaucracies) and the dominant party expands the likelihood of policy changes, especially if elites support innovative programs. Under this condition, party activists back more drastic, immediate changes than do civil servants, who favor incremental modifications of existing policies.

How well do these hypotheses explain the greater health policy changes initiated by the Thatcher administration in Britain during the 1980s, compared with the French and Japanese governments' more incremental adjustments? In all three societies, unitary states and powerful bureaucracies made key decisions. Two major parties or interparty alliances competed for office: Conservative vs. Labour in Britain, RPR-UDF vs. Socialists in France, and the Liberal Democrats vs. Socialists in Japan. Physicians operated as independent entrepreneurs. Despite these similarities, the British government enacted the most sweeping changes in the health care system at the end of the 1980s. What structural conditions linked to the institutionalist framework explain these policy variations among Britain, France, and Japan?

The 1990 National Health Service and Community Care Act brought significant organizational changes to England. The nationally-financed tax system remained; it provided publicly accessible and fairly comprehensive health benefits, except for dental care, eye treatments, and some prescription drugs. Yet, as we saw in Chapter 4, the NHS structure changed. Health providers — physicians, hospitals — became separated from purchasers, including district health authorities and GP fundholding practices. General practitioners, particularly the GP fundholders, gained greater authority over hospital specialists. Under informal contract arrangements, hospital consultants competed for patients referred to them by the general practitioners. Management centralization placed more power in the NHS Executive. Local authorities and district health authorities lost their former control over GPs and hospitals. District health authorities and family health service authorities merged into local health commissions (authorities).

The Thatcher administration could implement these changes because government agencies wielded autonomous, cohesive power; the central government and the Conservative Party maintained an interdependent relationship. Social groups and the opposition Labour Party remained more fragmented. Although the Conservatives won only 42 percent of the UK popular vote during the 1987 election, it secured 61 percent of the seats in the House of Commons. This large majority enabled the dominant party to translate its leaders' policy preferences into government decisions. Only a few elites — Prime Minister Thatcher, Secretary of State for Health, Chancellor of the Exchequer, NHS managers, and promarket technocrats from Conservative Party research institutes — formulated the policy proposal. Determined to eliminate socialist influences from Britain, these elites stood united behind an entrepreneurial health program that would bring more internal market competition and privatization to the NHS. Even though public opinion, physicians'associations, nurses, the Labour Party, and unions rejected these policy changes, fragmented power hindered their effectiveness. Representing specialists, the British Medical Association voiced different interests than did most general practitioners. The royal medical colleges were split into different specialties. Ideological disputes weakened Labour Party cohesion. High unemployment and antiunion policies pursued by the Conservative Party lessened trade union influence; between 1980 and 1990 union membership as a share of the total labor force fell from 50 percent to under 40 percent. Along with this union decline, ideological disputes fragmented Labour Party cohesion. By contrast, the Conservative Party remained more unified and autonomous from social group pressures, even those from business. Elected Conservative Party cabinet members maintained an interdependent relationship with Tory activists, who held an intense ideological commitment to the promarket health plans advocated by the Thatcher regime. Unlike previous prime ministers, Mrs Thatcher diminished the policy influence of the senior civil servants, particularly those in the Health Department. Supported by the three-fifths Conservative majority in Commons, the cabinet wielded the extensive institutional power needed to gain parliamentary approval for its health policy changes.[9]

Although a powerful civil service supposedly dominates the French nation-state, the policy process actually reveals a more complex, fragmented, incohesive pattern that gives interest groups extensive influence over health care decisionmaking. Analysts like David Wilsford exaggerate the centralized control wielded by cabinet ministries and the bureaucracy.[10] At the national level, the Ministries of Finance, Health, Social Affairs, and Education compete for influence; they scarcely present a united stand toward appropriate health policies. During the early 1980s the Socialist administration decentralized authority to regional and local (*département*, communal) governments. Regional governments gained influence over hospital planning. Local governments tackled preventive services, immunizations, and care for children, the elderly, and the handicapped. Various private organizations helped implement health care programs. These included private hospitals, nonprofit health insurance funds, mutual insurance funds, commercial insurance corporations, and private pharmacies. Earning a fee-for-service, most physicians operated as independent entrepreneurs. Even if divided into several medical associations, doctors still maintained extensive professional and clinical autonomy. The central government regulated their public reimbursements but wielded greater control over hospital budgets. Rather than tightly monitoring private health care providers, the central bureaucracy and ministries concentrated on determining national goals, formulating national standards for hospitals, and financing the expensive health system. Given these structural conditions of incohesive governmental institutions and fairly autonomous social groups, health policies changed more slowly in France than in Britain. Although government officials altered some financing procedures, the administrative organization remained stable.

Unlike British parties, the governing French political parties lacked the power to mobilize support behind policy transformations. Rather than functioning in an interdependent way, ruling parties depended on the French government. Whereas the British parliamentary government fused legislative with executive power, the French system divided power between an elected president and the National Assembly. Appointed by the president, the prime minister represented the dominant party or parties in the Assembly. Although the president exercised dominant power, his authority stemmed from his position as head of the French nation-state, not as leader of his party. Even when the president and National Assembly majority represented the same party, its activists rarely dictated final policy proposals. Instead, the president, prime minister, cabinet ministers, and high-ranking civil servants played the key role. The major political parties — the Rassemblement pour la République (RPR), the Union pour la Démocratie Française (UDF), and the Socialists — lacked the resources, cohesion, and organizational mechanisms to effectively shape health policies. Ideological factionalism fragmented all parties. On the left, the Socialists competed with the weakened Communists. The two main nonsocialist parties, the RPR and UDF, formed coalitions to control the National Assembly. During the 1981–1995 period, the Socialists held the presidency but formed an Assembly majority from June 1981 to March 1986 and from June 1988 to March 1993. At other times — March 1986–June 1988 and March 1993–April 1995, — the two nonsocialist parties held a majority of seats in the National Assembly. Hence, President François Mitterrand had to appoint an RPR legislator as prime minister. This divided party control between the presidency and legislature weakened the power of any political party to dominate the policy process. When the president and prime minister came from divergent parties, only incremental reforms or policy deadlocks could emerge from the incohesive structural conditions.[11]

Compared with French political leaders, Japanese officials have placed greater emphasis on consensual policymaking. Few open conflicts divided policy participants. Instead, they encouraged compromise, cooperation, and accommodation of differences — a policy style that led to incremental changes in health programs. During the post-World War II era, three organizations — the central civil service, the Liberal Democratic Party (LDP), and private business conglomerates (*keiretsu*) — dominated the policy process. Yet these elites scarcely wielded unified control. Personal rivalries, factionalism, and patron-client ties split their cohesion. Even if the government and party were interdependent, the Japanese civil service wielded greater authority over the LDP than did the British bureaucracy over the governing Conservative Party elites. Because Japanese LDP cabinet ministers had to negotiate compromises with both the bureaucracy and the *keiretsu*, they enacted marginal adjustments to health policies, rather than fundamental changes.

Neither the government bureaucracy nor the Liberal Democratic Party, which governed Japan from 1955 through 1993, wielded autonomous power. Instead, they depended on resources from the *keiretsu* and from health providers, especially the Japan Medical Association (JMA). Despite its extensive influence, the civil service needed support from top LDP legislators and private corporations. Whereas the Finance Ministry sympathized with business demands for cost containment, the Ministry of Health and Welfare allied with the Japan Medical Association in its preference for clinical and economic autonomy. Even though the Finance Ministry succeeded in lowering reimbursements to physicians, the JMA still retained significant influence. However great the rivalries between older general practitioners, which the JMA represented, and younger hospital specialists, doctors maintained control over drug prescriptions, diagnostic testing, and ownership of small hospitals and clinics. Hence, they possessed the resources to help shape policies proposed by the LDP and implemented by the Ministry of Health and Welfare. The LDP depended on farmers for electoral support and on private business corporations for funds. Besides factional rivalries, extensive corruption led to its electoral setbacks in 1993. Although it temporarily lost control of government, it still remained the dominant political party. Other political parties, including the Social Democrats and Communists, remained far weaker than the LDP. Unions lacked independence from corporate control. Hence, no leftist groups had the cohesion and autonomy to mobilize low-income classes for fundamental changes in the Japanese health care system.[12]

MARXISM: THE STATE AND CLASS MOBILIZATION

Marxist theorists assume that the capitalist class controls state institutions. Some Marxists like Vicente Navarro and Ralph Miliband view the state as the instrument for capitalist class rule. As Marx and Engels wrote in the *Manifesto of the Communist Party*: 'The executive of the modern state is but a committee for managing the common affairs of the whole bourgeoisie.'[13] Controlling the major means of production, large-scale corporations, especially monopolies and oligopolies, rely on the state as their instrument for furthering their class interests: higher profits, greater productivity, expanded capital accumulation, exploitation of labor-power. Other Marxist analysts such as Nicos Poulantzas claim that the state has some potential autonomy from the dominant classes. Even if not directly controlled by specific corporate heads, it upholds the long-term interests of capitalism but not necessarily the policy preferences of particular class fractions. Thus in contemporary industrialized societies, public health policies help reproduce the capitalist system. For the capitalists, good health means the ability to work hard and raise productivity, so that corporations can compete effectively in the world market. Health programs that increase labor productivity, promote advanced medical technology, and subsidize new pharmaceuticals not only expand capital accumulation but also bring higher profits to the corporate conglomerates. By providing health care benefits to the working class, public health policies help legitimate the existing political regimes dominated by the capitalist class.[14]

From the Marxist perspective, the dominant conflicts in capitalist societies revolve around class struggles. Gender, ethnic, and religious cleavages play a subordinate part in shaping government decisions. The dominant conflict pits the capitalists against the working class — between those who control the means of production and those who must sell their labor-power. Because the capitalists control the state, government officials enact health policies that secure unequal benefits for diverse employees, with unskilled laborers gaining far fewer services than do top-level managerial elites. Given these pervasive class conflicts, how do political institutions secure the order needed to further capital accumulation? Marxist theories assume that order derives from both coercive and consensual mechanisms. Particularly when high unemployment prevails and unions hold weak power in the factory or office, economic exploitation — low wages, few fringe benefits, unhealthy working conditions — deters workers from protesting their relative deprivation. The military and police use repression to protect capitalist interests, including the sanctity of private property. Legislation bans strikes by public health personnel. Police quell demonstrations staged by striking nurses and physicians.

As the Italian Marxist Antonio Gramsci indicated, cultural hegemony maintains the capitalist order through more consensual techniques. By controlling the major means of communication operated by the government, educational institutions, churches, and private enterprises, capitalist representatives define human, economic, and political reality, specifically the nature of illness and appropriate ways to attain health. Media messages propagate the notions that illness derives primarily from defective individual lifestyles or from biological (genetic) defects. Health becomes an individual responsibility, not an issue for collective political action that challenges the capitalist medical industrial complex. The mass media exclude certain issues — class domination of health policies, collective sources of personal illness, dangerous side-effects of medications on personal health — from placement on the political agenda. Swayed by this cultural hegemony, illness and health become privatized. Individuals take a fatalistic view about changing an unhealthy environment, defer to medical-industrial authorities, or concentrate on diet, exercise, medications, and self-healing as the ways to overcome ill health. Under these cultural conditions, interclass consensus emerges from the ideological hegemony.

If capitalists wield such great influence over the economic, political, and cultural systems, then how do health policy changes ever result? Marxists assume that class struggles, political conflicts, and ideological challenges produce the structural conditions required for new policies. Economic contradictions reinforce the struggle between labor and capital to control productive forces. These contradictions maintain a system in the short-run but undermine structural patterns over the long-run. For example, competition among small-scale health insurance companies may temporarily increase their profits. Over the longer-range period, however, lower prices, reduced wages, and falling profits lead to numerous bankruptcies. As smaller firms go bankrupt, the conglomerates gain greater control over the health care market. As Marx expected, capital becomes more centralized, concentrated, and internationalized. Growing contradictions between the productive forces (capital, labor-power, raw materials, technology) and the relations of production (economic classes controlling investment, workers, their use of machinery) cause increased economic misery. Private capitalist class relations impede capital accumulation and the fulfillment of human needs. Toxic waste, pollution, and ecological devastation worsen popular health. Economic inequalities, class exploitation, unsafe working conditions, dilapidated overcrowded housing, and material deprivation generate alienation form the capitalist system.

Political struggles intensify as workers and their class allies try to gain control over the government institutions that make public policies. When capitalist production becomes more social with larger workplaces and greater interdependence among urban employees, the structural opportunities for political mobilization increase. Solidary, autonomous sociopolitical networks among workers raise their expectations about political success. Seeking alliances with other classes, particularly white-collar employees and public-sector professionals, they rally behind unions and leftwing political parties for egalitarian changes in health policies.

If workers achieve dominance over the means of ideological production — mass media, parties, unions, schools, informal communications channels, — capitalist ideological hegemony no longer shapes political discourse. Their media try to deconstruct capitalist interpretations of political reality, reconstruct a more egalitarian class consciousness, and educate supporters in transformative attitudes. If the new values become internalized during the learning process, fatalism yields to personal and political efficacy. Rather than accepting capitalist authority, workers challenge capitalist role relationships and struggle to transform sociopolitical conditions. Egalitarian cooperation supersedes atomized individualism. Through exposure to mass media messages and participation in leftwing organizations, workers gain increased attitudinal solidarity, especially the awareness that the fate of the individual depends on cooperative political action. Instead of blaming themselves for sickness, they realize that illness stems from the socioeconomic and political environment — unhealthy workplaces, bad housing, inadequate education, ineffective government regulations of toxic wastes. These conditions reflect the capitalist mode of production and class domination of the state. Mobilizing behind solidary symbols that link improved personal health with political programs to change the environment, workers and their interclass allies cooperate to elect policymakers who will implement egalitarian changes in health programs.[15]

Several specific hypotheses derive from these general Marxist assumptions about the sources of policy change. First, the greater the capitalist control over the means of political power, the means of economic production (work environment), and the means of communication, the less likely that policymakers will enact policy changes that secure comprehensive, generous, egalitarian, and universal health benefits. Policy changes will produce greater privatization, lower public health care expenditures, more regressive financing, reduced benefits, and narrower coverage of individuals. Second, if a nation has a centralized, unified, inclusive, wealthy labor movement linked to a powerful leftist political party that controls a high share of cabinet seats for a lengthy time, then policymakers will implement more egalitarian health policy changes: higher public expenditures, more progressive financing, expanded benefits, and wider coverage of individuals. Third, if the dominant mass media stress that illness stems primarily from individual lifestyles or genetic defects, leftwing organizations face greater difficulties realizing egalitarian health policy changes. Under these cultural conditions, class differences impede access to public health care; those who wield the least control over productive forces, authority, and expertise receive the fewest health benefits. If, however, the dominant cultural interpretations highlight the collective environmental causes of illness that stem from class relations and the capitalist mode of production, the working class and its allies will have greater incentives to mobilize behind egalitarian policy changes. Leftwing political parties —

Socialist, Social Democratic, Labor — and unions will have greater political power to expand access to health facilities and to implement programs that secure high-quality care for the working poor and other low-income citizens.

How plausibly do these Marxist hypotheses explain the different policy changes implemented by US, Canadian, and Swedish governments during the last two decades? As we have seen, Sweden has the most public and egalitarian health programs. Swedes receive the most universal, comprehensive, and generous benefits. Canada represents an intermediate case; its provincial governments administer relatively comprehensive plans that include all citizens and supply somewhat generous services. United States officials enact the least egalitarian and the most private commercial programs. Forprofit health insurance corporations, hospitals, and pharmaceutical corporations wield extensive influence over the public policy process. As a result, public programs include only a limited segment of the population, mainly the elderly, low-income persons, veterans, and Native Americans. Neither the Medicare nor particularly the Medicaid programs provides comprehensive, generous health services. Many children, youths, and part-time, temporary employees lack access to either public programs or to private health insurance plans administered by private firms.[16]

Not only in North America and Sweden but throughout the industrialized capitalist world, structural conditions intensified economic inequalities and pressured policymakers during the 1980–2000 era to institute cost-containment programs that reduced health care services. Capitalist economies became more globalized; expansionary policies that had helped produce more equality and lower joblessness during the 'golden age' (1950–1975) no longer worked so effectively. As the power of the national government to stimulate the economy declined, regional organizations such as the European Union and the North American Free Trade Agreement gained greater influence over policies made by national finance, economics, and health ministries. Multinational corporations increased their leverage over unions; business executives no longer seemed so willing to negotiate compromises with union heads over wages and such fringe benefits as health care. Even socialist and other leftwing parties adopted many neoliberal policies that emphasized financial deregulation, wage flexibility (lower wages geared to productivity), privatization, regressive or proportional taxes, and lower expenditures for social services, including pensions, family allowances, unemployment compensation, public assistance, education, and health care. As central banks and businesses won greater influence over the economic policy process, controlling inflation took priority over accelerating economic growth, lowering unemployment, and especially expanding income equality. Trade and capital investment moved from industrialized nations to the rapidly-growing economies overseas, particularly those in East Asia, where low wages and high skills maximized profitability.

The domestic industrial structure changed from one based on manufacturing to a service-oriented economy. Whereas the manufacturing sector had greater wage equality, stronger unions, larger corporations, more full-time jobs, and greater occupational homogeneity, the service sector featured increased wage differences. Employees worked in smaller-scale firms with weaker unions. Individuals who held part-time and temporary jobs comprised a larger share of the labor force. Occupational differentiation fragmented worker solidarity. Professionals skilled at information processing had a high demand for their services. Regarded as functionally essential for further capitalist accumulation, they included administrators, managers, management consultants, financiers, investment bankers, corporate lawyers, scientists, engineers, computer specialists, and technocrats. These professionals received high salaries, gained close access to government officials, and wielded extensive influence over the policy process. By contrast, a larger number of people who provided personal services — secretaries, clerks, cashiers, retail salespeople, janitors, maids, hospital orderlies, waiters — earned low wages. Women and youths performed a large share of these jobs. Working in small-scale firms, they held more part-time temporary employment and labored under unhealthier working conditions than did either the university-educated professionals or skilled manufacturing employees. When the service sector came to include over 70 percent of the labor force during the early 1990s, these personal service workers bore the brunt of reduced public health care services and higher personal payments.[17]

Faced with these developments in the world capitalist economy, Swedish leaders enacted fewer inegalitarian policy changes than did their North American counterparts. In all three societies, health policy administration became more decentralized. Decreased government expenditures for health care led to reduced benefits and higher personal payments by patients. Swedish policymakers resisted pressures to establish a more elitist system under which private hospitals, physicians, and insurance companies assume greater responsibilities. The commitment to universal coverage, comprehensive care, and public provision and financing, even for private treatments, remained. Except for the conservative Moderate Unity Party, few organizations favored a market-based health system dominated by profit-oriented agencies. Instead, incremental reforms reduced sickness insurance benefits, slightly increased patient payments, and expanded individuals' choice of physicians and hospitals across county boundaries.

In North America, especially the United States, fiscal constraints produced more drastic changes that hurt low-income persons. During the mid-1990s, the federal governments decentralized authority over health care to the US states and to the Canadian provinces. Under the 1996 Canada Health and Social Transfer program, the Canadian federal government allocated block grants to the provinces for health care, postsecondary education, and public assistance. Because of reduced grants, provincial leaders lowered expenditures for health care. Hospitals closed or converted into community health centers. Hospital physicians performed fewer operations each year; patients remained in the hospital for a shorter time. Provincial health ministries raised fees for some prescription drugs and removed others from the reimbursement list. Payments for out-of-country health services declined. In several provinces Canadians no longer received public funds for children's dental care, adult eye examinations, circumcisions, and sterilization reversals. Expenditure ceilings limited physicians' fees and hospital charges. Cost-containment policies caused shortages of registered nurses, who earned lower salaries but had to secure higher educational credentials. Even though the Canada Health and Social Transfer program redistributed resources from wealthier provinces like Ontario, Alberta, and British Columbia to the other seven poorer provinces, greater inequalities in the allocation of health services emerged. Benefits depended on provincial wealth and the political party controlling the government. Poorer citizens in the rural regions suffered the most from fiscal restraints.

Even greater inequalities emerged in the United States from the Republican domination of the federal legislature during 1995–1998. Approved by Congress and signed by President William Clinton, the 1996 Personal Responsibility and Work Opportunity Reconciliation Act abolished the Aid to Families with Dependent Children program and transformed it into a Temporary Assistance for Needy Families (TANF) plan. Under the TANF, block grants to the states gave their policymakers wide latitude to exclude low-income individuals from access to publicly-funded benefits. Several groups — noncitizen immigrants, poor adults, disabled children — lost their right to secure Medicaid or Supplemental Security Income benefits. State governments often denied Medicaid services to low-income mothers who secured a paid job, which usually provided no private health insurance. State officials delegated authority to county and city governments, which lacked the resources to finance treatments for the poor. County and municipal hospitals dismissed physicians, nurses, physical therapists, and social workers who handled home health care for individuals with AIDS. A higher percentage of private hospitals and physicians refused to treat Medicaid patients, who sought health care in understaffed public emergency clinics. As Medicaid benefits declined, small business expenses for health care rose. Under competitive pressures, these private firms often decreased wages, financed less generous health plans, or denied insurance coverage to their employees, especially part-time and temporary workers. The cutbacks in both Medicaid and private employers' health plans mainly affected smaller enterprises and brought the greatest losses to young low-income Latino Americans and African Americans. Medical savings accounts, which enabled employees in small firms to earn tax-deductible interest on plans with high deductibles, benefited mainly private commercial health insurance corporations and wealthy, healthy individuals. Reductions in the growth of federal expenditures for Medicare, along with higher premiums, deductibles, and copayments, meant increased out-of-pocket expenditures by the elderly — increases that particularly hurt the low-income aged. Financial incentives for Medicare recipients to join health maintenance organizations or other managed care plans helped the healthier aged, who posed fewer risks to forprofit HMOs. Sicker old persons, however, brought lower profits to the commercial health insurance corporations and hence represented greater actuarial risks.[18] In short, the US health policy changes enacted during the mid-1990s produced a more inegalitarian situation than occurred in either Canada or especially Sweden.

Linked to the class structure, the political influence of capitalist corporations, labor unions, and parties explain the different health policies pursued by North American and Swedish government leaders. Although all three societies have market economies, in the United States government institutions and nonprofit organizations play a less influential role than in Canada or Sweden. The US capitalist class dominates the medical system. Private commercial health insurance industries, hospital conglomerates, and pharmaceutical industries have all undergone mergers. Corporate institutions, such as the Carnegie and Rockefeller foundations, finance medical research. The American Medical Association establishes close links with corporate capitalists, who often serve on hospital boards. Interlocking directorates cement relations among heads of hospitals, insurance corporations, and drug manufacturing enterprises. Medical associations and business corporations also wield extensive influence over the presidency, legislature, and both major political parties. Through policy planning groups, networks, memberships on several executive boards, financial institutions, and coalitions — the Business Roundtable, the Washington Business Group on Health — capitalists forge a common stand on health care issues. Blue Cross/Blue Shield, Aetna, CIGNA, MetLife, Prudential, and the AMA provide extensive contributions to legislators who head key congressional committees dealing with health policy changes. These organizations oppose government regulation, price controls on health providers, universal access, and generous benefits. Campaign donations go to both political parties, especially the Republicans who share their policy positions. Through control over the major mass media, including television, radio, newspapers, and weekly magazines, capitalist corporations try to inculcate citizens with assumptions about individual responsibility for health. According to the biomedical model, illness stems from genetic defects and mainly from personal lifestyles, not from the sociopolitical environment and class relationships. Hence, individuals must assume responsibility to get vaccinated, practice a healthy lifestyle, avoid viruses, and see a physician regularly. Influenced by these hegemonic ideas, people perceive less need to participate in political action to change structural conditions that lead to disease. The relative weakness of unions and leftwing parties that could challenge these assumptions further strengthens capitalist control over the health system. As a result, policymakers feel little incentive to implement egalitarian changes.[19]

By contrast, the Canadian and particularly the Swedish political system gives labor unions and leftwing parties greater policy influence vis-à-vis the capitalist class than does the US system. Even in these two societies, business enterprises shape government decisions about health care issues. Yet the higher union density and the stronger socialist parties lead policymakers to implement more egalitarian programs. Unions wield the greatest authority over the workplace in Sweden, where they enrolled over 80 percent of wage and salary-earners during 1990, compared with 37 percent of Canadian employees and only 15 percent of Americans. Swedish unionists represent workers' demands to managers and participate on management boards. In Canada and particularly the United States, however, unions play a more limited role over investment decisions, personnel recruitment, and health and safety conditions in the factory or office. Swedish collective bargaining arrangements include all public employees and three-fourths of private sector workers. Similar data for Canada indicate coverage rates of 80 percent public and 30 percent private. In the United States slightly above two-fifths of public employees have collective bargaining rights, compared to only 13 percent of private wage-earners.[20]

The strength of leftwing political parties corresponds to the degree of union influence among the three nations. Since World War II the Swedish Social Democratic Party has secured a higher share of popular votes, legislative seats, and cabinet ministries than any other leftist party in the industrialized capitalist world. Controlling the government for all but nine years from 1932 to 1997, the SAP retained more structural cohesion than did the fragmented nonsocialist parties. Because a large percentage of Swedes worked in either large manufacturing firms or in local (county-city) government services, the SAP gathered a wide multiclass backing. Elections to the national, county, and municipal governments occurred at the same time. Hence, when the SAP won a plurality of seats in the national legislature, it usually secured control of county and municipal councils. Political leaders at all three government levels enacted egalitarian measures, including high expenditures for public employment services, labor market retraining, youth apprenticeships, publicly-subsidized jobs, unemployment compensation, pensions, aid to the disabled, and health care. These generous policies secured greater wage and income equality for Swedes than for North Americans.

Leftist parties wielded less policy influence in Canada and especially the United States. Even though Democratic party activists supported egalitarian health policy changes, Democratic legislators and presidential staff depended on private health insurance corporations and medical associations for campaign donations and support for health proposals. These financial pressures deterred Democrats from implementing more comprehensive, universal, generous, and egalitarian health programs. Few policy innovations emerged from the state governments. Controlled by legislators from rural and suburban areas, states represented business and oligarchical interests more than the demands of low-income, uneducated, and sick people. State government expenditures went mainly to highway constructors, businesses, and wealthy farmers, not to the disabled, nursing home residents, and sick mothers and their children. Even egalitarian state government officials faced difficulties achieving health policy changes that would benefit low-income, sick people.

The Canadian federal system, however, provided structural opportunities for more egalitarian policy innovations. Although the socialist New Democratic Party never gained more than 15 percent of the seats in the federal House of Commons, it did secure executive power in several provinces, including Saskatchewan, British Columbia, Ontario, and Manitoba. Yet faced with business opposition, NDP governments in these provinces enacted policies that clashed with its egalitarian social democratic rhetoric. Influenced by the financial sector and the promarket Howe Institute, NDP officials implemented cost-containment programs. Although progressive taxes on the wealthy rose in British Columbia and Ontario, government expenditures for health, education, and income assistance decreased. Policies limited wage increases for government civil servants and reduced the number of public employees, including nurses, hospital assistants, and health care workers. Progressive-Conservative governments in Alberta and Ontario enacted even more stringent limitations on government expenditures for public health.

Although the Canadian leaders retained a more comprehensive, universal, generous, and egalitarian health care system than prevails in the United States, domestic fiscal pressures, increased competition in the world capitalist economy, and greater integration into the United States market under the North American Free Trade Agreement pressured Canadian policymakers during the 1990s to support policy changes that provided fewer health benefits to low-income citizens.

Even if capitalist corporations control the mass media in all three societies, the Swedes gain the greatest exposure to messages that attribute illness to environmental conditions and that promote collective political action as a way to improve public health. According to national sample surveys, over one-half the Swedish population expects that society and the government should assume responsibility for economic security and healthy living standards. Most Swedes support policies that secure comprehensive health care administered by county and city governments. Yet as individualists they uphold the need for free choice of health providers. The aspiration for personal independence from paternalistic family constraints shapes the Social Democrats' policy commitment to day-care centers, paid parental leaves, and health care. Compared with physicians, who stress that illness derives from unhealthy personal lifestyles, Swedish patients place greater importance on the structural conditions leading to poor health: housing inequalities and exposure to toxic paints at the workplace. These structural assumptions stem from the greater influence of unions and the Social Democratic Party over communications media than in Canada or the United States, where capitalist ideological hegemony seems more pervasive. Television news programs broadcast from the US and seen by most Canadians highlight the individualist causes of social problems. Rather than blaming unemployment, poverty, and illness on social stratification or public policies, news media focus on personal character defects and reckless, deviant lifestyles. Hence, viewers feel little incentive to struggle for egalitarian policy changes that might improve public health.[21]

CONCLUSION

Although Marxists, institutionalists, and pluralists try to clarify the structural conditions behind health policy changes, all three theories reveal certain limitations. Marxist explanations exaggerate the degree of class solidarity while underestimating class differentiation and heterogeneity. Both the capitalists and especially the workers show weak class cohesion. Economic differences fragment their solidarity. Intraclass fragmentation impedes union efforts to mobilize workers behind egalitarian health programs. For example, employed by small firms and earning low wages, US construction worker unions prefer a multiple-payer health insurance plan jointly administered by employers and unions. By contrast, the civil servants in the American Federation of State and Municipal Employees gain higher salaries; they favor a more egalitarian single-payer health plan within each state. Even in Sweden, workers with divergent skills, occupations, and incomes voice different policy positions toward social service policies. Although more unified than workers, capitalists also perceive divergent stakes in particular health proposals. US small firms and small health insurance companies have more fervently opposed a comprehensive, universal health plan than have larger corporations. These class divisions hinder a united capitalist front and often enable political party leaders, government officials, and health care technocrats to seize the initiative in framing new health plans.

Some Marxist analysts like Vicente Navarro have too high expectations about the positive impacts that result when socialist parties control government institutions and unions enroll a high share of the labor force. As we have seen, in all these market societies, national and multinational capitalists dominate productive forces and shape class relationships. Because they supply investment funds, provide employment, and finance government deficits, all policymakers, whatever their ideological orientation, need to retain business support. This need deters implementation of egalitarian health policies that will benefit the working class.

The empirical links between class position and actions to realize more egalitarian health policies remain ambiguous. Whereas Marxists conceive of 'class' as a relationship to the means of production, most empirical researchers operationalize class as occupation and income. As analytical (rational choice) Marxists like Erik Olin Wright have recommended, we need more precise indicators of workers' relative control over productive forces, including wealth, expertise, and authority. From this perspective, class position influences different opportunities and constraints, which shape individuals' consciousness about the expected costs and benefits of becoming politically active. The choice to support or oppose egalitarian changes in health policies emerges not only from class role relationships but from personal preferences, awareness of anticipated outcomes, and individual interpretations of messages transmitted by the capitalist mass media.[22]

Whereas Marxist theorists sketch a few assumptions simplifying empirical reality, the pluralist advocacy coalition framework of Paul Sabatier formulates a too descriptive approach that fails to explain the complex interactions among all the variables. The relationships among values, interests, and power remain particularly fuzzy. Focusing on deep core beliefs as the primary basis of a coalition's solidarity, Sabatier assumes that these shared core values remain stable for a lengthy time. Yet coalition members often reinterpret their values — freedom, equality, justice — to deal with new environmental conditions, such as challenges to their power and interests. He underestimates the importance of perceived interests — the tangible stakes that people have in government action or inaction toward health problems. Most US commercial health insurance companies place a high priority on attaining a profit. When allying with other groups to press for policy changes, to what extent does the pursuit of profits represent an instrumental strategy or an ultimate value? In what ways does the equation of an egalitarian, public, comprehensive, universal health program with 'socialized medicine' justify the interest-based preferences to achieve a private, forprofit health care system? Taking an elitist view, Sabatier stresses the importance of technical, professional, hierarchical expertise in the policy process but downplays the populist movements that often mobilize change from below. As a pluralist, he also assumes too optimistic a position toward achieving incremental reforms through dispersed power and moderate conflict. From his perspective, the greatest policy changes will emerge from group leaders, government officials, and experts who contend over implementing strategies, rather than deep core values, in professional forums. Yet how does the analyst measure 'moderate, informed' conflict as distinct from 'extreme, uninformed' clashes over opposing values? At times ideological polarization can produce extensive health policy changes, as happened in the 1980s when the Conservative administration of Prime Minister Margaret Thatcher had the ideological will and the institutional power to reorganize the National Health Service toward enhanced internal market competition. At other times, moderate conflicts among coalitional partners who hold fragile power lead to policy stalemates, not incremental reforms.[23]

Highlighting the cohesion and autonomy of the nation-state, institutionalists like Theda Skocpol, David Wilsford, and Ellen Immergut optimistically assume that government agencies and political parties can break policy deadlocks and secure policy changes, even against the opposition of powerful social groups. Viewing the state as a collective actor, they minimize the divisions among government officials and their ties with social group leaders. Institutionalists also exaggerate the degree of state control over such groups as health provider associations. Outcomes often diverge from policymakers' intentions. For example, the 1991 organizational changes in the National Health Service aimed to separate purchasers from providers and establish greater state managerial control over physicians. Nevertheless, this trend toward centralized management mobilized opposition from medical professionals who wanted to retain their autonomy. The General Medical Council upgraded standards of physician competency. NHS managers and hospital consultants accommodated some differences. Managers relied on physicians for technical information about health care provision. Doctors depended on the government for professional authorization and funds. Even if managers wielded greater authority than before 1991, physicians reasserted their control over medical practice. Instead of exerting autonomous power, NHS managers and doctors maintained an interdependent relationship. Finally, when analyzing negotiations between government agencies and social groups, institutionalists understate the importance of the personal preferences, motives, perceptions, and attitudes of individual policymakers. As rational choice theorists remind us, institutional power constrains behavior but also expands opportunities for political action. Influenced by these structural conditions, individual intentions and strategic interactions then shape policy choices. Hence, if we want to ascertain the precise impact of institutions on health policy changes, we need to ascertain policymakers' incentives, perceptions, and expectations.[24]

7 Rational Choice and Market Efficiency

As Charles Dickens illustrated in *Hard Times*, economic conditions shape people's health. Written in the mid-nineteenth century, the novel described life in Coketown, a standardized commercial center dedicated to rapid economic growth and efficiency. Town life revolved around pragmatic usefulness:

> You saw nothing in Coketown but what was severely workful . . . . The jail might have been the infirmary, the infirmary might have been the jail, the townhall might have been either, or anything else . . . . Relations between master and man were all fact, and everything was fact between the lying-in hospital and the cemetery, and what you couldn't state in figures, or show to be purchaseable in the cheapest market and saleable in the dearest, was not, and never should be, world without end, Amen.[1]

For the Coketown elites, economic efficiency took priority over popular health. Smoke, dust, and a black mist enveloped the town. Most people lived in miserable homes, suffered deplorable working conditions, and rarely breathed pure air. Millworkers labored until an early death. Businessmen, teachers, and government officials justified these conditions by appeals to self-interest. Adopting a calculating mentality, Bitzer, a young clerk, proclaimed: 'The whole system is a question of self-interest . . . . I was made in the cheapest market, and have to dispose of myself in the dearest.'[2]

According to this utilitarian perspective, a person's health depended on individual choices, not on environmental conditions such as pollution. Health would come to individuals only if they followed certain rules, learned cognitive skills, and practiced healthy lifestyles. Personal norms dictated a commitment to individual responsibility, hard work, and self-sufficiency. Local ministers enjoined the laity to practice purity and clean living. The Teetotal Society campaigned against alcohol. Pharmacists warned about the dangers of opium. Teachers proclaimed the need for rational individuals to gain more factual information about healthy living, so that they could accurately estimate the consequences of their actions, particularly the risks of consuming too much liquor or opium. Rational role-playing involved calculating the costs and benefits of optional lifestyles. Economic life focused on bargaining and the pursuit of concrete payoffs. Mill owners sought higher profits. Workers strove for a living wage and safe working conditions. In Coketown reason took precedence over the emotions. Self-interest supplanted concern for the public good, particularly the health of the wider community. Quantification superseded any qualitative commitment to compassion, empathy, and regard for other people's health needs. Through statistical measurements, uniform standards, and abstract concepts like cost-benefit ratios, entrepreneurs forged capital accumulation, transformed the physical environment, and controlled the population. Workers became regarded as 'human capital', as factors of production that could be quantified, standardized, and mechanized. As Dickens foresaw, during the twentieth century, not only capitalists but also public policymakers have stressed the most efficient ways to stimulate labor productivity. Today public health programs concentrate on strategies that will contain costs, maximize benefits, and raise productivity in a competitive world capitalist economy.[3]

Writing 140 years after *Hard Times*, Steven Lukes in his novel *The Curious Enlightenment of Professor Caritat* narrated the pilgrimage of the professor through several utopias, including Utilitaria. Modeled after Margaret Thatcher, the Prime Minister of Utilitaria Hilda Juggernaut proclaimed the key policy priority of her administration as the production of more utility. Her cabinet colleague Priscilla Yardstick, Minister of Health, linked health policies to this utilitarian aim: 'That's what my job essentially amounts to. Maintaining the quality of stock. Maximizing its productivity — its capacity to produce goods and services that generate utility — and maintaining its capacity to enjoy those goods and services and to obtain satisfaction! It's all a question of maximizing efficiency.'[4] For this Minister of Health, efficiency resulted when health experts weighed alternatives, calculated the consequences, and measured the degree of expected utility.

Probing the efficiency of health care markets, Chapter 7 explores three issues. First, what assumptions do rational choice theorists make about the personal and structural conditions that guide policy officials' decisions? Second, in what ways does the operation of the health care market clash with the ideal conditions of perfect competition? Third, how do health policies affect economic efficiency? What policies have most effectively restrained health care costs? What benefits result from these cost-containment policies? Which groups have secured the most gains and borne the greatest losses?

THE MEANING OF RATIONALITY

Rational choice theories offer a useful guide for evaluating the degree of efficiency in a health care market. They make several assumptions about the choices of health providers, patients, and insurers. First, adopting a methodological individualist perspective, these theorists assume that individuals, not groups, institutions, or society, constitute the primary decisionmaker. Only individuals act and make choices about ways to improve health. They, rather than any government bureaucrat or medical expert, can best judge their own interests. Individuals' goals, preferences, expectations, perceptions, motivations, and beliefs about the causal impacts of their alternative actions explain specific decisions. Their choices reflect a desire to optimize their expected utility — the net health advantages gained from selecting particular alternatives, such as the decision to stop smoking.

Second, individuals act rationally in social life; they use reason instrumentally to choose the most effective, efficient, feasible means to attain a goal. For rational choice theorists, rationality denotes a *means* to realize a preferred end, not the goal itself. From this instrumentalist view, individuals can clearly distinguish means from objectives. When evaluating the effects of all options, they act in a prudential, calculating, utilitarian, and strategic way. With clear consistent goals, they rank order their policy preferences. Consider a citizen who expects government officials to place highest priority on increasing access to public health care benefits, perceives lower taxes as less important, and ranks foreign assistance to Uganda at the bottom of her policy hierarchy. A voter with these ordered preferences will back the candidate and the political parties most strongly supporting higher health expenditures. Rational individuals can also ascertain feasible options to achieve their goals. They can accurately estimate and evaluate the costs and benefits of each alternative, choosing the option that leads to the greatest net advantages — that is, to outcomes where benefits exceed costs. For example, a rational person who values health as a top priority calculates the risks of engaging in such activities as smoking cigarettes, consuming excessive alcohol, and eating fatty foods. If the risks to health seem excessive, she may switch lifestyles and instead eat more vegetables, chew gum, and drink cranberry juice, rather than vodka. If poor health continues, she may change jobs, consult a family practitioner, or perhaps try alternative treatments, such as herbs or acupuncture. A politically active citizen would join some organization that pressures policymakers for changes in health programs, such as bans on cigarette advertising, reduced access to alcohol, and stricter enforcement of antipollution regulations. This assumption about prudential, calculating behavior implies that the rational individual has complete, accurate, relevant information about available options and their likely consequences. By wisely interpreting the information, she chooses the option with the highest probability of goal attainment.

The likelihood of realizing one's priorities also depends on strategic considerations. Rational individuals need reliable information about the preferences, power, and expected actions of other players in the political game. Enhanced political participation occurs when individuals perceive that collective action will maximize their personal utility, such as improved health, greater access to health providers, or lower health care costs. Organizational effectiveness not only depends on an association's resources, solidarity, and control over its own members but also on the power of opposition groups. The opposition's resources, commitment to valued objectives, and ability to use resources enable it to mobilize members, coordinate activities, and overcome opponents. Hence, those individuals who join an organization such as the Physicians for a National Health Program (PNHP) that advocates a more egalitarian, universal, comprehensive, accessible public health program for American citizens must consider this association's political power as well as the strategic reactions of opposition organizations like the Health Insurance Association of America. The perceived balance of power shapes the degree of political efficacy felt by PNHP members, their anticipated costs of associational participation, and their expected personal and policy benefits resulting from their collective action. Particularly when organizational members perceive that expected benefits from a health policy will remain concentrated among themselves but that expected costs (taxes) will be dispersed, then they will support that proposed policy.

Third, rational choice theorists link efficiency to actions that minimize marginal costs but maximize marginal benefits. To calculate cost-benefit ratios, the analyst must compare the financial costs of supplying each additional unit of health care — for example, a drug — with the marginal benefits of improved health, as measured by each additional 'quality adjusted year' of life expectancy. Under the most efficient conditions, the optimal price for a drug occurs when its marginal benefits (gains in quality adjusted life years) equal the marginal costs of developing, producing, and distributing the drug. From a policy perspective, efficiency increases when private associations and governments take actions that lower transaction (exchange) costs, expand information, stimulate technological innovations, and promote competition among autonomous political and economic participants. Particularly when government laws and informal customs enforce property rights, stabilize contracts, and provide political order, impersonal exchanges can more easily take place. Under such conditions, the rule of law limits arbitrary, monopolistic power. The competitive market operates efficiently.

In certain respects, the general assumptions about methodological individualism, instrumental rationality, and marginal efficiency only partially apply to health care policymaking. As methodological individualists, neoclassical economists like Alain Enthoven, Martin Feldstein, and Gordon Tullock downplay the importance of collective public goods — for example, a healthy community — that transcend individual preferences. Rather than just satisfy individual interests or promote market efficiency, political organizations define the moral purposes, cultural values, and normative expectations shared by society. Symbolic values linked to 'health' as well as concepts of a 'just' health care system shape individuals' interpretation of their self-interests. Not only in North America but also in Western Europe and particularly Japan, these shared meanings influence policymakers' goals and choices. Rather than derived from an aggregate of individual preferences, their decisions also reflect structural conditions: class relationships, political party pressures, government agencies' influence over social groups, and personal interactions within small group networks. Thus the meaning that government leaders attribute to 'utility' — for example, improved health — as well as their judgments about the most efficient policies to maximize utility depend on the cultural-structural context.

The rational choice stress on instrumental rationality offers a limited view of the health policy process. Neoclassical theorists equate rationality with efficient, feasible means to attain goals. Policymakers rank order all their preferences, compare the expected outcomes of all options, and then choose the policy option that will attain the highest priority objective — one that will most efficiently minimize costs while maximizing benefits. Yet particularly in the health sector, policy objectives often are inconsistent, rather than clearly ordered. Political leaders take an ambivalent stance toward several incompatible goals. For example, how can they best maximize consumers' access and use, physicians' clinical freedom, and economic efficiency? Policymakers also cannot accurately estimate the likely effects of all alternative strategies for improving community health. They lack information about the expected behavior of all the people who shape community health: patients, physicians, nurses, other medical personnel, friends, relatives, workmates, business executives, union leaders, health insurers, political party activists, government ministers, and so forth. Accurate feedback information about the outcomes of policy options remains elusive. Officials cannot readily predict long-term outcomes. Unexpected historical contingencies occur. As social situations change, so do people's preferences. Hence, the task of choosing the most efficient policy that will minimize losses but maximize gains becomes difficult.

The neoclassical equation of efficiency with Pareto optimality ignores the distribution of people's utilities. According to the Italian economist Vilfredo Pareto, public policies most efficiently ensure social well-being when they bring marginal gains to some people but make no one worse off than before. Pareto assumed a competitive market would maximize efficient exchanges, so that prices would reflect an equilibrium between marginal revenue and marginal costs. For example, the most efficient health policy would improve the health status (secure one more year of life expectancy) of some individuals without harming (decreasing the life expectancy) of any other person. Committed to profit maximization, health providers would charge prices so that marginal costs of treatments equaled their marginal revenue.

Unlike automobile dealers, however, health personnel cannot so easily estimate the marginal costs and benefits of their products or services. The Pareto concept of efficiency also takes an inegalitarian stance toward public policies. Few health programs that seek to expand comprehensive benefits to low-income persons can benefit a few individuals without bringing disadvantages, like higher taxes, to wealthier others. Pareto optimality accepts the existing distribution of resources but downplays the impact of concentrated industries, unemployment, social stratification, and political powerlessness on individuals' health. Its interpretation of efficiency thereby inhibits governmental attempts to secure societal transformations that would significantly improve community health.[5]

HEALTH CARE MARKETS AND COMPETITION: ASSUMPTIONS VS. ACTUAL OPERATION

Despite the empirical limitations of the rational choice model, neoclassical economists still assert that enhanced competition will produce greater efficiency in health care markets. Why? Incentives for productive investment rise. Seeking to lower costs and expand consumer satisfaction, health care providers have the incentive to seek more innovative, flexible techniques for supplying services under decentralized conditions. When competition among health providers (physicians, hospitals, laboratories, pharmacies) increases and they become differentiated from institutions (insurance agencies, government health authorities) that purchase health care benefits for consumers, decisions respond to price elasticity. Health providers, purchasers, and patients possess information about prices, benefits, and the quality of health care services. As prices decline, purchases of benefits rise. When prices increase, providers supply more high-quality health services. Under these competitive conditions, providers face pressures to reduce costs and expand benefits. Technical and allocative efficiency results. Health personnel use fewer resources (money, time, energy) to produce more services at the lowest opportunity costs. The allocation of resources among alternative uses secures the greatest health improvements. For example, a two-hour confrontational interview produces a greater reduction in alcohol consumption than does a month-long educational program.[6]

According to the model of perfect competition, the following conditions promote efficient decisionmaking. (1) Individuals seek to maximize their profits, so that revenues exceed costs. (2) A pluralist market structure decentralizes the decision process. Large numbers of providers and purchasers, mainly private forprofit organizations, share power; a single firm comprises only a small part of the market. These organizations retain the freedom to enter and exit the market. Enterprises seeking higher profits can freely move from one market to another. No oligopolistic agency restricts the entry of new firms into a market for highly-demanded services. (3) The competitive market lowers transaction costs that involve collecting information, negotiating contracts, and supervising implementation, outcomes, and contract compliance. Providers, purchasers, and consumers have extensive information about prices, costs, and quality of services, such as treatments, medical equipment, and pharmaceuticals. The costs of negotiating contracts, monitoring their compliance, and mediating disputes remain lower than the benefits of exchange relationships. (4) Price competition guides purchasers, who buy a service for its low price, not for its noneconomic aspects. Prices respond to changes in demand for a service and to the quantities supplied. When demand (spending) for a service declines or the supply of a highly demanded service increases, an enterprise lowers its price. Price competition produces an equilibrium between supply and demand. (5) Competitive markets promote extensive control by consumers. They can choose health purchasers (different insurance plans) and health providers, exit one market, and shop for new suppliers.

However widespread the neoclassical support for competitive markets as a method for producing greater efficiency, actual health care markets depart from the assumptions of perfect competition. First, few health providers seek only to maximize their profits; rather than just pursuing greater income, most personnel also place a high priority on intrinsic goals: the personal satisfaction that comes from improving people's health. As demonstrated by their efforts to prevent the outbreak of diseases, community well-being also motivates medical personnel. Compared with automobile dealers, health providers thus seek more universal, communal, and intrinsic objectives, rather than only monetary utility.

Second, health care markets remain less pluralistic than the model assumes. Particularly in Canada, West Europe, and Japan, public and nonprofit institutions dominate the health care market. As mergers increase, oligopolies gain greater control over the provision of health care services. Even in the United States, government health authorities, medical associations, hospitals, and especially private health insurance corporations restrict competition. Neither health providers nor health purchasers retain unlimited rights to enter and exit the market.

Third, high transaction costs hinder the efficiency of most health care markets. Consumers know less about the prices of their health care than about the prices of fruits, cars, television sets, computers, and homes. Health providers, particularly physicians, hold the greatest information about the diagnosis of health problems, alternative treatments, and expected outcomes. Policymakers can rarely obtain inexpensive information about doctors' diagnoses, treatments, and effects of their treatments, especially the most effective or efficient procedures. Unanticipated contingencies impede attempts to ascertain the links between treatments and patients' health status. Health providers cannot control the personal attitudes, lifestyles, genetic predispositions, and environmental conditions affecting individual health. Increased information about all these determinants may depend on more cooperation among health providers, not on greater competition. High transaction costs hinder efficient exchanges on the health care market. Health purchasers, such as sickness insurance funds, government health ministries, or private insurance corporations, incur high administrative costs when they negotiate and enforce contracts with health providers. Because the outcomes of specific procedures — chemotherapy, radiation, surgery, drugs — remain elusive, policymakers cannot easily ascertain the impact that these treatments wield on improving a patient's health. Hence, the tasks of monitoring and evaluating physicians' activities become expensive.

Fourth, neither price competition nor price elasticity guides the purchase of most health care services. Health benefits diverge on more aspects than just their price. They vary according to a health provider's training, experience, personality, and style. Consumers usually seek a physician who provides high-quality treatment, not just a low fee. If only the cash nexus shaped the interaction between a doctor and patient, this profit-maximizing orientation would violate the trusting attitude that forms a crucial aspect of effective medical care. Moreover, the prices of health care services stem from more conditions than just changes in supply and demand. Government institutions, medical associations, hospital administrations, pharmaceutical corporations, and health insurance agencies all influence prices, often independent of quantities available or willingness to pay for these services. Given this lack of price competition and elasticity, a disequilibrium between supply and demand ensues. Decisions made by physicians, government health agencies, and insurance organizations control demand for health care services. Policymakers often contend with too few nurses and general practitioners but too many medical specialists.

Fifth, consumers wield limited control over the health care market. Physicians, not patients, largely determine the demand for specific treatments, medical equipment, drugs, and hospital care. Decisions made by health ministries, insurance agencies, hospital administrations, and pharmaceutical corporations control the supply of hospitals, clinics, laboratories, and drugs. A patient's admission to a hospital and release from it depends not only on hospital administrators and physicians but also on accountants and managers who operate health-purchasing organizations, whether governmental institutions, forprofit corporations, or nonprofit agencies. Facing this oligarchical control, few patients have the freedom to choose among a wide variety of health purchasers or providers. In short, most consumers lack sufficient influence over the provision of health services to promote market efficiency.[7]

EFFICIENCY OF HEALTH CARE SYSTEMS: MEANING AND MEASUREMENT

Policy analysts can more easily define efficiency than they can devise reliable, valid techniques for measuring the cross-national efficiency of health care markets. Rational choice theorists assume that efficiency occurs when minimal inputs (costs of production) generate maximum benefits — gains in personal well-being. Most government actions focus on ways to contain costs for the government, insurance agency, and individual patient. Major costs include money spent for medical and paramedical services, inpatient hospital care, pharmaceuticals, and administration. Administrative costs involve the following tasks: transacting exchanges (billing, processing claims, making reimbursements, auditing), supplying information about benefits, advertising and selling health insurance programs, assessing the use of health care services, and monitoring compliance with government regulations about taxes, licenses, hygiene, safety, waste management, and the qualifications of health providers. The benefits refer to the health treatments' positive outcomes on individual health. Looking at the health providers' activities — their treatments, procedures, tests, — the analyst compares the marginal gains of using a specific new drug with the marginal benefits from alternative treatments, such as a different drug, a vaccine, or exposure to a health education service. How many quality adjusted life years does each ounce of the drug or day of health education exposure save for a similar group in a randomized controlled trial? Health-related qualitative benefits comprise physical, mental, and social well-being. If treatment X leads to a higher energy level, greater physical abilities, enhanced optimism, increased cognitive skills, and the capacity to perform more diverse roles, then we assume that this treatment produced more benefits than any alternative ones, as assessed by a health professional or the individual herself. According to cost-benefit ratios, efficiency results when one treatment (drug, medical equipment, vaccine, health education program) secures greater benefits but incurs fewer costs than any alternative procedures or 'interventions'.

Despite the consensus on the verbal definition of efficiency, rational choice theorists disagree about ways to measure either monetary or particularly nonmonetary cost-benefit ratios across several nations. How do investigators formulate similar, accurate, valid, reliable 'operational indicators' for fiscal costs? Exchange ratios, purchasing power parities, expenditures for each person, and expenditures as a share of the gross domestic product reflect only a few operational indicators. Yet the activities included within these quantitative indicators are ambiguous. The aggregate measures for the whole nation obscure the micro interactions that link individual health personnel to their specific patients. The quality of personal health connotes conditions beyond the cash nexus. Measuring efficiency as the price for each additional life year gained scarcely indicates the quality of life, whether determined by functional abilities or by the individual's subjective self-assessment. Indicators of 'good health' become meaningful only in a specific historical context. Hence, comparative analysts cannot easily ascertain the efficiency of health care policies across several nations at different time periods.[8]

Given these measurement problems of linking macro policies to the micro improvements in a person's health, the next sections make tentative general assessments about the efficiency of health care programs, rather than explore the outcomes of specific treatments or procedures. Rational choice theorists make the following hypotheses about the relative efficiency of health care policies. First, as transaction costs decline, efficiency in providing health care services rises. Second, the greater the competition in supplying health care services, the higher the efficiency. Geared toward innovation, health providers lower their production costs. Patients become more sensitive to the prices of health services; hence, greater demand elasticity promotes a more efficient market. Third, committed to the competitive market model, rational choice theorists hypothesize that entrepreneurial systems produce greater efficiencies than do either organic corporatist or social democratic systems.[9] We probe the plausibility of these hypotheses by focusing on three issues: What policies restrain the costs of physician services, hospital care, pharmaceuticals, and administration? Which groups experience the most benefits and suffer the greatest losses from cost containment programs? Which type of political system implements the most efficient health care policies?

Cost containment policies focus on efficient ways to restrain demand (expenditures) and control supplies of health care benefits. Limitations on expenditures apply to medical personnel, hospitals, and pharmaceutical manufacturers. For example, government health ministries impose caps (budget ceilings) on reimbursements to physicians. Both doctors and hospital administrators submit to expenditure targets; if exceeded, they lose revenues. Governments formulate general global budgets for hospitals. Public policy officials try to curtail drug costs by implementing price controls, limiting manufacturers' profits, and removing certain drugs from the list for government reimbursement. Physicians who prescribe drugs above a certain ceiling secure fewer government funds. Demand deflation also occurs when consumers must pay higher deductibles, user charges, and copayments for medical services, hospital care, and pharmaceuticals. Limits on health care benefits reduce the number of services available as well as the proportion of people eligible to receive them. Most often, policymakers decrease public financing for certain drugs, dental care, and eyeglasses, particularly those used by adults from eighteen to sixty. Physicians and hospitals no longer secure government funds for some diagnostic tests, medical equipment, and hospital beds. Measures encourage the provision of less expensive health care services, such as generic drugs, instead of brand-name versions. The elderly receive nursing care in residences for the aged and at home, rather than in hospitals.

Government officials who prefer market models assume that enhanced competition will best restrain administrative costs. According to their perspective, government regulators oversee negotiations of contracts between purchasing agents and health care suppliers. These contracts promote competition among hospitals, insurance organizations (private corporations, nonprofit insurance agencies), and private enterprises that sell cleaning services, medical equipment, and meals to hospitals. Rational choice theorists expect that market competition will heighten the incentives for health care providers to reduce transaction costs and hence increase administrative efficiency.[10] How effectively have these cost containment strategies worked in entrepreneurial, organic corporatist, and social democratic systems?

Entrepreneurial Systems

Canada and particularly the United States most fully embody the entrepreneurial model with its attachment to competitive markets. In the US private, forprofit health insurance corporations compete for clients. Compared with the Canadian, Japanese, or European situation, fewer government regulations restrain the operation of the health care market. Managed care plans operated by health maintenance organizations (HMOs), independent practice associations, preferred provider organizations, and point-of-service organizations grew more popular during the 1990s. In 1995 they enrolled about three-fourths of all US employees with health insurance and over one-third of Medicaid beneficiaries. Among the national HMOs, forprofit plans showed the fastest growth. Faced by high government deficits, Canadian policymakers, especially in Ontario and Alberta, also backed competitive market plans.

Despite their support for entrepreneurial market values, North Americans have faced a sharper rise of total health care costs than have people in the other six nations. As indicated by Table 7.1, from 1960 through 1995, total health expenditures as a share of the gross domestic product (GDP) increased most rapidly in the United States. During the 1960–1995 period these costs nearly tripled from 5.3 percent of the GDP to over 14 percent. Between 1980 and the early 1990s, total health expenses also escalated in Canada, even though at a slower rate than for its southern neighbor.[11] Compared with US government officials, Canadian policymakers implemented more effective measures to contain the costs incurred by medical personnel, hospital executives, drug manufacturers, and program administrators.

Table 7.1 Health expenditures as a percentage of GDP, 1960-1995

	1960	1965	1970	1975	1980	1985	1990	1995
Canada								
Total	5.5	6.0	7.1	7.2	7.4	8.5	9.5	9.6
Public	2.3	3.1	5.0	5.5	5.5	6.4	6.8	6.9
France								
Total	4.2	5.2	5.8	6.9	7.6	8.5	8.9	9.8
Public	2.4	3.5	4.4	5.4	6.0	6.5	6.6	7.7
Germany								
Total	4.8	5.1	5.9	8.1	8.4	8.7	8.3	10.4
Public	3.2	3.6	4.1	6.3	6.3	6.4	6.0	8.2
Japan								
Total	3.0	4.5	4.6	5.6	6.6	6.6	6.8	7.2
Public	1.8	2.7	3.2	4.1	4.6	4.8	4.8	5.7
Netherlands								
Total	3.8	4.3	5.9	7.4	7.9	7.8	8.0	8.8
Public	1.3	2.9	4.9	5.4	5.9	5.9	5.7	6.8
Sweden								
Total	4.7	5.6	7.2	7.9	9.4	8.8	8.6	7.2
Public	3.4	4.4	6.2	7.2	8.7	8.0	6.9	5.9
United Kingdom								
Total	3.9	4.1	4.5	5.5	5.8	6.0	6.2	6.9
Public	3.3	3.5	3.9	5.0	5.2	5.2	5.2	5.9
United States								
Total	5.3	5.9	7.4	8.4	9.2	10.5	12.4	14.2
Public	1.3	1.5	2.7	3.5	3.9	4.4	5.2	6.6

Sources: Organisation for Economic Cooperation and Development, *New Orientations for Social Policy* (Paris: OECD, 1994), 70–73; 'OECD in Figures 1997 Edition,' *OECD Observer*, no. 206 (June/July 1997): 48–49.

Through negotiations between provincial ministries of health and provincial medical associations, Canadian political leaders have gained greater control over physicians' fees and expenditures. Some provincial governments such as Quebec limit physicians' income; if doctors exceed that limit, their reimbursement fees decline. Canadian general practitioners comprise around 50 percent of all physicians. Committed to income equality, provincial officials negotiate higher fee increases for generalists, rather than for specialists. As a result, doctors' yearly income rise has approximated the general inflation rate. By contrast, in the United States, physicians' annual income from 1970 to 1994 increased faster than the general consumer price rise. Wider income disparities among physicians occur in the United States than in Canada. Over two-thirds of US doctors work as specialists. Surgeons, radiologists, and anesthesiologists earn higher salaries and secure greater gains in their annual income than do family practitioners, pediatricians, and those in internal medicine. Specialists perform the highest volume of services and secure the largest profits for each cataract operation or heart surgery. Hence, a wide income gap not only divides US physicians but also differentiates them from the income received by most employees.

The Canadian judicial system limits physicians' costs by discouraging malpractice suits. In Canada, unlike the United States, patients file fewer malpractice suits, win fewer cases, and gain lower monetary settlements for negligence that caused harm to the patient. The physician-administered Canadian Medical Protective Association, not a private health insurance corporation operated by non-physicians, supplies malpractice insurance. Some provincial governments subsidize this insurance. Hence, doctors pay lower premiums for insurance against malpractice, usually levied against specialists performing major surgery. Even though recent legal changes have made physicians more accountable for negligence, Canadian judicial procedures limit personal injury awards. Nongovernmental colleges of physicians and surgeons, not a court, render most decisions. The generous workers' compensation and public health programs that finance treatment for disabilities discourage malpractice suits. By contrast, in the United States the courts impose fewer judicial restrictions on litigation and on the income gained from a successful claim. Compared with Canadians, Americans file a greater number of claims and receive higher monetary settlements. American patients show less deference to their doctors than do Canadians. US physicians use newer, more advanced medical equipment that may lead to greater possible harm. Combined with the less generous US public health programs, all these structural conditions strengthen patients' incentive to file malpractice suits, thereby raising doctors' overall expenses.

Canadian officials have implemented policies that produce lower hospital costs than in the United States. Provincial governments enact a global budget for operating expenses and also finance capital expenditures. The high capacity use (between 80 percent and 90 percent of beds occupied), the large number of nonprofit hospitals, and the low administrative expenses constrain costs. Because the provincial government pays for all hospital expenditures except for private rooms financed by supplemental private health insurance plans, administrative costs remain fairly low. The standardized reimbursement formulae limit the need for administrators, accountants, and secretaries to process claims. Policies toward advanced technological equipment also deter cost increases. Canadian hospitals use less advanced medical equipment for every one million patients than do US health facilities. Magnetic resonance imaging, radiation therapy, lithotripsy, and organ transplantation occur mainly in urban teaching hospitals; rural hospitals lack advanced technology. Unlike US hospital physicians, Canadian doctors use fewer radiology tests, such as computed tomography scanning and magnetic resonance imaging, particularly for patients over 85 years old. Although Canadian and American hospital personnel earn similar salaries, extensive unionization leads to higher, more equal incomes for nurses in Canada than in the United States.

The more pluralist, competitive, and inegalitarian US health care system has neither restrained hospital costs nor enhanced efficiency. Compared with the Canadian situation, a greater wage gap divides highly-paid head nurses from lower-paid housekeepers, food-service aides, and laboratory technicians. More US hospitals contain advanced medical technology but use this equipment at a lower rate than in Canada. Competition for patients induces hospital administrators throughout the nation to purchase the latest, advanced, expensive medical equipment. Not only equipment but other aspects of capacity usage remain low. Only around two-thirds of hospital beds are occupied; hence costs increase. The decentralized, dispersed regulation of hospital expenditures achieves only limited success. Whereas in Canada the provincial ministry of health controls hospital expenditures, in the United States government officials wield less extensive control. State health personnel regulate hospital reimbursements from Medicaid. The Health Care Financing Administration regulates hospital fees charged to Medicare. Yet private insurance corporations implement the greatest cost controls over hospital expenditures. Their decisions, rather than a governmental global hospital budget, largely determine the efficiency of most hospitals. Although the growth of investor-owned, forprofit hospital conglomerates has eliminated some duplicate services, it has neither reduced costs nor increased efficiency. Administrative expenditures as a share of total expenditures are higher in forprofit hospitals than in public or private nonprofit hospitals. Commercial hospitals have also faced rapid increases in administrative costs, especially for marketing, advertising, billing health providers, and processing information for governments and health insurance corporations. The numerous financial providers — insurance companies, health maintenance organizations, Medicare, Medicaid — rely on different reimbursement and use formulae, thereby increasing the number of clerks, secretaries, accountants, computer technicians, lawyers, and other administrators required to process the claims. The movement away from nonprofit hospitals has enriched the salaries of top executives heading the hospital conglomerates that have the power to shift resources from one health market to another. As a result, profit margins have risen, contributing to greater economic inequality but higher costs within the US hospital sector.

During the 1980s neither the Canadian nor the US governments restrained the rapid rise of pharmaceutical expenditures, even though prices for the same drugs cost less in Canada than in the United States. The Patented Medicine Prices Review Board tried to limit prices on new Canadian drugs. Canadian policies also oversaw more compulsory licensing of generic drugs. Yet government controls over the prescription of drugs remained weak. From 1980 through 1990 the yearly average prices for pharmaceuticals increased faster than for hospital charges or medical personnel services. The United States had a more concentrated drug industry; the major pharmaceutical manufacturers controlled a larger share of the market than in Canada. Lower price competition led to higher drug prices and profits. From 1980 through 1994 the US drug industry gained the highest profit rate of any manufacturing industry. The after-tax yearly profits of US pharmaceutical corporations averaged around thirteen cents for every dollar of sales — over three times as high as the general manufacturing average of four cents. Whereas the Pharmacare program for elderly and low-income Canadian citizens financed a major portion of their drug expenses, in the United States most Americans had to purchase prescription drugs through personal payments and private insurance plans. Medicaid and Medicare paid for only a small share of these charges.

High administrative costs and profit margins for the US health care industry have produced a less egalitarian but more inefficient health care system than the Canadian system. During 1994 the health industry earned a larger return on equity (earnings per share) than any other corporation. Administrative expenditures brought major economic rewards to such business-professional elites as managers, consultants, lawyers, advertisers, accountants, economists, and chief executive officers. The dispersion of responsibility for health care among numerous agencies — federal government, state government, health maintenance organizations, private health insurance corporations — raised transaction and information costs. Administrators within both government and private institutions filed claims, billed providers and patients, adjudicated claims, made reimbursements, reviewed service use, marketed benefits, determined eligibility for benefits, and negotiated price discounts with hospital managers and physicians. Transacting all these exchanges among health personnel, purchasing agents, and consumers scarcely promoted lower costs or greater managerial efficiency. Instead, different organizations duplicated the same activities, such as cost accounting. High advertising costs by forprofit hospitals, HMOs, and private health insurance corporations increased overall health care expenditures. Information costs rose as administrators gathered and analyzed data about health providers, including their fees, payroll costs, use of facilities (medical equipment, laboratories), administrative expenses, and decisions regarding hospital admission and discharge. The high proportion (around 17 percent) of Americans with no public or private insurance coverage included the chronically ill, the disabled, the unemployed, and low-income workers and their children. Suffering from undertreatment, they suffered greater illnesses and incurred higher costs, particularly at hospital emergency rooms. By contrast, wealthier, healthier Americans benefited from overtreatment, especially from expensive but often unnecessary surgery. As a result of this dispersed, complex, differentiated, inegalitarian system, administrative expenses as a percentage of total health care expenditures exceeded those in Canada. From the early 1970s through the mid-1990s, the number of administrators (managers, clerks) as a share of total health personnel rose at a faster rate in the United States, especially its hospitals, than in Canada. Compared with private US health insurance corporations, public health institutions, especially the Medicare program, incurred lower administrative costs.

Canada's lower administrative costs derive from its more cohesive health policies that simplify program operations within each province. The provincial ministry of health pays physicians' fees and hospital charges. A global hospital budget separates current operating expenditures from capital expenditures. Private forprofit health insurance corporations finance only supplemental care, such as private hospital rooms, cosmetic surgery, and dental treatments. Because the provincial ministry of health handles most administrative tasks and one party usually controls the provincial government, accountability for limiting costs becomes more unified than in the United States, where several dispersed organizations fragment the policy process. Numerous purchasing agencies — state government, federal government institutions, municipalities, private businesses, private health insurance corporations — try to shift costs to other payers. Insurance companies use different forms and act under diverse procedures for reimbursing hospitals and medical personnel. Hospitals depend on insurance corporations, governmental agencies, and patients for their revenues, hence increasing administrative costs for processing claims and paying health care providers. As forprofit health insurance corporations gain greater influence over nonprofit organizations, administrative costs mount. Salaries of managers and chief executives soar. These corporate leaders impede the movement for a more cohesive, comprehensive public health program that would expand coverage but lower administrative expenses, as in Canada.[12]

In the United States the fragmented policy process, the weak governmental role, and the extensive power wielded by private corporations over the health care sector have led to the emergence of health maintenance organizations (HMOs) as the major impetus behind cost containment strategies. Despite their supporters' assumption that enhanced competition will lower costs and expand service quality, HMOs have achieved greater success in limiting expenditures for physicians' salaries, hospital charges, and pharmaceuticals than in raising benefits, particularly those gained by low-income, chronically ill persons. Supported by the federal government, state governments, both major political parties, private businesses, and private health insurance corporations, HMOs rely on managers to monitor the use of specific services (tests, check-ups, surgery) at hospitals and physicians' offices. Receiving a set monthly fee for each patient, doctors earn bonuses for lowering expenditures but incur sanctions for spending above a prescribed target. Monetary incentives deter physicians from hospitalizing patients for long periods. Physicians with larger numbers of patients secure discounts on prescription drugs. The HMO establishes a 'formulary', a list of prescription drugs eligible for full reimbursement. During the early 1990s, all these cost-containment measures caused HMO premiums to increase at a slower rate than did insurance premiums for fee-for-service health plans. In densely populated metropolitan areas with high competition among HMOs, insurance premiums showed the lowest rate of increase.

However great the cost savings, HMOs have mainly benefited wealthy, healthy persons, rather than the sick and poor. The largest share of HMO enrollees include high-income individuals aged 25 to 44 years old who live in urban-suburban areas throughout New England and the Far West. Few members reside in isolated, sparsely populated rural areas of the Midwest. HMOs also aim to attract healthy elderly persons. By 1995 10 percent of all Medicare patients belonged to an HMO, which enrolled younger individuals (aged 65–75) with fewer chronic illnesses. Older, sicker persons needing inpatient hospital care remained with fee-for-service physicians, who gained higher Medicare reimbursements. For each client managed-care plans receive government payments that equal 95 percent of the average costs of non-HMO claimants. Hence, the enrollment of the healthy elderly who need minor health services — physical examinations, vision tests, immunizations — hardly saves money. Instead, these plans gain revenues from their low-risk, inexpensive patients. HMOs restrict the free choices of both consumers and health providers. Under most HMOs, the employer in a large public or private organization dictates the doctors participating in the plan. Patients cannot select a specialist without their primary care physician's approval. The HMO plan will not reimburse a patient who sees a general practitioner or specialist outside the plan. Individuals cannot easily change their health plans. Compared with fee-for-service physicians, HMO doctors wield less control over their practices, including diagnoses, treatments, referrals to specialists, hospital admissions, hospital discharges, and use of expensive medical technology. HMO mangers may dismiss a physician who complains about plan operations. Faced with these competitive pressures, many physicians establish their own health plans and operate them as business managers. Yet small-scale programs rarely survive; corporate HMO conglomerates purchase them. Managers, rather than doctors, operate the HMOs. Doctors must submit to the regulations imposed by bureaucratic administrators who define and enforce their interpretations of the general interest as it applies to health care provision. Despite the focus on efficiency realized through economies of scale, the corporate HMOs incur higher administrative costs than do smaller fee-for-service practices, which must finance mainly office expenses. Particularly in the forprofit HMOs, marketing health plans, monitoring providers' treatments, and overseeing patients' use of services raise transaction costs. Managers and chief executive officers gain higher incomes. Americans secure less equal access to health care benefits than do Canadians or individuals in organic corporatist systems.[13]

Organic Corporatist Systems

Organic corporatist systems implement health policies that blend divergent structural conditions: elitist management with egalitarian access, social solidarity with individual choice, and regulated competition with private clinical autonomy. Governmental officials and private health providers — physicians, hospital executives, pharmaceutical manufacturers — administer the health care system through extensive negotiations. Nonprofit agencies play the leading role; private forprofit health insurance corporations wield only limited influence. The complex institutional arrangements, especially in Germany, France, and the Netherlands, raise administrative costs. Although more efficient than the United States' programs, corporatist pluralism produces greater inefficiencies than the simplified, streamlined Canadian programs that allocate responsibility to the provincial governments. Emphasizing social solidarity more than competitive individualism, corporatist policies promote relatively equal access to health care services. Citizenship and health care needs, rather than income, determine access to medical providers. Limited competition occurs among physicians, hospitals, insurance companies, and sickness funds. To restrain costs, however, German policymakers have recently encouraged greater competition among sickness funds. French government leaders seek enhanced competition among private and public hospitals. During the last decade Dutch officials have enacted the most competitive policies toward insurance companies. With the weakest commitment to competition, Japanese leaders have achieved greater efficiency than have policymakers in the other three organic corporatist states. As Tables 7.1 indicates, Japan during the early 1990s spent less money on health care as a percentage of the gross domestic product. From 1960 through 1990 Japanese expenditures on hospitals, medical and paramedical services, and pharmaceuticals rose at a lower rate. Public administrative costs as a share of public spending on health in Germany, France, and the Netherlands were higher than in Japan.[14]

Japanese policies toward physicians' fees, hospital charges, drug prices, and administrative costs largely explain the effective cost containment strategies. Compared with other national employees, physicians in Japan earn a more egalitarian income than they do in Germany. Influenced by the Ministry of Finance, the Central Social Insurance Medical Care Council and the Ministry of Health and Welfare determine a uniform fee schedule for various procedures, treatments, services, medical equipment, and drugs. These fee schedules prohibit a physician from billing above a fairly low prescribed target. Representing office physicians, the Japan Medical Association ensures that reimbursement decisions grant general practitioners higher fees than hospital specialists, who wield a limited impact on health policies. The system encourages patients to seek care at the physician's office, not at a hospital. Rewarding preventive medicine and inexpensive procedures by clinical doctors in primary care, the fee schedules give no monetary incentives for expensive surgery that uses advanced technological equipment. Besides the national Ministry of Health and Welfare, regional agencies in the prefectures take actions that limit physician and hospital costs. By assessing doctors' claims for reimbursements, prefectural panel peer review boards monitor physicians' expenses. Prefectural health planning committees approve the expansion of hospital capacity and the construction of new hospitals. Increased copayments for admission to public teaching hospitals further restrain hospital cost rises. Even if public policies have effectively restrained hospital expenditures, efforts to curtail drug prices have proven less effective. Private pharmaceutical manufacturers maintain close ties with Ministry of Health and Welfare officials. Government regulators grant higher reimbursements for drugs and diagnostic tests than for medical treatments, operations, and consultations. Doctors both prescribe and dispense drugs. Because the reimbursement rate for new drugs exceeds the discounted price charged by the pharmaceutical manufacturer, physicians earn a profit by selling new medications like anticancer drugs to their patients. Faced with low fee schedules, physicians earn the largest share of their income from dispensing medications and administering diagnostic tests — procedures that merit higher reimbursements. Despite the fee-for-service system, Japanese administrative costs remain low. The streamlined system run by the national and prefectural governments reduces transaction costs. A single uniform fee schedule eliminates the expenses of processing claims. Few malpractice suits occur. Mandatory coverage in one plan administered by employers or government officials reduces competition among insurers. Along with the weak influence of forprofit insurance companies, this policy cohesion reduces marketing expenses.

From a cost-benefit perspective, Japanese health policies restrain expenses but also incur a few liabilities. Its main assets include the low costs and egalitarian access. A progressive payment system subsidizes low-income people, the elderly, and public teaching hospitals. Limitations include short consultation times with doctors, who must treat too many patients. Individuals also face long waits in teaching hospitals for outpatient care. Many Japanese offer bribes to gain early admission and treatment by a senior hospital specialist. The elderly also suffer from the hospital system. The limited public financial assistance for home health services and for nursing homes means an overreliance on hospitals to care for the elderly. Many old people spend over three months in hospitals that lack sufficient nurses. Rather than stressing physical therapy and rehabilitation, hospital physicians overprescribe medications and administer extensive laboratory tests — activities that bring the highest reimbursements. Neither the government nor health insurance programs provide sufficient funds for home care by health aides. Instead, extended family members care for elderly relatives at their own expense. Given the limited concern to finance psychiatric hospitals, occupational therapy, and professional caregiving, mentally-ill persons secure little public care. They too must rely on extended family members for assistance. In short, Japanese leaders administer a relatively efficient, egalitarian health care system, but significant liabilities still remain, especially in the benefits provided to the elderly and those with mental illnesses.[15]

Unlike the Japanese, who operate a cohesive health care system, French and German officials face greater difficulties securing efficiencies under their more fragmented policy structures. Several organizations — central government agencies, regional authorities, different political parties, private nonprofit organizations, forprofit businesses — disperse authority over the health sector. Accountability remains elusive. Neither the central government nor a dominant political party like the Japanese Liberal Democratic Party coordinates the policy process. Private health agencies receive extensive government subsidies. Because private physicians retain clinical autonomy and private sickness funds wield considerable independence from central government control, public officials cannot easily limit these reimbursements. Costs escalate.

Whereas German political leaders have followed a consensual strategy toward cost containment, French policymakers adopt a more conflictual approach toward health providers. German physicians and hospitals wield more organized influence than do their French counterparts; hence, German expenditures for hospitals, physician services, and drugs increased at a higher rate from 1960 through 1990. In Germany physicians earn a high income relative to the salaries of most national employees. To constrain doctors' fee increases, sickness insurance funds, associations of physicians, and governmental health ministries negotiate prices, insurance premiums, benefits, and patient copayments. Despite opposition from specialists, both German and

French government leaders have tried to allocate greater resources to family practitioners. Whereas German physicians' associations negotiated these disputes with representatives from the Länder governments and regional sickness insurance funds, in France central government attempts to lower doctors' fees and to discourage patients from consulting with a specialist stimulated street demonstrations in Paris during late 1995. German policymakers specify targets for physicians' fees; according to these expenditure limits, the reimbursements made by sickness insurance funds to a specific doctor should not greatly exceed the average income growth of physicians during the last two years or the income earned by doctors in a specialty. If physicians exceed these targets, then they secure lower payments. Cost containment measures also limit hospital expenditures in both nations by raising hospital patients' fees and enacting ceilings on hospital expenditures. From 1995 through 1997, these measures stimulated protests and strikes by French hospital staff, hospital heads, medical interns, general practitioners, and specialists. Regional authorities, which largely control capital spending on hospitals, discourage the introduction of expensive medical technology. Government authorities attempt to restrain drug prices by implementing price freezes, limiting the number of reimbursable drugs, reducing doctors' prescriptions, and raising patients' copayments. From 1960 through 1990 these regulations more effectively limited pharmaceutical spending in France than in Germany.[16]

Even though political leaders expect that greater competition among insurance agencies and hospitals will lower administrative expenses, the fragmented policy process that regulates competition scarcely reduces administrative costs. Competition raises marketing expenses as health providers and purchasing agencies seek new customers. Offers of more generous health care services increase, rather than lower, costs. The overhead expenditures needed to monitor health providers' performance by dispersed organizations in both the public and private sectors also exacerbate the transaction costs of making economic exchanges on the market. Settling conflicts through confrontation or negotiation requires a complex administrative structure. Particularly when government officials link competitive strategies with higher cost sharing by consumers, then lower-income individuals secure the least benefits, as demonstrated by the French and German experiences.[17]

A more pluralist society than either France or Germany, the Netherlands during the last decade has shown greater enthusiasm for competitive cost-containment policies. Influenced by the neoclassical economist Alain Enthoven, Dutch leaders since 1988 have tried to implement the Dekker Commission proposals. This plan advocated greater competition among private, nonprofit insurance companies, expanded their influence over health providers (physicians, hospitals), and gave the consumer enhanced freedom to choose a health insurer. According to this regulated competition proposal, government officials enforce contractual agreements between health insurers and providers and allocate subsidies to the private insurance agencies. Yet the dispersed power situation and fragmented policy arrangements impeded adoption of the Dekker proposals. Even though the government limits physicians' fees, especially those of surgeons, imposes a global budget on hospital expenditures, and sets a maximum reimbursement price for drugs, weak coordination hinders regulatory authority. Government monitoring institutions remain ineffective. Insurance and provider associations ally with ministries of Health, Social Affairs, and Finance as well as with the Central Agency for Health Care Charges that establishes physicians' fees. The Association of Medical Specialists defends high fees and office expenditures. Within the parliamentary governing coalitions, different parties — Christian Democratic Appeal, Labor, Liberal — articulate opposing policy stands about the most effective ways to contain rising health care costs. Committed to reaching a consensus amidst the conflicting interests, the process of negotiating compromises takes a long time. Policy stalemates have ensued. The dispersed, fragmented policy process in a pluralist corporatist society like the Netherlands thus hinders the implementation of competitive policies that secure market efficiency.[18]

Social Democratic Systems

Operating more unified public health care programs, Swedish and English leaders have achieved relatively efficient systems. The English centralize authority for health policies in the Department of Health, especially the NHS Executive. The Department of Health coordinates the policy process. It remains accountable for the health system's performance, even though the 1990 NHS and Community Care Act produced greater fragmentation among several purchasers and providers. Unlike English officials, Swedish policymakers have decentralized greater authority over health care decisions to county and municipal governments. Compared with the British Conservative Party leaders who advocated enhanced competition among hospital trusts for patients, Swedish policymakers, particularly Social Democratic Party officials, prefer that cooperation, not competition, guide health providers' behavior. During the early 1990s a few county governments, as in Stockholm, divided purchasing activities from the provision of health care services. Stressing the need for increased competition between public and private hospitals, county officials negotiated contracts with some private health clinics. Between 1980 and 1995 Sweden represented the only nation among the eight that *decreased* its total expenditures on health care from 9.4 percent of the GDP to 7.2 percent. Public expenditures as a share of total expenditures also declined. Britain during the early 1990s spent a low proportion (around 7 percent) of its GDP on health care. In both countries, physicians' incomes, compared with the incomes of other employees, were more egalitarian than in the United States, Germany, Japan, and Canada. Hospital costs as a share of total health expenditures remained high, especially in Sweden. Like Swedish officials, British policymakers faced greater difficulties restraining hospital costs than limiting drug prices. Price controls, lower reimbursements, higher patient copayments, and restrictions on drug profits all helped curtail pharmaceutical spending. Besides Japan and Canada, these two nations most effectively controlled administrative costs. With their unified, coordinated, publicly administered systems, Sweden and Britain have thus attained a fairly efficient health care market, despite the limited competition from private, forprofit organizations.[19] Publicly financed systems ensured egalitarian access to health care facilities. Especially in Sweden, inclusive coverage and comprehensive benefits minimized the health disparities between rich and poor.

However great the accomplishments of the National Health Service, when the Conservative Party gained government power in 1979, Prime Minister Thatcher and her ministerial colleagues began reorganizing the NHS with the aim of privatizing some health services, establishing greater competition, and creating an internal health market oriented toward efficiency. Determined to lessen the impact of socialist values on public policymaking, the Thatcher government upheld the market virtues of conflict, profit, and cost containment. Health care became a commodity sold on the market, purchased by consumers, lost during accidents or diseases, and found when individuals changed their personal lifestyles. Along with Prime Minister Thatcher, neoclassical economists like Alain Enthoven assumed that an internal or 'managed' market would promote greater efficiency by reducing costs, encouraging more innovation, dispersing power, and expanding consumers' choices.

The 1990 NHS and Community Care Act blended elements of managed competition with continued state regulation. Although the new policies borrowed some aspects from US health maintenance organizations — diagnostic related groups, medical audits, performance reviews, and separation of health purchasers from providers, — government managers within the NHS Executive, rather than private administrators, monitored the British system. They oversaw the separation of purchasers (health authorities, general practitioner fundholders) from health care suppliers: physicians, nurses, hospital trusts, diagnostic laboratories, community health services. Contracts between NHS purchasers and hospital trusts represented internal service agreements subject to arbitration, not legally enforceable documents adjudicated by courts. Health care provision became a separate activity from means-tested community social care that helped mentally ill and elderly persons. Hospitals formerly managed by health authorities transformed into independent trusts supervised by the NHS Executive. The British health care system thus moved from a simple, unified, cohesive system toward a more fragmented, pluralist, functionally differentiated system. General practitioner fundholders, nonfundholding physicians, hospital trusts, health authorities, and a few private health insurance companies, hospitals, nursing homes, and clinics shared power. Despite the growth in private sector activities, such as financing hospital construction, running nursing homes, and supplying services to NHS hospitals, the national government still assumed the significant responsibility for financing health care services and managing their allocation. Regulations from the NHS Executive monitored competition among health providers.

Since the implementation of the internal market changes began in 1991, greater efficiency has scarcely emerged; instead, the more complex, fragmented system has faced problems limiting costs and expanding benefits. The NHS has allocated more funds to the general practitioner fundholders than to nonfundholding practices. Yet along with greater resources has come increased inequality, less clinical freedom, and higher administrative expenses. Fundholder GPs prefer to serve wealthier, healthier patients who live in suburban areas, rather than individuals who reside in poorer rural areas or the inner cities. Patients treated by fundholder GPs gain earlier admissions to hospitals, particularly at the year's end when the NHS trust lacks sufficient revenues. Regulated by the NHS Executive managers, fundholders enjoy less clinical autonomy and freedom to challenge the bureaucratic system. Although their influence over hospital consultants has increased, fundholders confront higher clerical, administrative costs for negotiating contracts with hospital trusts and medical suppliers. Hence, these general practitioners have less time to treat their patients.

Although the 1990 Act aimed to increase hospital efficiency by lowering costs, promoting competition among hospital consultants (specialists), expanding consumer choices, and managing hospitals as business enterprises, the expected efficiencies hardly resulted during the early 1990s. Policies to realize these goals included the allocation of fewer government resources, increased payments from privately-insured patients for current hospital expenditures, and greater reliance on private financial institutions to fund the design, construction, and management of new hospitals. Private financiers, who built new hospitals leased to the NHS trusts, employed ancillary staff responsible for laundry, catering, lighting, and waste disposal. These policies both lowered and raised hospitals' expenses. On the one hand, the NHS Executive managers imposed tight budgetary restraints on the hospital trusts. Shorter hospital stays, more outpatient day surgery, earlier discharges, and the refusal to admit many elderly people into hospital emergency units reduced costs. On the other hand, as pressures mounted for the closure or merger of small hospitals, inner-city facilities serving low-income persons suffered the most; quality care declined. Managers discouraged research, which meant lower productivity and innovation. Faced with poorly-equipped hospitals, British patients seeking urgent heart surgery had to wait longer times than did Americans, Canadians, and Swedes with similar health problems. During the 1990s patients waited shorter periods for minor surgery in small private hospitals than in NHS hospitals. Because NHS surgeons also conduct private practices, especially in London, the longest NHS waiting lists occurred where physicians performed the most surgery in private hospitals. Lengthy waits also indicated that the demand for beds, hospital space, operating rooms, intensive care units, and surgeons exceeded their supply. Too few hospital beds also posed difficulties for short-term patients who needed emergency care. Nursing shortages stemmed from overwork, exhaustion, low morale, and reduced pay and fringe benefits. Dominated by general mangers, hospitals granted nurses less autonomy than before the NHS trust system. Nurses' work load increased as they performed more unskilled tasks as well as more advanced medical activities that the junior doctor used to fulfill. Yet their salaries and job security declined when hospital managers cut costs. The main beneficiaries from the hospital trusts included the senior managers and private financiers. The minimal competition that arose from operating new hospitals brought high profits to private organizations that contracted with the hospitals to supply needed services, such as laundry, cleaning, and meals. Not only private funds but also public taxes financed these services as well as the capital costs of constructing new hospitals. Hence, high profits, such as a 25 percent return on investment, partly derived from public revenues.

During the early 1990s administrative health costs escalated. As a share of total health expenditures they doubled between 1991 and 1993. Over this period the number of NHS senior managers increased from only 500 to 20 000. These managers earned high salaries, certainly higher than NHS nurses, few of whom served as hospital managers. The fragmented new system required more clerical staff, accountants, computer specialists, management consultants, and contract negotiators. Fundholders needed more computer technicians to monitor budgets and to process morbidity information about patients. The emphasis on competition, rather than cooperation, between health purchasers and providers, led to service duplication and lower efficiency. Policy fragmentation meant overlapping jurisdictions, less overall planning, lower accountability, and higher costs. General practitioner fundholders acted as both health providers and purchasers. Hospitals, general practitioners, local authority social service departments, and private nursing homes served the frail elderly and the mentally ill. Faced with scarce resources, they all competed for NHS funds.

Managerial efforts to monitor health care performance within this fragmented system created high transaction costs. Managers could not easily formulate, implement, and enforce contracts between health providers and purchasers, who faced high transaction costs negotiating market exchanges. Purchasers, especially health authorities, lacked the information possessed by doctors and hospitals. Even among medical specialists, information about diagnoses (causes of illness), appropriate treatments, and prognoses remained uncertain. The costs of calculating the impact of health providers' treatments on improvements in their patients' health rose, especially when purchasers or NHS administrators tried to ascertain the quality of professional medical care. All these transaction costs lowered administrative efficiency.

From a cost-benefit perspective, the 1990 NHS and Community Care Act that established an internal health care market produced greater costs than benefits, particularly for the poor and sick. The policy changes saved some money on hospital expenses and reduced waiting times for elective surgery, especially for fundholding patients. Compared with nonfundholding general practitioners, fundholders during the 'first wave' (1991–1992) prescribed more generic drugs. Despite these financial savings, the NHS provided fewer benefits, such as dental services, eye examinations, and care for the elderly. The transfer of elderly patients from hospitals to private nursing homes raised expenditures paid by old people and their relatives. To publicize the new internal market arrangements, the Department of Health spent more public funds for advertising, which increased administrative costs. Private health insurers needed to advertise their plans and thereby recruit clients. Marketing strategies aimed to enroll healthy, wealthy individuals, who would ensure higher profits. Private financial institutions and other commercial businesses, such as diagnostic laboratories, manufacturers of medical equipment, and construction firms that built new NHS hospitals, also profited from the reorganized system. Greater inequality, however, emerged from these financial gains.[20]

CONCLUSION

Rational choice theorists hypothesize that efficiency stems from low transaction costs, extensive price competition, and entrepreneurial systems. To what extent do these hypotheses remain empirically plausible for the eight industrialized health care systems? As we have seen, competitive markets do not necessarily promote higher efficiency. Instead, policymakers have most effectively contained costs and expanded benefits in more coordinated systems such as Canada and Sweden, which reflect less market competition but rely on tax-financed public provision of health services. By contrast, the more fragmented entrepreneurial programs in the United States produce high administrative costs. Private forprofit health insurance corporations function as concentrated suppliers that limit both physicians' and consumers' choices. Bureaucratic managers within health maintenance organizations dominate medical professionals. Similarly, the British movement toward an internal health market with managed competition scarcely expanded efficiency. Instead, the physician relinquished clinical autonomy to managers from the NHS Executive. Their growth in numbers raised administrative expenses and produced greater inequalities in access to professional medical care. Although low transaction costs do expand efficiency, competitive market policies that limit government influence over the health care sector may not attain their intended outcomes. Under neoclassical rational choice assumptions, if government enforces contracts, protects private property rights, expands human capital (skills to make money), and alleviates negative externalities such as pollution, it will minimize transaction costs. Yet improvements in health depend on more than efficient market allocations. Instead, the most efficient systems such as the Swedish social democratic one plan their health policies for the public well being. Coordination, accountability, and responsibility for health policy performance remain clearer than in more fragmented, competitive market systems. Swedish macromanagement stresses the impact that housing conditions, the work situation, and income distribution wield on personal health.

Policy cohesion, rather than the type of political system, better explains the degree of efficiency in the health care arena. Greater variations occur within than between systems. Canada, Sweden, and Japan — parliamentary governments with the most cohesive policy processes — have realized greater administrative efficiencies than more fragmented systems like Germany, France, the Netherlands, and particularly the United States. Although pluralism expands information, dispersed power among several independent agencies impedes policymakers from taking consistent actions based on their information. Duplication of services results. Coordinating the divergent activities of agencies with overlapping jurisdictions requires numerous managers, who raise transaction costs.[21]

In conclusion, neoclassical rational choice theorists maximize parsimony and logical consistency at the expense of generalizability and empirical plausibility. As a deductive, axiomatic theory, it shows extensive parsimony and logical consistency. A few general propositions explain such dependent variables as efficient health policy performance. Specific hypotheses logically derive from general assumptions. Yet the assumptions rest on a weak empirical base, especially propositions about the impact that competition among private, profit-oriented health organizations wield on efficiency. Fragmented competition secures less accountability, efficiency, and equality. By contrast, policy cohesion based on shared civil values, cooperative norms, and interdependent, adaptive organizations more effectively improves people's health.

Part III

Evaluations of Health Policies and Outcomes

Part III probes two issues: the impact of public policies on people's health and different criteria for evaluating public health programs in the eight industrialized nations. Chapter 8 appraises the complex relationships among social stratification, public health policies, and the health status of nations, groups, and individuals. Why do persons with low socioeconomic status experience worse health than do people with higher education, income, and occupational prestige? What effects do public policies wield on individuals at different positions in the social stratification system? How can public health policies deal with the basic causes of illness, so that more egalitarian health outcomes result? The last chapter evaluates health programs according to several criteria. Which health systems — entrepreneurial, organic corporatist, social democratic — achieve the greatest success in realizing their objectives? In Chapter 7 we explored the impact of health policies on economic efficiency and freedom of choice. Chapter 9 focuses on three evaluative criteria: public satisfaction with national health programs, effectiveness in improving health, and equality of access, use, treatment, and health outcome.

8   Public Policies and Health

In his novel *The Plague*, Albert Camus viewed health as a public good and disease as a public evil. Written immediately after World War II, the novel portrays the diverse reactions to the plague that struck the Algerian port city of Oran. Perceiving the pestilence as inevitable, fatalists resigned themselves to suffering and eventual death. Roman Catholics who deferred to ecclesiastical authority sought solace in prayer. Although Father Paneloux regarded God's will as incomprehensible, he urged his parishioners to 'remain faithful and agree to rely on God', even when they could not understand the reasons for children's deaths.[1] Individualists who doubted the efficacy of prayer tried to escape the city. Those with greater optimism mobilized sanitary squads to improve public hygiene in the more congested areas of Oran. These egalitarian activists helped the official sanitary service disinfect the attics and cellars, so that rats could no longer infest residences with the bacteria that spread bubonic plague. Public policymakers, including the prefect and his subordinates, quarantined the city, fumigated houses, administered social services, and tried to maintain public order. The plague produced contradictory effects. Both solidarity and anomie resulted. Although the battle against a common threat apparently rallied solidarity among the besieged residents, the plague actually destroyed communal ties and thereby forced individuals back into a solitary existence. Not only inequality but also greater equality emerged. Even if the wealthier business districts eventually had to contend with the devastation, the poorest, most congested parts of Oran suffered the greatest losses from the plague. Yet in the crowded prisons equality prevailed. As the story's narrator Dr Bernard Rieux recounted:

> Despite the isolation of some prisoners, a prison is a community, as evidenced by what happened in our city jail: the same proportion of guards as prisoners succumbed to the plague. Under the exalted judgment of the plague, everyone from the warden down to the lowliest inmate was condemned. Perhaps for the first time, perfect justice reigned in the jail.[2]

Despite the absolute and relative deprivation, Camus still assumed a hopeful outlook. Even if he doubted the prospects for final victory over the plague, he remained committed to incremental reforms carried out by 'all who, while unable to act like saints but refusing to passively accept the plague and other calamities, strive to be healers'.[3]

Although infectious diseases such as bubonic plague, smallpox, and cholera no longer affect most people in the industrialized world, social stratification continues to produce unequal health outcomes. Individuals with the lowest socioeconomic status face the highest infant mortality rates, the shortest life expectancy, the greatest morbidity, and the worst self-assessed health. Why? Explanations for the relationship between health and social inequality revolve around interacting environmental and personal variables. The health of nations, social groups, and individuals reflects structural conditions within the environment, including the degree of income inequality, unemployment, workplace hazards, and residential deprivation. These environmental conditions interact with such personal variables as attitudes, perceptions, motivations, genetic predispositions, and individual lifestyles. Only by influencing these environmental and personal causes can public policies change the unequal health outcomes linked to social stratification. The following sections will probe the linkage between social inequality and health by formulating a theory of social opportunities, applying this framework to the causes of health, and evaluating the impact of health programs on these causes.

THEORY OF SOCIAL OPPORTUNITIES

According to the theory of social opportunities, the prospects for health depend on the interaction among cultural values, structural conditions in the environment, and individual attitudes, behaviors, and genetic predispositions. Certain conditions expand the opportunities for improved health. Dominant cultural values stress individual efficacy and egalitarian access to health care. Healthy societies have high income equality, low unemployment, safe working environments, and neighborhoods with minimal violence, pollution, and dilapidated housing. These cultural-structural variables promote risk-averse behavior. Yet whatever the environmental circumstances, individual will, predispositions, and actions also lead to health. Favorable genes help lengthen life expectancy if they interact with health-inducing personal behavior and social situations. Optimistic attitudes, self-esteem, personal efficacy, and a strong will to choose healthy lifestyles all contribute to well-being. Interacting with these attitudes, personal lifestyles reinforce the behaviors conducive to health. If individuals avoid smoking, consume little alcohol, exercise daily, and eat nutritious food, then their health should improve. The opposite conditions operate as constraints on health. Cultural values highlight fatalism — the belief that sickness and disease represent inevitable situations that neither the individual nor collectivity can control. Mass media urge deference to glamorous figures who exemplify risk-prone activities such as violence and promiscuity. Structural conditions constrain opportunities to lead healthy lives. Income inequalities and high unemployment rates limit the resources (money, information) needed to purchase quality health care, nutritious food, and safe, comfortable residences. Poor, unemployed people live in overcrowded, damp houses. Many lack the social support networks that reinforce healthy attitudes and lifestyles. Unable to control their objective environment, they express low self-esteem, feel inefficacious, and take a pessimistic view of future prospects.

Public policies shape individual, group, and national health when they effectively reduce the environmental risks that endanger people's health and when they expand the opportunities that lead to improved health. Policymakers can regulate environmental conditions (air pollution, hazardous wastes) and personal lifestyles, such as access to firearms, alcohol, and cigarettes. Public educational campaigns that portray certain behaviors as unhealthy — cigarette smoking, promiscuous sex, reckless driving — and others as beneficial — regular exercise, nutritious diets — uphold the attitudes reinforcing healthier lifestyles. By financing income redistribution measures, cancer screenings, research into the causes of health, and the provision of such health services as prenatal and elderly care, government policies can lower infant mortality and raise life expectancy. The effectiveness of these programs depends on policymakers' control over the causes of health. Financing prenatal care seems less difficult than controlling the behavior of an expectant mother. National government officials can more easily formulate regulations about air pollution than they can implement their local implementation. Broadcasts that warn against the dangers of smoking take fewer resources than programs to gain public compliance behind these media messages. Particularly in these eight pluralist democracies, policymakers lack the power or the authority to directly control all the environmental conditions and individual actions that produce health. Because the causes of health are cumulative, policies wield their greatest impact on people with low socioeconomic status — those who face the most health risks and have the fewest opportunities for healthy living. Yet because so many complex variables intervene among social stratification, public policies, individual behavior, and health, the policy explanations made by social scientists remain uncertain, tentative, and probabilistic, rather than deterministic. Unexpected contingencies arise that confound policymakers' intentions. Indefinite time lags occur between policy formulation — cessation of smoking in public places — and the anticipated outcome, such as declining lung cancer. Measurement errors, sampling of cases, and the use of divergent operational indicators for ambiguous variables like 'health' or 'equality' impede attempts to make precise generalizations about the impact of public policies on health.[4]

Despite the difficulties of ascertaining the interactions among social stratification, public policies, and health, we can probe the credibility of the following hypotheses that derive from social opportunities theory. First, if individuals rank low in the social stratification system, then they will face the greatest illness. Health researchers use education, income, and occupational prestige as the main indicators of an individual's socioeconomic status (SES). Divergent causes explain the impact of social status on health. Most social scientists focus on environmental conditions: income inequality, unemployment rates, the workplace situation, and housing standards. Others examine the interaction between these structural conditions and personal characteristics: genetic predispositions, individual values, motives, attitudes, personal lifestyles, and the use of health care services. We will analyze the plausibility of all these variables that suggest how SES affects individual and group health. Second, as the national income gap widens, health inequalities increase. Third, if public officials implement universal, comprehensive health policies, fewer inequalities will occur between the health status of low and high socioeconomic groups.[5]

Causal analyses of these hypotheses involve the following steps. First, the researcher assumes a high correlation between an independent variable X, such as policy changes, and a dependent variable Y like improved health. Certain policy changes — expanded access to health care, increased vaccinations, higher taxes on cigarettes and alcohol — lead to health improvements, as measured by lower infant mortality rates, longer life expectancy, decreased morbidity, and higher self-reported well-being. Second, the cause precedes the effect. Declining socioeconomic status comes before deteriorating health. Policies that raise joblessness cause greater illness among the unemployed. Third, controls for antecedent variables associated with both X and Y ensure that no other factors 'explain away' the original strong correlation that links cause to effect. For example, a high statistical association may exist between per capita use of acute hospital care (average bed-days for each person) and the death rate for every 100 000 individuals. Yet we would not assume that hospitalization causes death. Instead, both variables derive from a common antecedent — the spread of an infectious disease. Similarly, when gasoline consumption declines, so do highway fatalities. Why? A policy decision that lowers the legal speed limit reduces gas consumption, promotes safer driving, and leads to fewer vehicular fatalities. Fourth, because many causes explain an effect, health scientists seek to uncover those variables wielding the greatest impact. As variables causing improved health, how important are structural conditions (socioeconomic opportunities, constraints), personal orientations (personal efficacy, risk aversion, commitment to health), and individual behaviors (lifestyles)? How do public policies affect all these variables?

Particularly when comparing several nations, social scientists cannot easily validate the causal explanations linking social stratification, public policies, and health. First, weak correlations obscure the expected causal relationship between policy changes and health changes. Sometimes neither the independent variable (increased government expenditures for prenatal care) nor the dependent variable (declining infant mortality) varies by a large amount. The strength of the correlations depends on specific time periods, the groups sampled for investigation, and the techniques for measuring crucial variables. The impact of a policy — increased access to preventive or curative health services — often varies according to divergent groups: wealthy vs. poor, rural vs. urban, men vs. women. Generalizations about the correlation among social status, smoking, and health may change over time; that is, before the 1960s higher SES men smoked more cigarettes a day than did poorer men. After that period, inverse correlations occurred: the lower the SES, the higher the smoking rates.

When comparing health across nations, different operational indicators plague the search for valid causal explanations. How should we measure 'health'? Possibilities include such indicators as mortality rates, morbidity rates (restricted activity days, sickness absence days, incidence of chronic illness), life expectancy, quality adjusted life years, and self-assessed health. Individuals, physicians, and official statisticians supply this evidence, much of which refers to illness, disease, and death, rather than to health or well-being. Both the reliability and validity of these indicators vary not only within the same country but across nations. How comparable and accurate are the official statistics for infant morality rates? Whereas in the United States medical personnel register births, in other industrialized societies parents assume the responsibility for reporting their infants' births, whether live or dead. US physicians register a higher percentage of low-birthweight babies (under 1500 grams), babies who died 24 hours after birth, and infants dying before seven weeks of their mother's gestation; hence, US infant mortality rates exceed those of Japan and Europe, where officials classify some infant deaths as 'late fetal deaths' or 'false stillbirths'. Divergent methods of registering, reporting, and classifying births lead to some, if not all, the varying infant mortality rates of North America, West Europe, and Japan. At the other end of the age scale, estimates of life expectancy provide only limited information about the health of individuals at ages 70, 80, and 90. Measurements of equality also remain ambiguous. 'Equality' may indicate access to health care, use of health services, treatment by medical providers, distribution of health services according to need, and expenditures for different groups (socioeconomic, gender, ethnic) after controls for health status. Mortality rates and self-reported chronic illnesses show greater group inequalities than do morbidity rates. Thus the strength of correlations partly depends on the specific operational indicators used to measure ambiguous health variables.

Second, rather than the causal variable preceding the effect, feedback processes usually affect national, group, and individual health. Reciprocal causation occurs. For example, unemployment may produce worsened health, which in turn hinders the future job prospects of the sick person. Time lags also impede researchers' efforts to predict the future impact of policy changes or even to explain the link between a policy and its intended effect. Social scientists can more easily ascertain the short-term costs of a new health program than explain its long-term benefits. If public policies ban cigarette advertising and smoking in public places, how long will that injunction lead to reduced lung cancer, which usually emerges more than 30 to 40 years after an individual begins smoking? For these reasons, valid causal explanations require longitudinal analyses, both to uncover time lags as well as detect all the complex variables that link a public policy to people's health.

Third, because social scientists cannot designate or measure all the antecedent and intervening variables that explain the complex interactions among socioeconomic status, public policies, and health, misspecified equations impede attempts to make causal explanations. Measuring environmental conditions poses fewer problems than finding valid, reliable indicators for such personal variables as genetic predispositions or attitudes, which most investigators omit from their analyses. Yet if health derives from both opportunities and the willingness to act, these individual variables become important. The decision to abandon smoking depends not only on public policies like higher taxes on cigarettes and on positive reinforcements from social support networks in the immediate environment but also on the personal motivation to stop smoking. Mental orientations and genetic predispositions interact with environmental conditions to shape the likelihood of succumbing to heart disease.

Fourth, multicollinearity plagues the search for causal explanations. Neither national nor personal health stems from just one independent variable; instead, several variables interact to produce better health. Weighing their importance becomes difficult because most show strong correlations. For example, highly-educated persons usually earn sizable incomes and work in prestigious occupations. Poverty areas with high unemployment also reveal dilapidated, overcrowded housing, interpersonal violence, hazardous wastes, and water pollution. Which of these interdependent variables wields the strongest impact on people's health? The analytical problems magnify when investigators try to trace the interaction between socioeconomic and personal variables. The ecological fallacy confounds collective dimensions with attributes of group members. Relationships that characterize the group — for instance, the inverse correlation between socioeconomic status and smoking — hardly remain valid for every member of that group. Whereas some wealthy persons smoke over five packs of cigarettes a day, numerous low-income individuals never start smoking. Hence, health researchers face difficulties uncovering the causal interactions among SES, smoking, and such illnesses as lung cancer or heart disease. To ascertain causal explanations, social scientists must distinguish antecedent variables affecting nearly all members of the same group — contaminated water supply in a low-income area — from more particularistic factors, like limited wealth or formal education, that shape the health status of only a proportion of group members. Moreover, rather than merely compiling a list of important causes, analysts need to formulate a general theory that explains the interactions among independent variables. If we assume that the operation of social structures influences individual choices, we must designate the causal mechanisms that produce an effect such as health. According to the theory of social opportunities, crucial intervening variables include the commitment to health as a positive outcome, strong feelings of personal efficacy (expectations of success), and beliefs that structural opportunities outweigh environmental constraints. These variables not only mediate the relationship between structural conditions and health but also can produce changes in sociopolitical structures.[6] Guided by these assumptions, social scientists hope that even if policymakers cannot achieve final victory over disease, they can contribute to the incremental healing process, as Camus anticipated.

SOCIAL STRATIFICATION AND THE CAUSES OF HEALTH

During the early 1990s Japan compiled a better health record than did European nations or the two North American societies. The Japanese experienced the lowest infant mortality rates, the highest life expectancy, and few deaths from circulatory diseases (mainly heart fatalities, strokes), malignant neoplasms (cancers), and homicides. (See Table 8.1.) By contrast, the United States and the United Kingdom fared less well. Americans faced especially high infant mortality and homicide rates. On all measures except

Table 8.1   Life expectancy and causes of death, 1993

Country	Life Expectancy at Birth (Years)		Infant Mortality (Deaths under One Year per 1000 Live Births)			Malignant Neoplasms (Age-Standardized Death Rate per 100 000 Persons)		Circulatory Diseases (Age-Standardized Death Rate per 100 000 Persons)		Homicides (Death Rate per 100 000 Persons)	
	Male	Female	Total	Male	Female	Male	Female	Male	Female	Male	Female
Canada	74.6	81.0	6.3	6.9	5.7	244	160	330	195	2.5	1.2
France	73.8	82.1	6.5	7.5	5.4	293	129	254	149	1.4	0.8
Germany	72.8	79.3	5.8	6.6	5.1	271	162	472	297	1.4	1.0
Japan	76.5	83.1	4.3	4.7	4.0	226	111	257	172	0.8	0.5
Netherlands	74.0	80.0	6.3	7.2	5.3	292	162	384	220	1.8	0.7
Sweden	75.5	80.9	4.8	5.4	4.1	194	144	420	242	1.8	0.8
United States[a]	72.2	78.8	8.4	9.3	7.4	248	162	399	247	16.1	4.3
United Kingdom	73.5	78.9	6.3	7.0	5.6	267	179	449	267	1.7	0.8
England & Wales	73.8	79.2	6.3	7.0	5.6	263	176	439	259	1.3	0.8
Scotland	71.4	76.9	6.5	7.4	5.6	309	203	549	341	2.7	0.7
Northern Ireland	72.5	78.2	7.1	7.8	6.3	266	179	502	297	9.9	1.3

[a]The age-standardized death rates for malignant neoplasms and circulatory diseases in the United States refer to 1992.

Sources: World Health Organisation, *World Health Statistics Annual 1994, 1995* (Geneva: World Health Organisation, 1995, 1996); 'Report of Final Mortality Statistics, 1995,' *Monthly Vital Statistics Report* 45 (12 June 1997): 19, 66; US Bureau of the Census, *Statistical Abstract of the United States: 1996,* 116th ed. (Washington, DC: Government Printing Office, 1996), 96; United Nations, *Demographic Yearbook 1994,* 46th ed. (New York: United Nations, 1996), 393.

homicide, Canadians led healthier lives than did the British. Among the four continental European countries, the Dutch, Germans, and French had similar infant mortality, life expectancy, and homicide rates. Swedes endured low incidences of cancer but greater heart fatalities. Like Japanese infants, few Swedish babies died during the first year. The average Japanese woman lived until 82 years old.

In all eight nations people's health shows a close correlation with socioeconomic status. University graduates who earn more than twice the median income and who work as professionals, senior executives, managers, administrators, and employers enjoy the best health. By contrast, individuals who achieve only a primary education, earn one-half the median national income, and work in unskilled and semiskilled jobs suffer the worst health. Even at birth, they endure the highest infant mortality rates.

Ethnic stratification shapes health mainly through its close linkage with socioeconomic status. Ethnic minorities and migrant workers, who generally experience worse health than indigenous ethnic majorities, achieve less formal education, earn lower wages, labor in less prestigious jobs, and face higher unemployment. Concentrated in dangerous, unsafe occupations like construction and textile production, they suffer from loud noise, toxic pollutants, and hazardous equipment. Despite their frequent industrial accidents and disabilities, they enjoy limited access to rehabilitation services and to disability benefits. Policy officials often restrict their rights to employment, housing, and social service benefits. As a result, many ethnic minority members must live in overcrowded, dilapidated, damp housing. Along with deteriorating residences, difficulties in securing early prenatal care from a qualified general practitioner lead to high infant mortality rates among migrant workers and low-income ethnic minorities.

Despite their subordinate position in the social stratification system, women attain superior health vis-à-vis men. As Table 8.1 showed, more male babies die during their first year. In these eight countries women live from six to seven years longer than men. From 1950 to 1995 this gender gap increased. Rates for heart disease, cancer, stroke, motor accidents, suicide, and homicide all reveal higher male fatalities. Yet when we compare men and women with similar socioeconomic backgrounds, the gender health differences fade. True, education and occupation wield a stronger impact over male health. Highly-educated men and women in prestigious occupations enjoy more similar health than do lower-status persons of both sexes. Nevertheless, the odds for superior health increase when men and women work as professionals, escape unemployment, and earn high salaries. Regardless of gender, the sickest individuals work in unskilled factory jobs and the personal services, secure low wages, and function outside the official paid labor force as homemakers or unemployed persons. Whether men or women, these people enjoy the fewest structural opportunities to lead healthy lives.[7]

Both environmental conditions and individual characteristics explain the linkage between social stratification and health. Environmental conditions include such structural variables as a nation's income inequalities, unemployment rate, workplace situation, and residential deprivation, which constrain the opportunities for improved health among persons with low socioeconomic status. In his poem 'A Worker's Speech to a Doctor,' Bertolt Brecht blamed illness on economic exploitation, bad housing, and malnutrition. When the physician urged the thin, feeble worker to gain more weight, Brecht linked this injunction to warning a bullrush about the dangers of getting wet.[8] Nevertheless, a person's health not only depends on structural conditions within the nation, on the job, at home, and in the neighborhood but also derives from individual attitudes, motives, and lifestyles that interact with sociopolitical structures. According to the individualist rationale, if a person eats fresh fruit and vegetables, jogs before dawn, walks the dog at dusk, gets eight hours sleep a day, avoids stress, stays clean, and abstains from toxic drugs, cigarettes, alcohol, and unprotected sex, good health will result — maybe even wealth. Benjamin Franklin, an exponent of competitive individualism, advocated: 'Early to bed and early to rise makes a man healthy, wealthy, and wise.' In his fable about two chipmunks and the shrike, James Thurber, however, took a skeptical view about the favorable outcomes of personal prudence. One morning the female chipmunk convinced her mate to rise early: 'You can't be healthy if you lie in bed all day and never get any exercise.' Before that morning, the male chipmunk had left the house only at night, when darkness prevented the shrike, a predatory bird, from killing him. Unfortunately, when the two chipmunks took a stroll after breakfast, the shrike killed them both. Thurber moralized: 'Early to rise and early to bed makes a male healthy and wealthy and dead.'[9] As the fable illustrates, even if individuals retain some choice over their future destiny, environmental conditions also shape health, mortality, and life expectancy. The following section examines the relative importance of these two interacting variables that explain national, group, and individual health. Of the two causes, sociopolitical structures wield a stronger impact than do personal lifestyles, which have a weaker, more contingent link to both social stratification and health.[10]

Environmental Causes

National income inequalities affect infant mortality rates, homicide fatalities, heart disease, self-reported health, and life expectancy. According to data collected during the late 1980s by the Luxembourg Income Study, Sweden had the most egalitarian household income, followed by Germany, the Netherlands, Canada, France, and the United Kingdom. The United States showed the least income equality, as measured by the widest gaps in total disposable income (wages, salaries, rents, dividends, interest, government cash transfers) minus income taxes and social security contributions. American children also faced the greatest poverty, which referred to families with less than one-half the median income. Consistent with the income distribution figures, Swedish, Dutch, and German children lived under the least poverty. From 1979 through 1990 both the United States and the United Kingdom experienced not only increased child poverty but also growing income inequality. Particularly among men, real wages declined in both nations during this period. The Luxembourg Income Study did not include Japan. Whereas Japanese men secured higher wages, women and workers in smaller firms earned lower incomes than did full-time employees of large corporations. Yet the Japanese experienced minimal poverty and relatively low unemployment rates. The gap between the lowest-paid workers and the highest-paid corporate executives remained lower in Japan and Sweden than in Britain or especially the United States.

A wide gap between rich and poor leads to worse health among low-income persons. They suffer from hazardous working conditions, higher unemployment rates, more dilapidated rental housing, and reduced access to postsecondary education. Families cannot afford to purchase nutritious food, which costs more in poorer than wealthier neighborhoods. The least egalitarian nation

— the United States — supplies less generous, comprehensive social benefits than do more egalitarian societies like Sweden and the Netherlands. As a result, the United States showed higher infant mortality and homicide rates during the early 1990s. Babies born to low-income mothers, especially African-American and native American women, died most often at birth. The greater the gap between rich and poor in an American state, the higher the infant mortality and particularly the homicide rate, which particularly affected African-American and Latino young men. As urban income inequality rose among Latinos, the number of murders for every 100 000 persons also increased. The fragile social cohesion, low per capita medical expenditures, limited health insurance, and high unemployment within the least egalitarian areas reinforced the deteriorating health situation.

As income inequality rises, so does the health gap between rich and poor. Social cohesion declines. Aggression and family disruption increase. Civic trust wanes. Lower-income individuals participate less in civic associations such as churches, unions, and political parties. Governments spend a smaller share of the national income on health care, schools, and municipal services (libraries, public transportation, musical events). From this decline in civic solidarity results higher homicide rates, suicides, alcohol-related deaths, and traffic accidents — fatalities particularly suffered by young men of low socioeconomic status.[11]

Even if crossnational rankings of income inequality and unemployment rates show only weak correlations, the poorest *groups* also face the greatest dangers of losing their jobs. From 1960 through 1991, Sweden and especially Japan experienced the lowest unemployment — measured as working-age individuals (16–64) who have no job and actively seek employment as a proportion of the total labor force. From the early 1980s on, France, the United Kingdom, Canada, and Germany endured higher joblessness. Whereas during the early 1990s unemployment rates fell in the United States and the Netherlands, they rose in Germany, France, and particularly Sweden. Throughout this period, immigrants, ethnic minorities, semiskilled and unskilled workers, and persons with less than a secondary education endured the greatest unemployment.

Whatever the nation or time period, as national unemployment rates rose, general health deteriorated among those who lost their job. They, particularly men, experienced higher general mortality rates, increased heart disease, and shorter life expectancy. Unemployed men under thirty years old showed higher homicide rates and more motor accident fatalities than did their employed colleagues. Long-term unemployment over a year led to more chronic illnesses and to severe mental depression, with lower-income persons suffering the most depression. Social support networks shaped unemployed persons' response to losing their job. Those with the most supportive relatives, friends, neighbors, and workmates coped most effectively. Lacking social support, unemployed homemakers displayed worse health than did full-time employed men and women, whose higher education and occupational status gave them enhanced optimism, self-esteem, and perceived ability to control their lives and manage stressful situations. Along with social networks, reference group ties influenced individuals' responses to job loss. Unemployed persons who compared themselves with job-holding individuals experienced greater self-blame, lower self-esteem, and more depression. By contrast, those who compared their jobless fate with other unemployed people blamed government policies, rather than themselves. As a result, they displayed higher self-esteem, lower depression, and better general health.[12]

Besides unemployment, the workplace environment shapes health. Workers who labor under the most dangerous, hazardous, unsafe conditions face the greatest mortality rates, long-term illnesses, injuries, and disabilities. These include metal workers, roofers, construction employees, miners, loggers, timber cutters, farm workers, fishers, airline pilots, truck drivers, and taxi drivers. Their deaths stem from malfunctioning machinery, falls, homicides, and highway accidents. By contrast, professionals (teachers, doctors, lawyers), administrators, managers, executives, engineers, financiers, and realtors hold safer, less monotonous positions giving them a higher degree of control over the environment. Compared with unskilled manual workers, professionals achieve higher formal education, income, job security, home ownership, and political participation. All these resources give them the opportunities to lead healthy lives.

Even among prestigious salaried employees such as British civil servants, working conditions at different grades contribute to health, as measured by the fewest sickness absence days a week. The highest grade administrators — executives, permanent and deputy secretaries — take fewer absences than do clerks, clerical assistants, and office support staff. Top civil servants experience more consensual demands, perceive greater control over their occupational activities, use more diverse skills on the job, receive stronger social support, and express higher job satisfaction. Better health results. Lower-ranking clerks, however, receive more conflicting demands but perceive less control over the workplace situation. Performing more monotonous tasks that require few complex skills, they feel less satisfied with their jobs. Social networks provide limited support. Hence, depression and anxiety lead to more sickness absences, particularly among women. Yet within the British civil service, occupational rank wields a greater impact on men's than on women's health.[13]

Stratification not only affects the workplace but also the residential environment, which influences the opportunities for health. In all eight nations, people who live in neighborhoods with a high educational level, superior housing, and a sizable proportion of wealthy technical and professional employees experience longer life expectancy, fewer chronic illnesses, and lower infant mortality rates. By contrast, areas with high unemployment rates, inadequate educational facilities, and numerous unskilled laborers who earn minimal incomes suffer high mortality rates from coronary heart disease, lung cancer, tuberculosis, homicide, and AIDS. Reflecting the general economic deprivation among these neighborhoods, damp, cold, overcrowded, and dilapidated houses expose their residents, particularly low-income renters, to risks. Cluttered with broken glass, used syringes, beer cans, and dog feces, the physical environment hardly enhances health. Instead, pathogens, chemical wastes, carcinogens, mutagens, and other toxins pollute living conditions. The social environment features weak solidarity and few social support networks strengthening healthy behavior. Even in Britain, which has a comprehensive, public, universal National Health Service, health facilities serving low-income urban neighborhoods remain understaffed. Fewer young general practitioners or specialists serve these areas; instead, they locate in wealthier suburbs. The Indians who populate Canada's rural hinterlands endure low life expectancy. Compared with higher-income urban residents, they must cope with less formal education, more unemployment, and greater disabilities when employed as forest workers. Weak social integration magnifies chronic illnesses. Lacking the professionalized health services available to city dwellers, these

First Nation peoples make fewer visits to a medical provider relative to their health needs. Ethnic stratification also interacts with residential inequalities to shape group health in the United States. As urban housing segregation increases — that is, as African Americans become more residentially isolated from European Americans, — the black infant mortality and male homicide rates rise. These segregated neighborhoods usually lack job opportunities, superior educational institutions, and high-quality health services. Dilapidated rental housing exposes residents to numerous risks. Social support networks rarely promote healthy lifestyles. From environmental constraints and insufficient resources emerge feelings of vulnerability: low self-esteem, high fatalism, risk-prone behavior, and perceived powerlessness to change the deprived situation. Poor health results.[14]

Individual Causes

Despite the high correlation between social stratification and health, individual characteristics still partly explain the health of specific group members. Socioeconomic conditions applicable to a collectivity — occupation, ethnicity, gender — do not necessarily remain valid for every person within that group. The same structures exert divergent impacts on different individuals, who retain some choice over their responses to environmental conditions. Even if they cannot always change their sociopolitical situation, they can change their attitudes toward it. The most important individual reasons for health include genetic predispositions, attitudes, personal lifestyles, and use of health services. Yet, as we shall see in the following sections, their links with social stratification and health remain murky, variable, and contingent, particularly when we consider the effect of genes and lifestyles.

Although genetic predispositions certainly shape individuals' health, they have an unpredictable outcome on most diseases. Inherited from both parents, genes constitute protein segments of DNA molecules. Rather than causing a behavioral pattern, they represent *predispositions* that interact with environmental stimuli, mental orientations, emotions, other genes, and biochemical compounds to shape people's behavior. Just as genetic predispositions may lead individuals to respond to environmental experiences in a particular way, the environment can change genetic predispositions. Hence, one 'good' gene scarcely causes health; another 'bad' gene hardly determines disease. Most diseases like cancer drive mainly from environmental situations. DNA mutations wield greater impact over cystic fibrosis and sickle cell anemia. Yet, genes represent individual, not group, tendencies. Neither socioeconomic nor ethnic groups inherit these predispositions. Even though African Americans suffer from sickle cell anemia more than do European Americans, the 'anemic gene' accounts for under 1 percent of all excess black deaths. Environmental conditions, not gene sequences, explain the health status of most ethnic groups throughout the world.[15]

Whereas individuals cannot determine their genetic predispositions, they have greater control over the attitudes that frame their worldviews. Unlike genes, subjective orientations show a closer link to social stratification. Individuals who have the highest socioeconomic status — income, occupational status, formal education — express the strongest *empowerment*, defined as the perceived ability to understand, control, and change the environment. Cognitively, they can meaningfully interpret the complex world, including the reasons for health and illness as well as the future consequences of their present conduct. They have the general information, expertise, and skills to cope with health problems, especially effective ways to handle stress and overcome illness. From the affective standpoint, empowered individuals radiate a positive self-image: hope, optimism, self-esteem, personal efficacy. In their interpersonal relationships, they learn how to use resources effectively for goal attainment, to share decisionmaking, and to rely on others for social support. Relatives, friends, neighbors, and workmates reinforce life-enhancing behavior. Active participation in civic voluntary associations, political parties, unions, occupational organizations, and churches reinforces the positive impact of supportive social networks. From this empowerment emerges improved health. By contrast, individuals with lower SES feel less powerful, more fatalistic, and less able to master their present situation. Depressed, angry, and hostile, they report poorer health and experience higher mortality rates, particularly heart fatalities. When powerlessness increases, their health deteriorates. Because the causes of health are cumulative, life-enhancing attitudes can exert a positive outcome on low-income, uneducated, unskilled individuals who confront numerous structural constraints to better health. If they learn cognitive skills, gain a positive self-image, and participate in social support networks that strengthen the norms of healthy living, their ability to cope with stressful situations should rise, thereby causing improved health.[16]

Even though social scientists have uncovered a clear link between socioeconomic status and attitudes such as personal efficacy, the interactions among SES, individual lifestyles, and health remain more obscure. To what extent do the personal lifestyles of low SES people explain their greater illness? Few would deny that heavy smoking and excessive alcohol consumption heighten the risks of cancer and heart disease. Nevertheless, how significant is this impact? Lung cancer probably demonstrates the strongest link between lifestyle and health. For the last 40 years, a higher proportion of low SES persons have smoked cigarettes and thus succumbed to lung cancer. Yet moderate drinking, rather than total abstinence, may lower susceptibility to coronary heart fatalities. The effect of personal lifestyles varies across time, nation, and social group membership. As contingent variables, they derive from norms that prescribe proper, appropriate routines for people in diverse roles, whether occupational, ethnic, gender, or age. Role expectations specify the patterns of exercise, nutrition, and sexual behavior deemed proper for group members. Because these normative expectations depend on social position, the correlation between lifestyles — alcohol consumption, smoking, diet, exercise — and health wanes when we examine individuals with the same education, income, and occupational status.

Although well-educated, prosperous professionals enjoy better health than do unskilled manual workers, lifestyle differences explain only part of this outcome. From the 1960s on, cigarette smoking declined as socioeconomic status rose. Before that time, however, wealthier, higher educated persons smoked more heavily; yet, they still lived longer than their poorer colleagues. Alcohol consumption occurs more frequently among the educated wealthy, whose volume of intake varies across nations. 'Binge drinking' occurs among young men at opposite ends of the social stratification totem pole: highly-educated, wealthy fraternity members as well as unemployed workers with low incomes and education. Even the association linking exercise to SES remains ambiguous. Manual workers get more physical exercise on the job;

professionals exercise during their 'leisure' time. Assuming that cumulative causes explain health, researchers find that lifestyles exert a stronger impact on high SES individuals, who face fewer structural constraints against a long, healthy life. Hence, cessation of smoking and alcohol abuse may improve professionals' health more than manual workers' well-being.

Compared with men, who smoke more heavily and consume a greater volume of alcohol, women practice less risky lifestyles. These gender patterns partly account for females' lower rate of lung cancer and heart disease as well as for their longer life expectancy. Infant mortality also stems from lifestyle behavior. Women who smoke over ten cigarettes a day face a higher probability that their babies will die at birth. Gender interacts with occupation to shape the linkage between smoking and health. Whereas professional women either never smoked or stop smoking, a higher proportion of unskilled, semi-skilled female employees or housewives who face financial difficulties continue to smoke. As a result, their health deteriorates.[17]

Only a weak correlation prevails between national mortality rates and the volume of liquor or cigarette use. For instance, among the eight countries, the French consume the most pure alcohol. Yet they have the lowest incidence of heart disease. Few Japanese women smoke; their babies rarely die at birth. Even though Dutch, Canadian, and Swedish women have higher smoking rates, they suffer only slightly greater infant death rates. Personal lifestyles explain *individual* health differences better than national variations. National mortality rates depend primarily on such structural conditions as socioeconomic deprivation and on public policies shaping access to health facilities.[18]

THE IMPACT OF PUBLIC POLICIES ON HEALTH

Government policies can improve people's health when they effectively influence the two major causes of illness — individual characteristics and environmental conditions. The will to frame specific public health programs partly depends on elite political culture, especially on the way that policymakers interpret the causes of illness. Leaders stressing individual responsibility for personal health often support government measures to encourage healthier lifestyles. Strict controls on the sale of alcohol and cigarettes, severe punishment for drunk driving, requirements for use of automobile airbags, and educational campaigns that promote exercise and nutrition may enhance national health. Yet central governments have greater power to formulate regulations and to communicate moral injunctions than to secure compliance with these edicts. Financing health care services becomes easier for policymakers than changing people's attitudes toward health. Those who perceive that the primary reasons for good health stem from the environment, instead of personal lifestyles, take a more optimistic view of the prospects for policy effectiveness. According to this rationale, public policies have greater potential to transform the collective causes of illness. Government officials can more readily mandate the pasteurization of milk than ensure that every individual boil raw milk each morning. During the twentieth century governments have formulated various policies intended to promote a healthier environment — for example, fluoridation of water, clearance of mosquitoes from swamps, bans on smoking in public places, elimination of toxic chemicals from work sites, sanitary treatment of raw sewage, and reduction of damp, overcrowded, dilapidated housing.

Regulatory, educational, and financial policies all try to improve health conditions. Aimed at controlling not only the environment but also individual behavior, regulatory measures shape workplace health and safety, air and water pollution, violent actions, and such lifestyles as consumption of cigarettes, alcohol, and toxic drugs. National policymakers face fewer difficulties formulating these regulations than implementing them and guaranteeing compliance. Educational policies also face a gap between intentions and outcomes. Government officials can transmit messages to the public about the need to stop smoking, abandon alcohol, exercise daily, eat a nutritious diet, and maintain optimistic, efficacious attitudes toward coping with stress. Yet the effectiveness of such educational campaigns depends on comprehension of media messages, willingness to accept the injunctions, and social support networks that reinforce healthy behaviors. Despite constraints posed by financial recession, public policymakers have the greatest authority to implement fiscal programs that provide health services, including cancer screenings, immunizations, surgery, therapy, and radiation. Prenatal care, postnatal care, and child benefits help reduce infant mortality rates during the first year of birth. Whether at home, in nursing residences, or in hospitals, care for the elderly may lengthen life expectancy. Since World War II policies to decrease infant mortality have achieved greater success than programs to raise life expectancy. The latter policies involve greater control over individual lifestyles and environmental conditions. People from higher socioeconomic backgrounds can more effectively surmount the structural obstacles to better health. Because they live in a healthier, safer environment, they experience fewer illnesses. To the extent that public policies can treat the individual and environmental causes of disease, they will narrow the socioeconomic differences in life expectancy. Fiscal programs that expand income equality and decrease unemployment should also secure more equal health among diverse social groups and thereby raise a nation's overall health. Even if regulatory, educational, and fiscal policies have failed to attain all their objectives, they have contributed to improved health conditions.[19] In the following sections, we will first examine the impact of health policies on the environment and then probe their outcomes on individual characteristics.

Policies toward Income Equality

Political leaders can most effectively implement public policies to expand income equality and achieve full employment when they possess a strong will to act and sufficient power vis-à-vis groups resisting egalitarian measures. Where unions wield extensive policy influence and leftwing parties control national government finance, economic, and health ministries, egalitarian measures result. When political leaders place a high priority on social equality and assume that government actions can change not only environmental conditions but also personal behavior, we expect the passage of programs narrowing the gap that separates rich from poor. During the postwar era these conditions particularly prevailed in Sweden and to a lesser extent in the Netherlands. The Swedish government allocated comparatively high expenditures for social services and transfer payments, especially cash grants for pensions and health care. These public transfers greatly increased the incomes of single-parent families and the elderly; income distribution after government expenditures was far more equal than the pre-spending patterns. Compared with cash transfers, in-kind (noncash) benefits for post-primary education, medical care, and subsidized housing exerted a weaker effect on reducing income inequalities. Taxes had even less an egalitarian impact; Swedish tax policies were only slightly progressive. Social Democratic Party leaders and LO union heads strove for wage solidarity. Male manufacturing workers as well as men and women performing similar jobs received more equal wages in Sweden than in any other industrialized capitalist nation. Women, even part-time employees, benefited from union membership, from highly-paid public sector service positions in education, health care, and social work, and from state-financed fringe benefits like health care, dental services, day-care, and home assistance. Dutch governmental officials implemented somewhat similar, if less comprehensive, programs. As a result, Sweden and the Netherlands achieved comparatively high income equality during the 1980s. The generous social service policies helped lower infant mortality and improve general health conditions.

Japanese government leaders showed a weaker policy commitment to income equality than did Swedish or Dutch officials. Public expenditures concentrated on expanding economic growth, instead of redistributing income. Social service spending, including public health benefits, remained a small share of the national income. For example, in 1995 public health expenditures as a share of the gross domestic product totaled only 5.7 percent. Individuals depended on their family for financial support when they became old and sick. Nevertheless, compared with U.S. and British leaders, Japanese elites supported a narrower income gap between corporate executives and unskilled workers like a dishwasher.[20]

Workplace and Housing Regulations

Political leaders in Britain, the United States, and Canada enact looser regulations over the workplace and urban residences than in continental Europe, especially Sweden, Germany, and the Netherlands. Influenced by social democratic and Christian democratic principles, continental European government officials show a strong commitment to maintaining their cities as vital centers of civic life. Because city mayors often serve in national legislatures, municipal governments secure influence over the central policy process. European officials support the construction of extensive public housing. By granting housing allowances to residents and disbursing loans to local government agencies, cooperatives, and nonprofit housing associations, central governments promote more equal access to adequate housing for all citizens, thereby improving their health. Supported by Social Democrats and Christian Democrats, unions play an influential role in regulating the workplace environment. Particularly in Germany, the Netherlands, and Sweden, works councils promote health and safety and involve employees in some managerial activities. Government officials, employers, and union activists cooperate to offer integrated health services, with a focus on preventive medicine. Physicians, nurses, physiotherapists, safety engineers, and behavioral scientists coordinate their activities. In Sweden the Social Democratic Party and LO unions promote active worker involvement, which enhances greater trust, efficacy, and job stimulation — occupational attitudes leading to better health. Unions operate health and safety committees. Safety stewards make recommendations to the local government labor inspector and to health committees at each worksite. Comprising a working class majority, these health committees can stop dangerous industrial operations, inspect medical records and work conditions, supervise each enterprise's occupational health service, appoint physicians and sanitary engineers, and veto plans for new machines that injure workers' health. Within a factory, safety stewards can suspend production if they perceive dangers to health. Rather than imposing detailed legal regulations, government officials stress the need for informal cooperation among managers, union heads, and local government safety inspectors. Even though small businesses resist this consensual approach toward workplace democracy and less business-labor cooperation occurs today than twenty years ago, these health and safety committees operating under the works councils have reduced dangers from health hazards, increased sensitivity to safety issues, and made the workplace less vulnerable to accidents.

Britain, the United States, and Canada, however, have made less progress in improving health conditions within the working environment than has Sweden. Weaker, more decentralized unions and stronger opposition from management have impeded the promotion of a healthy, safe workplace. Dependent on the employer's will, health services place less emphasis on preventive medicine. During the 1980s the British Conservative government loosened regulations over the workplace. The Health and Safety Commission as well as factory inspectorates received fewer funds; civil service staff reductions limited their operations. Some regulatory agencies underwent privatization. Policies reduced government grants for union-sponsored health and safety training activities. Anxious to compete internationally for low-wage labor, Tory ministers during the 1990s opposed European Union directives about enforcing health and safety standards at workplaces. Canadian unionists also wield limited control over the working environment. Joint health and safety committees have most effectively reduced injury and illness rates in manufacturing firms where strong unions and management support these committees. In most cases, however, they defer to managers, particularly in small enterprises. Even though authorized by provincial governments, these health agencies need the employer's consent to investigate unsafe working conditions. As in the United States, many occupational fatalities occur in small-scale, nonunionized firms. Young, inexperienced workers suffer the greatest job hazards.

Compared with Canadian leaders, US policymakers have shown greater reluctance to promote healthier workplace situations. Opposed by Republican party activists, business executives, and even some Democrats, regulatory agencies — the Occupational Safety and Health Administration (OSHA), the Food and Drug Administration (FDA), the Food Safety and Inspection Service (FSIS), the Environmental Protection Agency — remain underfunded and understaffed. Ineffective enforcement of regulations thus results. Because only a few OSHA, FDA, and FSIS inspectors regulate private businesses, weak compliance with health standards results. Employers found guilty of violating health regulations incur low fines. Unions represent under one-fifth the labor force. Few US factories have health and safety committees. Managers, rather than workers, dominate these committees, which possess only limited authority to veto injurious work practices and remove defective machinery. When legal suits arise against manufacturers, the courts usually side with the corporations. US workers thus face more severe job hazards on the job than do Swedes, Germans, and Dutch.

American officials have shown only a weak commitment to expanding safe public housing for the poor. Private banks, realtors, and home builders resist regulations to upgrade housing standards, so that low-income residents can avoid the deleterious conditions that result from damp, overcrowded, dilapidated residences. Cities gain weak leverage over decisions made by the federal or state governments. Instead, wealthy suburban residents dominate the national House of Representatives and state legislatures. Urban officials, who need financial resources to upgrade city neighborhoods, rarely receive needed funds from either state or national administrations. The health of low-income urbanites, especially ethnic minorities, hence suffers from violence and residential decay.[21]

Public Policies, Individual Attitudes, and Personal Lifestyles

Policymakers face greater obstacles changing personal attitudes and lifestyles than transforming environmental conditions. In all these industrialized nations, pluralism constrains the power of government officials over individuals and social groups. Public educational campaigns to teach healthier attitudes occur mainly in the mass media, schools, and workplaces. Despite noble intentions to persuade people to assume personal responsibility for their health, educational policies can neither directly control personal attitudes nor change behavior. Government officials lack the authority to monitor doctor-patient interactions, particularly the hope, optimism, and feeling of mastery that a health provider may instill in patients. Media messages wield the greatest impact on university graduates in high-status professions, rather than on less-formally-educated male manual workers with the greater risks of lung cancer and heart disease. Facing fewer small-group reinforcements against smoking, they show the least receptivity to communications about the negative health consequences of smoking and about the need to change lifestyles.[22]

If policymakers want to change personal lifestyles, they must concentrate on altering cultural norms and structural situations as well as on modifying an individual's personal conduct. For example, educational campaigns highlight the dangers of smoking cigarettes and articulate new norms about prestigious role behavior — the role expectation that high-status people will avoid cigarettes. Bans on cigarette advertising and prohibition of smoking in public places represent policy efforts to change structural situations. Higher taxes on cigarettes may lead individuals to reduce the number smoked each day. Nicotine patches may induce a person to cease smoking. Greater information about the health risks of smoking, especially about the dangers of dying from lung cancer and heart disease at an early age, operates as a disincentive to continue deleterious behavior. Nevertheless, the outcomes of these education, regulatory, and fiscal policies often diverge from their intentions. To change personal lifestyles requires not only the opportunities but the will to act. Individuals need information about the most effective ways to stop smoking. Yet those with the highest smoking rates possess the least formal education, which constrains their access to information, their interpretation of it, and strategies for action. Motives to take action also influence the decision to abandon smoking. The value placed on health, the perceived threat from diseases like lung cancer, and the expectation that option A (cease smoking) will secure a more beneficial health outcome than option B (continue smoking) influence personal motives. As we have seen, public policies cannot easily transform motives. Individuals have diverse intentions; prevention of disease represents only one goal, perhaps one with low salience for many persons who smoke. They seek to maintain peer group approval from friends, relatives, and workmates who also smoke. For some teenagers, smoking may seem 'cool', a hot way to affirm an adult identity. Others find that smoking relieves the stress linked to socioeconomic deprivation. Fatalistic attitudes often hinder some individuals from changing their behavior. Structural constraints, especially those in social support networks, impede choices to realize preferences, such as the desire to stop smoking. For all these reasons, policy attempts to reduce such personal lifestyles as smoking achieve only limited success.[23]

Despite all these difficulties, cigarette consumption has declined during the last two decades; public policies deserve some credit. For example, in the United States, Canada, Britain, and Sweden, antismoking campaigns, higher sales taxes on cigarettes, increased regulation of tobacco advertising, and bans on smoking in public places and worksites all led to declining tobacco consumption. As cigarette taxes rose and expenditures on television broadcasts against smoking increased, cigarette sales declined. Compared with restrictions on smoking in public places, higher taxes wielded the greater impact, especially on low-income youths. The Swedes implemented a particularly comprehensive campaign. Material about smoking hazards appeared in pharmacies, schools, and workplaces. City leaders sponsored Quit and Win antismoking contests. County health centers and occupational health services conducted smoking cessation classes. All these programs helped reduce cigarette consumption and thereby the incidence of lung cancer.[24]

Dutch officials have implemented extensive programs to mitigate the effects of drug abuse, especially from cocaine, heroin, and marijuana. Whereas US politicians adopt a more punitive approach, Dutch policymakers stress the need for education, counseling, and consultations with health professionals. Viewing drug use as a medical problem, not a crime, they employ preventive measures and administer methadone treatments. Physicians, nurses, psychiatrists, and social workers provide therapy, counsel addicts, and educate them about the dangers of drugs, including vulnerability from AIDS for those who inject drugs with unclean needles. Both the Ministry of Justice as well as the Ministry of Welfare, Health, and Cultural Affairs administer these drug treatment programs; while the former ministry handles coordination, the latter agency takes responsibility for implementation. In the highly pluralistic Dutch political system, members of *junkiebond*, the junkies' union, voice their policy preferences before the Dutch parliament. Egalitarian pluralism encourages both rich and poor to participate in the drug treatment-prevention programs. Consensual treatment also occurs in drug-free detention centers, where persons addicted to heroin and cocaine spend three to six months. Not only experts and guards but the addicts themselves participate in activities designed to help overcome addiction. Drug addicts work outside the center for a private employer, can take weekend leaves, and have free movement within the center. After release from detention, they receive clinical treatment, employment opportunities, financial assistance, and supervised housing. As a partial result of these comprehensive, nonpunitive policies, the Netherlands, compared with the United States, has experienced a lower incidence of AIDS by drug addicts and a lower rate of violent crimes, such as robberies and homicides.

By contrast, American leaders have placed higher priority on punitive policies toward drug users. Viewing drug consumption as a criminal activity, American government officials impose punitive sanctions as a way to curb demand and achieve total abstinence. Unlike Dutch addicts, most American users, particularly African-American youth, receive costly fines and long prison sentences. The federal Department of Justice and local law enforcement agencies handle the drug problem. Policymakers allocate most funds to police forces and prisons, spending less money on treatment or prevention. Whereas low-income users cannot easily secure public health services that can help them overcome their addiction, wealthier individuals gain treatments through job-based private health insurance plans. Because of these inegalitarian policies, American youths contract AIDS and commit violent crimes at a higher rate for 100 000 people than in the other seven nations, particularly the Netherlands.[25]

Punitive policies have also failed to curb violent lifestyles in the United States. During the early 1990s only Northern Ireland approached the high US murder rate for every 100 000 persons. (See Table 8.1.) From 1984 through 1994 male youths between 15 and 24 committed an increasingly large proportion of homicides, mainly directed against other young men. In Sweden, Germany, the Netherlands, France, Canada, England/Wales, and Japan, the young male homicide rate approximated the rate for all men. In the United States, however, it was twice as high. Young African American men and to a lesser degree Puerto Ricans became most involved in the rising homicide rate, both as perpetrators and as victims. Unlike other national leaders, US government officials imposed more punitive sanctions: longer prison sentences and far greater use of capital punishment. Nevertheless, from 1975 through 1990, the number of executions and the prison population for every 100 000 persons within a state failed to significantly reduce state-level homicide rates. Instead, low poverty and high yearly AFDC payments in a state wielded a stronger impact on curbing murder rates. Similarly, from a cross-national perspective, higher expenditures for social service programs — family allowances, unemployment benefits, work-related injuries — led to lower homicide rates during the 1980s. Stronger solidarity, lower anomie, and greater controls over violent behavior emerged from egalitarian public policies.

A person's motive to commit homicide depends on three types of controls: inner moral restraints, state punishment, and informal pressures from small-group networks. Structural opportunities and constraints not only shape but also reinforce these incentives. Some individuals internalize cultural values that restrain the resort to violence. Learned from family, churches, and books, moral restraints embedded in the conscience inhibit violent crime. The decision to murder also stems from political controls imposed by police, judges, and prison officials. Fear of punishment by government agencies motivates nonviolent behavior. The values articulated by small-group leaders, as well as the rewards and punishments meted out by such social networks as the family, neighborhood, youth gangs, or workmates, shape the expression of aggression. Individuals may either gain acceptance from the group by acting violently in a stressful situation or else lose small-group approval when they commit violent actions. Because individuals directly participate in these social networks, the values, rewards, and sanctions experienced in the small-group setting more effectively restrain potential homicidal behavior than do punitive state policies. Pressured to lower violent crime, public policymakers face a dilemma: the conditions most directly under the control of government officials appear least responsible for homicide. They can more easily add police officers to the force, increase the legal sentences for homicide, and increase the number of yearly executions than they can change cultural values, internal moral restraints, and small-group reinforcements. Yet the values justifying the use of violence originate in the family and other small-group settings, such as neighborhood gangs. Because most individuals learn risk-prone violent attitudes in small group networks, public policies in democratic societies can wield only limited impact on reshaping the reinforcements and cultural values reinforcing aggressive lifestyles.

Compared with the United States, in Japan and Sweden more lenient public policies, higher income equality, and greater social integration have minimized youthful violence. Rather than imposing punitive policies, Swedish and Japanese leaders rely on social integration as a major way to strengthen peaceful behavior. Small-group controls restrain citizens from using violence as a way to alleviate stress, handle conflicts, and attain goals. Especially in Japan, the individual functions within a tight group network. Family associations, neighborhood clubs, crime prevention associations, and vocational unions establish informal social pressures that restrain aggressive behavior, especially by young men under 25. Like the Japanese, the Swedes belong to various groups, including labor unions, political parties, sports federations, study circles, civic associations, and cooperatives of producers and consumers. Providing solidarity, these group networks also reinforce the norms of law-abiding behavior. Cultural values uphold the need to cooperate with social group members, respect the legitimacy of existing government institutions, show self-discipline, and abide by the law. Governmental regulations restrict access to guns. Few Japanese or Swedish murder victims die from gunshot wounds. Unlike the US situation, neither the possession nor use of firearms symbolizes independence, adult status, and the assertion of authority against established institutions. From 1960 through 1991, the high income equality and low unemployment rates, including those for young men under 25, provided legitimate opportunities to earn money and gain the status that comes from employment. Hence, few Swedes or Japanese male youth felt the need to engage in violent criminal activity as a way to gain higher social mobility. Influenced by greater economic opportunities, stronger community solidarity, and more stringent small-group networks to act nonviolently, Swedes and Japanese had a far lower homicide rate than did US citizens.[26]

Access to Public Health Care
Services for Mothers and Infants

The same public policies and socioeconomic conditions explaining the low murder rate in Sweden and Japan also account for the low infant mortality rates. In these two economically egalitarian societies, mothers make use of the egalitarian, comprehensive prenatal and postnatal health services sponsored by government agencies. Among the five West European nations, Sweden attains the lowest infant death rate. Swedish political leaders implement generous cash benefits. In-kind services provide comprehensive, accessible, inexpensive, and universal benefits. Nearly all mothers receive extensive prenatal care at maternity health centers and child health centers. For the first two years after a baby's birth, over 97 percent of all mothers visit a child health clinic, where pediatric nurses and pediatricians administer physical examinations, diagnostic tests, immunizations, counseling, and screenings for possible diseases. Public health nurses conduct home visits. Public schools and health agencies supply extensive information about family planning, sex education, and the use of contraceptives, so that only 3 percent of all pregnancies occur to teenagers. Around 85 percent of children are born to women between 20 and 35 years old, the period with the fewest low birthweight (under 1500 grams) babies, premature deliveries (under 33 weeks), and infant deaths. Generous cash benefits — long paid maternal leaves, maternal disability payments, child allowances, paid leaves for sick children — and day care services enable poor women to continue working outside the home but still provide for their young children. Because Sweden provides universal health care to all mothers, whatever their country of origin, infant mortality rates show few ethnic differences.

By contrast, the British government provided less generous cash benefits and in-kind services for mothers and their children. Particularly during Conservative party rule (1979–1997), the administration reduced the public provision of social services: day care, home assistance, district nursing. Stressing individual, collective responsibility for health care, Tory policymakers urged women to change their personal lifestyles through diet, exercise, and cessation of smoking. Means-tested benefits for low-income women became more common; yet the reduced allowances for children hardly provided enough money to meet health care needs, especially those of single mothers. By the late 1980s nearly three times as many British children lived in poverty (under one-half the median income) as in Sweden. Just as unemployment rates and income inequality grew during the 1980s, so did the proportion of British children living in poverty. Compared with Swedish leaders, British officials funded fewer child health centers. During the first year of life, fewer British children than Swedes visited a physician or a public health nurse. As hospital services became more centralized under NHS reorganization into trusts, low-income women faced greater economic difficulties traveling to a hospital. Stingy, short maternity leaves left the working poor with only minimal resources to care for their babies. Along with high joblessness, increased income inequality, and greater child poverty, the scarcity of specialized child health services endangered low income British children, who suffered higher infant mortality rates during their first year than did Swedish or Japanese babies. Unlike Sweden, in the United Kingdom ethnicity wielded a greater impact on infant mortality. South Asians, especially Bangladeshis, suffered the most from poverty and high infant death rates.

Among the three Pacific Rim countries, the United States has the highest infant mortality rate, while the more comprehensive, universal, egalitarian health systems of Canada and Japan implement policies producing fewer infant deaths for every 1000 live births. From 1969 to 1971 Canadian provincial governments introduced a national health insurance program for physician care. This program provided more egalitarian, extensive, accessible prenatal than postnatal services, which depend to a greater extent on family income. As a result, the overall infant mortality rate declined, even though unmarried, low-income mothers aged 15 through 19 still suffered more infant deaths than did wealthier, better educated urban professional women. Provincial government health departments sponsor programs for family planning, prenatal care, and nutrition. In local communities public health nurses offer maternal care at child health centers, hospitals, clinics, schools, and homes. Most provincial legislatures require employers to grant mothers a maternity leave both before and after a child's birth. During the 1990s, however, as the fiscal deficit grew and cost containment measures became widespread, the federal government allocated fewer funds to the provincial governments for health care and income support assistance. The policy influence of the New Democratic Party declined not only at the federal level but also within the provinces. At all government levels, both Conservative and Liberal policymakers reduced cash benefits for social services. As in the United States, stringent means-tested programs, including ones for child allowances, harmed low-income women. Maternal leaves covered only one-half a working woman's salary — a far less generous payment than in Sweden, France, Germany, and especially the Netherlands. As a partial result, child poverty increased, even though it still remained below US levels. These policy developments threatened the comprehensive, egalitarian, universal health policies that had helped produce relatively low infant mortality.

Because the United States governments administer partial, inaccessible, expensive, and inegalitarian health programs, infant mortality rates have shown wider social group differences than in Europe, Canada, or Japan. Extensive child poverty meant that a mother's income influenced the likelihood that her baby will die during the first year. Wealthy European American parents secured private health insurance for their children, who showed the best health. Education, income, and ethnicity shaped reliance on prenatal services. As eligibility for Medicaid benefits expanded from 1984 through 1990, poor mothers made greater use of prenatal care during the first three months of their pregnancy. Their infant mortality rates declined. Yet many state governments refused to allocate sufficient Medicaid finances for prenatal care. States spending the lowest expenditures on Medicaid for every poor child faced the highest infant mortality rates. Lacking health insurance, many poor women, especially African Americans and Native Americans, secured prenatal services only during the third trimester of their pregnancy. As a result of malnutrition and inaccessible care, low birthweight babies and premature deliveries resulted; many died at birth or during the first year. Government policies that restricted access to contraceptives led to a higher proportion of teenage pregnancies than in Western Europe or Japan. Niggardly child allowances brought few economic benefits to poor women, especially single teenage mothers. When state legislatures limited finances, low-income women endured the greatest health costs. They rarely secured home visits by public health nurses. Only around 70 to 80 percent of all one-year-old children obtained vaccinations against diphtheria, polio, and measles, compared with rates of over 90 percent in Sweden and the Netherlands. Combined with growing income inequality and child poverty, US public policies thus widened the infant mortality gap among mothers with polarized incomes.

Living in a more homogeneous, egalitarian society with comprehensive health programs, Japanese women experience low infant mortality rates. Comprehensive prenatal and postnatal care takes place at public health centers, hospitals, clinics, and schools. These agencies as well as public health nurses visiting the home administer vaccinations, checkups, and screenings for possible diseases. Expectant mothers consult a doctor around 14 times — a higher number than in the United States. Compared with American female employees, Japanese women secure longer paid maternal leaves from their work. Yet even if they benefit from comprehensive health services, they enjoy fewer economic or political rights vis-à-vis female Americans. Japanese women gain prestige as mothers. Few work for money between 25 and 35 years old, the period when 90 percent of births occur. Nearly all babies begin their lives in two-parent families. High income equality, low unemployment, limited child poverty, and extensive social integration, along with the comprehensive maternal and child care programs, all contribute to Japan's impressive infant health record.[27]

CONCLUSION

As we have seen in this cross-national examination of eight industrialized nations, complex interactions shape the impact of social stratification and public policies on health outcomes. Historical contingencies, socioeconomic conditions, political power relationships, policymakers' priorities, and individual characteristics influence the health of nations, social groups, and specific persons. Which hypotheses about health retain the greatest validity? First, people ranking low in political power, income, and status generally experience the most severe illness. They show the highest infant mortality rates, the greatest morbidity, the worst self-assessed health, and the shortest life expectancy. Yet women represent an exception to this trend. On all indicators except self-reported well-being, women seem healthier than men. Despite recent female gains in government representation, employment opportunities, and prestige, women still hold lower positions in the social stratification system. Fewer workplace hazards, healthier lifestyles, and greater use of medical services may partly explain women's better health. The relationship between ethnicity and health also reveals a few anomalies. Despite their working-class backgrounds, individuals born in the Caribbean but now living in England experience relatively low mortality rates, especially from heart disease. The healthiest ethnic groups in Canada comprise non-European immigrants. Highly educated but with lower incomes, they suffer fewer disabilities and live longer than does the Canadian-born population. The ethnic gap in infant mortality that separates African Americans from European Americans looms larger among wealthy mothers than among poor women.

Second, income inequalities within a nation account for at least some health differences that separate rich from poor. Particularly in the United States, which has more economic inequality than the other seven countries, low-income, less-formally-educated groups have the worst health. When income inequality rose in Britain and the US during the 1980s, the health gap between different income groups also increased. From 1983 through 1993 as educational equality declined in the Netherlands, the perceived health status among those with only an elementary education deteriorated vis-à-vis university graduates.

Third, nations with less comprehensive public health systems, especially the United States, reveal the greatest divergence in health achieved by high and low SES persons. Comprehensive programs in the other seven countries provide universal, accessible, and egalitarian care. Yet social stratification also affects their health status. Equality of access to health care and use of these programs appears more widespread than equality of health. Despite the implementation of the British National Health Service after World War II, British occupational inequalities in health status have widened since the early 1930s. A similar trend has emerged in the United States, where access to public health care services expanded after World War II.

Attempts to validate these hypotheses and formulate plausible causal explanations pose several difficulties. A correlation between certain public policies and health outcomes does not necessarily imply a causal relationship. Weak correlations plague health research. Some problems stem from methodological issues. How can we devise similar operational indicators that will accurately measure such ambiguous concepts as 'class', 'ethnicity', 'equality', and 'health' across several nations? These concepts all have divergent operational definitions not only in the same society but across different countries. Group members assign different interpretations to their occupational, ethnic, and gender identities, which are socially constructed and thus change over time. Not all individuals within the same group share similar attitudes or behaviors. As these pluralist, industrialized societies become more ethnically heterogeneous, a larger proportion of individuals shares a mixed ethnic heritage. Throughout their lives, people change their occupations or hold two jobs with divergent prestige. Hence, social scientists cannot easily link group membership to health, mainly because so many complex variables — individual attitudes, personal values, lifestyles, workplace conditions, residential environment, education, use of health services, public health policies — confound the interaction between social stratification and health.

Rather than the cause (social stratification, public policies) preceding the effect (health status), often these variables show a reciprocal, symmetrical relationship. Even if unemployment worsens health, the resulting illness may impede the prospects of finding a new job. Sickness and marginal social stratification thus simultaneously reinforce each other. The time sequences between attitudes and behavior also remain murky. Do optimistic attitudes cause healthy behavior? Or do healthy personal lifestyles lead to efficacious attitudes? Public policies reflect a group's position in the social stratification system; that is, wealthier, better educated, higher status groups wield the greatest political power to translate their preferences into public health programs. Yet particularly in such nations as Sweden and the Netherlands, public policymakers can partially transform the social stratification system toward more egalitarian opportunities.

Furthermore, spurious relationships mar attempts to ascertain the causal linkages among stratification, policies, and health. We cannot easily discover the antecedent variables linked to both a cause like ethnic lifestyles and some health outcome such as infant mortality. To what extent does socioeconomic status — formal education, income, occupation, unemployment, workplace environment, housing conditions — explain this interaction, as distinct from public policies that reinforce exclusionary practices against ethnic group members? Which specific socioeconomic variables exert the greatest impact? How do they relate to public policies and to personal behaviors, such as cigarette consumption, alcohol use, physical exercise, and choosing a low-fat diet of fresh fruits, vegetables, fish, and whole wheat bread? The impact of public policies on health remains ambiguous because of the gap between policy formulation and implementation. Political leaders often formulate vague policies that government officials implement at a regional or municipal level. Policy reversals and delays occur as the power and preferences of key political actors change. Because most health officials in these eight pluralist democracies make incremental changes, analysts cannot easily ascertain the long-term effect of a particular decision. Rather than rely on cross-sectional designs, we need more longitudinal studies among different countries to clarify how several antecedent variables affect personal and group health.

Finally, even though the general theory of social opportunities highlights the significance of several interacting variables that shape health, researchers have yet to ascertain their precise weight or importance. Structural conditions — socioeconomic opportunities and constraints — probably wield a greater effect than do genetic predispositions or personal lifestyles, which reveal no consistent relationship among groups or across time. Yet along with individual attitudes, such personal characteristics do at least partly shape one's health. The social scientist must disentangle their exact significance and also explain the importance of public policies. Exactly how do policies influence not only the environment but also personal attitudes and behavior? Which specific programs are most effective in lowering infant mortality, raising life expectancy, and preventing disease? Cross-national, time-series investigations have found that only by shaping environmental conditions and personal behavior can public policies improve general national health.[28] As Albert Camus reminded us, although political leaders have scarcely achieved final victory over disease, they have enacted incremental policy reforms that expanded opportunities for healthier lives.

9 Evaluating Public Health Policies

The motion picture *Casablanca* takes place at Rick's Café Americain, a chic nightclub adjacent to the airport in the Moroccan city. It is December 1941, just before full-scale warfare erupted between the Allied and Axis powers. Rick Blaine, the American owner of the cafe, gazes at the airport's beacon light. Captain Louis Renault, a French police prefect appointed by the Vichy regime, sits at a table on the cafe terrace. He asks Rick: 'And what in heaven's name brought you to Casablanca?' Rick replies: 'My health. I came to Casablanca for the waters.' Because the Saharan Desert occupies the southern part of Morocco, Renault wonders: 'Waters? What waters? We're in the desert.' Rick counters: 'I was misinformed.'[1]

Before analysts can fairly evaluate public policies, they need accurate descriptive information. Without accurate information about specific outcomes and their assumed policy causes, the credibility of explanations remains obscure. Evaluation rests on plausible explanations that specify the relationships among organizational power, cultural beliefs, and personal attitudes and behaviors. For example, if we fail to explain the linkages between health care programs and low infant mortality, we cannot claim that the health policies implemented in Sweden more effectively reduced the infant death rate than did those in Britain. Hence, explanation and evaluation both depend on accurate information.

Policy evaluation involves three steps. First, the social scientist specifies the criteria used to judge a policy process — standards such as equality, effectiveness in improving health, and satisfaction with health policies. Second, the evaluator devises empirical indicators to measure these general criteria. Third, the analyst matches empirical observations to the criteria of worth, thereby rank-ordering different political systems on their policy performance. Assume that we evaluate the eight nations on their equality of access to policy benefits. If we secure empirical evidence on the degree to which every individual gains similar access to health care services, we can rank countries on an equality scale and try to ascertain the comparative performance of different systems.

Several problems face the policy analyst who evaluates health care performance. The objectives and structures of public health programs reflect a complex pattern. Policymakers often seek different objectives that may come into conflict. Systems that uphold egalitarian access may cause overloaded health providers to neglect patients with the greatest need for treatment. Furthermore, among these pluralist societies, several organizations participate in the formulation and especially the implementation of health policies. The central government frames general goals, raises revenues, allocates expenditures, and specifies guidelines for health treatments. Usually it delegates authority to decentralized government agencies — Swedish counties, US states, Canadian provinces, German Länder, Japanese prefectures, Dutch cities, French regions, and British health authorities. In Germany, the Netherlands, Japan, and France, semipublic insurance funds review claims and pay benefits. US private health insurance corporations help administer government programs such as Medicare. Particularly in Canada, the United States, Germany, and the Netherlands, church-administered hospitals receive public funds. Throughout these pluralist societies, physicians and other health providers exert extensive professional autonomy. Private medical associations play an active role in the health policy process. Various personnel — doctors, nurses, insurance agents, government leaders at different levels — assume responsibility for preventive and curative medicine. Because of this dispersed power situation, the evaluator cannot easily pinpoint accountability for a health policy outcome such as effectiveness in improving people's health.

When making health policies, all participants face uncertainties about the linkages between policy inputs and health outcomes. To what degree will a decentralized administration, increased public health expenditures, and expanded scope of health care services upgrade national or group health? Factors other than public policies that shape health include environmental conditions — housing, the workplace situation, income equality, unemployment levels — and personal behavior, such as diet, exercise, hygiene, and use of health services. Particularly in these pluralist systems, policymakers can hardly control all the environmental conditions or individual behaviors that produce a healthier population.

Even though policy evaluation rests on an empirical base, it also involves a subjective dimension that arouses contention among different investigators. Not all analysts agree on the specific values that should constitute the evaluative standards. Should equality take priority over efficiency? Even if researchers agree on the same criteria for evaluation, disagreements often emerge about the most reliable, valid procedures for measuring general values. For instance, effectiveness in improving health may refer to widely used operational indicators like infant mortality rates and years of life expectancy. If during a 30-year time span Japan experiences greater reductions in infant mortality and higher gains in life expectancy than does Britain, we assume that Japan has shown more effectiveness in improving popular health. These indicators, however, reflect death rates, not necessarily the quality of life. People may survive for a long time but be sick during half that period. Yet cross-national information about morbidity, particularly about quality of life, remains difficult to obtain and interpret. Given all these evaluative problems, health researchers must clearly define their standards of worth and specify the precise operational indicators used to measure the standards.[2]

This concluding chapter focuses on three evaluative questions. First, which systems have most effectively improved people's health, realized egalitarian ideals, and attained the greatest public satisfaction with health care policies? Why do some systems — entrepreneurial, organic corporatist, social democratic — rank higher on some values than on others? Second, what specific policies have most fully achieved priorities such as equality, effectiveness, and satifaction? What impact do administrative, fiscal, and benefits programs exert on these values? Third, social stratification not only shapes public health policies but also is affected by them. Which social groups have gained the most benefits and incurred the greatest losses from health policies? This issue focuses on the equality dimension of policy performance.

EQUALITY

Equality of health services pertains to several components. At the least stringent level, it means access or availability. All individuals, regardless of their income, occupational status, ethnicity, gender, age, and religious affiliation, have the same access to health providers: physicians, dentists, hospitals, and other medical facilities. Inclusive access also means that health providers are geographically available, so that those needing health care incur no high transportation costs. A second dimension involves equal use of health services vis-à-vis individual need. People with the same illnesses, disabilities, and chronic limitations make the same number of visits to a physician's office, health clinic, or hospital. Third, equality denotes similar health treatments. Individuals with the same health problems receive high-quality treatments, as measured by physicians' competence, adequacy of hospital facilities (medical equipment, supplies), and availability of effective medicines. Interpersonal relations between health providers and citizens reveal mutual respect. Fourth, equality of health implies that all persons, whatever their socioeconomic status, experience similar physical, emotional, and mental well-being.[3]

Public policymakers can more easily promote equal access to health care services than they can ensure equality of health. Nearly everyone in the eight nations except the United States can gain access to publicly-financed health facilities. Rural inhabitants find health benefits less immediately available than do urban and particularly suburban residents. Nevertheless, low-income ill persons can usually secure health care at a hospital emergency department if not always at a specialist's office. The United States' health system provides the least equal access. At a single point during the year, nearly 17 percent of Americans lack health insurance coverage. Over a two-year period, as many as 30 percent under 65 years go uninsured. Young people (18 to 24), Mexican Americans, African Americans, low-income individuals, those with less than a high school education, and employees in agriculture, personal services, retail trade, and construction comprise the major groups lacking employer-based health insurance. From the early 1980s through the late 1990s, this uninsured population increased. As the economy shifted from manufacturing toward service sector dominance, real wages declined. Workers could secure fewer full-time jobs. Unions enrolled a lower share of the labor force. Facing rising health care costs, employers either imposed higher premiums or stopped offering private health insurance. Public health benefits failed to compensate for the loss of private insurance coverage. The more unequal access to health benefits meant that low-income sick individuals delayed seeking medical treatment. When finally admitted to a hospital, they faced a higher probability of dying than did those with private insurance.

Even though in all eight nations the elderly (over 65 years old), people with long-term illnesses, and women most frequently use medical facilities, low-income persons hardly receive equal treatment. Manual workers, renters, and the unemployed have more consultations with general practitioners and stay in hospitals for longer periods than do the wealthy because poor people are sicker. Yet better educated, wealthier patients secure greater access to specialists. Even in egalitarian Sweden, wealthy urbanites can visit a private health clinic, where they receive more immediate, specialized care unavailable to low-income rural Swedes.

Despite the increased equality of health care access and use, if not treatment, since the Second World War, the health of national populations has scarcely shown such an egalitarian advance. As we have seen, people's health depends on more variables than public policies toward equality. Environmental conditions as well as individual characteristics shape one's health. These circumstances usually remain beyond policymakers' control, even in systems like Sweden and the Netherlands that have the greater income equality and more equal health among social groups than do France, Germany, or the United States. Today as before World War II, persons with the highest formal education, income, and occupational prestige still enjoy the best health.

Success in realizing health equality partly depends on the way that policy officials choose to allocate health care services. Leaders governing entrepreneurial systems base this allocation on individuals' financial ability to pay for private health insurance. Organic corporatists implement different nonprofit insurance plans for diverse occupations. Social Democrats view health care as a universal right that all citizens should enjoy. From this cultural perspective, entrepreneurial systems, particularly the United States, implement the least egalitarian programs. Health care benefits for those under 65 largely depend on individual income, specifically on the financial resources to purchase private health insurance coverage. The organic corporatist systems, particularly Germany, France, and Japan, link health benefits to occupational status, with wealthier groups gaining greater services. Yet German officials have recently enabled working-class employees to secure the same benefits formally enjoyed by higher-status people. With its highly pluralist system, the Netherlands promotes the most egalitarian policies among the organic corporatist systems. Egalitarian social movements press for equal services for all Dutch. As the system that most fully embodies social democratic values, Sweden demonstrates the strongest commitment to equal access, use, and treatment. Regarding health care as a universal right, Swedish leaders implement egalitarian programs that ensure a generous scope of benefits. Comprehensive policies available to all citizens, rather than means-tested programs popular in the United States, ensure high-quality, egalitarian care, even if cost-containment measures have limited the generosity of some benefits like sickness disability payments.[4] As a partial result of these comprehensive policies, the Swedes have attained excellent health compared with people in all the other nations except Japan.

EFFECTIVENESS

How effectively do health care policies reduce infant mortality and raise life expectancy? Because these two health indicators reflect not only governmental actions but also environmental conditions and individual circumstances, analysts cannot easily ascertain the precise impact of specific policies. Generally, however, a nation's scope of benefits wields a more positive effect than do administrative or fiscal programs. As shown in Tables 9.1 and 9.2, the health differences within each system appear as great as the variations among systems. Consider the two social democratic systems, Sweden and Britain. From 1960 through 1995 Sweden ranked either first or second in both infant mortality rates and male life expectancy at birth. These favorable rates remained constant over the 35-year period. Indeed, as early as 1900, before the government instituted comprehensive health care policies, Swedes enjoyed the world's longest life expectancy and lowest infant mortality rates. By contrast, over the last 35 years, even back to the early twentieth century, Britain's record has deteriorated. Tory market-based health programs, high unemployment, and rising income inequality impeded progress toward a healthier population.

Table 9.1   Infant mortality, 1960–1995

Infant Mortality Rates
(Deaths under One Year per 1000 Live Births)

Country	1960	1970	1980	1990	1995
Canada	27.3	18.8	10.4	6.8	6.0
France	27.4	18.2	10.1	7.2	4.9
Germany	33.8	23.4	12.7	7.1	5.3
Japan	30.7	13.1	7.5	4.6	4.3
Netherlands	17.9	12.7	8.6	7.1	5.5
Sweden	16.6	11.0	6.9	6.0	4.0
United Kingdom	22.5	18.5	12.1	7.9	6.0
United States	26.0	20.0	12.6	9.1	7.6

Sources: Organisation for Economic Cooperation and Development, *OECD Health Systems: Facts and Trends 1960–1991*, vol. 1 (Paris: OECD, 1993), 69; 'OECD in Figures 1997 Edition,' *OECD Observer*, no. 206 (June/July 1997): 50–51; 'Report of Final Mortality Statistics, 1995,' *Monthly Vital Statistics Report* 45 (12 June 1997): 66; Office for Official Publications of the European Communities, *Eurostat Yearbook '96*, 2d ed. (Brussels: ECSC-EC-EAEC, 1996), 32; Gerard F. Anderson, 'In Search of Value: An International Comparison of Cost, Access, and Outcomes,' *Health Affairs* 16 (November/December 1977): 170.

   Among the four organic corporatist systems, Japan has shown the most dramatic health improvements since World War II. Whereas in 1960 Japanese suffered from the second highest infant morality rates and had the shortest life expectancy, by 1995 few Japanese babies died before the first year. Life expectancy for men and women placed them at the top. Unlike Japan, the other major Axis power Germany did not fare so well after the war. German life expectancies remained comparatively short from 1960 through 1995. During the 1990s, however, infant mortality ratings did improve vis-à-vis France and Canada. The French scored the greatest advancements in women's life expectancy. By 1994 they ranked second just below the Japanese. Throughout the 35-year period, the Dutch infant death rate stayed relatively low; yet their initially favorable life expectancy records declined during the 1990s.

Table 9.2   Life expectancy, 1960–1995

Life Expectancy at Birth (Years)

Country	1960 Women	1960 Men	1970 Women	1970 Men	1980 Women	1980 Men	1990 Women	1990 Men	1995 Women	1995 Men
Canada	73.0	68.0	76.2	69.3	78.9	71.4	80.4	73.8	81.3	75.3
France	73.6	67.0	76.1	68.6	78.4	70.2	80.9	72.7	81.9	73.9
Germany	72.4	66.9	73.8	67.4	76.6	69.9	79.2	72.7	79.5	73.0
Japan	70.2	65.5	74.7	69.3	78.8	73.4	81.9	75.9	82.8	76.4
Netherlands	75.5	71.6	76.6	70.9	79.2	72.4	80.1	73.8	80.4	74.6
Sweden	74.9	71.2	77.1	72.2	78.8	72.8	80.4	74.8	81.5	76.2
United Kingdom	74.2	68.3	75.2	68.6	75.9	70.2	78.5	73.0	79.7	74.3
United States	73.1	66.6	74.7	67.1	77.4	70.0	78.8	72.0	79.2	72.5

Sources: Organisation for Economic Cooperation and Development, *OECD Health Systems: Facts and Trends 1960-1991*, vol. 1 (Paris: OECD, 1993), 54–5; 'OECD in Figures 1997 Edition,' *OECD Observer*, no. 206 (June/July 1997): 50–1; World Health Organization, *Annual Epidemiological and Vital Statistics, 1960* (Geneva: WHO, 1963), 25–8; *World Health Statistics Annual* (Geneva: WHO, 1970, 1982, 1983, 1984, 1991, 1992, 1993, 1994, 1995).

Since 1960 Canada has consistently experienced lower infant mortality and higher life expectancy than the United States, which has pursued more entrepreneurial health policies. Canadian comprehensive, universal, generous, and egalitarian policies partly explain this difference. Whereas Americans under 65 lack comprehensive public health programs, older citizens secure Medicare and Social Security benefits that upgrade their health. Even though in 1990 the United States recorded the lowest life expectancy at birth and the highest infant mortality rate, at age 80 Americans could expect to live more years than any senior citizens among the other seven nations except Canada. American survivors thus showed the resilience to surmount the market-based pressures of competitive individualism — pressures that have hindered the establishment of comprehensive health programs for all citizens.[5]

SATISFACTION

Popular satisfaction with public health policies depends on the congruence between citizens' expectations about systemic performance and their perceived treatment by those responsible for implementing these programs. If citizens expect equal access, efficiency, freedom of choice, and effectiveness in securing improved health, then high satisfaction will result if health providers, insurance agents, and government officials actually meet these expectations. Greater dissatisfaction emerges when the gap widens between expectations and perceived performance. Particularly if individuals hold egalitarian values but view the health system as operating in an elitist way, dissatisfaction will mount. Individualists valuing free choice become dissatisfied when public policies deny them the right to choose a physician and hospital or impose rigid bureaucratic rules that raise personal expenses. Although fatalists take a distrustful view of all institutions, their low personal efficacy leads to resignation, if not acceptance, of institutional operations. Elderly, religious people show the greatest satisfaction because of their deferential attitude toward established authority. Throughout the eight nations, citizens voice greater enthusiasm for their personal physicians than for hospital treatments or particularly the performance of the national health system.[6]

Evaluations of national health policies stem from attitudes toward administration, fiscal burdens, and scope of benefits. If people perceive that the administrators treat them in a cold impersonal way, impose rigid rules, and hinder prompt treatments, dissatisfaction rises. Discontent also increases when policymakers reduce health care benefits but enact higher taxes, insurance premiums, and user fees. Viewing health care as a salient issue, low-income egalitarian voters for leftwing parties oppose measures that limit access to health services, particularly when rightwing parties control the government. Wealthier individualists supporting private health provision resent high taxes, limits on personal choices, and bureaucratic government regulations. Assuming deferential attitudes toward established authority, older religious persons who support Conservative or Christian Democratic parties usually express the greatest satisfaction with existing health policies. They still vote for a conservative government party, regardless of their attitudes toward health care policies or their experience of reduced personal benefits. For these hierarchs, such issues as crime and defense represent a more important reason for their vote.

During the last 20 years, organic corporatist leaders have generated the greatest support for their public health programs. Even if Japanese citizens resent high medical expenditures and long waits to see a clinic physician or to secure care at a teaching hospital, they respect the medical community. Their deferential attitudes minimize overt opposition against physicians who prescribe and sell an extensive amount of drugs. Compared with Japanese, Germans adopt more egalitarian, individualist worldviews. Yet particularly the older citizens defer to authority, appreciate generous health benefits like spa treatments, and support federal government health agencies. Among all German institutions, only the universities, schools, and armed forces elicit greater trust than does the health system. Like the Germans, the French remain fairly satisfied with existing health programs, opposing government plans to curtail services and raise fees. Of the four organic corporatist regimes, the Netherlands implements the most popular policies. Its pluralist system that blends generous public benefits with administration by both government and private agencies appeals to Dutch holding egalitarian, individualist, and hierarchical values. Compared with the Germans and French, the Dutch offer more favorable evaluations of their health system, complain the least about lengthy waits to see a physician, and voice the strongest support for the legal right to free public health care.

In the two entrepreneurial systems Canada and the United States, dissatisfaction with national health policies has recently grown. Despite their value differences, both Canadians and Americans favor expanded government benefits for such social services as pensions, education, and health care. Americans reject proposals to curtail Social Security payments and Medicare services; Medicaid programs attract less enthusiasm. Whatever their value orientations, nearly all Americans worry about the high costs of medical care, especially about rising private insurance premiums and out-of-pocket payments for nursing home care. Most prefer larger government expenditures that would finance a greater share of personal expenses. Egalitarians — mainly Democrats, self-styled 'liberals,' and low-income persons — seek fundamental transformations in the health system, particularly policies that would expand access to health services. They blame high costs on profits secured by private health insurance corporations. By contrast, individualists, Republicans, self-defined 'conservatives,' and business executives prefer incremental reforms: lower taxes, expanded personal choice, greater portability of benefits from one job to another, and less government regulation. For them, governmental waste, fraud, and abuse represent the major sources behind rising health costs.

Compared with the US citizenry, Canadians have more favorably evaluated their national health care system. During the late 1980s they voiced greater satisfaction than people from the other seven nations; Americans perceived the need for the most transformative changes. After 1992, however, North Americans' attitudes began to converge, even though Canadians still retained their more positive outlook. Canadian federal government reductions in health expenditures to the provinces aroused antagonism. Popular support behind the health system eroded as provincial health ministries limited benefits. Particularly in the poorer Atlantic provinces, Canadians resented lower access to their family physician, nursing shortages in hospitals, and longer waits for hospital surgery and for admission to emergency departments. From 1988 to 1994 the proportion of Canadians favoring minor changes in their health system fell by one-half. Supporters of major changes nearly doubled. Along with highly-educated managers and professionals, Progressive-Conservatives and Reform Party voters most strongly favored a two-tiered system that would finance basic health services with government revenues but would require private funds for additional services. Holding more egalitarian values, Liberals and especially the New Democrats expressed greater opposition to this proposal for partial privatization.

Among the two social democratic systems, Britain has faced more dissatisfaction with its public health system than has Sweden. Most British, particularly low-income persons and Labour voters, reject Conservative government measures that have privatized some features of the National Health Service, closed hospitals, introduced market-based competition, and limited public benefits, including those for elder care. Opposition to these policies stems from the incongruence between the egalitarian social democratic values linked to the NHS and the neoliberal entrepreneurial values upheld by Tory leaders. By contrast, the values between Swedish policymakers and citizens show greater agreement. Both give priority to egalitarian and individualist values. Supporting universal, public health programs that ensure equal access, Swedes also favor greater choice of physicians and hospitals. Whereas citizens over 60 want the freedom to choose their physicians, younger, well-educated urban citizens place more importance on egalitarian values, especially the right to participate with doctors in making decisions about medical treatments. Responding to these public preferences, Swedish policymakers enacted reforms that blended expanded personal choices with egalitarian public financing and opportunities for influencing health care decisions. Responsive policy performance thus led Swedes to maintain greater satisfaction with their national health programs than the British have shown toward the NHS.[7]

CONCLUSION

This evaluation of health policy performance has highlighted three general themes. First, despite the trend toward policy convergence among the eight industrialized societies, they still reveal important differences. Developments in the world capitalist economy have placed cost containment at the top of the policy agenda. Low growth rates, high unemployment, large fiscal deficits, expanded international competition, and the rising influence of multinational corporations and regional organizations all impose fiscal constraints on national health policymakers. They have less autonomy than before to implement generous, comprehensive, universal, egalitarian health care benefits. As benefits decline, taxes, user fees, and insurance premiums increase. Everywhere the public becomes more discontent with these trends. Yet, political leaders in diverse countries formulate different strategies for coping with the same fiscal problems. Although privatization measures arouse some enthusiasm, only in the United States do private forprofit insurance corporations wield such extensive policy influence. Elsewhere, government health officials and nonprofit groups — health insurance funds, hospitals, churches — negotiate needed policy changes. Particularly on the European continent and in Japan, organic corporatist and social democratic values influence policy participants to regard health care provision as a public service, not only a business enterprise. American officials who administer the US entrepreneurial system place the highest priority on managing health institutions as efficient private corporations. This neoliberal trend also has influenced Canadian and especially Conservative British policymakers; yet they retain a stronger commitment to competition among public and private nonprofit organizations, instead of only commercial enterprises.

Second, all policy officials face limits realizing a healthier population. Public health programs chosen for implementation reflect the interaction between leaders' subjective will and objective conditions — constraints and opportunities — less subject to policy control. Objective conditions include a nation's historical context, its position in the world capitalist economy, cultural values transmitted from past generations, and the politicoeconomic power of labor unions, private businesses, and health providers' associations. In pluralist democracies no government can easily control family and peer group networks that affect an individual's health. Even after policy implementation, outcomes may diverge from formulators' original intentions. Effective goal attainment depends on clear policy preferences, consensual policy priorities, a strong motivation to realize these priorities, and the organizational opportunities to reach policy objectives. Because many diverse groups participate in the health policy process, goals often remain ambiguous. Leaders cannot agree on priorities. Complex variables intervene between an implemented policy and an outcome like individual or group health improvements. Hence, analysts face problems trying to ascertain the precise causal links between a policy and its intended effects.

Comparative assessments indicate that no nation secures a highly favorable ranking on all evaluative criteria. With its cohesive political system usually run by the Social Democratic Party, Sweden probably enacted the most effective, egalitarian programs. Strong labor unions, cooperatives, workers' education associations, schools, and health associations helped the Social Democrats implement policies, educate the populace about preventive health measures, and secure fairly equal health among all social groups. Along with the Japanese, Swedes hence attained low infant mortality and high life expectancy rates. Yet Swedish physicians maintained less economic freedom than their medical colleagues in Germany, Japan, and Canada. The Canadian health system seems fairly efficient; as in other countries, however, measures to curtail costs limited egalitarian access to health facilities and reduced the freedom of low-income individuals, especially rural residents, to gain needed care. Committed to internal market reforms, British Tory elites sought more efficient management of the National Health Service. Despite this policy priority, the recruitment of more senior managers to the NHS Executive raised administrative costs and limited the freedom of hospital consultants. Increased competition among hospital trusts scarcely raised their productivity. Public dissatisfaction with the NHS rose. Prizing freedom and entrepreneurial innovation, American leaders supported managed competition, particularly health maintenance organizations, as the most effective means to maximize efficiency. Yet corporate mergers and managerial dominance by private commercial health insurance managers reduced the freedom formerly enjoyed by physicians and their patients. Since 1995 popular dissatisfaction with managed care has grown, especially about such problems as decreased time with doctors, greater difficulty in seeing a specialist, and declining quality of health care for the sick. The poorest and sickest persons feel particularly disenchanted with managed care programs.[8]

Third, a reciprocal interaction occurs between social stratification and policy performance. Social inequality not only shapes public health programs but is affected by them. Groups at the top of the social hierarchy — managers, administrators, professionals — have greater resources and stronger motives to influence public policies than do individuals with less political power, wealth, and status. No matter how egalitarian the society, the most active policy participants comprise those with the most education, income, and organizational ties. In turn, public policies shape the social stratification system. Since World War II they made health care more available to all citizens, thereby lowering infant mortality rates and raising life expectancy. Lower-income persons particularly gained from these programs. Yet groups with the highest SES still secure the best-quality health care. Despite the growth of comprehensive plans, they have greater access to urban specialists. Everywhere rural residents, the urban poor, individuals with little formal education, and ethnic minorities — immigrant workers throughout Europe, Canada's First Nation peoples, and African Americans, Latinos, and Native Americans — receive the fewest benefits relative to their health needs. Increased access to health care facilities hardly secures equal health among diverse socioeconomic groups. Finally, social status affects the degree of satisfaction with the health care system. Besides managers and professionals, the wealthy, healthy elderly voice the strongest approval. Low-income unskilled workers feel most discontented.[9] Confronting the greatest incidence of disabling diseases and the lowest life expectancy, they seek healing waters but find that social inequality still plagues public health systems.

Notes

I Introduction

1. Henrik Ibsen, *An Enemy of the People, The Wild Duck, Rosmersholm*, ed. and trans. James McFarlane (New York: Oxford University Press, 1988), 73, 47. See too Solomon Posen, 'The Portrayal of the Physician in Non-Medical Literature — the Physician and Politics,' *Journal of the Royal Society of Medicine* 87 (April 1994): 237–41.

2. J. H. Sebus and A. K. Iderwald, 'Metaphors in Medicine,' *Curare* 14, no. 3 (1991): 119–26; David Armstrong, 'Public Health Spaces and the Fabrication of Identity,' *Sociology* 27 (August 1993): 393–410; Fritz Efaw, 'Toward a Critical History of Methodological Individualism,' *Review of Radical Political Economics* 26 (September 1994): 103–10.

3. See Jeffrey C. Alexander, 'Modern, Anti, Post and Neo,' *New Left Review*, no. 210 (March/April 1995): 63–101; Risto Heiskala, 'Modernity and the Intersemiotic Condition,' *Social Science Information* 32 (Fall 1993): 581–604; Pauline Vaillancourt Rosenau, 'Health Politics Meets Post-Modernism: Its Meaning and Implications for Community Health Organizing,' *Journal of Health, Politics and Law* 19 (Summer 1994): 303–33; Robin Marantz Henig, 'Medicine's New Age,' *Civilization* 4 (April/May 1997): 42–9; Per-Gunnar Svensson and Patricia Stephenson, 'Health Care Consequences of the European Economic Community in 1993 and Beyond,' *Social Science and Medicine* 35 (August 1992): 525–9; Rory Watson, 'European Parliament Flexes Its Muscles over Health,' *British Medical Journal* 310 (28 January 1995): 214; Bertrand Rossert and Peter Goate, 'The Role of the European Community,' in *Financing Health Care*, vol. 2, ed. Ullrich K. Hoffmeyer and Thomas R. McCarthy (Dordrecht, The Netherlands: Kluwer Academic Publishers, 1994), 1295–1392.

4. Michael Moran, 'Reshaping the Health-Care State,' *Government and Opposition* 29 (Winter 1994): 48–63; David Mechanic, 'Social Research in Health and the American Sociopolitical Context: The Changing Fortunes of Medical Sociology,' *Social Science and Medicine* 36 (January 1993): 95–102; Jeremy Hurst and Jean-Pierre Poullier, 'Paths to Health Reform,' *OECD Observer*, no. 179 (December 1992/January 1993): 4–7.

5. Kenneth C. Calman, 'Equity, Poverty, and Health for All,' *British Medical Journal* 314 (19 April 1997): 1187–91; Frances Baum, 'Researching Public Health: Behind the Qualitative — Quantitative Methodological Debate,' *Social Science and Medicine* 40 (February 1995): 459–68; Chris Ham, 'Analysis of Health Policy — Principles and Practice,' *Scandinavian Journal of Social Medicine*, Supplement, 46 (1991): 62–6; Charles F. Andrain and David E. Apter, *Political Protest and Social Change: Analyzing Politics* (London: Macmillan Press, 1995), 125–31, 225–32, 278–80; Dietrich Rueschemeyer and Theda Skocpol, eds., *States, Social Knowledge, and the Origins of Modern Social Policies* (Princeton, NJ: Princeton University Press and New York: Russell Sage Foundation, 1996), esp. Dietrich Rueschemeyer

236

and Theda Skocpol, 'Conclusion,' 296–312; Bradford H. Gray and Sarah R. Phillips, 'Medical Sociology and Health Policy: Where Are the Connections?' *Journal of Health and Social Behavior* 36 (Extra Issue 1995): 170–81; David Mechanic, 'Emerging Trends in the Application of the Social Sciences to Health and Medicine,' *Social Science and Medicine* 40 (June 1995): 1491–6; Barbara Stocking, 'Why Research Findings Are Not Used by Commissions — And What Can Be Done about It,' *Journal of Public Health Medicine* 17 (December 1995): 380–2; Seymour Martin Lipset, 'The State of American Sociology,' *Sociological Forum* 9 (June 1994): 199–220.

6. Tomas Faresjö, 'Social Environment and Health,' *Scandinavian Journal of Primary Health Care* 10 (June 1992): 105–10; Sally Macintyre, 'Understanding the Social Patterning of Health: The Role of the Social Sciences,' *Journal of Public Health Medicine* 16 (March 1994): 53–9; Denny Vågerö, 'Health Inequalities as Policy Issues — Reflections on Ethics, Policy and Public Health,' *Sociology of Health and Illness* 17 (January 1995): 1–19; Abdelmonem A. Afifi and Lester Breslow, 'The Maturing Paradigm of Public Health,' in *Annual Review of Public Health 1994*, vol. 15, ed. Gilbert S. Omenn, Jonathan E. Fielding, and Lester B. Lave (Palo Alto, CA: Annual Reviews, Inc., 1994), 223–35; Donald L. Patrick and Pennifer Erickson, *Health Status and Health Policy: Quality of Life in Health Care Evaluation and Resource Allocation* (New York: Oxford University Press, 1993), 101, 381–2; Jeremy Hurst and OECD Secretariat, *The Reform of Health Care: A Comparative Analysis of Seven OECD Countries* (Paris: Organisation for Economic Cooperation and Development, 1992), 14–17.

Part I

1. Gøsta Esping-Andersen, *The Three Worlds of Welfare Capitalism* (Princeton, NJ: Princeton University Press, 1990). For applications and evaluations of his models, see Luis Duran-Arenas and Michael Kennedy, 'The Constitution of Physicians' Power: A Theoretical Framework for Comparative Analysis,' *Social Science and Medicine* 32, no. 6 (1991): 643–8; Gregg M. Olsen, 'Locating the Canadian Welfare State: Family Policy and Health Care in Canada, Sweden, and the United States,' *Canadian Journal of Sociology* 19 (Winter 1994): 1–20; Hans Keman and Paul Pennings, 'Managing Political and Societal Conflict in Democracies: Do Consensus and Corporatism Matter?' *British Journal of Political Science* 25 (April 1995): 271–81; Markus M. L. Crepaz and Arend Lijphart, 'Linking and Integrating Corporatism and Consensus Democracy: Theory, Concepts and Evidence,' *British Journal of Political Science* 25 (April 1995): 281–8; Robert C. Kloosterman, 'Three Worlds of Welfare Capitalism? The Welfare State and the Post-Industrial Trajectory in the Netherlands after 1980,' *West European Politics* 17 (October 1994): 166–89. As Kloosterman points out, Esping-Andersen includes different specific countries (the Netherlands, Germany) under the same general model (corporatism). By underestimating the impact of external economic conditions, like the world capitalist economy, on domestic programs, he also downplays the policy changes that have occurred during the last two decades. As Charles C. Ragin indicates in 'A Qualitative Comparative Analysis of Pension Systems,' in *The Comparative Political Economy of the Welfare State*, ed. Thomas Janoski and Alexander M. Hicks (New York: Cambridge University Press, 1944), 320–42, Esping-Andersen downplays the diversities within a single regime, especially the corporatist

type. Although the United States and Canada clearly belong in the entrepreneurial camp and Swedish policies reflect the social democratic model, Germany, Japan, the Netherlands, and the United Kingdom represent more mixed cases. This analysis of health policies confirms the mixed features of the different governmental systems.

2. Anne Mills, 'Decentralization and Accountability in the Health Sector from an International Perspective: What Are the Choices?' *Public Administration and Development* 14 (August 1994): 281–92; Uwe E. Reinhardt, 'Reforming the Health Care System: The Universal Dilemma,' *American Journal of Law and Medicine* 19, nos. 1–2 (1993): 21–36; David Wilsford, *Doctors and the State: The Politics of Health Care in France and the United States* (Durham, NC: Duke University Press, 1991), 221–91; Charles F. Andrain and David E. Apter, *Political Protest and Social Change: Analyzing Politics* (London: Macmillan, 1995), 30–43, 49–51, 81–2, 132–54, 172–82.

2   The Entrepreneurial Model

1. Deborah A. Stone, 'The Struggle for the Soul of Health Insurance,' in *The Politics of Health Care Reform: Lessons from the Past, Prospects for the Future*, ed. James A. Morone and Gary S. Belkin (Durham, NC: Duke University Press, 1994), 26–56.

2. Theodore R. Marmor, *Understanding Health Care Reform* (New Haven, CT: Yale University Press, 1994), 179–94; Gregg M. Olsen, 'Locating the Canadian Welfare State: Family Policy and Health Care in Canada, Sweden, and the United States,' *Canadian Journal of Sociology* 19 (Winter 1994): 1–20.

3. Mary Ruggie, 'The Paradox of Liberal Intervention: Health Policy and the American Welfare State,' *American Journal of Sociology* 97 (January 1992): 919–44; Mary Ruggie, *Realignments in the Welfare State: Health Policy in the United States, Britain, and Canada* (New York: Columbia University Press, 1996), esp. 1–27, 77–271.

4. Mary L. Fennell and Jeffrey A. Alexander, 'Perspectives on Organizational Change in the US Medical Care Sector,' in *Annual Review of Sociology*, vol. 19, ed. Judith Blake and John Hagen (Palo Alto, CA: Annual Reviews, Inc., 1993), 89–112.

5. See Laura A. Scofea, 'The Development and Growth of Employer-Provided Health Insurance,' *Monthly Labor Review* 117 (March 1994): 3–10; Steffie Woolhandler and David U. Himmelstein, 'Clinton's Health Plan: Prudential Choice,' *International Journal of Health Services* 24, no. 4 (1994): 583–92; Vicente Navarro, 'The Politics of Health Care Reform in the United States, 1992–1994: A Historical Review,' *International Journal of Health Services* 25, no. 2 (1995): 185–202; Robert Sherrill, 'The Madness of the Market,' *Nation* 260 (January 9/16, 1995): 64–72; J. Warren Salmon, 'A Perspective on the Corporate Transformation of Health Care,' *International Journal of Health Services* 25, no. 1 (1995): 11–42; Julius B. Richmond and Rashi Fein, 'The Health Care Mess: A Bit of History,' *Journal of the American Medical Association* 273 (4 January 1995): 69–71; Douglas R. Wholey, Jon B. Christianson, and Susan M. Sanchez, 'The Effect of Physician and Corporate Interests on the Formation of Health Maintenance Organizations,' *American Journal of Sociology* 99 (July 1993): 164–200; Larry Makinson, 'Political Contributions from the Health and Insurance Industries,' *Health Affairs* 11 (Winter 1992): 119–34; and the following three essays in *The Politics of*

Health Care Reform, ed. Morone and Belkin: Cathie Jo Martin, 'Together Again: Business, Government, and the Quest for Cost Control,' 224–58; Nancy S. Jecker, 'Can an Employer-Based Health Insurance System Be Just?' 259–75; Lawrence D. Brown, 'Dogmatic Slumbers: American Business and Health Policy,' 205–23.

6. Ronald L. Caplan, 'The Commodification of American Health Care,' *Social Science and Medicine* 28, no. 11 (1989): 1139–48; Sherrill, 'The Madness of the Market,' 60–64; US Bureau of the Census, *Statistical Abstract of the United States* (Washington, DC: US Government Printing Office, 1984, 1986, 1988, 1989, 1992, 1994, 1995), 549 ('84), 535 ('86), 516 ('88), 539 ('89), 543 ('92), 561 ('94), 565 ('95); Warren E. Leary, 'Government Gives Up Right to Control Prices of Drugs It Helps Develop,' *New York Times*, 12 April 1995, p. A11.

7. Lawton R. Burns, 'The Transformation of the American Hospital: From Community Institution toward Business Enterprise,' in *Comparative Social Research*, vol. 12, ed. Craig Calhoun (Greenwich, CT: JAI Press, 1990), 77–112; Allen W. Imershein, Philip C. Rond III, and Mary P. Mathis, 'Restructuring Patterns of Elite Dominance and the Formation of State Policy in Health Care,' *American Journal of Sociology* 97 (January 1992): 970–93; David Dranove, Mark Shanley, and William D. White, 'Price and Concentration in Hospital Market: The Switch from Patient-Driven to Payer-Driven Competition,' *Journal of Law and Economics* 26 (April 1993): 179–204; Ruggie, 'The Paradox of Liberal Intervention,' 922–41; Salmon, 'A Perspective on the Corporate Transformation of Health Care,' 13–27; Public Citizen Health Research Group, 'The Failure of 'Private' Regulation of Hospitals,' *Health Letter* 12 (August 1996): 1–6;

8. Yael Yishai, 'Physicians and the State in the U.S.A. and Israel,' *Social Science and Medicine* 34 (January 1992): 129–39; John K. Iglehart, 'Health Policy Report: Physicians and the Growth of Managed Care,' *New England Journal of Medicine* 331 (27 October 1994): 1167–71; Carol J. Simon, David Dranove, and William D. White, 'The Impact of Managed Care on the Physician Marketplace,' *Public Health Reports* 112 (May/June 1997): 223; Makinson, 'Political Contributions from the Health and Insurance Industries,' 119–23, 130–1.

9. Russell L. Hanson, 'Health-Care Reform, Managed Competition, and Subnational Politics,' *Publius: The Journal of Federalism* 24 (Summer 1994): 49–68; Russell L. Hanson, 'Defining a Role for States in a Federal Health Care System,' *American Behavioral Scientist* 36 (July 1993): 760–81; Colleen M. Grogan, 'Political-Economic Factors Influencing State Medicaid Policy,' *Political Research Quarterly* 47 (September 1994): 589–622; Colleen M. Grogan, 'Federalism and Health Care Reform,' *American Behavioral Scientist* 36 (July 1993): 741–59; Robert G. Frank, Michael J. Sullivan, and Patrick H. DeLeon, 'Health Care Reform in the States,' *American Psychologist* 49 (October 1994): 855–67; Virginia Gray, 'Federalism and Health Care,' *PS: Political Science and Politics* 27 (June 1994): 217–20; Michael S. Sparer, 'The Unknown States,' in *The Politics of Health Care Reform*, ed. Morone and Belkin, 430–40.

10. Jacob S. Hacker and Theda Skocpol, 'The New Politics of Health Policy,' *Journal of Health Politics, Policy and Law* 22 (April 1997): 315–38; Lawrence D. Brown, 'The Politics of Medicare and Health Reform, Then and Now,' *Health Care Financing Review* 18 (Winter 1996): 163–8; John K. Iglehart, 'Republicans and the New Politics of Health Care,' *New England*

Journal of Medicine 332 (6 April 1995): 972–5; David C. Vladeck and Thomas O. McGarity, 'Paralysis by Analysis: How Conservatives Plan to Kill Popular Regulation,' *American Prospect*, no. 22 (Summer 1995): 78–83.

11. Mark A. Peterson, 'Congress in the 1990s: From Iron Triangles to Policy Networks,' in *The Politics of Health Care Reform*, ed. Morone and Belkin, 103–47; Rand E. Rosenblatt, 'The Courts and the Reconstruction of American Social Legislation,' in *The Politics of Health Care Reform*, ed. Morone and Belkin, 165–202; Brown, 'Dogmatic Slumbers: American Business and Health Policy,' 205–22; Linda A. Bergthold, 'American Business and Health Care Reform,' *American Behavioral Scientist* 36 (July 1993): 802–12; Cathie Jo Martin, 'Markets, Medicare, and Making Do: Business Strategies after National Health Care Reform,' *Journal of Health Politics, Policy and Law* 22 (April 1997): 557–93; Cathie Jo Martin, 'Nature or Nurture? Sources of Firm Preference for National Health Reform,' *American Political Science Review* 89 (December 1995): 898–913; Joan Retsinas, 'Small Businesses: The Health Insurance Bind,' *Journal of Health and Social Policy* 6, no. 3 (1995): 1–12; Carol S. Weissert and William G. Weissert, *Governing Health: The Politics of Health Policy* (Baltimore, MD: Johns Hopkins University Press, 1996), esp. 257–324.

12. Nancy S. Jecker and Eric M. Meslin, 'United States and Canadian Approaches to Justice in Health Care: A Comparative Analysis of Health Care Systems and Values,' *Theoretical Medicine* 15 (June 1994): 181–200.

13. Ronald W. Watts, 'The American Constitution in Comparative Perspective: A Comparison of Federalism in the United States and Canada,' *Journal of American History* 74 (December 1987): 769–91; Jonathon S. Rakich, 'The Canadian Health Care Model and How It Differs from the U.S. System,' *American Review of Canadian Studies* 23 (Spring 1993): 17–35; Anne Crichton, 'Health Insurance and Medical Practice Organization in Canada: Findings from a Literature Review,' *Medical Care Review* 51 (Summer 1994): 149–71; Jonathan Lomas, John Woods, and Gerry Veenstra, 'Devolving Authority for Health Care in Canada's Provinces: 1. An Introduction to the Issues,' *Canadian Medical Association Journal* 156 (1 February 1997): 371–7; Jonathan Lomas, Gerry Veenstra, and John Woods, 'Devolving Authority for Health Care in Canada's Provinces: 2. Backgrounds, Resources and Activities of Board Members,' *Canadian Medical Association Journal* 156 (15 February 1997): 513–20; Louis Demers and Clermont Bégin, 'Pouvoirs et contre-pouvoirs dans le secteur de la santé: Deux cas de fusion,' *Recherches sociographiques* 21 (September–December 1990): 381–404; Raynald Pineault, Paul A. Lamarche, François Champagne, André-Pierre Contandriopoulos, and Jean-Louis Denis, 'The Reform of the Quebec Health Care System: Potential for Innovation?' *Journal of Public Health Policy* 14 (Spring 1993): 198–219; Raynald Pineault, Brigitte Maheux, Jean Lambert, François Béland, and Anne Lévesque, 'Characteristics of Physicians Practicing in Alternative Primary Care Settings: A Quebec Study of Local Community Service Center Physicians,' *International Journal of Health Services* 21, no. 1 (1991): 49–58; Michel O'Neill, 'Community Participation in Quebec's Health System: A Strategy to Curtail Community Empowerment,' *International Journal of Health Services* 22, no. 2 (1992): 287–301.

14. David Coburn, 'Canadian Medicine: Dominance or Proletarianization?' *Milbank Quarterly* 66, supplement 2 (1988): 92–116; David Coburn, 'State Authority, Medical Dominance, and Trends in the Regulation of the Health

Professions: The Ontario Case,' *Social Science and Medicine* 37 (July 1993): 129–38; David Coburn, Susan Rappolt, and Ivy Bourgeault, 'Decline vs. Retention of Power through Restratification: An Examination of the Ontario Case,' *Sociology of Health and Illness* 19 (January 1997): 1–22; Vincent Lemieux and France Gagnon, 'La maîtrise des modes de décision: le cas de la répartition géographique des effectifs médicaux au Québec,' *Canadian Public Policy* 19 (September 1993): 311–24; Adrianne H. Cohen, Robert Cohen, Bryce R. Taylor, and Richard K. Reznick, 'Health Care System and Medical Education in Canada, 1. Review of the Health Care Context in a Time of Change,' *World Journal of Surgery* 18 (September/October 1994): 672–5; David M. Rayside and Every A. Lindquist, 'AIDS Activism and the State in Canada,' *Studies in Political Economy*, no. 39 (Autumn 1992): 37–76; John D. Blum, 'Universality, Quality and Economics: Finding a Balance in Ontario and British Columbia,' *American Journal of Law and Medicine* 20 (Spring–Summer 1994): 203–29; Seymour Martin Lipset, 'Trade Union Exceptionalism: The United States and Canada,' *Annals of the American Academy of Political and Social Science* 538 (March 1995): 115–30; Seymour Martin Lipset, *Continental Divide: The Values and Institutions of the United States and Canada* (New York: Routledge, 1990).

15. François Pétry, 'The Party Agenda Model: Election Programmes and Government Spending in Canada,' *Canadian Journal of Political Science* 28 (March 1995): 51–84; Leslie S. Laczko, 'Canada's Pluralism in Comparative Perspective,' *Ethnic and Racial Studies* 17 (January 1994): 20–41; R. Kent Weaver, 'Political Institutions and Conflict Management in Canada,' *Annals of the American Academy of Political and Social Science* 538 (March 1995): 54–68; Antonia Maioni, 'Parting at the Crossroads: The Development of Health Insurance in Canada and the United States, 1940–1965,' *Comparative Politics* 29 (July 1997): 411–31; Jamie Portman, 'And Not by Bread Alone: The Battle over Canadian Culture,' in *Canada and the United States: Differences that Count*, ed. David Thomas (Ontario, Canada: Broadview Press, 1991), 343–63; *OECD Economic Outlook*, no. 59 (June 1996): A4, A25, A33; Jill Rafuse, 'Private-Sector Share of Health Spending Hits Record Level,' *Canadian Medical Association Journal* 155 (15 September 1996): 749–50; Mary Janigan, 'Dustup over Dollars,' *Maclean's* 110 (19 May 1997): 20–2.

16. Robert Sass, 'Labor Policy and Social Democracy: The Case of Saskatchewan, 1971–1982,' *International Journal of Health Services* 24, no. 4 (1994): 763–91; Robert Sass, 'The Work Environment Board and the Limits of Social Democracy in Canada,' *International Journal of Health Services* 23, no. 2 (1993): 279–300; Mary Janigan, 'Mike the Knife: Ontario's New Premier Has a Mandate to Cut Taxes and Slash Government,' *Maclean's* 108 (19 June 1995): 10–13; Brian Bergman and Mary Nemeth, 'Pregnant Moms and a Medicare War,' *Maclean's* 109 (26 August 1996): 18–19; Charlotte Gray, 'Government Cost Cutting Means Expansion Opportunities for Companies like Liberty Health,' *Canadian Medical Association Journal* 155 (15 October 1996): 1142–5.

17. Marmor, *Understanding Health Care Reform*, 179–94; Robert G. Evans, 'Canada: The Real Issues,' in *The Politics of Health Care Reform*, ed. Morone and Belkin, 463–86; Robert G. Evans, 'Less Is More: Contrasting Styles in Health Care,' in *Canada and the United States*, ed. Thomas, 21–41; Robert G. Evans, 'Going for the Gold: The Redistributive Agenda behind Market-Based Health Care Reform,' *Journal of Health Politics, Policy and Law* 22

(April 1997): 427–65, esp. 450–9; Colleen M. Grogan, 'Who Gets What? Levels of Care in Canada, Britain, Germany, and the United States,' in *The Politics of Health Care Reform*, ed. Morone and Belkin, 443–62; Lipset, *Continental Divide*, 136–51, 193–227; Organisation for Economic Cooperation and Development, *OECD Health Systems: Facts and Trends 1960–1991*, vol. 1 (Paris: OECD, 1993), 252; Arnold Bennett and Orvill Adams, eds., *Looking North for Health: What We Can Learn from Canada's Health Care System* (San Francisco: Jossey-Bass, 1993), especially the essays by Robert G. Evans, 'Health Care in the Canadian Community,' 1–27; Jerry R. Estill, 'From Inside the System: A Physician, Hospital Administrator, and Business Executive Talk about Their Work in Canada,' 40–60; Rosalie A. Kane, 'Delivering and Financing Long Term Care in Canada's Ten Provinces,' 89–101; Orvill Adams, 'Understanding the Health Care System that Works,' 113–41; Ron Pollack, 'Eleven Lessons from Canada's Health Care System,' 142–76.

3 **The Organic Corporatist Model**

1. Robert Nisbet, *Conservatism: Dream and Reality* (Minneapolis: University of Minnesota Press, 1986); Leif Lewin, 'The Rise and Decline of Corporatism: The Case of Sweden,' *European Journal of Political Research* 26 (June 1994): 59–70; Hans Keman and Paul Pennings, 'Managing Political and Societal Conflict in Democracies: Do Consensus and Corporatism Matter?' *British Journal of Political Science* 25 (April 1995): 271–81.

2. Stefan Kirchberger, 'Health Care Technology in the Federal Republic of Germany,' *Health Policy* 30, nos. 1–3 (1994): 163–205; Ullrich Hoffmeyer, 'The Health Care System in Germany,' in *Financing Health Care*, vol. 1, ed. Ullrich K. Hoffmeyer and Thomas R. McCarthy (Dordrecht, the Netherlands: Kluwer Academic Publishers, 1994), 421–512; Udo Schagen, 'Medicine in Germany, Austria, and Switzerland,' in *The Oxford Medical Companion*, ed. John Walton, Jeremiah A. Barondess, and Stephen Lock (New York: Oxford University Press, 1994), 547–52; Klaus-Dirk Henke, Claudia Ade, and Margaret A. Murray, 'The German Health Care System: Structure and Changes,' *Journal of Clinical Anesthesia* 6 (May/June 1994): 252–62; Marian Döhler and Philip Manow-Borgwardt, 'Gesundheitspolitische Steuerung zwischen Hierarchie und Verhandlung,' *Politische Vierteljahresschrift* 33, no. 4 (1992): 571–96; Marian Döhler, 'Comparing National Patterns of Medical Specialization: A Contribution to the Theory of Professions,' *Social Science Information* 32 (June 1993): 185–231; Marian Döhler, 'The State as Architect of Political Order: Policy Dynamics in German Health Care,' *Governance* 8 (July 1995): 380–404; Susan Giaimo, 'Health Care Reform in Britain and Germany: Recasting the Political Bargain with the Medical Profession,' *Governance* 8 (July 1995): 354–79; Hanna Behrend, 'Dismantling Germany's Welfare State,' *New Politics* 6 (Summer 1996): 111–22; Deborah A. Stone, 'German Unification: East Meets West in the Doctor's Office,' *Journal of Health Politics, Policy and Law* 16 (Summer 1991): 401–12; Richard Freeman, 'Prevention in Health Policy in the Federal Republic of Germany,' *Policy and Politics* 22 (January 1994): 3–16; Susan Tester, 'Implications of Subsidiarity for the Care of Older People in Germany,' *Social Policy and Administration* 28 (September 1994): 251–62; Francis D. Powell, 'Government Participation in Physician Negotiations in German Economic Policy as Applied to Universal

Health Care Coverage in the United States,' *Social Science and Medicine* 38 (January 1994): 35–43; J.-Matthias Graf v.d. Schulenburg, 'Germany: Solidarity at a Price,' *Journal of Health, Politics and Law* 17 (Winter 1992): 715–38; J.-Matthias Graf von der Schulenburg, 'Economic Evaluation of Medical Technologies from Theory to Practice — the German Perspective,' *Social Science and Medicine* 45 (August 1997): 621–33; Jeffrey L. Jackson, 'The German Health System,' *Archives of Internal Medicine* 157 (27 January 1997): 155–60; Wolfgang Greiner and J.-Matthias Graf v.d. Schulenburg, 'Germany,' in *Health Care and Reform in Industrialized Countries*, ed. Marshall W. Raffel (University Park: The Pennsylvania State University Press, 1997), 77–104; Nicholas Tanti-Hardouin, *L'hospitalisation privée* (Paris: Notes et études documentaires, La documentation française, 1996), 121, 132–4.

3. For analyses of liberal, communal, and radical pluralism as well as civil values, see Charles F. Andrain and David E. Apter, *Political Protest and Social Change* (London: Macmillan, 1995), 96–7, 172–96.

4. Frederik T. Schut, 'Health Care Systems in Transition: The Netherlands, Part 1: Health Care Reforms in the Netherlands: Miracle or Mirage?' *Journal of Public Health Medicine* 18 (September 1996): 278–84; Einte Elsinga and Frans F. H. Rutten, 'Economic Evaluation in Support of National Health Policy: The Case of the Netherlands,' *Social Science and Medicine* 45 (August 1997): 605–20; Arno van Raak and Ingrid Mur-Veeman, 'Home Care Policy in the Netherlands,' *Health Policy* 36 (April 1996): 37–51; Graham Shuttleworth, 'The Health Care System in the Netherlands,' in *Financing Health Care*, ed. Hoffmeyer and McCarthy, 697–765; Bradford L. Korkman-Liff, 'Health Insurance Values and Implementation in the Netherlands and the Federal Republic of Germany,' *Journal of the American Medical Association* 265 (15 May 1991): 2496–2502; Harm Lieverdink and Hans Maarse, 'Negotiating Fees for Medical Specialists in the Netherlands,' *Health Policy* 31 (February 1995): 81–101; Michael Bos, 'Health Care Technology in the Netherlands,' *Health Policy* 30, nos. 1–3 (1994): 207–55; Peter P. Groenewegen, 'The Shadow of the Future: Institutional Change in Health Care,' *Health Affairs* 13 (Winter 1994): 137–48; Peter P. Groenewegen and Jack B. F. Hutten, 'The Influence of Supply-Related Characteristics on General Practitioners' Workload,' *Social Science and Medicine* 40 (February 1995): 349–58; Frederik T. Schut, 'Workable Competition in Health Care: Prospects for the Dutch Design,' *Social Science and Medicine* 35 (December 1992): 1445–55; A. J. P. Schrijvers, 'The Netherlands Introduces Some Competition into the Health Services,' *Journal of the American Medical Association* 266 (23/30 October 1991): 2215–17; Richard B. Saltman and Adrian A. de Roo, 'Hospital Policy in the Netherlands: The Parameters of Structural Stalemate,' *Journal of Health Politics, Policy and Law* 14 (Winter 1989): 773–95; Chris Ham and Mats Brommels, 'Health Care Reform in the Netherlands, Sweden, and the United Kingdom,' *Health Affairs* 13 (Winter 1994): 106–19; Ronald Naaborg, 'Changing the Health Care System in the Netherlands: The End of a Period of Cost Containment?' *International Social Security Review* 44, no. 3 (1991): 23–37; Eddy Van Doorslaer, Adam Wagstaff, and Richard Janssen, 'The Netherlands,' in *Equity in the Finance and Delivery of Health Care: An International Perspective* (New York: Oxford University Press, 1993), 166–80; Henk A. M. J. ten Have and Helen Keasberry, 'Equity and Solidarity: The Context of Health Care in the Netherlands,' *Journal of*

Medicine and Philosophy 17 (August 1992): 463–77; Wouter M. de Jong, 'Policy on AIDS and Drug Users: The State of Affairs in the Netherlands,' *Health Promotion International* 6, no. 4 (1991): 257–61; Reuven Y. Hazan, 'Attacking the Centre: 'Moderate-Induced Polarization' in Denmark and the Netherlands,' *Scandinavian Political Studies* 18, no. 2 (1995): 73–95; Marja A. Pijl, 'The Dutch Welfare State: A Product of Religious and Political Pluralism,' *Social Policy Review* 5 (1993): 288–304; Robert C. Kloosterman, 'Three Worlds of Welfare Capitalism? The Welfare State and the Post-Industrial Trajectory in the Netherlands after 1980,' *West European Politics* 17 (October 1994): 166–89; Peter Mair, 'The Correlates of Consensus Democracy and the Puzzle of Dutch Politics,' *West European Politics* 17 (October 1994): 97–123; Hugh Compston, 'Union Participation in Economic Policy-Making in Austria, Switzerland, the Netherlands, Belgium and Ireland, 1970–1992,' *West European Politics* 17 (January 1994): 123–45; Bruce Western, 'A Comparative Study of Working-Class Disorganization: Union Decline in Eighteen Advanced Capitalist Countries,' *American Sociological Review* 60 (April 1995): 179–201, esp. 181; Thomas T. Mackie and Richard Rose, *The International Almanac of Electoral History*, 3d ed. (Washington, DC: Congressional Quarterly, 1991), 322–6, 337–9; 'OECD in Figures 1997 Edition,' *OECD Observer*, no. 206 (June/July 1997): 29, 45, 67; United Nations Development Programme, *Human Development Report 1994* (New York: Oxford University Press, 1994), 198; International Labour Office, *The Cost of Social Security: Fourteenth International Inquiry, 1987–1989* (Geneva: International Labour Office, 1996), 72–5; Organisation for Economic Cooperation and Development, *New Orientations for Social Policy* (Paris: OECD, 1994), 59–61.

5. Richard C. Rapp and Kyoko Shibuya, 'The Health Care System in Japan,' in *Financing Health Care*, vol. 1, ed. Hoffmeyer and McCarthy, 646; Chalmers Johnson, *Japan: Who Governs? The Rise of the Developmental State* (New York: W. W. Norton, 1995), esp. 21–68, 157–82.

6. Naoki Ikegami, 'Overview: Health Care in Japan,' in *Containing Health Care Costs in Japan*, ed. Naoki Ikegami and John Creighton Campbell (Ann Arbor: University of Michigan Press, 1996), 8–18; Naoki Ikegami, 'Efficiency and Effectiveness in Health Care,' *Daedalus* 123 (Fall 1994): 113–25; Sumiko Oshima, 'Japan: Feeling the Strains of an Aging Population,' *Science* 273 (5 July 1996): 44–5; Hisashi Teramatsu, 'Japan's Health Care System in the 21st Century,' *Tokai Journal of Experimental and Clinical Medicine* 20 (September 1995): 151–6; Rapp and Shibuya, 'The Health Care System in Japan,' 585–696; Toshihide Tsuda, Hideyasu Aoyama, and Jack Froom, 'Primary Health Care in Japan and the United States,' *Social Science and Medicine* 38 (February 1994): 489–95; Y. Watanabe, 'Japan,' in *The Reform of Health Care Systems: A Review of Seventeen OECD Countries* (Paris: Organisation for Economic Cooperation and Development, 1994), 205–18; John Creighton Campbell, *How Policies Change: The Japanese Government and the Aging Society* (Princeton, NJ: Princeton University Press, 1992), 282–312; Yasuki Kobayashi, 'Health Care Expenditures for the Elderly and Reforms in the Health Care System in Japan,' *Health Policy* 29 (September 1994): 197–208; Yasuki Kobatashi, 'Health Care Financing for the Elderly in Japan,' *Social Science and Medicine* 37 (August 1993): 343–53; Naoko T. Miyaji and Margaret Lock, 'Monitoring Motherhood: Sociocultural and Historical Aspects of Maternal and Child Health in Japan,' *Daedalus* 123 (Fall 1994): 87–112; José Antiono Crespo, 'The Liberal Democratic Party in

Japan: Conservative Domination,' *International Political Science Review* 16 (April 1995): 199–209; Laurene A. Graig, *Health of Nations*, 2d ed. (Washington, DC: Congressional Quarterly, 1993), 129–46; Scott A. Kupor, Yong-chuan Liu, Jungwoo Lee, and Aki Yoshikawa, 'The Effect of Copayments and Income on the Utilization of Medical Care by Subscribers to Japan's National Health Insurance System,' *International Journal of Health Services* 25, no. 2 (1995): 294–312; Haruhiro Fukui and Shigeko N. Fukai, 'Japan in 1996: Between Hope and Uncertainty,' *Asian Survey* 27 (January 1997): 22–8.

7. For analyses of different aspects of the French health care system, see Claude Le Pen, 'Pharmaceutical Economy and the Economic Assessment of Drugs in France,' *Social Science and Medicine* 45 (August 1997): 635–43; Serge-Allain Rozenblum, 'Santé enjeux et défis,' *Revue politique et parlementaire* 99 (March–April 1997): 28–40; Alexander Dorozynski, 'Report Criticises French Health Ministry,' *British Medical Journal* 314 (1 February 1997): 325; Jonathan E. Fielding and Pierre-Jean Lancry, 'Lessons from France — "Vive la Différence,"' *Journal of the American Medical Association* 270 (11 August 1993): 748–56; Victor G. Rodwin and Simone Sandier, 'Health Care under French National Health Insurance,' *Health Affairs* 12 (Fall 1993): 111–31; J. P. Moatti, C. Chanut, and J. M. Benech, 'Researcher-Driven versus Policy-Driven Economic Appraisal of Health Technologies: The Case of France,' *Social Science and Medicine* 38 (June 1994): 1625–33; Stephen Bach, 'Managing a Pluralist Health System: The Case of Health Care Reform in France,' *International Journal of Health Services* 24, no. 4 (1994): 593–606; Mike Burstall and Konrad Wallerstein, 'The Health Care System in France,' in *Financing Health Care*, vol. 1, ed. Hoffmeyer and McCarthy, 345–418; Martine Bungener and Geniève Paicheler, 'Social Trajectories and Diversity of Careers: Two Aspects of the Evolution of the Medical Profession in France (1925–1989),' *Social Science and Medicine* 38 (May 1994): 1439–47; Monica Steffen, 'Les professions libérales de la santé en France,' *Regards sur l'actualité*, no. 175 (November 1991): 3–32; Pierre-Jean Lancry, 'Le secteur 2 de la médecine libérale: Un élément de marché?' *Revue d'économie politique* 99 (November–December 1989): 854–70; Béatrice Majnoni d'Intignano, 'Les paradoxes de la médecine libérale,' *Revue française des affaires sociales* 44 (April–June 1990): 9–29; Anne Vega, 'La crise identitaire des infirmières hospitalières françaises,' *La pensée*, no. 291 (January–February 1993): 59–81; Christine Guyomar, 'Le partage de clintèle entre hôpital et clinique,' *Économie et statistique*, no. 265, no. 5 (1993): 53–62; D. Patrick Redmon and Paul J. Yaboboski, 'The Nominal and Real Effects of Hospital Global Budgets in France,' *Inquiry* 32 (Summer 1995): 174–83; Jean Deramon, 'Deux décennies d'expansion des dépenses de santé,' *Économie et statistique*, no. 265, no. 5 (1993): 9–16; Tanti-Hardouin, *L'hospitalisation privée*, 38–51, 189; Bernard Bonnici, *L'hôpital: Enjeux politiques et réalités économiques* (Paris: Notes et études documentaires, La documentation française, 1992); Philippe Batifoulier, 'Financement du système de soins et appauvrissement de la politique économique,' *Revue française des affaires sociales* 47 (April–June 1993): 7–27; M. Manciaux, C. Jestin, M. Fritz, and D. Bertrand, 'Child Health Care Policy and Delivery in France,' *Pediatrics* 86 (December 1990):1037–43; Laurent Caussat et Michel Glaude, 'Dépenses médicales et couverture sociale,' *Économique et statistique*, no. 265, no. 5 (1993): 31–43; Pierre Mormiche, 'Les disparités de recours aux soins en 1991,' *Économique et statistique*, no. 265, no. 5 (1993):

45–52; François Tonnelier, 'Accès aux soins et types de communes en France,' *Espace, Populations, Sociétés* (1992–1993): 297–311; Andrée Mizrahi and Arié Mizrahi, 'Le cumul des handicaps,' *Informations sociales*, no. 26 (1993): 16–21; Jean-Claude Henrard, Bernard Cassou, and Dominique Le Disert, 'The Effects of System Characteristics on Policy Implementation and Functioning of Care for the Elderly in France,' *International Journal of Health Services* 20, no. 1 (1990): 125–39; Claire Lachaud and Lise Rochaix, 'France,' in *Equity in the Finance and Delivery of Health Care*, ed. van Doorslaer, Wagstaff, and Rutten, 117–33; Rory Watson, 'The French Way of Controlling Drug Costs,' *British Medical Journal* 310 (22 April 1995): 1028; David Wilsford, *Doctors and the State: The Politics of Health Care in France and the United States* (Durham, NC: Duke University Press, 1991), esp. 221–306.

8. 'OECD in Figures 1997 Edition,' 8–9.

4   The Social Democratic Model

1. Jim Kemeny, 'Theories of Power in *The Three Worlds of Welfare Capitalism*,' *Journal of European Social Policy* 5, no. 2 (1995): 87–96.

2. Charles F. Andrain, *Comparative Political Systems: Policy Performance and Social Change* (Armonk, NY: M. E. Sharpe, 1994), 49–59; Leif Lewin, 'The Rise and Decline of Corporatism: The Case of Sweden,' *European Journal of Political Research* 26 (July 1994): 59–79; Hans Keman and Paul Pennings, 'Managing Political and Societal Conflict: Do Consensus and Corporatism Matter?' *British Journal of Political Science* 25 (April 1995): 271–81; Rianne Mahon and Rudolf Meidner, '"System Shift"; Or, What Is the Future of Swedish Social Democracy?' *Socialist Review* 23, no. 4 (1994): 57–77; Wallace Clement, 'Exploring the Limits of Social Democracy: Regime Change in Sweden,' *Studies in Political Economy*, no. 44 (Summer 1994): 95–123; Sven E. Olsson and Suzanne McMurphy, 'Social Policy in Sweden: The Swedish Model in Transition,' *Social Policy Review* 5 (1993): 248–69; Stefan Svallfors, 'The End of Class Politics? Structural Cleavages and Attitudes to Swedish Welfare Politics,' *Acta Sociologica* 38, no. 1 (1995): 60; Charles W. Mueller, Sarosh Kuruvilla, and Roderick D. Iverson, 'Swedish Professionals and Gender Inequalities,' *Social Forces* 73 (December 1994): 555–73; *OECD Economic Outlook* 61 (June 1997): A4, A19, A25, A33.

3. Stefan Szücs, 'Democratization and the Reorganization of the Welfare State,' *Annals of the American Academy of Political and Social Science* 540 (July 1995): 105–17; Howard Glennerster and Manos Matsaganis, 'The English and Swedish Health Care Reforms,' *International Journal of Health Services* 24, no. 2 (1994): 231–51; Vibeke Erichsen, 'States and Health Care: Scandinavian Welfare State Research,' *European Journal of Political Research* 23 (June 1993): 387–405; Rolf Å. Gustafsson, 'Open the Black Box: Paradoxes and Lacunas in Swedish Health Care Reforms,' *International Journal of Health Services* 25, no. 2 (1995): 243–58; Helen Hansagi, Johan Calltorp, and Sven Andréasson, 'Quality Comparisons between Privately and Publicly Managed Health Care Centres in a Suburban Area of Stockholm, Sweden,' *Quality Assurance Health Care* 5 (March 1993): 33–40; Richard B. Saltman, 'Emerging Trends in the Swedish Health System,' *International Journal of Health Services* 21, no. 4 (1991): 615–23; Richard B. Saltman, 'Competition and Reform in the Swedish Health System,' *Milbank Quarterly* 68, no. 4 (1990): 597–618; Finn Diderichsen, 'Market Reforms in Swedish

Health Care: A Threat to or Salvation for the Universalistic Welfare State?'
International Journal of Health Services 23, no. 1 (1993): 185–8; Finn
Diderichsen, 'Market Reforms in Health Care and Sustainability of the
Welfare State: Lessons from Sweden,' *Health Policy* 32 (April–June 1995):
141–53; Elianne Riska, 'They Don't Care: Unemployed Physicians in the
Nordic Countries,' *International Journal of Health Services* 25, no. 2 (1995):
259–69; Stig Bengmark and Bengt Jeppson, 'Swedish Health Care Delivery
System and Its Effects on Surgical Education,' *World Journal of Surgery* 18
(September/October 1994): 707–12; Daniel M. Fox, Patricia Day, and Rudolf
Klein, 'The Power of Professionalism: Policies for AIDS in Britain, Sweden,
and the United States,' *Daedalus* 118 (Spring 1989): 93–112; Ullrich
Hoffmeyer, 'The Health Care System in Sweden,' in *Financing Health Care*,
vol. 2, ed. Ullrich K. Hoffmeyer and Thomas R. McCarthy (Dordrecht, The
Netherlands: Kluwer Academic Publishers, 1994), 889–943; Swedish
Planning and Rationalization Institute, 'Sweden,' in *The Reform of Health
Care Systems: A Review of Seventeen OECD Countries* (Paris: Organisation
for Economic Cooperation and Development, 1994), 265–84.

4. Peter Garpenby, 'Health Care Reform in Sweden in the 1990s: Local
Pluralism versus National Coordination,' *Journal of Health Politics, Policy
and Law* 20 (Fall 1995): 695–717; Peter Garpenby, 'Implementing Quality
Programmes in Three Swedish County Councils: The Views of Politicians,
Managers and Doctors,' *Health Policy* 39 (March 1997): 195–206; Bengt
Jönsson, 'Economic Evaluation of Medical Technologies in Sweden,' *Social
Science and Medicine* 45 (August 1997): 597–604; Anders Anell, 'The
Monopolistic Integrated Model and Health Care Reform: The Swedish
Experience,' *Health Policy* 37 (July 1996): 19–33; Bo Burström, Bo JA
Haglund, Per Tillgren, Lars Berg, Eva Wallin, Henrik Ullén, and
Christopher Smith, 'Health Promotion in Schools: Policies and Practices in
Stockholm County, 1990,' *Scandinavian Journal of Social Medicine* 23
(March 1995): 39–46; Egon Jonsson and H. David Banta, 'Health Care
Technology in Sweden,' *Health Policy* 30, nos. 1–3 (1994): 257–94; US
Department of Health and Human Services, Social Security Administration,
Office of Research and Statistics, *Social Security Programs throughout the
World — 1993*, Research Report #63 (Washington, DC: Government Printing
Office, 1994), 310–13; Ilene R. Zeitzer, 'Recent European Trends in
Disability and Related Programs,' *Social Security Bulletin* 57 (Summer
1994): 21–26; Sveb Ikav Daatland, 'Stress and Strategies in Care Systems:
The Scandinavian Experience,' *Social Science and Medicine* 38 (April 1994):
867–74; Jan Sundquist, 'Ethnicity as a Risk Factor for Consultations in
Primary Health Care and Out-Patient Care,' *Scandinavian Journal of
Primary Health Care* 11 (September 1993): 169–73; Harald Runblom,
'Swedish Multiculturalism in a Comparative European Perspective,'
Sociological Forum 9 (December 1994): 623–40; Joan Higgins and Marilynn
Rosenthal, 'The Development of Private Medicine in Britain and Sweden:
Two Cases of Economic Necessity,' in *Research in the Sociology of Health
Care*, vol. 10, ed. Jennie Jacobs Kronenfeld and Rose Weitz (Greenwich, CT:
JAI Press, 1993), 47–69.

5. Charles Webster, 'Conflict and Consensus: Explaining the British Health
Service,' *Twentieth Century British History* 1, no. 2 (1990): 115–51; Carol
Sakala, 'The Development of National Medical Care Programs in the United
Kingdom and Canada: Applicability to Current Conditions in the United
States,' *Journal of Health Politics, Policy and Law* 15 (Winter 1990): 709–53;

Patricia Day and Rudolf Klein, 'Constitutional and Distributional Conflict in British Medical Politics: The Case of General Practice, 1911–1991,' *Political Studies* 40 (September 1992): 462–78.

6. Alain C. Enthoven, 'Internal Market Reform of the British National Health Service,' *Health Affairs* 10 (Fall 1991): 60–70; Penny Newman, 'Interview with Alain Enthoven: Is There Convergence between Britain and the United States in the Organisation of Health Services?' *British Medical Journal* 310 (24 June 1995): 1652–5; Andrain, *Comparative Political Systems*, 58–67; David Mechanic, 'The Americanization of the British National Health Service,' *Health Affairs* 14 (Summer 1995): 51–67.

7. Calum Paton, 'Devolution and Centralism in the National Health Service,' *Social Policy and Administration* 27 (June 1993): 83–108; David Hughes, 'The Reorganisation of the National Health Service: The Rhetoric and Reality of the Internal Market,' *Modern Law Review* 54 (January 1991): 88–103; Tim Blackman, 'Recent Developments in British National Health Policy: An Emerging Role for Local Government?' *Policy and Politics* 23 (January 1994): 31–48; Jackie Spiby, 'Health Care Technology in the United Kingdom,' *Health Policy* 30, nos. 1–3 (1994): 295–334; Lynn Ashburner and Liz Cairncross, 'Membership of the "New Style" Health Authorities: Continuity or Change?' *Public Administration* 71 (Autumn 1993): 357–75; Anthony Cook, 'Financial Accounting in the NHS,' *British Medical Journal* 310 (4 February 1995): 312–16; Philip Hunt, 'Accountability in the National Health Service,' *Parliamentary Affairs* 48 (April 1995): 297–305; Patricia Day, 'The State, the NHS, and General Practice,' *Journal of Public Health Policy* 13 (Summer 1992): 165–79; Rudolf Klein, 'The NHS Reforms So Far,' *Annals of the Royal College of Surgeons of England* 75 (March 1993): 74–8; Allyson M. Pollock, 'Where Should Health Services Go: Local Authorities versus the NHS?' *British Medical Journal* 310 (17 June 1995): 1580–9; Stephen Harrison, 'Working the Markets: Purchaser/Provider Separation in English Health Care,' *International Journal of Health Services* 21, no. 4 (1991): 625–35; Rob Baggot, 'Reforming the British Health Care System: A Permanent Revolution?' *Policy Studies* 15 (Autumn 1994): 35–47; Charles D. Shaw, 'Quality Assurance in the United Kingdom,' *Quality Assurance in Health Care* 5 (June 1993): 107–18; Ken Judge and Nicholas Mays, 'Allocating Resources for Health and Social Care in England,' *British Medical Journal* 308 (21 May 1994): 1363–6; Brian Salter, 'The Politics of Community Care: Social Rights and Welfare Limits,' *Politics and Policy* 22 (April 1994): 119–30; Brian Salter, 'The Politics of Purchasing in the National Health Service,' *Policy and Politics* 21 (July 1993): 171–84; M. Impallomeni and J. Starr, 'The Changing Face of Community and Institutional Care for the Elderly,' *Journal of Public Health Medicine* 17 (June 1995): 171–8; Linda Challis and Melanie Henwood, 'Equity in Community Care,' *British Medical Journal* 308 (4 June 1994): 1496–9; Tim Booer, 'The Health Care System in the United Kingdom,' in *Financing Health Care*, ed. Hoffmeyer and McCarthy, 1076–1116.

8. Justin Keen, 'Should the National Health Service Have an Information Strategy?' *Public Administration* 72 (Spring 1994): 33–53; Mike Dent, 'Professionalism, Educated Labour and the State: Hospital Medicine and the New Managerialism,' *Sociological Review* 41 (May 1993): 244–73; Rob Flynn, 'Coping with Cutbacks and Managing Retrenchment in Health,' *Journal of Social Policy* 20 (April 1991): 215–36; John Bailey, 'Time for Change in Traditional Working Practices?' *British Medical Journal* 310 (25 March

1995): 788–90; Brian Salter, 'Change in the British National Health Service: Policy Paradox and the Rationing Issue,' *International Journal of Health Services* 24, no. 1 (1994): 45–72; Michael Calnan and Simon Williams, 'Challenges to Professional Autonomy in the United Kingdom? The Perceptions of General Practitioners,' *International Journal of Health Services* 25, no. 2 (1995): 219–41; Martin McKee and Nick Black, 'Does the Current Use of Junior Doctors in the United Kingdom Affect the Quality of Medical Care?' *Social Science and Medicine* 34 (March 1992): 549–58; Sarah Hayward and Elizabeth Fee, 'More in Sorrow than in Anger: The British Nurses' Strike of 1988,' *International Journal of Health Services* 22, no. 3 (1992): 397–415.

9. Michael Drummond, Jonathan Cooke, and Tom Walley, 'Economic Evaluation under Managed Competition: Evidence from the U.K.,' *Social Science and Medicine* 45 (August 1997): 583–95; John Butler, 'The Privatization of the National Health Service,' *Journal of the Royal Society of Medicine* 90 (January 1997): 3–7; Chris Ham, 'Population-Centered and Patient-Focused Purchasing: The U.K. Experience,' *Milbank Quarterly* 74 (June 1996): 191–214; David Hughes, 'Health Policy: Letting the Market Work?' *Social Policy Review* 5 (1993): 104–24; Margaret Brazier, Jill Lovecy, Michael Moran, and Margaret Potton, 'Falling from a Tightrope: Doctors and Lawyers between the Market and the State,' *Political Studies* 41 (June 1993): 197–213; Ewan Ferlie, 'The Creation and Evolution of Quasi Markets in the Public Sector: Early Evidence from the National Health Service,' *Policy and Politics* 22 (April 1994): 105–12; Bob Hudson, 'Quasi-Markets in Health and Social Care in Britain: Can the Public Sector Respond?' *Policy and Politics* 20 (April 1992): 131–42; Alastair Mason and Kieran Morgan, 'Purchaser-Provider: The International Dimension,' *British Medical Journal* 310 (28 January 1995): 231–5; Stephen Harrison, 'The Dynamics of Health Care Organisation in Britain,' *Journal of Public Health Policy* 15 (Autumn 1994): 283–97; Howard Glennerster and Julian Le Grand, 'The Development of Quasi-Markets in Welfare Provision in the United Kingdom,' *International Journal of Health Services* 25, no. 2 (1995): 203–18; Nancy North, 'Alford Revisited: The Professional Monopolisers, Corporate Rationalisers, Community and Markets,' *Policy and Politics* 23 (April 1995): 115–25; Brian Salter, 'The Private Sector and the NHS: Redefining the Welfare State,' *Policy and Politics* 23 (January 1995): 17–30; Carol Propper, 'Agency and Incentives in the NHS Internal Market,' *Social Science and Medicine* 40 (June 1995): 1683–90; Carol Propper, 'Equity and the UK National Health Service: A Review of the Evidence,' *Economic and Social Review* 25 (July 1994): 343–65; Owen O'Donnell, Carol Propper, and Richard Upward, 'United Kingdom,' in *Equity in the Finance and Delivery of Health Care: An International Perspective*, ed. Eddy Van Doorslaer, Adam Wagstaff, and Frans Rutten (New York: Oxford University Press, 1993), 326–61; Booer, 'The Health Care System in the United Kingdom,' 1076–81, 1090–1104, 1113–21; Peggy Foster, 'Improving the Doctor/Patient Relationship: A Feminist Perspective,' *Journal of Social Policy* 18 (July 1989): 337–61.

10. Mike Pringle, 'An Opportunity to Improve Primary Care,' *British Medical Journal* 314 (22 February 1997): 595–7; Eddy Van Doorslaer and Adam Wagstaff, 'Equity in the Finance of Health Care: Methods and Findings,' in *Equity in the Finance and Delivery of Health Care*, ed. Van Doorslaer, Wagstaff, and Rutten, 20–48, esp. 47–8; Maria Evandrout, Jane

Falkingham, Julian Le Grand, and David Winter, 'Equity in Health and Social Care,' *Journal of Social Policy* 21 (October 1992): 489–523; Booer, 'The Health Care System in the United Kingdom,' in *Financing Health Care*, ed. Hoffmeyer and McCarthy, 1077–84; Robin Haynes, 'Inequalities in Health and Health Service Use: Evidence from the General Household Survey,' *Social Science and Medicine* 33, no. 4 (1991): 361–8; Margaret Whitehead, 'Who Cares about Equity in the NHS?' *British Medical Journal* 308 (14 May 1994): 1284–7.

11. US Department of Health and Human Services, *Social Security Programs throughout the World — 1993*, 340–3; Zeitzer, 'Recent European Trends in Disability and Related Programs,' 22–3; Hartley Dean and Peter Taylor-Gooby, 'Statutory Sick Pay and the Control of Sickness Absence,' *Journal of Social Policy* 19 (January 1990): 47–67; Organisation for Economic Cooperation and Development, *OECD Health Systems: Facts and Trends 1960–1991*, vol. 1 (Paris: OECD, 1993), 252–75; Organisation for Economic Cooperation and Development, *Revenue Statistics of OECD Member Countries, 1965–1993* (Paris: OECD, 1994), 192–3; Jonas Pontusson, 'Explaining the Decline of European Social Democracy: The Role of Structural Economic Change,' *World Politics* 47 (July 1995): 495–533, esp. 530–1; George J. Shieber, 'Preconditions for Health Reform: Experiences from the OECD Countries,' *Health Policy* 32 (April–June 1995): 279–93.

12. See the articles by John Warden: 'Labour Finds Power Is Heaven on Earth,' *British Medical Journal* 314 (17 May 1997): 1438; 'Dobson Is New Health Secretary,' *British Medical Journal* 314 (10 May 1997): 1366; 'Ending "Two Tierism" Is Top Priority for New Health Secretary,' *British Medical Journal* 314 (17 May 1997): 1434; 'Labour Acts to Cut NHS Costs,' *British Medical Journal* 314 (17 May 1997): 1574.

Part II

1. See Charles F. Andrain and David E. Apter, *Political Protest and Social Change: Analyzing Politics* (London: Macmillan Press, 1995), 9–10; James B. Rule, *Theory and Progress in Social Science* (New York: Cambridge University Press, 1977), esp. 23–119, 173–242; Ernan McMullian, 'Underdetermination,' *Journal of Medicine and Philosophy* 20 (June 1995): 233–52; Gary King, Robert O. Keohane, and Sidney Verba, *Designing Social Inquiry: Scientific Inference in Qualitative Research* (Princeton, NJ: Princeton University Press, 1994), 34–49; Bernard Cohen, 'Sociological Theory: The Half-full Cup,' in *Formal Theory in Sociology: Opportunity or Pitfall?* ed. Jerald Hage (Albany: State University of New York Press, 1994), 66–83.

5   Political Culture and the Meaning of Health

1. Bernard Shaw, *Major Critical Essays: Doctors' Delusions, Crude Criminology, Sham Education*, vol. 22 (New York: Wm. H. Wise and Company, 1932), 1.

2. Ibid., 4–12, 42–69, 157. See too Murray T. Pheils, 'Thank You, Mr. Shaw,' *British Medical Journal* 309 (24–31 December 1994): 1724–6.

3. For analyses of the functions of political ideology in the policy process, see Charles F. Andrain and David E. Apter, *Political Protest and Social Change* (London: Macmillan Press, 1995), 13–25; Louise G. White, 'Policy Analysis

as Discourse,' *Journal of Policy Analysis and Management* 13 (Summer 1994): 506–25.

4. Mary Douglas, 'Governability: A Question of Culture,' *Millennium* 22 (Winter 1993): 463–81; Michael Thompson, Richard Ellis, and Aaron Wildavsky, *Cultural Theory* (Boulder, CO: Westview Press, 1990), esp. 1–100; Dennis J. Coyle and Richard J. Ellis, eds., *Politics, Policy, and Culture* (Boulder, CO: Westview Press, 1994), particularly the following essays: Richard J. Ellis and Denis J. Coyle, 'Introduction,' 1–14, Richard P. Boyle and Richard M. Coughlin, 'Conceptualizing and Operationalizing Cultural Theory,' 191–218; Aaron Wildavsky, 'Can Norms Rescue Self-Interest or Macro Explanations Be Joined to Micro Explanations?' *Critical Review* 5 (Summer 1991): 301–23; Aaron Wildavsky, 'Why Self-Interest Means Less Outside of a Social Context: Cultural Contributions to a Theory of Rational Choices,' *Journal of Theoretical Politics* 6 (April 1994): 131–59; Christopher Hood, 'Control over Bureaucracy: Cultural Theory and Institutional Variety,' *Journal of Public Policy* 15 (September–December 1995): 207–30, esp. 208–12; Sharon Hays, 'Structure and Agency and the Sticky Problem of Culture,' *Sociological Theory* 12 (March 1994): 57–72; Kathryn Vance Staiano, 'The Semiotic Perspective,' in *The Social Construction of Illness: Illness and Medical Knowledge in Past and Present*, ed. Jens Lachmund and Gunnar Stollberg (Stuttgart, Germany: Franz Steiner Verlag, 1992), 173–80.

5. Susan T. Fiske and Shelley E. Taylor, *Social Cognition*, 2d ed. (New York: McGraw-Hill, 1991), 22–95, esp. 48–54, 83–8.

6. Douglas, 'Governability,' 470–80; Wildavsky, 'Why Self-Interest Means Less Outside of a Social Context,' 141–57; Wildavsky, 'Can Norms Rescue Self-Interest or Macro Explanations Be Joined to Micro Explanations?' 302–22; Russell Caplan, 'The Importance of Social Theory for Health Promotion: From Description to Reflexivity,' *Health Promotion International* 8, no. 2 (1993): 147–57; Betsy L. Fife, 'The Conceptualization of Meaning in Illness,' *Social Science and Medicine* 38 (January 1994): 309–16; Adam Wagstaff and Eddy Van Doorslaer, 'Equity in the Finance and Delivery of Health Care: Concepts and Definitions,' in *Equity in the Finance and Delivery of Health Care: An International Perspective*, ed. Eddy Van Doorslaer, Adam Wagstaff, and Frans Rutten (New York: Oxford University Press, 1993), 7–19.

7. M. Angeles Mora and Víctor Urruela, 'Salud y Sociedad: Influencia de las Corrientes de Pensamiento en los Modelos Sanitarios,' *Revista Española de Investigaciones Sociológicas*, no. 53 (January–March 1991): 19–27; Hubert Oppl and Ernst von Kardorff, 'The National Health Care System in the Welfare State,' *Social Science and Medicine* 31, no. 1 (1990): 43–50; Dean C. Hammer, 'Cultural Theory and Historical Change: The Development of Town and Church in Puritan New England,' in *Politics, Policy, and Culture*, ed. Coyle and Ellis, 137–56.

8. William C. Cockerham, Thomas Abel, and Günther Lüschen, 'Max Weber, Formal Rationality, and Health Lifestyles,' *Sociological Quarterly* 34 (August 1993): 413–25; Deborah Stone, 'At Risk in the Welfare State,' *Social Research* 56 (Autumn 1989): 591–633; James M. Buchanan, 'Economic Science and Cultural Diversity,' *Kyklos* 48, no. 2 (1995): 193–200; Peter Minowitz, *Profits, Priests, and Princes: Adam Smith's Emancipation of Economics from Politics and Religion* (Stanford, CA: Stanford University Press, 1993), 218–26; Jerry Z. Muller, *Adam Smith in His Time and Ours: Designing the Decent Society* (Princeton, NJ: Princeton University Press,

1993), 100–12; Sheldon S. Wolin, *Politics and Vision: Continuity and Innovation in Western Political Thought* (Boston: Little, Brown, 1960), 343–5.

9. Anatole France, *Le Lys rouge* (Paris: Calmann-Lévy, 1923), 117–18.

10. Mora and Urruela, 'Salud y Sociedad,' 19–27; Gary Lee Malecha, 'A Cultural Analysis of Populism in Late-Nineteenth-Century America,' in *Politics, Policy, and Culture*, ed. Coyle and Ellis, 93–116; Andrain and Apter, *Political Protest and Social Change*, 191–4.

11. Albert O. Hirschman, *The Rhetoric of Reaction: Perversity, Futility, Jeopardy* (Cambridge, MA: Belknap Press of Harvard University Press, 1991), 43–80; Richard J. Ellis, 'The Social Construction of Slavery,' in *Politics, Policy, and Culture*, ed. Coyle and Ellis, 117–35.

12. Lawrence R. Jacobs, 'Institutions and Culture: Health Policy and Public Opinion in the U.S. and Britain,' *World Politics* 44 (January 1992): 179–209; Lawrence R. Jacobs, *The Health of Nations: Public Opinion and the Making of American and British Health Policy* (Ithaca, NY: Cornell University Press, 1993), esp. 217–36.

13. For sample surveys of national attitudes toward social services, see the following sources: (1) *World Opinion Update* 21 (February 1997): 22; 20 (March 1996): 30–2; 20 (January 1996): 9–10; 19 (November 1995): 126–9; 19 (August 1995): 95; 19 (July 1995): 82; 19 (March 1995): 31–2; 19 (January 1995): 2–3; 18 (September 1994): 103; 17 (October 1993): 116–17; 17 (May 1993): 57–8, 60; 17 (April 1993): 39–40; 17 (January 1993): 2–3; 16 (November 1992): 127–8; 16 (July 1992): 77; 16 (May 1992): 57; 16 (March 1992): 29–30; 16 (February 1992): 19; 16 (January 1992): 10–11; (2) Elizabeth Hann Hastings and Philip K. Hastings, eds., *Index to International Public Opinion, 1995–1996* (Westport, CT: Greenwood Press, 1997): 44, 114–24, 138, 152–6; *Index to International Public Opinion, 1994–1995* (Westport, CT: Greenwood Press, 1996): 52–4, 80–1, 97–8, 133, 141–7, 165, 170–87; *Index to International Public Opinion, 1993–1994* (Westport, CT: Greenwood press, 1995): 78–9; 131–9, 148–51, 157–60, 168–77, 409, 709, 711–13; *Index to International Public Opinion, 1992–1993* (Westport, CT: Greenwood Press, 1994): 60–1, 145–6, 153, 162–4, 329, 356, 408, 412–15; *Index to International Public Opinion, 1991–1992* (Westport, CT: Greenwood Press, 1993): 112–15, 136, 144–7, 153–7, 170, 356–7, 374, 379, 381, 391–3, 427–30; *Index to International Public Opinion, 1990–1991* (Westport, CT: Greenwood Press, 1992): 122–8, 147–9, 306, 409, 413; (3) *Gallup Poll Monthly*, no. 365 (February 1996): 9–12; no. 354 (March 1995): 26–7; no. 352 (January 1995): 3, 7–8, 26; no. 348 (September 1994): 30; no. 347 (August 1994): 17, 47–8; no. 346 (July 1994): 14–15; (4) *Public Perspective* 6 (October/November 1995): 14–17; 6 (April/May 1995): 2, 29; 4 (January/February 1993): 8–9. See too *American Enterprise* 5 (July/August 1994): 95–108; Lawrence R. Jacobs and Robert Y. Shapiro, 'Public Opinion's Tilt against Private Enterprise,' *Health Affairs* 13 (Spring 1994): 285–98; Lawrence R. Jacobs, Robert Y. Shapiro, and Eli C. Schulman, 'The Polls — Poll Trends: Medical Care in the United States — An Update,' *Public Opinion Quarterly* 57 (Fall 1993): 394–427; Lawrence R. Jacobs and Robert Y. Shapiro, 'Questioning the Conventional Wisdom on Public Opinion toward Health Reform,' *PS: Political Science and Politics* 27 (June 1994): 208–14; Susan A. MacManus, 'Taxing and Spending Politics: A Generational Perspective,' *Journal of Politics* 57 (August 1995): 607–29, esp. 624–5; Robert J. Blendon, Tracey Stelzer Hyams, and John Benson, 'Health Care

and the 1996 Election,' *Inquiry* 33 (Spring 1996): 10–14; Robert J. Blendon, Drew E. Altman, John Benson, Matt James, Diane Rowland, Patricia Neuman, Robert Leitman, and Tracey Stelzer Hyams, 'The Public's View of the Future of Medicare,' *Journal of the American Medical Association* 274 (22/29 November 1995): 1645–8; Robert J. Blendon, John Marttila, John M. Benson, Matthew C. Shelter, Francis J. Connolly, and Tom Kiley, 'The Beliefs and Values Shaping Today's Health Reform Debate,' *Health Affairs* 13, no. 1 (1994): 274–84; Robert J. Blendon, Karen Donelan, Albert J. Jovell, Laura Pellisé, and Enrique Costas Lombardia, 'Spain's Citizens Assess Their Health Care System,' *Health Affairs* 10 (Fall 1991): 220–4; Elim Papadakis and Clive Bean, 'Popular Support for the Welfare State: A Comparison between Institutional Regimes,' *Journal of Public Policy* 13 (July–September 1993): 227–54; Stefan Björk and Per Rosén, 'Setting Health Care Priorities in Sweden: The Politician's Point of View,' *Health Policy* 26, no. 2 (1993): 141–54; Stefan Svallors, 'The End of Class Politics? Structural Cleavages and Attitudes to Swedish Welfare Policies,' *Acta Sociologica*, no. 1 (1995): 53–74; Edeltraud Roller, 'Ideological Basis of the Market Economy: Attitudes toward Distribution Principles and the Role of Government in Western and Eastern Germany,' *European Sociological Review* 10 (September 1994): 111.

14. Loek Halman, 'Individualism in Individualized Society? Results from the European Values Surveys,' *International Journal of Comparative Sociology* 37 (December 1996): 195–214; James R. Kluegel and Masaru Miyano, 'Justice Beliefs and Support for the Welfare State in Advanced Capitalism,' in *Social Justice and Political Change: Public Opinion in Capitalist and Post-Communist States*, ed. James R. Kluegel, David S. Mason, and Bernd Wegener (New York: Aldine de Gruyter, 1995), 81–105; James R. Kluegel, György Csepeli, Tamás Kolosi, Antal Örkény, and Mária Neményi, 'Accounting for the Rich and Poor: Existential Justice in Comparative Perspective,' in *Social Justice and Political Change*, 179–207; Beate M. Huseby, 'Attitudes toward the Size of Government,' in *The Scope of Government*, ed. Ole Borre and Elinor Scarbrough (New York: Oxford University Press, 1995), 87–118; Maria A. Confalonieri and Kenneth Newton, 'Taxing and Spending: Tax Revolt or Tax Protest?' in *The Scope of Government*, 121–48; Achille Ardigó, 'Public Attitudes and Changes in Health Care Systems: A Confrontation and a Puzzle,' in *The Scope of Government*, 388–406; Everett Carll Ladd, 'Every Country Is Unique, but the U.S. Is Different,' *Public Perspective* 6 (April/May 1995): 14–20; *Public Perspective* 6 (February/March 1995): 39; *American Enterprise* 5 (July/August 1995): 101–2; Peter E. Abrahamson, 'Welfare and Poverty in the Europe of the 1990s: Social Progress or Social Dumping?' *International Journal of Health Services* 21, no. 2 (1991): 237–64; Marie R. Haug, Hiroko Akiyama, Georgeanna Tryban, Kyoichi Sonoda, and May Wykle, 'Self Care: Japan and the U.S. Compared,' *Social Science and Medicine* 33, no. 9 (1991): 1011–22; Seymour Martin Lipset, *American Exceptionalism: A Double-Edged Sword* (New York: W. W. Norton, 1996), 211–63; Seymour Martin Lipset, *Continental Divide: The Values and Institutions of the United States and Canada* (New York: Routledge, 1990), 117–51, 212–27; Scott C. Flanagan, Shinsaku Kohei, Ichiro Miyake, Bradley M. Richardson, and Joji Watanuki, *The Japanese Voter* (New Haven, CT: Yale University Press, 1991), 84–142; Donald S. Kellermann, Andrew Kohut, and Carol Bowman, *The Pulse of Europe: A Survey of Political and Social Values and Attitudes* (Washington, DC: Times Mirror Center for the People and the Press, 1991), section IX,

Questionnaire, 96, 117–20; Robert Y. Shapiro and John T. Young, 'Public Opinion toward Social Welfare Policies: The United States in Comparative Perspective,' in *Research in Micropolitics*, vol. 3, ed. Samuel Long (Greenwich, CT: JAI Press, 1990), 143–86.

15. Jacob S. Hacker, 'National Health Care Reform: An Idea Whose Time Came and Went,' *Journal of Health Politics, Policy and Law* 21 (Winter 1996): 647–96.

16. Lawrence R. Jacobs and Robert Y. Shapiro, 'Don't Blame the Public for Failed Health Care Reform,' *Journal of Health Politics, Policy and Law* 20 (Summer 1995): 412–13.

17. Andrain and Apter, *Political Protest and Social Change*, 149–60, 269–79; Jacques Thomassen, 'Empirical Results into Political Representation: Failing Democracy or Failing Models?' in *Elections at Home and Abroad: Essays in Honor of Warren E. Miller*, ed. M. Kent Jennings and Thomas E. Mann (Ann Arbor: University of Michigan Press, 1994), 237–60; *Index to International Public Opinion, 1995–1996*, 44, 122–3, 365; *World Opinion Update* 20 (October 1996): 116; Adam Swift, Gordon Marshall, Carole Burgoyne, and David Routh, 'Distributive Justice: Does It Matter What the People Think?' in *Social Justice and Political Change*, ed. Kluegel, Mason, and Wegener, 32–40; Kenneth Newton and Maria A. Confalonieri, 'Politics, Economics, Class, and Taxation,' in *The Scope of Government*, ed. Borre and Scarbrough, 149–64; Edeltraud Roller, 'The Welfare State: The Equality Dimension,' in *The Scope of Government*, 165–97; Per Arnt Pettersen, 'The Welfare State: The Security Dimension,' in *The Scope of Government*, 198–233; Flanagan, et al., *The Japanese Voter*, 112–24; Adrian Furnham, 'Explaining Health and Illness: Lay Perceptions on Current and Future Health, the Causes of Illness, and the Nature of Recovery,' *Social Science and Medicine* 39 (September 1994): 715–25; François Pétry, 'The Party Agenda Model: Election Programmes and Government Spending in Canada,' *Canadian Journal of Political Science* 28 (March 1995): 51–84; Paul M. Sniderman, Joseph F. Fletcher, Peter H. Russell, and Philip E. Tetlock, *The Clash of Rights: Liberty, Equality, and Legitimacy in Pluralist Democracy* (New Haven, CT: Yale University Press, 1996), 80–155; David Wilsford, 'Path Dependency, or Why History Makes It Difficult but Not Impossible to Reform Health Care Systems in a Big Way,' *Journal of Public Policy* 14 (July–December 1994): 251–83; Papadakis and Bean, 'Popular Support for the Welfare State,' 237–49; Roller, 'Ideological Basis of the Market Economy,' 112; Mark D. Smith, Drew E. Altman, Robert Leitman, Thomas W. Moloney, and Humphrey Taylor, 'Taking the Public's Pulse on Health System Reform,' *Health Affairs* 11 (Summer 1992): 125–33; William G. Jacoby, 'Public Attitudes toward Government Spending,' *American Journal of Political Science* 38 (May 1994): 336–61; *Gallup Monthly*, no. 354 (March 1995): 26; *Public Perspective* 6 (April/May 1995): 28; Robert B. Smith, 'Ideology, Partisanship, and the New Political Continuum,' *Society* 34 (March/April 1997): 13–18; Blendon et al., 'Beliefs and Values Shaping Today's Health Reform Debate,' 278; Charles F. Andrain, *Social Policies in Western Industrial Societies* (Berkeley, CA: Institute of International Studies, University of California, Berkeley, 1985), 149–60.

18. Peter Taylor-Gooby, 'Paying for Welfare: The View from Europe,' *Political Quarterly* 67 (April–June 1996): 116–26; Peter Taylor-Gooby, 'The Future of Health Care in Six European Countries: The Views of Policy Elites,' *International Journal of Health Services* 26, no. 2 (1996): 215–17; *Index to*

International Public Opinion, 1995–1996, 14, 155; *Index to International Public Opinion, 1994–1995*, 180–1; *Index to International Public Opinion, 1992–93*, 344; John D. Moynahan, Jr., 'Revising the Health Care System: Over 2,000 Opinion Leaders Speak Out,' *Statistical Bulletin* 72 (July–September 1991): 2–9; Joel C. Cantor, Nancy L. Barrand, Randolph A. Desonia, Alan B. Cohen, and Jeffrey C. Merrill, 'Business Leaders' Views about Health Care,' *Health Affairs* 11 (Spring 1991): 98–105; Robert J. Blendon and Jennifer N. Edwards, 'Caring for the Uninsured: Choices for Reform,' *Journal of the American Medical Association* 265 (15 May 1991): 2563, 2565; Vicente Navarro, *The Politics of Health Policy: The U.S. Reforms, 1980–1994* (Cambridge, MA: Blackwell, 1994), 171–93; Jochen Clasen and Arthur Gould, 'Stability and Change in Welfare States: Germany and Sweden in the 1990s,' *Policy and Politics* 23 (July 1995): 189–201; Bruce Western, 'Institutional Mechanisms for Unionization in Sixteen OECD Countries: An Analysis of Social Survey Data,' *Social Forces* 73 (December 1994): 497–519; Jonas Pontusson, 'Explaining the Decline of European Social Democracy: The Role of Structural Economic Change,' *World Politics* 47 (July 1995): 495–533, esp. 530–1; Marja A. Pijl, 'The Dutch Welfare State: A Product of Religious and Political Pluralism,' *Social Policy Review* 5 (1993): 288–9; Michael Fogarty, 'How Dutch Christian Democracy Made a New Start,' *Political Quarterly* 66 (July–September 1993): 138–55; Stephen A. Borrelli and Terry J. Royed, 'Government "Strength" and Budget Deficits in Advanced Democracies,' *European Journal of Political Research* 28 (September 1995): 225–60, esp. 239; Robert F. O'Neil, 'Corporate Social Responsibility and Business Ethics: A European Perspective,' *International Journal of Social Economics* 13, no. 10 (1986): 64–76; Michael Ornstein, 'The Political Ideology of the Canadian Capitalist Class,' *Canadian Review of Sociology and Anthropology* 23 (May 1986): 182–209; Andrain, *Social Policies in Western Industrial Societies*, 160–88; Göran Therborn, 'Karl Marx Returning: The Welfare State and the Neo-Marxist, Corporatist and Statist Theories,' *International Political Science Review* 7 (April 1986): 131–64.

19. Tjeerd Tymstra and Margriet Andela, 'Opinions of Dutch Physicians, Nurses, and Citizens on Health Care Policy, Rationing, and Technology,' *Journal of the American Medical Association* 270 (22–29 December 1993): 2995–9; Hesook Suzie Kim, Inger Margrethe Holter, Margarehte Lorensen, Mitsuko Inayoshi, Sadao Shimaguchi, Reiko Shimazaki-Ryder, Yuko Kawaguchi, Ryoko Hori, Kumiko Takezaki, Helena Leino-Kilpi, and Maarit Munkki-Utunen, 'Patient-Nurse Collaboration: A Comparison of Patients' and Nurses' Attitudes in Finland, Japan, Norway, and the U.S.A.,' *International Journal of Nursing Studies* 30 (October 1993): 387–401; Gregory J. Hayes, Steven C. Hayes, and Thane Dykstra, 'Physicians Who Have Practiced in Both the United States and Canada Compare the Systems,' *American Journal of Public Health* 83 (November 1993): 1544–8; Rodney A. Hayward, Richard L. Kravitz, and Martin F. Shapiro, 'The U.S. and Canadian Health Care Systems: Views of Resident Physicians,' *Annals of Internal Medicine* 115 (15 August 1991): 308–14; A. Paul Williams, Eugene Vayda, May L. Cohen, Christel A. Woodward, and Barbara M. Ferrier, 'Medicine and the Canadian State: From the Politics of Conflict to the Politics of Accommodation?' *Journal of Health and Social Behavior* 36 (December 1995): 303–21; Léo-Paul Landry, 'Physicians Want More Private-Sector Spending on Health Care, CMA Survey Reveals,' *Canadian Medical Association Journal* 151 (1 December 1994): 1633–5; Amy Scanlan, Stephen

256 *Notes*

J. Zyzanski, Susan A. Flocke, Kurt C. Strange, and Inese Grava-Gubins, 'A Comparison of US and Canadian Family Physician Attitudes toward Their Respective Health Care Systems,' *Medical Care* 34 (August 1996): 837–44; Leighton Ku and Dena Fisher, 'The Attitudes of Physicians toward Health Care Cost-Containment Policies,' *Health Services Research* 25 (April 1990, Part I): 25–42; *World Opinion Update* 17 (May 1993): 57–8; Jeffrey Schnipper and Robert A. Dorwart, 'Medical Students' Opinions of Health System Reform,' *Journal of the American Medical Association* 273 (4 January 1995): 80–1; Michael S. Wilkes, Samuel A. Skootsky, Carol S. Hodgson, Stuart Slavin, and LuAnn Wilkerson, 'Health Care Reform as Perceived by First Year Medical Students,' *Journal of Community Health* 19 (August 1994): 253–69; Michael S. Wilkes, Samuel A. Skootsky, Stuart Slavin, Carol S. Hodgson, and LuAnn Wilkerson, 'Entering First-Year Medical Students' Attitudes toward Managed Care,' *Academic Medicine* 69 (April 1994): 307–9; Carol S. Hodgson, Michael S. Wilkes, and LuAnn Wilkerson, 'Students' Attitudes toward Health Care: First-Year Medical Students' Attitudes toward Access to Medical Care and Cost Containment,' *Academic Medicine* 68 (October Supplement 1993): S70–S72; Richard M. Levinson, Edward W. McCranie, Graham Scambler, and Annette Scambler, 'Physician Authority and the Autonomy of Nurses and Patients: Attitudes of British and U.S. Medical Students,' in *Research in the Sociology of Health Care: Patients, Consumers, Providers, and Caregivers*, vol. 12, ed. Jennie Jacobs Kronenfeld (Greenwich, CT: JAI Press, 1995), 355–68.

20. See Sven Steinmo and Jon Watts, 'It's the Institutions, Stupid! Why Comprehensive National Health Insurance Always Fails in America,' *Journal of Health, Politics and Law* 20 (Summer 1995): 329–72; Hacker, 'National Health Care Reform,' 647–96; John R. Zaller, *The Nature and Origins of Mass Opinion* (New York: Cambridge University Press, 1992), 310–32; Jacobs, *The Health of Nations*; Jacobs, 'Institutions and Culture,' 179–209; William M. Reisinger, 'The Renaissance of a Rubric: Political Culture as Concept and Theory,' *International Journal of Public Opinion* 7 (Winter 1995): 328–52; Marco Verweij, 'Cultural Theory and the Study of International Relations,' *Millennium* 24 (Spring 1995): 87–111.

6 Political Power and Policy Changes

1. Robert Tressell, *The Ragged Trousered Philanthropists* (New York: Monthly Review Press, 1962), 157. See also 29, 138–9, 219, 505, 628–30. According to a 1994 survey, one-third of Labour Party members in the House of Commons stated that Robert Tressell had the greatest influence on their political beliefs. R. H. Tawney and the Bible ranked second and third. See Steve Platt and Julia Gallagher, 'From Bevan to the Bible,' *New Statesman and Society* 7 (30 September 1994): 22–3.
2. A. J. Cronin, *The Citadel* (Boston: Little, Brown, 1937), esp. 133, 188–95.
3. See Paul A. Sabatier and Hank C. Jenkins-Smith, eds., *Policy Change and Learning: An Advocacy Coalition Approach* (Boulder, CO: Westview Press, 1993), esp. 1–56, 211–35; Hank C. Jenkins-Smith and Paul A. Sabatier, 'Evaluating the Advocacy Coalition Framework,' *Journal of Public Policy* 14 (April–June 1994): 175–203; Paul A. Sabatier and Hank C. Jenkins-Smith, 'The Advocacy Coalition Framework: An Assessment' (paper presented at the annual meeting of the American Political Science Association, San Francisco, August 1996).

4. Jenkins-Smith and Sabatier, 'Evaluating the Advocacy Coalition Framework,' 198–9; Paul A. Sabatier and Hank C. Jenkins-Smith, 'The Advocacy Coalition Framework: Assessment, Revisions, and Implications for Scholars and Practitioners,' in *Policy Change and Learning*, ed. Sabatier and Jenkins-Smith, 211–34.

5. Thomas Poguntke, 'Germany,' *European Journal of Political Research* 26 (December 1994): 305–12.

6. Philipp Genschel, 'The Dynamics of Inertia: Institutional Persistence and Change in Telecommunications and Health Care,' *Governance* 10 (January 1997): 43–66; Frederik T. Schut, 'Health Care Reform in the Netherlands: Balancing Corporatism, Statism, and Market Mechanisms,' *Journal of Health Politics, Policy and Law* 20 (Fall 1995): 615–52; Karl Hinrichs, 'The Impact of German Health Insurance Reforms on Redistribution and the Culture of Solidarity,' *Journal of Health Politics, Policy and Law* 20 (Fall 1995): 653–87; David Wilsford, 'States Facing Interests: Struggles over Health Care Policy in Advanced, Industrial Democracies,' *Journal of Health Politics, Policy and Law* 20 (Fall 1995): 571–613; Michael Fogarty, 'How Dutch Christian Democracy Made a New Start,' *Political Quarterly* 66 (July–September 1995): 138–55; Marja A. Pijl, 'The Dutch Welfare State: A Product of Religious and Political Pluralism,' *Social Policy Review* 5 (1993): 288–304; Peer Scheepers, Jan Lammers, and Jan Peters, 'Religious and Class Voting in the Netherlands 1990–1991: A Review of Recent Contributions Tested,' *Netherlands Journal of Social Sciences* 30 (August 1994): 5–24; Jelle Visser, 'Works Councils and Unions in the Netherlands: Rivals or Allies?' *Netherlands Journal of Social Sciences* 29 (June 1993): 64–92; Joel Rogers and Wolfgang Streeck, 'Workplace Representation Overseas: The Works Councils Story,' in *Working under Different Rules*, ed. Richard B. Freeman (New York: Russell Sage Foundation, 1994), 112–21; Wim Groot and Annette van den Berg, 'Why Union Density Has Declined,' *European Journal of Political Economy* 10 (December 1994): 749–63; 'In Group Participation: Still a Nation of Joiners,' *Public Perspective* 6 (April/May 1995): 21; Barbara J. Coleman, 'European Models of Long-Term Care in the Home and Community,' *International Journal of Health Services* 25, no. 3 (1995): 455–74; Wynand P. M. M. van de Ven and Frederik T. Schut, 'The Dutch Experience with Internal Markets,' in *Health Care Reform through Internal Markets*, ed. Monique Jérôme Forget, Joseph White, and Joshua M. Wiener (Washington, DC: Brookings Institution, 1995), 95–117; Susan Giaimo, 'Health Care Reform in Britain and Germany: Recasting the Political Bargain with the Medical Profession,' *Governance* 8 (July 1995): 354–79; Marian Döhler, 'The State as Architect of Political Order: Policy Dynamics in German Health Care,' *Governance* 8 (July 1995): 380–404; Ulrike Götting, Karin Haug, and Karl Hinrichs, 'The Long Road to Long-Term Care Insurance in Germany,' *Journal of Public Policy* 14 (July–December 1994): 285–309; Jochen Clasen and Arthur Gould, 'Stability and Change in Welfare States: Germany and Sweden in the 1990s,' *Policy and Politics* 23 (July 1995): 189–201; Jens Alber, 'A Framework for the Comparative Study of Social Services,' *Journal of European Social Policy* 5, no. 2 (1995): 131–49; Ullrich Hoffmeyer, 'The Health Care System in Germany,' in *Financing Health Care*, vol. 1, ed. Ullrich K. Hoffmeyer and Thomas R. McCarthy (Dordrecht, the Netherlands: Kluwer Academic Publishers, 1994), 421–93; Graham Shuttleworth, 'The Health Care System in the Netherlands,' in *Financing Health Care*, vol. 1, 699–754.

7. See Theda Skocpol, *Protecting Soldiers and Mothers: The Political Origins of Social Policy in the United States* (Cambridge, MA: The Belknap Press of Harvard University Press, 1992), 42; Theda Skocpol, *Boomerang: Clinton's Health Security Effort and the Turn against Government in U.S. Politics* (New York: W. W. Norton, 1996); David Wilsford, *Doctors and the State: The Politics of Health Care in France and the United States* (Durham, NC: Duke University Press, 1991), 1–28, 221–91; Ellen M. Immergut, *Health Politics: Interests and Institutions in Western Europe* (New York: Cambridge University Press, 1992), 1–79, 226–44.

8. R. Kent Weaver and Bert A. Rockman, 'When and How Do Institutions Matter?' in *Do Institutions Matter? Government Capabilities in the United States and Abroad*, ed. R. Kent Weaver and Bert A. Rockman (Washington, DC: The Brookings Institution, 1993), 445–61; James G. March and Johan P. Olsen, *Rediscovering Institutions: The Organizational Basis of Politics* (New York: The Free Press, 1989); James G. March and Johan P. Olsen, *Democratic Governance* (New York: The Free Press, 1995); James G. March and Johan P. Olsen, 'Institutional Perspectives on Political Institutions,' *Governance* 9 (July 1996): 247–64; Jonas Pontusson, 'From Comparative Public Policy to Political Economy: Putting Political Institutions in Their Place and Taking Interests Seriously,' *Comparative Political Studies* 28 (April 1995): 117–47; B. Guy Peters, 'Political Institutions, Old and New,' in *A New Handbook of Political Science*, ed. Robert E. Goodin and Hans-Dieter Klingemann (New York: Oxford University Press, 1996), 205–20; Charles F. Andrain and David E. Apter, *Political Protest and Social Change: Analyzing Politics* (London: Macmillan Press, 1995), 144-54.

9. Jean Blondel, 'Toward a Systematic Analysis of Government-Party Relationships,' *International Political Science Review* 16 (April 1995): 127–43; R. Kent Weaver and Bert A. Rockman, 'Assessing the Effects of Institutions,' in *Do Institutions Matter?* ed. Weaver and Rockman, 11–41; Jonas Pontusson, 'Explaining the Decline of European Social Democracy: The Role of Structural Economic Change,' *World Politics* 47 (July 1995): 530–1; Thomas T. Mackie and Richard Rose, *The International Almanac of Electoral History*, 3d ed. (Washington, DC: Congressional Quarterly, 1991), 453, 455; Rudolf Klein, 'Big Bang Health Care Reform — Does It Work? The Case of Britain's 1991 National Health Service Reforms,' *Milbank Quarterly* 73 (September 1995): 299–337; Patricia Day and Rudolf Klein, 'Constitutional and Distributional Conflict in British Medical Politics: The Case of General Practice, 1911–1991,' *Political Studies* 40 (September 1992): 462–78; Bob Hudson, 'Joint Commissioning: Organisational Revolution or Misplaced Enthusiasm?' *Policy and Politics* 23 (July 1995): 233–49.

10. Wilsford, *Doctors and the State*, 263–72.

11. Wilsford, 'States Facing Interests,' 575–9; Caroline Weill, 'Health Care Technology in France,' *Health Policy* 30, nos. 1–3 (1994): 123–62; Stephen Bach, 'Managing a Pluralist Health System: The Case of Health Reform in France,' *International Journal of Health Services* 24, no. 4 (1994): 593–606; Jonathan E. Fielding and Pierre-Jean Lancry, 'Lessons from France — "Vive la Différence,"' *Journal of the American Medical Association* 270 (11 August 1993): 748–56; Mike Burstall, 'The Health Care System in France,' in *Financing Health Care*, vol. 1, ed. Hoffmeyer and McCarthy, 347–408.

12. John Creighton Campbell, *How Policies Change: The Japanese Government and the Aging Society* (Princeton, NJ: Princeton University Press, 1992), 282–312, 352–95; Chalmers Johnson, *Japan: Who Governs? The Rise of the*

Developmental State (New York: W. W. Norton, 1995), esp. 21–68, 115–56; Naoki Ikegami, 'Japanese Health Care: Low Cost through Regulated Fees,' *Health Affairs* 10 (Fall 1991): 87–109; Richard T. Rapp, 'The Health Care System in Japan,' in *Financing Health Care*, vol. 1, ed. Hoffmeyer and McCarthy, 587–670; José Antonio Crespo, 'The Liberal Democratic Party in Japan: Conservative Domination,' *International Political Science Review* 16 (April 1995): 199–209; Rei Shiratori, 'Japan,' *European Journal of Political Research* 26 (December 1994): 355–60.

13.   Karl Marx, *The Revolutions of 1848: Political Writings*, vol. 1, ed. David Fernbach (New York: Vintage Books, 1974), 69.

14.   Clyde W. Barrow, *Critical Theories of the State: Marxist, Neo-Marxist, Post-Marxist* (Madison: University of Wisconsin Press, 1993), 13–76; Karl Marx, *Surveys from Exile: Political Writings*, vol. 2, ed. David Fernbach (New York: Vintage Books, 1974), 236–49; Andrain and Apter, *Political Protest and Social Change*, 157–9; Richard Breen and David Rottman, 'Class Analysis and Class Theory,' *Sociology* 29 (August 1995): 453–73; Raju J. Das, 'State Theories: A Critical Analysis,' *Science and Society* 60 (Spring 1996): 27–57; Kevin White, 'The Sociology of Health and Illness,' *Current Sociology* 39 (Autumn 1991): 23–49.

15.   Ernest Mandel, 'Introduction,' in Karl Marx, *Capital: A Critique of Political Economy*, vol. 1, trans. Ben Fowkes (New York: Vintage Books, 1977), 11–86, esp. 23; Bertell Ollman, 'Putting Dialectics to Work: The Process of Abstraction in Marx's Method,' *Rethinking Marxism* 3 (Spring 1990): 26–74; Howard Waitzkin, 'Marxist Perspectives in Social Medicine,' *Social Science and Medicine* 28, no. 11 (1989): 1099–1101; Howard Waitzkin, 'Text, Social Context, and the Structure of Medical Discourse,' in *Current Research on Occupations and Professions*, vol. 6, ed. Helena Z. Lopata and Judith A. Levy (Greenwich, CT: JAI Press, 1991), 117–46; Deborah Lupton, 'Discourse Analysis: A New Methodology for Understanding the Ideologies of Health and Illness,' *Australian Journal of Public Health* 16 (June 1992): 145–50; Albert Bergesen, 'The Rise of Semiotic Marxism,' *Sociological Perspectives* 36 (Spring 1993): 1–22; William K. Carroll and R. S. Ratner, 'Between Leninism and Radical Pluralism: Gramscian Reflections on Counter-Hegemony and the New Social Movements,' *Critical Sociology* 20, no. 2 (1994): 3–26; Erik Olin Wright, *Interrogating Inequality: Essays on Class Analysis, Socialism and Marxism* (London: Verso, 1994), 32–106, 178–255; Erik Olin Wright, *Class Counts: Comparative Studies in Class Analysis* (Cambridge, England: Cambridge University Press, 1997), esp. 1–42, 373–546; Alvin Y. So, 'Recent Developments in Marxist Class Analysis: A Critical Appraisal,' *Sociological Inquiry* 65 (November 1995): 313–28.

16.   Gregg M. Olsen, 'Locating the Canadian Welfare State: Family Policy and Health Care in Canada, Sweden, and the United States,' *Canadian Journal of Sociology* 19 (Winter 1994): 1–20.

17.   See Andrea Botho, 'Western Europe's Economic Stagnation,' *New Left Review*, no. 201 (September–October 1993): 60–75; Enrico Pugliese, 'The Europe of the Unemployed,' *International Journal of Political Economy* 23 (Fall 1993): 13–36; Lars Osberg, 'Concepts of Unemployment and the Structure of Employment,' *Économie Appliquée* 48, no. 1 (1995): 157–81; Jonathan Michie and Frank Wilkinson, 'Wages, Government Policy and Unemployment,' *Review of Political Economy* 7 (April 1995): 133–49; Malcolm Sawyer, 'Unemployment and the Dismal Science,' *University of Leeds Review* 36 (1993/1994): 285–301; Charles F. Andrain, *Comparative*

Political Systems: Policy Performance and Social Change (Armonk, NY: M. E. Sharpe, 1994), 185–6; Michael Moran, 'Three Faces of the Health Care State,' *Journal of Health Politics, Policy and Law* 20 (Fall 1995): 767–81; Peter Taylor-Gooby, 'Citizenship, Dependency, and the Welfare Mix: Problems of Inclusion and Exclusion,' *International Journal of Health Services* 23, no. 3 (1993): 455–74.

18. Peter Garpenby, 'Health Care Reform in Sweden in the 1990s: Local Pluralism versus National Coordination,' *Journal of Health Politics, Policy and Law* 20 (Fall 1995): 695–717; Robert A. Spasoff, 'Health Department Administration of the Canadian Health Care Program,' *Journal of Health Policy* 16, no. 2 (1995): 141–51; Mary Janigan, 'Dustup over Dollars,' *Maclean's* 110 (19 May 1997): 20–2; Sharon Doyle Driedger, 'The Nurses,' *Maclean's* 110 (28 April 1997): 24–7; Karl Kronebusch, 'Medicaid and the Politics of Groups: Recipients, Providers, and Policy Making,' *Journal of Health Politics, Policy and Law* 22 (June 1997): 839–78; Demetrios Caraley, 'Dismantling the Federal Safety Net: Fictions versus Realities,' *Political Science Quarterly* 111 (Summer 1996): 225–58; Christopher Jencks, 'The Hidden Paradox of Welfare Reform,' *American Prospect*, no. 32 (May–June 1997): 33–40.

19. Ronald L. Caplan, 'The United States Health Care Crisis: A Marxian Reappraisal,' *Rethinking Marxism* 4 (Winter 1991): 94–111; Hans A. Baer, 'The American Dominative Medical System as a Reflection of Social Relations in the Larger Society,' *Social Science and Medicine* 28, no. 11 (1989): 1103–12; David U. Himmelstein and Steffie Woolhandler, 'The Corporate Compromise: A Marxist View of Health Policy,' *Monthly Review* 42 (May 1990): 14–24; Vicente Navarro, *The Politics of Health Policy: The U.S. Reforms, 1980–1994* (Cambridge, MA: Blackwell, 1994), 111–216; Vicente Navarro, 'Why Congress Did Not Enact Health Care Reform,' *Journal of Politics, Policy and Law* 20 (Summer 1995): 455–62; Nancy Watzman and Patrick Woodhall, 'Managed Health Care Companies' Lobbying Frenzy,' *International Journal of Health Services* 25, no. 3 (1995): 403–10; Beth Mintz, 'Business Participation in Health Care Policy Reform: Factors Contributing to Collective Action within the Business Community,' *Social Problems* 42 (August 1995): 408–28.

20. OECD, *Employment Outlook*, July 1994 (Paris: Organisation for Economic Cooperation and Development, 1994), 149–54, 173, 181–5.

21. Stephen A. Borrelli and Terry J. Royed, 'Government "Strength" and Budget Deficits in Advanced Democracies,' *European Journal of Political Research* 28 (September 1995): 238–9; Pontusson, 'Explaining the Decline of European Social Democracy,' 495–533; OECD, *Employment Outlook*, July 1995 (Paris: Organisation for Economic Cooperation and Development, 1995), 192, 209, 223, 228, 229; Francis Green, Andrew Henley, and Euclid Taskalotos, 'Income Inequality in Corporatist and Liberal Economies: A Comparison of Trends within OECD Countries,' *International Review of Applied Economics* 8 (September 1994): 303–31; Anthony B. Atkinson, Lee Rainwater, and Timothy M. Smeeding, *Income Distribution in OECD Countries: Evidence from the Luxembourg Income Study* (Paris: Organisation for Economic Cooperation and Development, 1995), 39–49; Paul Pierson, 'Fragmented Welfare States: Federal Institutions and the Development of Social Policy,' *Governance* 8 (October 1995): 449–78; Carol Sakala, 'The Development of National Medical Care Programs in the United Kingdom and Canada: Applicability to Current Conditions in the United States,' *Journal of Health*

Politics, Policy and Law 15 (Winter 1990): 709–53; Antonia Maioni, 'Nothing Succeeds Like the Right Kind of Failure: Postwar National Health Insurance Initiatives in Canada and the United States,' *Journal of Health Politics, Policy and Law* 20 (Spring 1995): 5–30; Mel Watkins, 'Ontario: Discrediting Social Democracy,' *Studies in Political Economy*, no. 43 (Spring 1994): 139–48; Marjorie Griffin Cohen, 'British Columbia: Playing Safe Is a Dangerous Game,' *Studies in Political Economy*, no. 43 (Spring 1994): 149–59; Phillip Hansen, 'Saskatchewan: The Failure of Political Imagination,' *Studies in Political Economy*, no. 43 (Spring 1994): 161–7; Marita Johanson, Ullabeth Sätterlund Larsson, Roger Säljö, and Kurt Svärdsudd, 'Lifestyle in Primary Health Care Discourse,' *Social Science and Medicine* 40 (February 1995): 339–48; Wright, *Class Counts*, 318–70; Andrain, *Comparative Political Systems*, 50; Shanto Iyengar, *Is Anyone Responsible? How Television Frames Political Issues* (Chicago: University of Chicago Press, 1991), 127–43.

22. Caplan, 'The United States Health Care Crisis,' 102–9; White, 'The Sociology of Health and Illness,' 45–49; Gregory Pappas, 'Some Implications for the Study of the Doctor-Patient Interaction: Power, Structure, and Agency in the Works of Howard Waitzkin and Arthur Kleinman,' *Social Science and Medicine* 30, no. 2 (1990): 199–204; Breen and Rottman, 'Class Analysis and Class Theory,' 461–8; Wright, *Interrogating Inequality*, 32–50, 88–106, 178–98; Michael A. Lebowitz, 'Analytical Marxism and the Marxian Theory of Crisis,' *Cambridge Journal of Economics* 18 (April 1994): 163–79; Cathie Jo Martin, 'Markets, Medicare, and Making Do: Business Strategies after National Health Care Reform,' *Journal of Health Politics, Policy and Law* 22 (April 1997): 557–93; Laurence A. Weil, 'Organized Labor and Health Reform: Union Interests and the Clinton Plan,' *Journal of Public Health Policy* 18, no. 1 (1997): 30–48.

23. Nikolaos Zahariadis, 'Comparing Lenses in Comparative Public Policy,' *Policy Studies Journal* 23 (Summer 1995): 378–82; Edella Schlager and William Blomquist, 'A Comparison of Three Emerging Theories of the Policy Process,' *Political Research Quarterly* 49 (September 1996): 651–72; Ken Lertzman, Jeremy Rayner, and Jeremy Wilson, 'Learning and Change in the British Columbia Forest Policy Sector: A Consideration of Sabatier's Advocacy Coalition Framework,' *Canadian Journal of Political Science* 29 (March 1996): 111–33.

24. Pontusson, 'From Comparative Public Policy to Political Economy,' 127–44; Klein, 'Big Bang Health Care Reform,' 299–37; Day and Klein, 'Constitutional and Distributional Conflict in British Medical Politics,' 462–78; Barrow, *Critical Theories of the State*, 125–45; Youssef Cohen, *Radicals, Reformers, and Reactionaries: The Prisoner's Dilemma and the Collapse of Democracy in Latin America* (Chicago: University of Chicago Press, 1994), esp. 1–52.

7 Rational Choice and Market Efficiency

1. Charles Dickens, *Hard Times* (New York: New American Library, 1961), 31.
2. Ibid., 282–3.
3. James C. Scott, 'The Role of Theory in Comparative Politics: A Symposium,' *World Politics* 48 (October 1995): 28–37.
4. Steven Lukes, *The Curious Enlightenment of Professor Caritat: A Comedy of Ideas* (London: Verso, 1995), 81. See also 76–98.

5. For assumptions and criticisms of rational choice theory, see Peter Zweifel and Friedrich Breyer, *Health Economics* (New York: Oxford University Press, 1977); Charles F. Andrain and David E. Apter, *Political Protest and Social Change: Analyzing Politics* (London: Macmillan Press, 1995), 261–5; Donald P. Green and Ian Shapiro, *Pathologies of Rational Choice Theory: A Critique of Applications in Political Science* (New Haven, CT: Yale University Press, 1994), 1–46, 179–204; Donald P. Green and Ian Shapiro, 'Pathologies Revisited: Reflections on Our Critics,' *Critical Review* 9 (Winter–Spring 1995): 235–76; Hamish Stewart, 'A Critique of Instrumental Reason in Economics,' *Economics and Philosophy* 11 (April 1995): 57–83; Gary S. Becker, 'Nobel Lecture: The Economic Way of Looking at Behavior,' *Journal of Political Economy* 101 (June 1993): 385–409; Michael Banton, 'Rational Choice Theories,' *American Behavioral Scientist* 38 (January 1995): 478–97; Magnus Johannesson, 'The Relationship between Cost-Effectiveness Analysis and Cost-Benefit Analysis,' *Social Science and Medicine* 41 (August 1995): 483–9; Paul J. Feldstein, 'An Economic Perspective on Health Politics and Policy,' *Quarterly Review of Economics and Business* 30 (Winter 1990): 117–35; Douglass C. North, 'The Historical Evolution of Polities,' *International Review of Law and Economics* 14 (December 1994): 381–91; William M. Dugger, 'Douglass C. North's New Institutionalism,' *Journal of Economic Issues* 29 (June 1995): 453–8; Donald Wittman, *The Myth of Democratic Failure: Why Political Institutions Are Efficient* (Chicago: University of Chicago Press, 1995), esp. 31–75, 87–114, 162–93; Robert E. Lane, 'What Rational Choice Explains,' *Critical Review* 9 (Winter–Spring 1995): 107–26; Thomas Rice, 'Can Markets Give Us the Health System We Want?' *Journal of Health Politics, Policy and Law* 22 (April 1997): 383–426; Jeff Worsham, Marc Allen Eisner, and Evan J. Ringquist, 'Assessing the Assumptions: A Critical Analysis of Agency Theory,' *Administration and Society* 28 (February 1997): 419–40; William Hildred and Larry Watkins, 'The Nearly Good, the Bad, and the Ugly in Cost-Effectiveness Analysis of Health Care,' *Journal of Economic Issues* 30 (September 1996): 755–75.

6. Alain C. Enthoven, 'Internal Market Reform of the British National Health Service,' *Health Affairs* 10 (Fall 1991): 60–70; Alain C. Enthoven, 'On the Ideal Market Structure for Third-Party Purchasing of Health Care,' *Social Science and Medicine* 39 (November 1994): 1413–24; Alain C. Enthoven and Sara J. Singer, 'Market-Based Reform: What to Regulate and by Whom?' *Health Affairs* 14 (Spring 1995): 100–19; Alain C. Enthoven, 'Why Managed Care Has Failed to Contain Health Costs,' *Health Affairs* 12 (Fall 1993): 27–43; Penny Newman, 'Interview with Alain Enthoven: Is There Convergence between Britain and the United States in the Organisation of Health Services?' *British Medical Journal* 310 (24 June 1995): 1652–5; Alain Enthoven, 'Enthoven Responds,' *Health Affairs* 16 (July/August 1997): 282–4; Zweifel and Breyer, *Health Economics*, 363–70; Matthew Sutton, 'Personal Paper: How to Get the Best Health Outcome for a Given Amount of Money,' *British Medical Journal* 315 (5 July 1997): 47–9; Robin G. Milne and Ben Torsney, 'The Efficiency of Administrative Governance: The Experience of the Pre-reform British National Health Service,' *Journal of Comparative Economics* 24 (April 1997): 161–80.

7. See Kenneth J. Arrow, 'Uncertainty and the Welfare Economics of Medical Care,' *American Economic Review* 53 (December 1963): 941–73; Casten von Otter and Richard B. Saltman, 'Towards a Swedish Health Policy for the 1990s: Planned Markets and Public Firms,' *Social Science and Medicine* 32,

no. 4 (1991): 473–81; Siegfried G. Karsten, 'Health Care: Private Good vs. Public Good,' *American Journal of Economics and Sociology* 54 (April 1995): 129–44; Sam Mirmirani and Richard N. Spivack, 'Health Care System Collapse in the United States: Capitalist Market Failure!' *De Economist* 141, no. 3 (1993): 419–31; Camilo Dagum, 'The Scope and Method of Economics as a Science,' *Il Politico* 60 (January–March 1995): 5–39; Phil Shackley and Mandy Ryan, 'What Is the Role of the Consumer in Health Care?' *Journal of Social Policy* 23 (October 1994): 517–41; Choong Sup Lee, 'Optimal Medical Treatment under Asymmetric Information,' *Journal of Health Economics* 14 (October 1995): 419–41; Julian Le Grand, 'The Evaluation of Health Care Systems Reforms,' *Il Politico* 58 (January–June 1993): 31–53; Manuel C. Pontes, 'Agency Theory: A Framework for Analyzing Physician Services,' *Health Care Management Review* 20 (Fall 1995): 57–67; Brian Ferguson and Justin Keen, 'Transaction Costs, Externalities and Information Technology in Health Care,' *Health Economics* 5 (January 1996): 25–36.

8. Victor R. Fuchs, 'What Every Philosopher Should Know about Health Economics,' *Proceedings of the American Philosophical Society* 140 (June 1996): 186–96; Alan M. Garber and Charles E. Phelps, 'Economic Foundations of Cost-Effectiveness Analysis,' *Journal of Health Economics* 16 (February 1997): 1–31; David Parkin, 'Comparing Health Service Efficiency across Countries,' *Oxford Review of Economic Policy* 5 (Spring 1989): 75–88; Peter J. Neumann and Magnus Johannesson, 'From Principle to Public Policy: Using Cost-Effectiveness Analysis,' *Health Affairs* 13 (Summer 1994): 206–14; Magnus Johannesson, 'A Note on the Depreciation of the Societal Perspective in Economic Evaluation of Health Care,' *Health Policy* 33 (July 1995): 59–66; Magnus Johannesson, 'Economic Evaluation of Health Care and Policymaking,' *Health Policy* 33 (September 1995): 179–90; Bernie O'Brien, 'Principles of Economic Evaluation for Health Care Programs,' *Journal of Rheumatology* 22 (July 1995): 1399–1402; Julien Forder, Martin Knapp, and Gerald Wistow, 'Competition in the Mixed Economy of Care,' *Journal of Social Policy* 25 (April 1996): 201–21; J. Richardson, 'Cost Utility Analysis: What Should Be Measured?' *Social Science and Medicine* 39 (July 1994): 7–21; Martin Feldstein, 'The Economics of Health and Health Care: What Have We Learned? What Have I Learned?' *American Economic Review* 85 (May 1995): 28–31; Cam Donaldson, 'Economics, Public Health and Health Care Purchasing: Reinventing the Wheel?' *Health Policy* 33 (August 1995): 79–90.

9. Robert D. Tollison and Richard E. Wagner, 'Self-Interest, Public Interest, and Public Health,' *Public Choice* 69 (March 1991): 323–43; Louis de Alessi, 'The Effect of Institutions on the Choices of Consumers and Providers of Health Care,' *Journal of Theoretical Politics* 1 (October 1989): 427–58; Enthoven, 'Why Managed Care Has Failed to Contain Health Costs,' 28–32, 37–42; Enthoven, 'On the Ideal Market Structure for Third-Party Purchasing of Health Care,' 1416–23.

10. Maitland MacFarlan and Howard Oxley, 'Reforming Health Care,' *OECD Observer*, no. 192 (February/March 1995): 23–6; Brian Abel-Smith and Elias Mossialos, 'Cost Containment and Health Care Reform: A Study of the European Union,' *Health Policy* 28 (May 1994): 89–132; Brian Abel-Smith, 'Cost Containment and New Priorities in the European Community,' *Milbank Quarterly* 70, no. 3 (1992): 393–416; Peter P. Groenewegen and Michael Calnan, 'Changes in the Control of Health Care Systems in Europe,'

European Journal of Public Health 5 (December 1995): 240–4; Richard B. Saltman, 'A Conceptual Overview of Recent Health Care Reforms,' *European Journal of Public Health* 4, no. 4 (1994): 287–93; I. H. Monrad Aas, 'Incentives and Financing Methods,' *Health Policy* 34 (December 1995): 205–20; William A. Glaser, 'How Expenditure Caps and Expenditure Targets Really Work,' *Milbank Quarterly* 71, no. 1 (1993): 97–127; Timothy Besley and Miguel Gouveia, 'Alternative Systems of Health Care Provision,' *Economic Policy*, no. 19 (1994): 199–258; John Hutton, Michael Borowitz, Inga Oleksy, and Byran R. Luce, 'The Pharmaceutical Industry and Health Reform: Lessons from Europe,' *Health Affairs* 13 (Summer 1994): 98–111; David J. Gross, Jonathan Ratner, James Perez, and Sarah L. Glavin, 'International Pharmaceutical Spending Controls: France, Germany, Sweden, and the United Kingdom,' *Health Care Financing Review* 15 (Spring 1994): 127–40; Nick Freemantle and Karen Bloor, 'Lessons from International Experience in Controlling Pharmaceutical Expenditure I: Influencing Patients,' *British Medical Journal* 312 (8 June 1996): 1469–71; Karen Bloor, 'Lessons from International Experience in Controlling Pharmaceutical Expenditure II: Influencing Doctors,' *British Medical Journal* 312 (15 June 1996): 1525–7; Karen Bloor, Alan Maynard, and Nick Freemantle, 'Lessons from International Experience in Controlling Pharmaceutical Expenditure III: Regulating Industry,' *British Medical Journal* 313 (6 July 1996): 33–5.

11.   George J. Schieber, Jean-Pierre Poullier, and Leslie M. Greenwald, 'Health System Performance in OECD Countries, 1980–1992,' *Health Affairs* 13 (Fall 1994): 101–3; Organisation for Economic Cooperation and Development, *New Directions in Health Care Policy: Health Policy Studies No. 7* (Paris: OECD, 1995), 9, 19; 'OECD in Figures 1997 Edition,' *OECD Observer*, no 206 (June/July 1997): 48–9.

12.   See Robert G. Evans, 'Canada: The Real Issues,' *Journal of Health Politics, Policy and Law* 17 (Winter 1992): 739–62; Robert G. Evans, Morris L. Barer, and Clyde Hertzman, 'The 20-Year Experiment: Accounting for, Explaining, and Evaluating Health Care Cost Containment in Canada and the United States,' in *Annual Review of Public Health 1991*, vol. 12, ed. Gilbert S. Omenn, Jonathan E. Fielding, and Lester B. Lave (Palo Alto, CA: Annual Reviews, 1991), 481–518; Morris L. Barer and Robert G. Evans, 'Interpreting Canada: Models, Mind-sets, and Myths,' in *National Health Care: Lessons for the United States and Canada*, ed. Jonathan Lemco (Ann Arbor: University of Michigan Press, 1994), 147–67; Pauline Vaillancourt Rosenau, 'Impact of Political Structures and Informal Political Processes on Health Policy: Comparison of the United States and Canada,' *Policy Studies Review* 13 (Autumn/Winter 1994): 293–314; Morris L. Barer, Jonathan Lomas, and Claudia Sanmartin, 'Re-Minding Our Ps and Qs: Medical Cost Controls in Canada,' *Health Affairs* 15 (Summer 1996): 216–34; Charles F. Andrain, *Social Policies in Western Industrial Societies* (Berkeley: Institute of International Studies, University of California, 1985), 106–12, 116–17; W. Pete Welch, Diana Verrilli, Steven J. Katz, and Eric Latimer, 'A Detailed Comparison of Physician Services for the Elderly in the United States and Canada,' *Journal of the American Medical Association* 275 (8 May 1996): 1410–16; Robert B. Sullivan, Mamoru Watanabe, Michael E. Whitcomb, and David A. Kindig, 'The Evolution of Divergences in Physician Supply Policy in Canada and the United States,' *Journal of the American Medical Association* 276 (4 September 1996): 704–9; Marc L. Rivo and David A.

Kindig, 'A Report Card on the Physician Work Force in the United States,' *New England Journal of Medicine* 334 (4 April 1996): 892–6; Naoki Ikegami and Yoshinori Hiroi, 'Factors in Health Care Spending: An Eight-Nation Comparison with OECD Data,' in *Containing Health Care Costs in Japan*, ed. Naoki Ikegami and John Creighton Campbell (Ann Arbor: University of Michigan Press, 1996), 39; Steven J. Katz, Stephen Zuckerman, and W. Pete Welch, 'Comparing Physician Fee Schedules in Canada and the United States,' *Health Care Financing Review* 14 (Fall 1992): 141–9; Peter C. Coyte, Donald N. Dewees, and Michael J. Trebilcock, 'Canadian Medical Malpractice Liability: An Empirical Analysis of Recent Trends,' *Journal of Health Economics* 10 (July 1991): 143–68; Donald N. Dewees, Michael J. Trebilcock, and Peter C. Coyte, 'The Medical Malpractice Crisis: A Comparative Empirical Perspective,' *Law and Contemporary Problems* 54 (Winter 1991): 217–51; Jeffrey Mullis, 'Medical Malpractice, Social Structure, and Social Control,' *Sociological Forum* 10 (March 1995): 135–63; OECD, 'Canada,' in *Internal Markets in the Making: Health Systems in Canada, Iceland, and the United Kingdom: Health Policy Studies No. 6* (Paris: Organisation for Economic Cooperation and Development, 1995), 29–69; Donald A. Redelmeier and Victor R. Fuchs, 'Hospital Expenditures in the United States and Canada,' *New England Journal of Medicine* 328 (18 March 1993): 772–8; Susan G. Haber, Jack Zwanziger, Jack Geoffrey M. Anderson, Kenneth E. Thorpe, and Joseph P. Newhouse, 'Hospital Expenditures in the United States and Canada: Do Hospital Worker Wages Explain the Differences?' *Journal of Health Economics* 11 (December 1992): 453–65; Dale A. Rublee, 'Medical Technology in Canada, Germany, and the United States: An Update,' *Health Affairs* 13 (Fall 1994): 113–17; Kathleen Gondek, 'Prescription Drug Payment Policy: Past, Present, and Future,' *Health Care Financing Review* 15 (Spring 1994): 1–7; OECD, *New Directions in Health Care Policy*, 19, 35; US Bureau of the Census, *Statistical Abstract of the United States* (Washington, DC: US Government Printing Office, 1984, 1986, 1988, 1989, 1992, 1994, 1995), 549 ('84), 535 ('86), 516 ('88), 539 ('89), 543 ('92), 561 ('94), 565 ('95); Joel Lexchin, 'After Compulsory Licensing: Coming Issues in Canadian Pharmaceutical Policy and Politics,' *Health Policy* 40 (April 1997): 69–80; Lynda Buske, 'Regulating the Price of Patented Drugs,' *Canadian Medical Association Journal* 156 (15 May 1997): 1512; Margaret H. Davis and Sally T. Burner, 'Three Decades of Medicare: What the Numbers Tell Us,' *Health Affairs* 14 (Winter 1995): 231–43; Jean-Pierre Poullier, 'Administrative Costs in Selected Industrialized Countries,' *Health Care Financing Review* 13 (Summer 1992): 167–72; Anne K. Gauthier, Deborah L. Rogal, Nancy L. Barrand, and Alan B. Cohen, 'Administrative Costs in the U.S. Health Care System: The Problem or the Solution?' *Inquiry* 29 (Fall 1992): 308–20; Terry Mizrahi, Robert Fasano, and Susan M. Dooha, 'Canadian and American Health Care: Myths and Realities,' *Health and Social Work* 18 (February 1993): 7–12; Steffie Woolhandler and David U. Himmelstein, 'The Deteriorating Administrative Efficiency of the U.S. Health Care System,' *New England Journal of Medicine* 324 (2 May 1991): 1253–8; David U. Himmelstein, James P. Lewontin, and Steffie Woolhandler, 'Who Administers? Who Cares? Medical Administrative and Clinical Employment in the United States and Canada,' *American Journal of Public Health* 86 (February 1996): 172–8; David U. Himmelstein and Steffie Woolhandler, *The National Health Program Book: A Source Guide for Advocates* (Monroe, ME: Common Courage Press, 1994),

111–38; 180–1; Steffie Woolhandler and David U. Himmelstein, 'Costs of Care and Administration at For-Profit and Other Hospitals in the United States,' *New England Journal of Medicine* 336 (13 March 1997): 769–74.

13. Gillian Fairfield, David J. Hunter, David Mechanic, and Flemming Rosleff, 'Managed Care: Origins, Principles, and Evolution,' *British Medical Journal* 314 (21 June 1997): 1823–6; Gillian Fairfield, David J. Hunter, David Mechanic, and Flemming Rosleff, 'Managed Care: Implications of Managed Care for Health Systems, Clinicians, and Patients,' *British Medical Journal* 314 (28 June 1997): 1895–8; John H. McArthur and Francis D. Moore, 'The Two Cultures and the Health Care Revolution: Commerce and Professionalism in Medical Care,' *Journal of the American Medical Association* 277 (26 March 1997): 985–9; Deborah A. Stone, 'The Doctor as Businessman: The Changing Politics of a Cultural Icon,' *Journal of Health Politics, Policy and Law* 22 (April 1997): 533–56; Jon Gabel, 'Ten Ways HMOs Have Changed during the 1990s,' *Health Affairs* 16 (May/June 1997): 134–45; Gail A. Jensen, Michael A. Morrisey, Shannon Gaffney, and Derek K. Liston, 'The New Dominance of Managed Care: Insurance Trends in the 1990s,' *Health Affairs* 16 (January/February 1997): 125–36; Janet M. Corrigan, Jill S. Eden, Marsha R. Gold, and Jeremy D. Pickreign, 'Trends toward a National Health Care Marketplace,' *Inquiry* 34 (Spring 1997): 11–28; Diana Rowland and Kristina Hanson, 'Medicaid: Moving to Managed Care,' *Health Affairs* 15 (Fall 1996): 150–2; Robert Friedland, 'Medicare: Short-Term Answers, Long-Term Questions,' *Challenge* 40 (January–February 1997): 30–45; Jonathan B. Oberlander, 'Managed Care and Medicare Reform,' *Journal of Health Politics, Policy and Law* 22 (April 1997): 595–631; Gerald Riley, Cynthia Taylor, Yen-pin Chiang, and Melvin Ingber, 'Health Status of Medicare Enrollees in HMOs and Fee-for-Service in 1994,' *Health Care Financing Review* 17 (Summer 1996): 65–76; Robert O. Morgan, Beth A. Virnig, Carolee A. DeVito, and Nancy A. Persily, 'The Medicare-HMO Revolving Door — The Healthy Go In and the Sick Go Out,' *New England Journal of Medicine* 337 (17 July 1997): 169–75; Paul G. Ginsburg and Jeremy D. Pickreign, 'Tracking Health Care Costs: An Update,' *Health Affairs* 16 (July/August 1997): 151–5; Donald W. Light, '*Homo Economicus*: Escaping the Traps of Managed Competition,' *European Journal of Public Health* 5, no. 3 (1995): 145–54; Alain C. Enthoven, 'Reply on Managed Competition,' *European Journal of Public Health* 5, no. 3 (1995): 155; Enthoven, 'Why Managed Care Has Failed to Contain Health Costs,' 27–43; Paula Braveman and Trude Bennett, 'Let's Take on the Real Dragon: Profiteering in Health Care,' *Journal of Public Health Policy* 16, no. 3 (1995): 261–8; Amy K. Taylor, Karen M. Beauregard, and Jessica P. Vistnes, 'Who Belongs to HMOs: A Comparison of Fee-for-Service versus HMO Enrollees,' *Medical Care Research and Review* 52 (September 1995): 389–408; Vernellia R. Randall, 'Impact of Managed Care Organizations on Ethnic Americans and Underserved Populations,' *Journal of Health Care for the Poor and Underserved* 5, no. 3 (1994): 224–36; Linda F. Wolf and John K. Gorman, 'New Directions and Developments in Managed Care Financing,' *Health Care Financing Review* 17 (Spring 1996): 1–5; Steven A. Schroeder, 'Cost Containment in U.S. Health Care,' *Academic Medicine* 70 (October 1995): 861–6.

14. William A. Glaser, 'The Competition Vogue and Its Outcomes,' *Lancet* 341 (27 March 1993): 805–12; OECD, *New Directions in Health Care Policy*, 19, 35.

15. See Toshihide Tsuda, Hideyasu Aoyama, and Jack Froom, 'Primary Health Care in Japan and the United States,' *Social Science and Medicine* 38 (February 1994): 489–95; Michael R. Reich, 'Why the Japanese Don't Export More Pharmaceuticals: Health Policy as Industrial Policy,' *California Management Review* 32 (Winter 1990): 124–50; Yasuki Kobayashi and Paul Harris, 'Mental Health Care in Japan,' *Hospital and Community Psychiatry* 43 (November 1992): 1100–3; Blake W. H. Smith, Ray Demers, and Linda Garcia-Shelton, 'Family Medicine in Japan,' *Archives of Family Medicine* 6 (January/February 1997): 59–62; Naoki Ikegami, 'Efficiency and Effectiveness in Health Care,' *Daedalus* 123 (Fall 1994): 113–25; and the following essays in Ikegami and Campbell, eds., *Containing Health Care Costs in Japan*: Ikegami and Hiroi, 'Factors in Health Care Spending,' 33–52; William C. Hsiao, 'Afterword: Costs — The Macro Perspective,' 45–52; Naoki Ikegami, Jay Wolfson, and Takanori Ishii, 'Comparison of Administrative Costs in Health Care between Japan and the United States,' 80–93; John M. Eisenberg and Nancy Foster, 'Aterword: Quality and Cost in Japanese and U.S. Medical Care,' 143–54; Naoki Ikegami and Takeshi Yamada, 'Comparison of Long-Term Care for the Elderly between Japan and the United States,' 155–71; John Creighton Campbell, 'The Egalitarian Health Insurance System,' 255–64; Mikitaka Masuyama and John Creighton Campbell, 'The Evolution of Fee-Schedule Politics in Japan,' 265–77.
16. J.-Matthias Graf von der Schulenburg, 'Forming and Reforming the Market for Third-Party Purchasing of Health Care: A German Perspective,' *Social Science and Medicine* 39 (November 1994): 1473–81; Klaus-Dirk Henke, Margaret A. Murray, and Claudia Ade, 'Global Budgeting in Germany: Lessons for the United States,' *Health Affairs* 13 (Fall 1994): 7–21; Ashley Files and Margaret Murray, 'German Risk Structure Compensation: Enhancing Equity and Effectiveness,' *Inquiry* 32 (Fall 1995): 330–9; Ikegami and Hiroi, 'Factors in Health Care Spending,' 39; Vicente Navarro, 'The West German Health System: A Critique,' *International Journal of Health Services* 21, no. 3 (1991): 565–71; Gross et al., 'International Pharmaceutical Spending Controls,' 127–40; Alexander Dorozynski, 'French Doctors Protest over Health and Welfare Reforms,' *British Medical Journal* 311 (9 December 1995): 1520; Alexander Dorozynski, 'French Protest at Health Budget Cuts,' *British Medical Journal* 311 (11 November 1995): 1247–8; Alexander Dorozynski, 'French Doctors Strike over Night Visits,' *British Medical Journal* 313 (12 October 1996): 898; Alexander Dorozynski, 'French Doctors' Strike Enters Third Week,' *British Medical Journal* 314 (5 April 1997): 993; Mike Burstall and Konrad Wallerstein, 'The Health Care System in France,' in *Financing Health Care*, vol. 1, ed. Ullrich K. Hoffmeyer and Thomas R. McCarthy (Dordrecht, the Netherlands: Kluwer Academic Publishers, 1994), 391–8; OECD, *New Directions in Health Care Policy*, 35.
17. Andrain, *Social Policies in Western Industrial Societies*, 114–16; Laurence Bloch and Pierre Ricordeau, 'La régulation du système de santé en France,' *Revue française d'économie* 11 (Winter 1996): 87–146.
18. Wynand P. M. M. van de Ven, 'Regulated Competition in Health Care: With or Without a Global Budget?' *European Economic Review* 39 (April 1995): 786–94; Wynand P. M. M. van de Ven and Frederik T. Schut, 'The Dutch Experience with Internal Markets,' in *Health Care Reform through Internal Markets*, ed. Monique Jérôme-Forget, Joseph White, and Joshua Wiener (Washington, DC: Brookings Institution, 1995), 95–117; Ham Lieverdink and Hans Maarse, 'Negotiating Fees for Medical Specialists in the

Netherlands,' *Health Policy* 31 (February 1995): 81–101; Graham Shuttleworth, 'The Health Care System in the Netherlands,' in *Financing Health Care*, vol. 1, ed. Hoffmeyer and McCarthy, 729–43; J.-P. A. Nicolai, 'Budget Caps and the Quality of Health Care in Holland,' *Plastic and Reconstructive Surgery* 96 (September 1995): 964–5; Tony Sheldon, 'Dutch Efficiency Savings Are Hitting Healthcare Quality,' *British Medical Journal* 313 (2 November 1996): 1104.

19. Clas Rehnberg, 'The Swedish Experience with Internal Markets,' in *Health Care Reform through Internal Markets*, ed. Jérôme-Forget, White, and Wiener, 49–73; J. Calltorp, 'Sweden: No Easy Choices,' *British Medical Bulletin* 51 (October 1995): 791–8; John Øvretveit, 'Beyond the Public-Private Debate: The Mixed Economy of Health,' *Health Policy* 35 (January 1996): 75–93; Juan Gérvas, Mercedes Pérez Fernández, and Barbara H. Starfield, 'Primary Care, Financing and Gatekeeping in Western Europe,' *Family Practice* 11 (September 1994): 307–17; 'OECD in Figures 1997 Edition,' 49; OECD, *New Directions in Health Care Policy*, 9, 19, 35; OECD, *Internal Markets in the Making*, 9; Ikegami and Hiroi, 'Factors in Health Care Spending,' 39; Gross et al., 'International Pharmaceutical Spending Controls,' 127–40; Timothy Stoltzfus Jost, David Hughes, Jean McHale, and Lesley Griffiths, 'The British Health Care Reforms, the American Health Care Revolution, and Purchaser/Provider Contracts,' *Journal of Health Politics, Policy and Law* 20 (Winter 1995): 885–908.

20. Health Policy Network of the National Health Service Consultants' Association and the National Health Service Support Federation, 'In Practice: The NHS Market in the United Kingdom,' *Journal of Public Health Policy* 16, no. 4 (1995): 452–91; Enthoven, 'On the Ideal Market Structure for Third-Party Purchasing of Health Care,' 1413–24; Alan Maynard, 'Can Competition Enhance Efficiency in Health Care? Lessons from the Reform of the U.K. National Health Service,' *Social Science and Medicine* 39 (November 1994): 1433–45; Michael J. Wilkinson, 'Love Is Not a Marketable Commodity: New Public Management in the British National Health Service,' *Journal of Advanced Nursing* 21 (May 1995): 980–7; Le Grand, 'The Evaluation of Health Care Systems Reforms,' 31–53; Chris Ham, 'Managed Markets in Health Care: The UK Experiment,' *Health Policy* 35 (March 1996): 279–92; Chris Ham, 'Population-Centered and Patient-Focused Purchasing: The U.K. Experience,' *Milbank Quarterly* 74 (June 1996): 191–214; Andrew Wall, 'Mine, Yours or Theirs? Accountability in the New NHS,' *Policy and Politics* 24 (January 1996): 73–84; Rowena Vickridge, 'NHS Reforms and Community Care — Means-Tested Health Care Masquerading as Consumer Choice?' *Critical Social Policy* 15 (Summer 1995): 76–80; Rob Flynn, Susan Pickard, and Gareth Williams, 'Contracts and the Quasi-Market in Community Health Services,' *Journal of Social Policy* 24 (October 1995): 529–50; David M. Rea, 'Unhealthy Competition: The Making of a Market for Mental Health,' *Policy and Politics* 23 (April 1995): 141–55; Trevor R. Hadley and Howard Goldman, 'Effect of Recent Health and Social Service Policy Reforms on Britain's Mental Health System,' *British Medical Journal* 311 (9 December 1995): 1556–8; Angela Coulter, 'Evaluating General Practice Fundholding in the United Kingdom,' *European Journal of Public Health* 5 (9 December 1995): 233–9; Stephen Harrison and Nabila Choudhry, 'General Practice Fundholding in the UK National Health Service: Evidence to Date,' *Journal of Public Health Policy* 17, no. 3 (1996): 331–45; Darrin L. Baines and David K. Whynes, 'Selection Bias in GP

Fundholding,' *Health Economics* 5 (March–April 1996): 129–40; Toby Gosden and David J. Torgerson, 'The Effect of Fundholding on Prescribing and Referral Costs: A Review of the Evidence,' *Health Policy* 40 (May 1997): 103–14; Toby Gosden, David J. Torgerson, and Alan Maynard, 'What Is to Be Done about Fundholding,' *British Medical Journal* 315 (19 July 1995): 170–1; Alan Earl-Slater and Colin Bradley, 'The Inexorable Rise in the UK NHS Drugs Bill: Recent Policies, Future Prospects,' *Public Administration* 74 (Autumn 1996): 393–411; Martin Chalkley and James M. Malcomson, 'Contracts for the National Health Service,' *Economic Journal* 106 (November 1996): 1691–1701; Jacob Glazer and Amir Shmueli, 'The Physician's Behavior and Equity under a Fundholding Contract,' *European Economic Review* 39 (April 1995): 781–5; Nick Evans and David Panter, 'Contracting through District Health Authorities,' *British Journal of Hospital Medicine* 54 (21 June –11 July 1995): 52–3; Allyson M. Pollock, 'The NHS Goes Private,' *Lancet* 346 (9 September 1995): 683–4; C. B. T. Adams, 'OxDONS Syndrome: The Inevitable Disease of the NHS Reforms,' *British Medical Journal* 311 (9 December 1995): 1559–61; Allyson M. Pollock, Matthew Dunnigan, Declan Gaffney, Alison Macfarlane, and F. Azeem Majeed, 'What Happens When the Private Sector Plans Hospital Services for the NHS: Three Case Studies under the Private Finance Initiative,' *British Medical Journal* 314 (26 April 1997): 1266–71; Richard J. Carroll, Susan D. Horn, Bjorn Soderfeldt, Brent C. James, and Lars Malmberg, 'International Comparison of Waiting Times for Selected Cardiovascular Procedures,' *Journal of the American College of Cardiology* 25 (1 March 1995): 557–63; Caroline Richmond, 'NHS Waiting Lists Have Been a Boon for Private Medicine in the UK,' *Canadian Medical Association Journal* 154 (1 February 1996): 378–81; Peter L. Bradshaw, 'The Recent Health Reforms in the United Kingdom: Some Tentative Observations on Their Impact on Nurses and Nursing in Hospitals,' *Journal of Advanced Nursing* 21 (May 1995): 975–9.

21. Rogers Hollingsworth, Robert Hanneman, Jerald Hage, and Charles Ragin, 'The Effect of Human Capital and State Intervention on the Performance of Medical Systems,' *Social Forces* 75 (December 1996): 459–84; Denny Vagerö, 'Equity and Efficiency in Health Reform: A European View,' *Social Science and Medicine* 39 (November 1994): 1203–10.

8 **Public Policies and Health**

1. Albert Camus, *La Peste* (Paris: Gallimard, 1947), 247.
2. Ibid., 187–8.
3. Ibid., 331.
4. Claudio Cioffi-Revilla and Harvey Starr, 'Opportunity, Willingness, and Political Uncertainty: Theoretical Foundations of Politics,' *Journal of Theoretical Politics* 7 (October 1995): 447–76; Charles F. Andrain and David E. Apter, *Political Protest and Social Change: Analyzing Politics* (London: Macmillan Press, 1995), xi–xii, 3–10, 311–17; Charles F. Andrain, *Social Policies in Western Industrial Societies* (Berkeley: Institute of International Studies, University of California at Berkeley, 1985), 90–1.
5. See Robert G. Evans and Gregory L. Stoddart, 'Producing Health, Consuming Health Care,' in *Why Are Some People Healthy and Others Not? The Determinants of Health of Populations*, ed. Robert G. Evans, Morris L. Barer, and Theodore R. Marmor (New York: Aldine de Gruyter, 1994), 27–64; Richard G. Wilkinson, *Unhealthy Societies: The Afflictions of Inequality* (London: Routledge, 1996); Michael G. Marmot, 'Social

Differentials in Health within and between Populations,' *Daedalus* 123 (Fall 1994): 197–216; John W. Frank and J. Fraser Mustard, 'The Determinants of Health from a Historical Perspective,' *Daedalus* 123 (Fall 1994): 1–19; Douglas Carroll, Paul Bennett, and George Davey Smith, 'Socio-Economic Health Inequalities: Their Origins and Implications,' *Psychology and Health* 8, no. 5 (1993): 295–316; Jonathan S. Feinstein, 'The Relationship between Socioeconomic Status and Health: A Review of the Literature,' *Milbank Quarterly* 71, no. 2 (1993): 279–322; Johannes Siegrist, 'Social Differentials in Chronic Disease: What Can Sociological Knowledge Offer to Explain and Possibly Reduce Them?' *Social Science and Medicine* 41 (December 1995): 1603–5.

6. Jerald Hage and Barbara Foley Meeker, *Social Causality* (Boston: Unwin Hyman, 1988), 20–5; Herman W. Smith, *Strategies of Social Research*, 3d ed. (Fort Worth, TX: Holt, Rinehart and Winston, 1991), 569–71; Andrain and Apter, *Political Protest and Social Change*, 299–30; L. R. Karhausen, 'The Logic of Causation in Epidemiology,' *Scandinavian Journal of Social Medicine* 24 (March 1996): 8–13; Neil D. Weinstein, 'Testing Four Competing Theories of Health-Protective Behavior,' *Health Psychology* 12 (July 1993): 324–33; Michael C. Wolfson, 'Toward a System of Health Statistics,' *Daedalus* 123 (Fall 1994): 181–95; Adam Wagstaff, Pierella Paci, and Eddy van Doorslaer, 'On the Measurement of Inequalities in Health,' *Social Science and Medicine* 33, no. 5 (1991): 545–7; Lars Lindholm, Måns Rosén, and Maria Emmelin, 'An Epidemiological Approach towards Measuring the Trade-Off between Equity and Efficiency in Health Policy,' *Health Policy* 35 (March 1996): 205–16; Sharon Schwartz, 'The Fallacy of the Ecological Fallacy: The Potential Misuse of a Concept and the Consequences,' *American Journal of Public Health* 84 (May 1994): 819–24; Samuel Sepkowitz, 'International Rankings of Infant Mortality and the United States' Vital Statistics Natality Data Collecting System — Failure and Success,' *International Journal of Epidemiology* 24 (June 1995): 583–8; Embry M. Howell and Béatrice Blondel, 'International Infant Mortality Rates: Bias from Reporting Differences,' *American Journal of Public Health* 84 (May 1994): 850–2; Korbin Liu, Marilyn Moon, Margaret Sulvetta, and Juhi Chawla, 'International Infant Mortality Rankings: A Look behind the Numbers,' *Health Care Financing Review* 13 (Summer 1992): 105–18.

7. Sally Macintyre, 'The Black Report and Beyond: What Are the Issues?' *Social Science and Medicine* 44 (March 1997): 723–45; Denny Vågerö and Raymond Illsley, 'Explaining Health Inequalities: Beyond Black and Barker,' *European Sociological Review* 11 (December 1995): 219–41; Viveca Östberg and Denny Vågerö, 'Socio-Economic Differences in Mortality among Children: Do They Persist into Adulthood?' *Social Science and Medicine* 32, no. 4 (1991): 403–10; J. P. Mackenbach, J. van den Bos, I. M. A. Joung, H. van de Mheen, and K. Stronks, 'The Determinants of Excellent Health: Different from the Determinants of Ill-Health?' *International Journal of Epidemiology* 23 (December 1994):1273–81; J. P. Mackenbach, 'Socio-Economic Health Differences in the Netherlands: A Review of Recent Empirical Findings,' *Social Science and Medicine* 34 (February 1992): 213–26; Uwe Helmert and S. Shea, 'Social Inequalities and Health Status in Western Germany,' *Public Health* 108 (September 1994): 341–56; Nelson Blank and Finn Diderichsen, 'Social Inequalities in the Experience of Illness in Sweden: A "Double Suffering,"' *Scandinavian Journal of Social Medicine* 24 (June 1996): 81–9; Yolande Obadia, Pierre Toubiana, Charlie Chanut, and Michel Rotily, 'L'état de santé des RMIstes dans les Bouches du Rhône: Enquête sur la morbidité déclarée,' *Revue française des affaires sociales* 48 (April–June 1994): 111–29; Pierre Aïach, 'La santé et ses inégalités,' *Esprit*, no. 229 (February 1997): 63–71; Alain Parant, 'Longévité et retraite en France,' *Futuribles*, no. 207 (March 1996): 49–54; Cameron A. Mustard, Shelley Derksen, Jean-Marie Berthelot,

Michael Wolfson, and Leslie L. Roos, 'Age-Specific Education and Income Gradients in Morbidity and Mortality in a Canadian Province,' *Social Science and Medicine* 45 (August 1997): 383–97; Paola Bollini and Harald Siem, 'No Real Progress towards Equity: Health of Migrants and Ethnic Minorities on the Eve of the Year 2000,' *Social Science and Medicine* 41 (September 1995): 819–28; H. P. Uniken Venema, H. F. L. Garretsen, and P. J. van der Mass, 'Health of Migrants and Migrant Health Policy: The Netherlands as an Example,' *Social Science and Medicine* 41 (September 1995): 809–18; Roland Rosmond, Leif Lapidus, and Per Björntorp, 'A Comparative Review of Psychosocial and Occupational Environment in Native Swedes and Immigrants,' *Scandinavian Journal of Social Medicine* 24 (December 1996): 237–42; Wilhelmina A. Leigh, 'The Health Status of Women of Color,' in *The American Woman 1994–95: Where We Stand, Women and Health*, ed. Cynthia Costello and Anne J. Stone (New York: W. W. Norton, 1994), 154–96; David R. Williams and Chiquita Collins, 'US Socioeconomic and Racial Differences in Health: Patterns and Explanations,' in *Annual Review of Sociology 1995*, vol. 21, ed. John Hagan and Karen S. Cook (Palo Alto: Annual Reviews, 1995), 349–86; Sally Macintyre, Kate Hunt, and Helen Sweeting, 'Gender Differences in Health: Are Things Really as Simple as They Seem?' *Social Science and Medicine* 42 (February 1996): 617–24; Susan Macran, Lynda Clarke, and Heather Joshi, 'Women's Health: Dimensions and Differentials,' *Social Science and Medicine* 42 (May 1996): 1203–16; Sara Arber, 'Comparing Inequalities in Women's and Men's Health: Britain in the 1990s,' *Social Science and Medicine* 44 (March 1997): 773–87.

8. Bertolt Brecht, *Bertolt Brecht Poems*, ed. John Willett, Ralph Manheim, and Erich Fried (London: Eyre Methuen, 1976), 292–3.

9. James Thurber, *Fables for Our Time and Famous Poems Illustrated* (New York: Harper and Brothers, 1940), 21–2.

10. See Sally Macintyre, 'Understanding the Social Patterning of Health: The Role of the Social Sciences,' *Journal of Public Health Medicine* 16 (March 1994): 53–9; Tomas Faresjö, 'Social Environment and Health: A Social Epidemiological Frame of Reference,' *Scandinavian Journal of Primary Health Care* 10 (June 1992): 105–10; Norman B. Anderson and Cheryl A. Armstead, 'Toward Understanding the Association of Socioeconomic Status and Health: A New Challenge for the Biopsychosocial Approach,' *Psychosomatic Medicine* 57 (May/June 1995): 213–25.

11. Orly Manor, Sharon Matthews, and Chris Power, 'Comparing Measures of Health Inequality,' *Social Science and Medicine* 45 (September 1997): 761–71; Wilkinson, *Unhealthy Societies*, 53–136, 153–92, 211–32; Richard G. Wilkinson, 'Health Inequalities: Relative or Absolute Material Standards?" *British Medical Journal* 314 (22 February 1997): 591–5; Sandra J. Mcisaac and Richard G. Wilkinson, 'Income Distribution and Cause-Specific Mortality,' *European Journal of Public Health* 7 (March 1997): 45–53; Ichiro Kawachi and Bruce P. Kennedy, 'Health and Social Cohesion: Why Care about Income Inequality?' *British Medical Journal* 314 (5 April 1997): 1037–40; Eddy van Doorslaer et al., 'Income-Related Inequalities in Health: Some International Comparisons,' *Journal of Health Economics* 16 (February 1997): 93–112; Mel Bartley, David Blane, and Scott Montgomery, 'Health and the Life Course: Why Safety Nets Matter,' *British Medical Journal* 314 (19 April 1997): 1194–6; Kevin Fiscella and Peter Franks, 'Poverty or Income Inequality as Predictor of Mortality: Longitudinal Cohort Study,' *British Medical Journal* 314 (14 June 1997): 1724–8; Anthony B. Atkinson, Lee Rainwater, and Timothy Smeeding, *Income Distribution in OECD Countries: Evidence from the Luxembourg Income Study* (Paris: Organisation for Economic Cooperation and Development, 1995), esp. 46, 49, 59–80; Peter Gottschalk and Timothy M. Smeeding, 'Cross-National Comparisons of Earnings and Income Inequality,' *Journal of Economic Literature* 35 (June 1997): 633–87; A.

B. Atkinson, 'Income Distribution in Europe and the United States,' *Oxford Review of Economic Policy* 12 (Spring 1996): 15–28; Paul Johnson, 'The Assessment: Inequality,' *Oxford Review of Economic Policy* 12 (Spring 1996): 1–14; Francis Green, Andrew Henley, and Euclid Tsakalotos, 'Income Inequality in Corporatist and Liberal Economies: A Comparison of Trends within OECD Countries,' *International Review of Applied Economics* 8 (September 1994): 303–31; Stephen Nickell and Brian Bell, 'Changes in the Distribution of Wages and Unemployment in OECD Countries,' *American Economic Review* 86 (May 1996): 302–8; Stephen Nickell and Brian Bell, 'The Collapse in Demand for the Unskilled and Unemployment across the OECD,' *Oxford Review of Economic Policy* 11 (Spring 1995): 40–62, esp. 51; David M. Gordon, *Fat and Mean* (New York: Free Press, 1996), esp. 29, 43–7, 80–6, 100–1, 143, 168–71, 210, 221; Lee Rainwater and Timothy M. Smeeding, 'Le Bien-être économique des enfants Européens: Une perspective comparative,' *Population* 49 (November 1994): 1437–50; John Lie, 'Sociology of Contemporary Japan,' *Current Sociology* 44 (Spring 1996): 35–45; Harriet Orcutt Duleep, 'Mortality and Income Inequality among Economically Developed Countries,' *Social Security Bulletin* 58 (Summer 1995): 34–50; Ramiro Martinez, Jr., 'Latinos and Lethal Violence: The Impact of Poverty and Inequality,' *Social Problems* 43 (May 1996): 131–45.

12. See *OECD Economic Outlook* 61 (June 1997): A25; OECD *Employment Outlook* (July 1995): 216–18; 'OECD in Figures 1997 Edition,' *OECD Observer*, no. 206 (June/July 1997): 8–13; Robert L. Jin, Chandrakant P. Shah, and Tomislav J. Svoboda, 'The Impact of Unemployment on Health: A Review of the Evidence,' *Canadian Medical Association Journal* 153 (1 September 1995): 529–40; Samuel E. D. Shortt, 'Is Unemployment Pathogenic? A Review of Current Concepts with Lessons for Policy Planners,' *International Journal of Health Services* 26, no. 3 (1996): 569–89; Robert A. Verheij, 'Explaining Urban-Rural Variations in Health: A Review of Interactions between Individual and Environment,' *Social Science and Medicine* 42 (March 1996): 923–35; Paschal Sheeran, Dominic Abrams, and Sheina Orbell, 'Unemployment, Self-Esteem, and Depression: A Social Comparison Theory Approach,' *Basic and Applied Social Psychology* 17 (August 1995): 62–82.

13. Mats Thorslund, Bo Wärneryd, and Piroska Östlin, 'The Work-Relatedness of Disease: Workers' Own Assessment,' *Sociology of Health and Illness* 14 (March 1992): 57–72; Jeffrey V. Johnson, Walter Stewart, Ellen M. Hall, Peeter Fredlund, and Tores Theorell, 'Long-Term Psychosocial Work Environment and Cardiovascular Mortality among Swedish Men,' *American Journal of Public Health* 86 (March 1996): 324–31; Joachim Vogel, 'Class and Inequality: The Swedish Experience,' *International Journal of Sociology* 23 (Spring 1993): 31–58; Nelson Blank and Finn Diderichsen, 'The Prediction of Different Experiences of Longterm Illness: A Longitudinal Approach in Sweden,' *Journal of Epidemiology and Community Health* 50 (April 1996): 156–61; Fiona M. North, S. Leonard Syme, Amanda Feeney, Martin Shipley, and Michael Marmot, 'Psychosocial Work Environment and Sickness Absence among British Civil Servants: The Whitehall II Study,' *American Journal of Public Health* 86 (March 1996): 332–40; Michael Marmot, Amanda Feeney, Martin Shipley, Fiona North, and S. L. Syme, 'Sickness Absence as a Measure of Health Status and Functioning: From the UK Whitehall II Study,' *Journal of Epidemiology and Community Health* 49 (February 1995): 124–30; S. A. Stansfeld, F. M. North, I. White, and M. G. Marmot, 'Work Characteristics and Psychiatric Disorder in Civil Servants in London,' *Journal of Epidemiology and Community Health* 49 (February 1995): 48–53; Guy Toscano and Tracy Jack, 'The Changing Character of Fatal Work Injuries,' *Monthly Labor Review* 117 (October 1994): 17–28.

14. Sally Macintyre, Sheila Maciver, and Anne Sooman, 'Area, Class and Health: Should We Be Focusing on Places or People?' *Journal of Social Policy* 22 (April 1993):

213–34; Vera Carstairs, 'Deprivation Indices: Their Interpretation and Use in Relation to Health,' *Journal of Epidemiology and Community Health* 49 (December 1995 Supplement 2): S3–S8; Jan Sundquist, Madhavi Bajekal, Brian Jarman, and Sven-Erik Johansson, 'Underprivileged Area Score, Ethnicity, Social Factors and General Mortality in District Health Authorities in England and Wales,' *Scandinavian Journal of Primary Health Care* 14 (June 1996): 79–85; Harriet L. MacMillan, Angus B. MacMillan, David R. Offord, and Jennifer L. Dingle, 'Aboriginal Health,' *Canadian Medical Association Journal* 155 (1 December 1996): 1569–77; Anthony P. Polednak, 'Trends in US Urban Black Infant Mortality, by Degree of Residential Segregation,' *American Journal of Public Health* 86 (May 1996): 723–6; Sheryl Thorburn Bird, 'Separate Black and White Infant Mortality Models: Differences in the Importance of Structural Variables,' *Social Science and Medicine* 41 (December 1995): 1507–12; Edward S. Shihadeh and Nicole Flynn, 'Segregation and Crime: The Effect of Black Social Isolation on the Rates of Black Urban Violence,' *Social Forces* 74 (June 1996): 1325–52.

15. Ruth Hubbard and R. C. Lewontin, 'Pitfalls of Genetic Testing,' *New England Journal of Medicine* 334 (2 May 1996): 1192–4; Ruth Hubbard, *Profitable Promises: Essays on Women, Science and Health* (Monroe, ME: Common Courage Press, 1995), 31–75; Winifred Gallagher, *I.D.: How Heredity and Experience Make You Who You Are* (New York: Random House, 1996), 61–72; 115–16; P. A. Baird, 'The Role of Genetics in Population Health,' in *Why Are Some People Healthy and Others Not?* ed. Evans, Barer, and Marmor, 133–59; Leigh, 'The Health Status of Women of Color,' 164; Hannah Bradby, 'Ethnicity: Not a Black and White Issue, A Research Note,' *Sociology of Health and Illness* 17 (June 1995): 407; David R. Williams, 'Race/Ethnicity and Socioeconomic Status: Measurement and Methodological Issues' *International Journal of Health Services* 26, no. 3 (1996): 493.

16. Christine M. Rodwell, 'An Analysis of the Concept of Empowerment,' *Journal of Advanced Nursing* 23 (February 1996): 305–13; Melvin Seeman and Susan Lewis, 'Powerlessness, Health and Mortality: A Longitudinal Study of Older Men and Mature Women,' *Social Science and Medicine* 41 (August 1995): 517–25; Aaron Antonovsky, 'The Salutogenic Model as a Theory to Guide Health Promotion,' *Health Promotion International* 11 (March 1996): 11–18; Gerry Larsson and Kjell O. Kallenberg, 'Sense of Coherence, Scoioeconomic Conditions and Health,' *European Journal of Public Health* 6 (September 1996): 175–80; Nelson Blank and F. Diderichsen, 'Inequalities in Health: The Interaction between Socio-economic and Personal Circumstances,' *Public Health* 110 (May 1996): 157–62; R. Jay Turner and Franco Marino, 'Social Support and Social Structure: A Descriptive Epidemiology,' *Journal of Health and Social Behavior* 35 (September 1994): 193–212; Lisa F. Berkman, 'The Role of Social Relations in Health Promotion,' *Psychosomatic Medicine* 57 (May/June 1995): 245–54; David S. Sobel, 'Rethinking Medicine: Improving Health Outcomes with Cost-Effective Psychosocial Interventions,' *Psychosomatic Medicine* 57 (May/June 1995): 234–44.

17. Kathryn Dean, Concha Colomer, and Santiago Pérez-Hoyos, 'Research on Lifestyles and Health: Searching for Meaning,' *Social Science and Medicine* 41 (September 1995): 845–55; Kathryn C. Backett and Charlie Davison, 'Lifecourse and Lifestyle: The Social and Cultural Location of Health Behaviours,' *Social Science and Medicine* 40 (March 1995): 629–38; Simon J. Williams, 'Theorising Class, Health and Lifestyles: Can Bourdieu Help Us?' *Sociology of Health and Illness* 17 (November 1995): 577–604; George Davey Smith, David Blane, and Mel Bartley, 'Explanations for Socio-Economic Differentials in Mortality: Evidence from Britain and Elsewhere,' *European Journal of Public Health* 4, no. 2 (1994): 131–44; Andrew Steptoe and Jane Wardle, 'What the Experts Think: A European Survey of Expert Opinion about the Influence of Lifestyle on Health,' *European Journal of Epidemiology* 10 (April 1994): 195–203; Karien

Stronks, H. Dike van de Mheen, Casper W. N. Looman, and Johan P. Mackenbach, 'Behavioural and Structural Factors in the Explanation of Socio-Economic Inequalities in Health: An Empirical Analysis,' *Sociology of Health and Illness* 18 (November 1996): 653–72; W. Philip, T. James, Michael Nelson, Ann Ralph, and Suzi Leather, 'The Contribution of Nutrition to Inequalities in Health,' *British Medical Journal* 314 (24 May 1997): 1545–9; Hilary Graham, 'Cigarette Smoking: A Light on Gender and Class Inequality in Britain?' *Journal of Social Policy* 24 (October 1995): 509–27; Anthony Glendinning, Leo Hendry, and Janet Shucksmith, 'Lifestyle, Health and Social Class in Adolescence,' *Social Science and Medicine* 41 (July 1995): 235–48; Anthony Glendinning, Janet Shucksmith, and Leo Hendry, 'Social Class and Adolescent Smoking Behaviour,' *Social Science and Medicine* 38 (May 1994): 1449–60; Lawrence D. Cohn, Susan Macfarlane, Claudia Yanez, and Walter K. Imai, 'Risk-Perception: Differences between Adolescents and Adults,' *Health Psychology* 14 (May 1995): 217–22; Henry Wechsler, George W. Dowdall, Andrea Davenport, and Sonia Castillo, 'Correlates of College Student Binge Drinking,' *American Journal of Public Health* 85 (July 1995): 921–6; Tomas Hemmingsson, Ingvar Lundberg, Anders Romelsjö, and Lars Alfredsson, 'Alcoholism in Social Classes and Occupations in Sweden,' *International Journal of Epidemiology* 26 (June 1997): 584–91; 'Drinking in America,' *The Public Perspective* 6 (April/May 1995): 34–6; Richard Peto, Alan D. Lopez, Jullian Boreham, Michael Thun, Clarke Heath, Jr., and Richard Doll, 'Mortality from Smoking Worldwide,' *British Medical Bulletin* 52 (January 1996): 12–21; Charlotte A. Schoenborn, 'Trends in Health Status and Practices: Canada and the United States,' *Canadian Social Trends*, no. 31 (Winter 1993): 16–21; Eric W. Single, Joan M. Brewster, Patricia MacNeil, Jeffrey Hatcher, and Catherine Trainor, 'The 1993 General Social Survey II: Alcohol Problems in Canada,' *Canadian Review of Public Health* 86 (November–December 1995): 402–7.

18. Ans Nicolaides-Bouman, Nicholas Wald, Barbara Forey, and Peter Lee, *International Smoking Statistics: A Collection of Historical Data from 22 Economically Developed Countries* (New York: Oxford University Press, 1993), xxxvi–xxxix, 74, 149, 176, 177, 271, 272, 294, 295, 388, 389, 441, 442, 467; Organisation for Economic Cooperation and Development, *OECD Health Systems: Facts and Trends 1960–1991*, vol. 1 (Paris: OECD, 1993), 80, 86, 90–2.

19. B. Balkau and E. Eschwege, 'Risk Factors and Their Identification: First Part, What Is a Risk Factor?' *Diabete et Metabolisme* 21 (February 1995): 69–75; Manuella Adrian, Neville Layne, and Joan Mereau, 'Can Life Expectancies Be Used to Determine if Health Promotion Works?' *American Journal of Health Promotion* 8 (July/August 1994): 449–61; John P. Bunker, 'Medicine Matters After All,' *Journal of the Royal College of Physicians of London* 29 (March/April 1995): 105–12; Andrain, *Social Policies in Western Industrial Societies*, 95–6.

20. Nico Wilterdink, 'Increasing Income Inequality and Wealth Concentration in the Prosperous Societies of the West,' *Studies in Comparative International Development* 30 (Fall 1995): 3–23; *The Cost of Social Security: Fourteenth International Inquiry, 1987–1989* (Geneva: International Labour Office, 1996), 72–5; Charles F. Andrain, *Comparative Political Systems: Policy Performance and Social Change* (Armonk, NY: M. E. Sharpe, 1994), 49–67, 184–6; Paul Pierson, 'The New Politics of the Welfare State,' *World Politics* 48 (January 1996): 143–79; Atkinson, Rainwater, and Smeeding, *Income Distribution in OECD Countries*, 103–11; *OECD Economic Outlook*, no. 61 (June 1997): A25; 'OECD in Figures 1997 Edition,' 44–9; Sidney Verba et al., *Elites and the Idea of Equality: A Comparison of Japan, Sweden, and the United States* (Cambridge, MA: Harvard University Press, 1987), 112–44.

21. Andrain, *Social Policies in Western Industrial Societies*, 101–2; Joel Rogers and Wolfgang Streeck, 'Workplace Representation Overseas: The Works Councils Story,'

in *Working under Different Rules*, ed. Richard B. Freeman (New York: Russell Sage Foundation, 1994), 97-156; Eric Tucker, 'Worker Participation in Health and Safety Regulation: Lessons from Sweden,' *Studies in Political Economy*, no. 37 (Spring 1992): 95-127; Anton Steen, 'Welfare-State Expansion and Conflicts in the Nordic Countries: The Case of Occupational Health Care,' *Scandinavian Political Studies* 18, no. 3 (1995): 159-86; Steve Tombs, 'Injury, Death, and the Deregulation Fetish: The Politics of Occupational Safety Regulation in U.K. Manufacturing Industries,' *International Journal of Health Services* 26, no. 2 (1996): 309-29; David R. Walters, 'Preventive Services in Occupational Health and Safety in Europe: Developments and Trends in the 1990s,' *International Journal of Health Services* 27, no. 2 (1997): 247-71; David Walters, 'Trade Unions and the Effectiveness of Worker Representation in Health and Safety in Britain,' *International Journal of Health Services* 26, no. 4 (1996): 625-41; Wayne Lewchuk, A. Leslie Robb, and Vivienne Walters, 'The Effectiveness of Bill 70 and Joint Health and Safety Committees in Reducing Injuries in the Workplace: The Case of Ontario,' *Canadian Public Policy* 22 (September 1996): 223-43; Joan M. Eakin and Nancy Weir, 'Canadian Approaches to the Promotion of Health in Small Workplaces,' *Canadian Journal of Public Health* 86 (March-April 1995): 109-13; Kurt J. Greenlund and Ray H. Elling, 'Capital Sectors and Workers' Health and Safety in the United States,' *International Journal of Health Services* 25, no. 1 (1995): 101-16; Daniel P. Puzo, 'Food Plant Inspections Decline,' *Los Angeles Times* 13 June 1996, p. H2; Thomas A. Burke, 'Strengthening the Role of Public Health in Environmental Policy,' *Policy Studies Journal* 23 (Spring 1995): 76-84; David McKay, 'Urban Development and Civic Community: A Comparative Analysis,' *British Journal of Political Science* 26 (January 1996): 1-24.

22   Sobel, 'Rethinking Medicine,' 234-44; Bunker, 'Medicine Matters After All,' 110-11; Bo Burström, Bo J. A. Haglund, Per Tillgren, Lars Berg, Eva Wallin, Henrik Ullén, and Christopher Smith, 'Health Promotion in Schools: Policies and Practices in Stockholm County, 1990,' *Scandinavian Journal of Social Medicine* 23 (March 1995): 39-46; Inger Brännström and Inga-Britt Lindblad, 'Mass Communication and Health Promotion: The Power of the Media and Public Opinion,' *Health Communication* 6, no. 1 (1994): 21-36; Wayne J. Millar, 'Reaching Smokers with Lower Educational Attainment,' *Canadian Social Trends*, no. 45 (Summer 1997): 18-23.

23.   Alfred Rütten, 'The Implementation of Health Promotion: A New Structural Perspective,' *Social Science and Medicine* 41 (December 1995): 1627-37; Brian R. Flay and John Petraitis, 'The Theory of Triadic Influence: A New Theory of Health Behavior with Implications for Preventive Interventions,' in *Advances in Medical Sociology: A Reconsideration of Health Behavior Change Models*, vol. 4, ed. Gary L. Albrecht (Greenwich, CT: JAI Press, 1994), 19-44; Roger Ingham, 'Some Speculations on the Concept of Rationality,' in *Advances in Medical Sociology*, vol. 4, 89-111.

24.   John P. Pierce, 'Progress and Problems in International Public Health Efforts to Reduce Tobacco Usage,' in *Annual Review of Public Health*, vol. 12, ed. Gilbert S. Omenn, Jonathan E. Fielding, and Lester B. Lave (Palo Alto: Annual Review, 1991), 383-400; Kenneth E. Warner, 'Behavioral and Health Effects of the Antismoking Campaign in the United States,' in *Research in Human Capital and Development*, vol. 7, ed. P. C. Huang, Ruey S. Lin, and L. P. Chow (Greenwich, CT: JAI Press, 1993), 135-48; Frank J. Chaloupka and Henry Wechsler, 'Price, Tobacco Control Policies and Smoking among Young Adults,' *Journal of Health Economics* 16 (June 1997): 359-73; Kenneth J. Meier and Michael J. Licari, 'The Effect of Cigarette Taxes on Cigarette Consumption, 1955 through 1994,' *American Journal of Public Health* 87 (July 1997): 1126-30; Murray J. Kaiserman and Byron Rogers, 'Tobacco Consumption Declining Faster in Canada than in the US,' *American Journal of Public Health* 81 (July 1991):

902–4; Per Tillgren, Bo J. A. Haglund, Lena Kanström, and Lars-Erik Holm, 'Community Analysis in the Planning and Implementation of the Stockholm Cancer Prevention Program,' *Health Promotion International* 7, no. 2 (1992): 89–97; Linda Gearhart Pucci and Bo Haglund, "Naturally Smoke Free': A Support Program for Facilitating Worksite Smoking Control Policy Implementation in Sweden,' *Health Promotion International* 9, no. 3 (1994): 177–87.

25. Roland DF Wolters, 'Crime, Disorder and Legal Pressure as a Result of Addiction Problems in the Netherlands,' *Medicine and Law* 14, nos. 7–8 (1995): 521–9; Bruce Billington, 'War and Peace: Drug Policy in the United States and the Netherlands,' *Crime, Law and Social Change* 22 (April 1995): 213–38; GHA van Brussel, 'Public Health Care Policies for Drug Addicts in Amsterdam,' *Acta Paediatrica* 83 (November 1994 Supplement): 72–4.

26. Charles F. Andrain, *Foundations of Comparative Politics: A Policy Perspective* (Monterey, CA: Brooks/Cole, 1983), 2–33; James A. Mercy, Mark L. Rosenberg, Kenneth E. Powell, Claire V. Broome, and William L. Roper, 'Public Health Policy for Preventing Violence,' *Health Affairs* 12 (Winter 1993): 7–29; Fred C. Pampel and Rosemary Gartner, 'Age Structure, Socio-Political Institutions, and National Homicide Rates,' *European Sociological Review* 11 (December 1995): 243–60; Steven F. Messner and Richard Rosenfeld, 'Political Restraint of the Market and Levels of Criminal Homicide: A Cross-National Application of Institutional-Anomie Theory,' *Social Forces* 75 (June 1997): 1393–1416; Kevin B. Smith, 'Explaining Variation in State-Level Homicide Rates: Does Crime Policy Pay?" *Journal of Politics* 59 (May 1997): 350–67; AMB Golding, 'Understanding and Preventing Violence: A Review,' *Public Health* 109 (March 1995): 91–7.

27. Andrain, *Social Policies in Western Industrial Societies*, 96–9; Bret C. Williams, 'Social Approaches to Lowering Infant Mortality: Lessons from the European Experience,' *Journal of Public Health Policy* 15 (Spring 1994): 18–25; Irene Wennemo, 'Infant Mortality, Public Policy and Inequality — A Comparison of 18 Industrialised Countries 1950–85,' *Sociology of Health and Illness* 15 (September 1993): 429–46; Kees Schaapveld, Astrid M. J. Chorus, and Rom J. M. Perenboom, 'The European Health Potential: What Can We Learn from Each Other?' *Health Policy* 33 (September 1995):205–17; United Nations Children's Fund, *The State of the World's Children 1995* (New York: Oxford University Press, 1995), 69, 71; Rainwater and Smeeding, 'Le Bien-être économique des enfants Européens,' 1441–2; OECD, *Employment Outlook*, July 1995, pp. 192–4; Eero Lahelma and Sara Arber, 'Health Inequalities among Men and Women in Contrasting Welfare States: Britain and Three Nordic Countries Compared,' *European Journal of Public Health* 4, no. 3 (1994): 213–26; Sara Arber and Eero Lahelma, 'Women, Paid Employment and Ill-Health in Britain and Finland,' *Acta Sociologica* 36, no. 2 (1993): 121–38; C. Patrick Chaulk, 'Preventive Health Care in Six Countries: Models for Reform?' *Health Care Financing Review* 15 (Summer 1994): 7–19; Pierre Buekens, Milton Kotelchuck, Beatrice Blondel, Finn Borlum Kristensen, Jian-Hua Chen, and Godelieve Masuy-Stroobant, 'A Comparison of Prenatal Care Use in the United States and Europe,' *American Journal of Public Health* 83 (January 1993): 31–6; Lennart Köhler, 'Infant Mortality: The Swedish Experience,' in *Annual Review of Public Health*, vol. 12, ed. Omenn, Fielding, and Lave, 177–93; E. C. Michael Oldenburg, Finn Rasmussen, and Niki Cotten, 'Ethnic Differences in Rates of Infant Mortality and Sudden Infant Death in Sweden, 1978–1990,' *European Journal of Public Health* 7 (March 1997): 88–94; Ruth Young, 'The Household Context for Women's Health Care Decisions: Impacts of U.K. Policy Changes,' *Social Science and Medicine* 42 (March 1996): 949–63; Maria J. Hanratty, 'Canadian National Health Insurance and Infant Health,' *American Economic Review* 86 (March 1996): 276–84; Maureen Baker, 'Eliminating Child Poverty: How

Does Canada Compare?' *American Review of Canadian Studies* 25 (Spring 1995): 79–110; Sharon M. Keigher, 'The Morning after Deficit Reduction: The Poverty of U.S. Maternal and Child Health Policy,' *Health and Social Work* 19 (May 1994): 143–7; David R. Morgan and James T. LaPlant, 'The Spending-Service Connection: The Case of Health Care,' *Policy Studies Journal* 24 (Summer 1996): 215–29; Janet Currie and Jonathan Gruber, 'Saving Babies: The Efficacy and Cost of Recent Changes in the Medicaid Eligibility of Pregnant Women,' *Journal of Political Economy* 104 (December 1996): 1263–96; US Department of Health and Human Services, *Health United States 1995* (Hyattsville, MD: National Center for Health Statistics, 1996), 86, 90, 99–101; Naoko T. Miyaji and Margaret Lock, 'Monitoring Motherhood: Sociocultural and Historical Aspects of Maternal and Child Health in Japan,' *Daedalus* 123 (Fall 1994): 87–112; Naoki Ikegami, 'Efficiency and Effectiveness in Health Care,' *Daedalus* 123 (Fall 1994): 113–25.

28.   Denny Vågerö, 'Inequality in Health — Some Theoretical and Empirical Problems,' *Social Science and Medicine* 32, no. 4 (1991): 367–71; Oliver Fein, 'The Influence of Social Class on Health Status: American and British Research on Health Inequalities,' *Journal of General Internal Medicine* 10 (October 1995): 577–86; Johan P. Mackenbach and Anton E. Kunst, 'Measuring the Magnitude of Socio-Economic Inequalities in Health: An Overview of Available Measures Illustrated with Two Examples from Europe,' *Social Science and Medicine* 44 (March 1997): 757–71; van Doorslaer et al., 'Income-Related Inequalities in Health,' 93–112; Peter J. Aspinall, 'The Conceptual Basis of Ethnic Group Terminology and Classifications,' *Social Science and Medicine* 45 (September 1997): 689–98; Michaela Benzeval, Ken Judge, and Chris Smaje, 'Beyond Class, Race, and Ethnicity: Deprivation and Health in Britain,' *Health Services Research* 30 (April 1995, Part II): 163–77; Chris Smaje, 'The Ethnic Patterning of Health: New Directions for Theory and Research,' *Sociology of Health and Illness* 18 (March 1996): 139–71; Jiajian Chen, Edward Ng, and Russell Wilkins, 'The Health of Canada's Immigrants in 1994–95,' Statistics Canada *Health Reports* 7 (Spring 1996): 33–45; Sarah Wild and Paul McKeigue, 'Cross Sectional Analysis of Mortality by Country of Birth in England and Wales, 1970–92,' *British Medical Journal* 314 (8 March 1997): 705–10; Marsha Lillie-Blanton, P. Ellen Parsons, Helene Gayle, and Anne Dievler, 'Racial Differences in Health: Not Just Black and White, But Shades of Gray,' in *Annual Review of Public Health 1996*, vol. 17, ed. Gilbert S. Omenn, Jonathan E. Fielding, and Lester B. Lave (Palo Alto, CA: Annual Reviews, 1996), 411–48; Madelon W. Kroneman and Jouke van der Zee, 'Health Policy as a Fuzzy Concept: Methodological Problems Encountered When Evaluating Health Policy Reforms in an International Perspective,' *Health Policy* 40 (May 1997): 139–55.

9   Evaluating Public Policies

1.   Julius Epstein, Philip Epstein, and Howard Koch, 'The Script,' in *Casablanca: Script and Legend*, ed. Howard Koch (Woodstock, NY: The Overlook Press, 1973), 59.

2.   Charles F. Andrain, *Social Policies in Western Industrial Societies* (Berkeley: Institute of International Studies, University of California, Berkeley, 1985), 5–7, 90–1; James G. March and Johan P. Olsen, *Democratic Governance* (New York: The Free Press, 1995), 157–8; Joao Pereira, 'What Does Equity in Health Mean?' *Journal of Social Policy* 22 (January 1993): 19–48.

3.   Martin Powell, 'The Strategy of Equality Revisited,' *Journal of Social Policy* 24 (April 1995): 163–85; Ronald M. Andersen, 'Revisiting the Behavioral Model and Access to Medical Care: Does It Matter?' *Journal of Health and Social Behavior* 36 (March 1995): 1–10; Abdullah A. Khan and Surinder M. Bhardwaj, 'Access to Health Care:

A Conceptual Framework and Its Relevance to Health Care Planning,' *Evaluation and the Health Professions* 17 (March 1994): 60–76; Andrain, *Social Policies in Western Industrial Societies*, 102–3.

4. John Holahan, Colin Winterbottom, and Shruti Rajan, 'A Shifting Picture of Health Insurance Coverage,' *Health Affairs* 14 (Winter 1995): 253–64; Paul Fronstin, 'The Decline in Health Insurance and Labor Market Trends,' Metropolitan Life *Statistical Bulletin* 77 (July–September 1996): 28–36; Katherine Swartz, 'Changes in the 1995 Current Population Survey and Estimates of Health Insurance Coverage,' *Inquiry* 34 (Spring 1997): 70–9; Karen Seccombe, 'Health Insurance Coverage among the Working Poor: Changes from 1977 to 1987,' in *Research in the Sociology of Health Care*, vol. 13 (Part A), ed. Jennie Jacobs Kronenfeld (Greenwich, CT: JAI Press, 1996), 199–227; Paul Fronstin and Sarah C. Snider, 'An Examination of the Decline in Employment-Based Health Insurance between 1988 and 1993,' *Inquiry* 33 (Winter 1996/97): 317–25; Steven A. Schroeder, 'The Medically Uninsured — Will They Always Be with Us?' *New England Journal of Medicine* 334 (25 April 1996): 1130–3; Ronald J. Angel and Jacqueline L. Angel, 'The Extent of Private and Public Health Insurance Coverage among Adult Hispanics,' *Gerontologist* 36 (June 1996): 332–40; Adela de la Torre, Robert Friis, Harold R. Hunter, and Lorena Garcia, 'The Health Insurance Status of US Latino Women: A Profile from the 1982–1984 HHANES,' *American Journal of Public Health* 86 (April 1996): 533–7; Rudy Fichtenbaum and Kwabena Gyimah-Brempong, 'The Effects of Race on the Use of Physicians' Services,' *International Journal of Health Services* 27, no. 1 (1997): 139–56; Mark W. Rosenberg and Neil T. Hanlon, 'Access and Utilization: A Continuum of Health Service Environments,' *Social Science and Medicine* 43 (September 1996): 975–83; Steven J. Katz, Timothy P. Hofer, and Willard G. Manning, 'Physician Use in Ontario and the United States: The Impact of Socioeconomic Status and Health Status,' *American Journal of Public Health* 86 (April 1996): 520–4; Noralou P. Roos and Cameron A. Mustard, 'Variation in Health and Health Care Use by Socioeconomic Status in Winnipeg, Canada: Does the System Work Well? Yes and No,' *Milbank Quarterly* 75, no. 1 (1997): 89–111; John Eyles, Stephen Birch, and K. Bruce Newbold, 'Delivering the Goods? Access to Family Physician Services in Canada: A Comparison of 1985 and 1991,' *Journal of Health and Social Behavior* 36 (December 1995): 322–32; A. J. Culyer and Adam Wagstaff, 'Equity and Equality in Health and Health Care,' *Journal of Health Economics* 12 (December 1993): 431–57; Eddy van Doorslaer and Adam Wagstaff, 'Equity in the Delivery of Health Care: Some International Comparisons,' *Journal of Health Economics* 11 (December 1992): 389–411; Anton E. Kunst, José J. M. Geurts, and Jaap van den Berg, 'International Variation in Socioeconomic Inequalities in Self Reported Health,' *Journal of Epidemiology and Community Health* 49 (April 1995): 117–23; Anton E. Kunst and Johan P. Mackenbach, 'The Size of Mortality Differences Associated with Educational Level in Nine Industrialized Countries,' *American Journal of Public Health* 84 (June 1994): 932–37; Inge M. B. Bongers, Joost B. W. van der Meer, Johannes van den Bos, and Johan P. Mackenbach, 'Socio-Economic Differences in General Practitioner and Outpatient Specialist Care in the Netherlands: A Matter of Health Insurance?' *Social Science and Medicine* 44 (April 1997): 1161–8; Joost B. W. van der Meer, Johannes van den Bos, and Johan P. Mackenbach, 'Socioeconomic Differences in the Utilization of Health Services in a Dutch Population: The Contribution of Health Status,' *Health Policy* 37 (July 1996): 1–18; Chris Smaje and Julian Le Grand, 'Ethnicity, Equity and the Use of Health Services in the British NHS,' *Social Science and Medicine* 45 (August 1997): 485–96; Émile Papiernik and Louis G. Keith, 'The Regionalization of Perinatal Care in France — Description of a Missing Policy,' *European Journal of Obstetrics & Gynecology and Reproductive Biology* 61 (August 1995): 99–103.

5. Kenneth Hill, 'The Decline of Childhood Mortality,' in *The State of Humanity*, ed. Julian L. Simon (Oxford, England: Blackwell, 1995), 41–2; Julian L. Simon, 'Introduction,' in *The State of Humanity*, 9; Angus Maddison, *Monitoring the World Economy 1820–1992* (Paris: Organisation for Economic Cooperation and Development, 1995), 27; Organisation for Economic Cooperation and Development, *OECD Health Systems: Facts and Trends 1960–1991*, vol. 1 (Paris: OECD, 1993), 60–1; Kenneth G. Manton and James W. Vaupel, 'Survival after the Age of 80 in the United States, Sweden, France, England, and Japan,' *New England Journal of Medicine* 333 (2 November 1995): 1232–3.

6. Peter H. Ditto, Kathleen A. Moore, James L. Hilton, and Jonathon R. Kalish, 'Beliefs about Physicians: Their Role in Health Care Utilization, Satisfaction, and Compliance,' *Basic and Applied Social Psychology* 17 (August 1995): 23–48; Anthony Scott, Alan Shiell, and Madeleine King, 'Is General Practitioner Decision Making Associated with Patient Socio-Economic Status?' *Social Science and Medicine* 42 (January 1996): 35–46; Canadian Medical Association, 'Core and Comprehensive Health Care Services: CMA Policy Summary,' *Canadian Medical Association Journal* 152 (1 March 1995): 740A–740B; Caroline K. Ross, Colette A. Steward, and James M. Sinacore, 'A Comparative Study of Seven Measures of Patient Satisfaction,' *Medical Care* 33 (April 1995): 392–406; Margo L. Rosenbach, Killard W. Adamache, and Rezaul K. Khandker, 'Variations in Medicare Access and Satisfaction by Health Status: 1991–93,' *Health Care Financing Reivew* 17 (Winter 1995): 29–49; G. Cohen, 'Age and Health Status in a Patient Satisfaction Survey,' *Social Science and Medicine* 42 (April 1996): 1085–93; M. Calnan, V. Katsouyiannopoulos, VK. Ovcharov, R. Prokhorskas, H. Ramic, and S. Williams, 'Major Determinants of Consumer Satisfaction with Primary Care in Different Health Systems,' *Family Practice* 11 (December 1994): 468–78; David J. Owens and Claire Batchelor, 'Patient Satisfaction and the Elderly,' *Social Science and Medicine* 42 (June 1996): 1483–91; Susan Williams, John Weinman, Jeremy Dale, and Stanton Newman, 'Patient Expectations: What Do Primary Care Patients Want from the GP and How Far Does Meeting Expectations Affect Patient Satisfaction?' *Family Practice* 12 (June 1995): 193–201; Ingvar Krakau, 'Satisfaction with Health Care in a Swedish Primary Care District,' *Scandinavian Journal of Primary Health Care* 9 (March 1991): 59–64; Ray Fitzpatrick, 'Patients' Assessments of the Outcomes of Primary Care Consultations,' *Scandinavian Journal of Primary Health Care* 11 (November 1993, Supplement 2): 68–71; Margareta Ehnfors and Björn Smedby, 'Patient Satisfaction Surveys Subsequent to Hospital Care: Problems of Sampling, Non-Response and Other Losses,' *Quality Assurance in Health Care* 5 (March 1993): 19–32; Paul D. Cleary, Susan Edgman-Levitan, Marc Roberts, Thomas W. Moloney, William McMullen, Janice D. Walker, and Thomas L. Delbanco, 'Patients Evaluate Their Hospital Care: A National Survey,' *Health Affairs* 10 (Winter 1991): 254–67; Cathy Charles, Mary Gauld, Larry Chambers, Bernie O'Brien, R. Brian Haynes, and Roberta Labelle, 'How Was Your Hospital Stay? Patients' Reports about Their Care in Canadian Hospitals,' *Canadian Medical Association Journal* 150 (1 June 1994): 1813–22; F. Goupy, O. Ruhlmann, O. Paris, and B. Thélot, 'Results of a Comparative Study of In-Patient Satisfaction in Eight Hospitals in the Paris Region,' *Quality Assurance in Health Care* 3, no. 4 (1991): 309–15.

7. Guenther Lueschen, Fred Stevens, Jouke van der Zee, William C. Cockerham, Joe Diederijks, Alphonse d'Houtaud, Manuel G. Ferrando, Ruud Peeters, and Steffen Niemann, 'Health Care Systems and the People: A Five-Nation Study in the European Union,' *International Sociology* 9 (September 1994): 337–62; John H. Kurata, Yoshiyuki Watanabe, Christine McBride, Keiichi Kawai, and Ronald Andersen, 'A Comparative Study of Patient Satisfaction with Health Care in Japan and the United States,' *Social Science and Medicine* 39 (October 1994): 1069–76; Alex Inkeles,

'Industrialization, Modernization and the Quality of Life,' *International Journal of Comparative Sociology* 34 (January–April 1993): 7–9; Harvard Community Health Plan, *An International Comparison of Health-Care Systems: Annual Report 1990* (Brookline, MA: Harvard Community Health Plan, 1990), 4–22; Robert J. Blendon, Robert Leitman, Ian Morrison, and Karen Donelan, 'Satisfaction with Health Systems in Ten Nations,' *Health Affairs* 9 (Summer 1990): 185–92; Robert J. Blendon, John Benson, Karen Donelan, Robert Leitman, Humphrey Taylor, Christian Koeck, and Daniel Gitterman, 'Who Has the Best Health Care System? A Second Look,' *Health Affairs* 14 (Winter 1995): 220–30; Karen Donelan, Robert J. Blendon, John Benson, Robert Leitman, and Humphrey Taylor, 'All Payer, Single Payer, Managed Care, No Payer: Patients' Perspectives in Three Nations,' *Health Affairs* 15 (Summer 1996): 254–65; Helen Halpin Schauffler and Tracy Rodriguez, 'Availability and Utilization of Health Promotion Programs and Satisfaction with Health Plan,' *Medical Care* 32 (December 1994): 1182–96; Robert J. Blendon and John M. Benson, 'Health Care Reform: The Public versus the Experts,' *Public Perspective* 4 (March/April 1993): 13–15; Alec Gallup and Lydia Saad, 'America's Top Health Care Concerns: Long-Term Care, Rising Costs,' *Gallup Poll Monthly*, no. 333 (June 1993): 2–5; Carol Kelly and Elise Gemeinhardt, 'Public Attitudes on Health Care Reform,' Metropolitan Life *Statistical Bulletin* 73 (October–December 1992): 2–10; Michael K. Le Roy, 'Participation, Size, and Democracy: Bridging the Gap between Citizens and the Swedish State,' *Comparative Politics* 27 (April 1995): 297–316; Bo Rothstein, 'The Crisis of the Swedish Social Democrats and the Future of the Universal Welfare State,' *Governance: An International Journal of Policy and Administration* 6 (October 1993): 492–517; Anders Anell, Per Rosén, and Catharina Hjortsberg, 'Choice and Participation in the Health Services: A Survey of Preferences among Swedish Residents,' *Health Policy* 40 (May 1997): 157–68; Lynda Buske, 'Public Attitudes on Access to Service,' *Canadian Medical Association Journal* 156 (1 June 1997): 1680; Karen D. Hughes, Graham S. Lowe, and Allison L. McKinnon, 'Public Attitudes toward Budget Cuts in Alberta: Biting the Bullet or Feeling the Pain?' *Canadian Public Policy* 22 (September 1996): 268–84. For sample surveys of national attitudes toward the health care system, see the following two sources: (1) *World Opinion Update* 21 (February 1997): 22; 20 (October 1996): 116; 20 (February 1996): 18–20; 20 (January 1996): 8–10; 19 (November 1995): 126–8; 19 (September 1995): 106; 19 (July 1995): 82; 19 (April 1995): 38; 19 (January 1995): 2–3; 18 (November 1994): 123, 128; 18 (May 1994): 50–2; 17 (July 1993): 80–2; 17 (March 1993): 33–4; 16 (June 1992): 70; 16 (January 1992): 8–11; 15 (November 1991): 125; 15 (September 1991): 108; 15 (August 1991): 88–9; (2) Elizabeth Hann Hastings and Philip K. Hastings, eds., *Index to International Public Opinion, 1995–1996* (Westport, CT: Greenwood Press, 1997), 120–4, 136, 148–63, 290, 365; *Index to International Public Opinion 1994–1995* (Westport, CT: Greenwood Press, 1996), 171, 180–7, 196–8, 387; *Index to International Public Opinion, 1993–1994* (Westport, CT: Greenwood Press, 1995), 132–9, 147–9, 168, 170–7, 310–11; *Index to International Public Opinion, 1992–1993* (Westport, CT: Greenwood Press, 1994), 55, 127–8, 157–8, 162–3, 174, 299–302, 307; *Index to International Public Opinion, 1991–1992* (Westport, CT: Greenwood Press, 1993), 114–15, 145–6, 152–7, 168–71, 285; *Index to International Public Opinion, 1990–1991* (Westport, CT: Greenwood Press, 1992), 139, 143–4, 147–8, 656–7.

8.   Margaret Whitehead, Maria Evadrou, Bengt Haglund, and Finn Diderichsen, 'As the Health Divide Widens in Sweden, What's Happening to Access to Care?' *British Medical Journal* 315 (18 October 1997): 1006–9; Neil Söderlund, Ivan Csaba, Alastair Gray, Ruairidh Milne, and James Rafery, 'Impact of the NHS Reforms on English Hospital Productivity: An Analysis of the First Three Years,' *British Medical Journal*

315 (1 November 1997): 1126–9; *World Opinion Update* 21 (October 1997): 113; Harris M. Allen, Jr. and William H. Rogers, 'The Consumer Health Plan Value Survey: Round Two,' *Health Affairs* 16 (July/August 1997): 156–66; David Olmos, 'Survey Finds Wide Distrust of HMO Care,' *Los Angeles Times*, 6 November 1997, pp. A1, A18; Richard B. Saltman, 'Equity and Distributive Justice in European Health Care Reform,' *International Journal of Health Services* 27, no. 3 (1997): 443–53.

9. Andrain, *Social Policies in Western Industrial Societies*, 120, 200–1; Richard G. Wilkinson, *Unhealthy Societies: The Afflictions of Inequality* (London: Routledge, 1996).

Index